Institutional Theory

Over the past three decades, Meyer, Jepperson, and colleagues have contributed to the development of one of the leading approaches in social theory, by analyzing the cultural frameworks that have shaped modern organizations, states, and identities. Bringing together key articles and new reflections, this volume collects the essential theoretical ideas of "sociological neoinstitutionalism." It clarifies the core ideas and situates them within social theory writ large. Among other topics, the authors discuss the changing nature of the "actors" that have operated within contemporary social structure. The book concludes with the evolving frameworks that have structured social activity in the post–World War II period of "embedded liberalism," in the more recent neoliberal period, and in an emergent post-liberal period that appears to be a radical departure.

RONALD L. JEPPERSON is Associate Professor of Sociology, emeritus, at the University of Tulsa, where he taught social science, philosophy, and critical thinking to undergraduates. Previously he was a faculty member at the University of Washington, and a visiting professor at Stanford University, the University of California-Berkeley, and the European University Institute.

JOHN W. MEYER is Professor of Sociology, emeritus, at Stanford University. His research has focused on comparative sociology, education, and formal organizations, employing and developing neo-institutional theory, emphasizing the dependence of modern social structure on wider and often global cultural frameworks. He has published widely and received many academic honors.

Institutional Theory

The Cultural Construction of Organizations, States, and Identities

RONALD L. JEPPERSON
University of Tulsa

JOHN W. MEYER
Stanford University, California

CAMBRIDGE
UNIVERSITY PRESS

University Printing House, Cambridge CB2 8BS, United Kingdom

One Liberty Plaza, 20th Floor, New York, NY 10006, USA

477 Williamstown Road, Port Melbourne, VIC 3207, Australia

314–321, 3rd Floor, Plot 3, Splendor Forum, Jasola District Centre, New Delhi – 110025, India

79 Anson Road, #06–04/06, Singapore 079906

Cambridge University Press is part of the University of Cambridge.

It furthers the University's mission by disseminating knowledge in the pursuit of education, learning, and research at the highest international levels of excellence.

www.cambridge.org
Information on this title: www.cambridge.org/9781107078376
DOI: 10.1017/9781139939744

© Ronald L. Jepperson and John W. Meyer 2021

This publication is in copyright. Subject to statutory exception and to the provisions of relevant collective licensing agreements, no reproduction of any part may take place without the written permission of Cambridge University Press.

First published 2021

A catalogue record for this publication is available from the British Library.

Library of Congress Cataloging-in-Publication Data
Names: Jepperson, Ronald L., author. | Meyer, John W., author.
Title: Institutional theory : the cultural construction of organizations, states, and identities / Ronald L. Jepperson, University of Tulsa, John W. Meyer, Stanford University, California.
Description: 1 Edition. | New York : Cambridge University Press, 2021. | Includes index.
Identifiers: LCCN 2020049470 (print) | LCCN 2020049471 (ebook) | ISBN 9781107078376 (hardback) | ISBN 9781139939744 (ebook)
Subjects: LCSH: Organizational sociology. | New institutionalism (Social sciences) | Sociology. | Culture and globalization.
Classification: LCC HM711 .M49 2021 (print) | LCC HM711 (ebook) | DDC 302.3/5–dc23
LC record available at https://lccn.loc.gov/2020049470
LC ebook record available at https://lccn.loc.gov/2020049471

ISBN 978-1-107-07837-6 Hardback
ISBN 978-1-107-43528-5 Paperback

Cambridge University Press has no responsibility for the persistence or accuracy of URLs for external or third-party internet websites referred to in this publication and does not guarantee that any content on such websites is, or will remain, accurate or appropriate.

Contents

List of Figures	*page* vii
Preface	ix
Credits	xii

Part I   Introduction

1 Introduction: Cultural Institutionalism 3
   J. MEYER AND R. JEPPERSON

Part II   Institutional Theory: Its Role in Modern Social Analysis

2 Society without Culture: A Nineteenth-century Legacy (1988) 27
   J. MEYER

3 Institutions, Institutional Effects, and Institutionalism (1991) 37
   R. JEPPERSON

4 The Development and Application of Sociological Neoinstitutionalism (2002) 67
   R. JEPPERSON

5 Reflections on Part II: Institutional Theory 126
   R. JEPPERSON AND J. MEYER

Part III   The Institutional Level of Analysis

6 Multiple Levels of Analysis and the Limitations of Methodological Individualisms (2011) 139
   R. JEPPERSON AND J. MEYER

7 The Limiting Effects of Analytical Individualism:
   Examples from Macrosocial Change (2007) 170
   R. JEPPERSON AND J. MEYER

8 Reflections on Part III: Levels of Analysis 196
   R. JEPPERSON AND J. MEYER

   Part IV Institutions of Modernity and Postmodernity:
            The Construction of Actors

9 The "Actors" of Modern Society: The Cultural
   Construction of Social Agency (2000) 209
   J. MEYER AND R. JEPPERSON

10 Institutional Theory and World Society (2009) 243
   J. MEYER

11 Reflections on Part IV: The Construction of Actors 281
   J. MEYER AND R. JEPPERSON

   Part V Conclusion

12 Concluding Reflections: Evolving Cultural Models
   in Global and National Society 297
   R. JEPPERSON AND J. MEYER

Index 322

Figures

3.1	Lines of theory in organizational analysis	*page* 50
6.1	Boudon–Coleman diagram	140
6.2	Typical reconstruction of Weber's "Protestant ethic thesis"	146
6.3	Possible pathways linking Protestantism and capitalism at different levels of analysis	156

Preface

Over the past thirty years the authors have produced a set of articles that draw upon and develop one of the main "new institutionalisms" in social science. The central concern of this line of thought is how broad contemporary cultural changes – for example, in religious or political ideas – are "institutionalized" in core social structures (such as legal systems, professions, and organizational structures), and construct both actors and collective action systems. Hence this research program, with the involvement of many scholars, examines the cultural bases of formal organizations, states, and identities. As a cultural institutionalism, the perspective is distinct from the more economics-inspired institutionalisms that have also emerged in recent decades. Put simply, this line of thought takes an "anthropological" view of modern society, in the connotative sense of the term.

The material in this book takes off from earlier institutionalist analyses, as we indicate throughout. Most directly, the work in this volume is based on the sociological neoinstitutionalism that influenced sociology beginning in the 1970s.[1]

This book presents both previously published articles (from 1988 through 2011) and newly written pieces. The previously published elements (some coauthored, some individually written) concern fundamental issues in social theory. They have separately received a good deal of attention. However, they were published in disparate outlets. Any given reader may only have easy access to some of them and may not be aware of companion pieces. Accordingly, this volume provides the articles as a set.

In addition, we add five newly written coauthored pieces. Chapter 1 provides a new basic introduction to the line of social theory and three other chapters provide current reflections on the topics of the previously published articles. A new concluding chapter (Chapter 12) applies the line of social theory by analyzing the cultural frameworks of three historical periods: the post–World War II period of "embedded liberalism," the more recent neoliberal period, and the emergent postliberal period.

The book is organized in the following way. After the introduction just mentioned, the chapters cluster around three topics: the foundations of institutional theory, the multiple levels of analysis involved in social theory, and the nature of the "actors" within contemporary social structure. These sections are followed by the concluding chapter described in the preceding paragraph. We introduce the specific chapters of the volume in more detail at the end of the introductory chapter.

A note on the use of the pronoun "we" in the coauthored pieces of this volume: It's just the editorial "we" used for convenience. It would be tedious and distracting to try to specify individual responsibility for statements or to indicate any differences in emphasis. We share equal responsibility for the new chapters in this book (Chapters 1, 5, 8, 11, and 12), those chapters going back and forth between us multiple times. Related, the ordering of author names for the book is merely alphabetical, reflecting the general shared responsibility for the volume.

The work in this book arises not only from our own efforts but also from the ideas and research of a community of institutionalist scholars. It has been a shared enterprise. We report the contributions of our collegial compatriots in the acknowledgments and citations in the separate chapters of this book.

We would also like to acknowledge the support and assistance of Valerie Appleby (commissioning editor at Cambridge University Press), Tobias Ginsberg (senior editorial assistant), and Liisa Salomaa (our research assistant for this book project). We also have benefited from the work of Laura Simmons, Gayathri Tamilselvan, Anitha Nadarajan, and Jim Diggins in the production of the book. Finally, we appreciate the permission to include previously published articles received from the University of Chicago Press, Greenwood Publishing Group, Oxford University Press, Rowman & Littlefield, SAGE Publications, and Stanford University Press.

Notes

1. J. Meyer, "The Effects of Education as an Institution," *American Journal of Sociology* (1977) 83:55–77; J. Meyer & B. Rowan, "Institutionalized Organizations: Formal Structure as Myth and Ceremony," *American*

Journal of Sociology (1977) 83:340–63; J. Meyer & B. Rowan, "The Structure of Educational Organizations," pp. 78–109 in *Environments and Organizations* (1978), edited by M. W. Meyer, San Francisco: Jossey-Bass; J. Meyer, "The World Polity and the Authority of the Nation-State," pp. 109–137 in *Studies of the Modern World-System* (1980), edited by A. Bergesen, New York, NY: Academic Press; J. Meyer & W. R. Scott, *Organizational Environments: Ritual and Rationality* (1983), Beverly Hills: SAGE.

Credits

Ch. 2 Originally published in *Rethinking the Nineteenth Century*, edited by F. Ramirez (Greenwood Press, 1988), pp. 193–201. Reprinted by permission of Greenwood Publishing Group, Inc.

Ch. 3 Originally published in *The New Institutionalism in Organizational Analysis*, edited by W. Powell and P. DiMaggio (University of Chicago Press, 1991), pp. 143–63. Reprinted by permission of the University of Chicago Press.

Ch. 4 Originally published in *New Directions in Contemporary Sociological Theory*, edited by J. Berger and M. Zelditch (Rowman & Littlefield, 2002), pp. 229–66. Reprinted by permission of Rowman & Littlefield Publishers.

Ch. 6 Originally published in *Sociological Theory*, vol. 29 (2011), pp. 54–73. Reprinted by permission of Sage Publications.

Ch. 7 An excerpt (pp. 281–99) from "Analytical Individualism and the Explanation of Macrosocial Change," originally published in *On Capitalism*, edited by V. Nee and R. Swedberg (Stanford University Press, 2007), pp. 273–304. Reprinted by permission of Stanford University Press.

Ch. 9 Originally published in *Sociological Theory*, vol. 18 (2000), pp. 100–20. Reprinted by permission of Sage Publications.

Ch. 10 Originally published in *World Society: The Writings of John W. Meyer*, edited by G. Kruecken and G. Drori (Oxford University Press, 2009), pp. 36–66. Reprinted by permission of Oxford University Press.

PART I
Introduction

1 | Introduction: Cultural Institutionalism

J. MEYER AND R. JEPPERSON

The "sociological neoinstitutionalism" of this volume is a creature of, reaction to, and interpreter of society in the postwar period. The line of thought developed in the 1970s.[1] It emphasizes the way that the "actors" of contemporary society – often taken for granted in both common discourse and (unfortunately) social theory – can usefully be seen as constructions of an evolving rationalistic and individualistic culture.

Informal ideas of this sort are commonplace in ordinary social life. People, even social scientists, wryly understand that those around them – the people they work with, the students they teach, or the troubled patients they counsel – vary greatly from those of the past, carrying thoughts, capacities, and expectations of an entirely distinct spirit. People after hours comment on the different ways in which one must act and talk under changed contemporary cultural conceptions: the new gender dynamics of contemporary life, the new rules of organizational life, the new understanding of problems of the natural environment, or the new demands for transparency in business or personal relationships. These rapidly changing routines in fact reflect dramatic cultural changes that reach all the way up to the global level – for instance, to sweepingly universalistic discussions of human rights in UNESCO and other organs of world society. Such cultural changes have their own history, reflecting the efforts of movements, themselves embedded in previous cultural frames, to change the meaning systems under which social life proceeds.

Noticing such changes, describing them analytically, and attempting to explain them have been the core concerns of the neoinstitutionalism reflected in this book. This introductory chapter provides a brief intellectual history that situates the line of thought.

1.1 Sociology after Mid-century: The Marginalization of Culture

The emergent field of sociology in the early twentieth century routinely invoked broad cultural frameworks in its explanations. Ideas of folkways and mores, embedded in habits, were standard (Camic 1986). Groups were seen as having customs derived from the past, or from broad religious, political, and legal doctrines that themselves had long histories. National societies were seen as having highly distinctive and causally powerful cultures. People were envisioned as natives and role occupants within their communities, deeply embedded within them in both their identities and mentalities.

Early twentieth-century political science also had a cultural-institutional character. The textbooks of the time typically featured compressed national histories that one was to use to make sense of differences in political dynamics and political behavior. A reference to a then-current French protest would naturally invoke a protest repertoire originating in 1789, or explicate tensions among clerical, aristocratic, and statist models of order. A mid-century text continued to emphasize the abiding French tension between plebiscitary democratic and pseudodemocratic Bonapartist models of political order (Wright 1954).

Various cultural institutionalisms remained standard in social science through the mid-twentieth century. A good example of the explanatory imagery is provided by S. M. Lipset's studies of US/Canada differences (Lipset 1990). Lipset emphasized how the different foundational histories of the two polities – one self-consciously breaking with European ties and traditions, the other not – were reified into distinct "organizing principles," deeply built into a variety of social structures from family to religious groups to the political order. Canadian elites saw themselves as sustaining Tory ideas of rule and social order, just as US ones saw themselves as separating from a stigmatized European Old World. The divergent organizing principles generated different practices of leadership, social control, and welfare.

Related, Talcott Parsons offered a sweeping survey of cultural evolution and its institutionalization in social structures, in *The System of Modern Societies* (an analysis independent from but unfortunately overshadowed by his [in]famous systems theory). S. N. Eisenstadt compared world civilizations over a long career, emphasizing the institutionalization of distinct "cultural premises" (Eisenstadt 1966, 1996).

This form of explanation remains standard in social science, if less present in social theory. For instance, textbook discussions of Japanese society naturally discuss the varying influence of Buddhist, Confucian, and Shinto models in establishing the institutional matrix of Japan (e.g., Schneider and Silverman 2012: ch. 1). The Meiji period is then presented as a stark historical break, opening to external models, while at the same time recovering and refashioning old ideas of imperial sovereignty.

Elements of an explicit social theory of varying cultural-institutional "life-worlds" were synthesized in Berger and Luckmann's *Social Construction of Reality* (1966; also Berger 1963). Distinct cultural worlds were seen as carried and reproduced by various institutional machineries (economy, polity, education), but were also seen as institutionalizations of evolving cultural mythologies (e.g., Durkheim's [1969] "cult of the individual," or American Protestant visions of community). In this picture people inhabit entire "symbolic universes" of folk knowledge and rituals. The lifeworlds contain both standardized identities for people (e.g., in the contemporary system, individual, person, and actor) and the main lines of action for these identities (e.g., occupational, educational, marital, and political choices). Much individual activity is enactment of highly scripted identities, within highly ritualized social dramas (e.g., dramas of progress, at the national level; dramas of self-development and success, at the individual level).

In this "phenomenological" imagery, the cultural system – the particular "life-world" – is causally primary and fundamentally ideological in nature. The identities and lines of behavior of individuals and associations are constructed and derivative from a social scientific standpoint. After all, in the great scheme of things, few people vote when there is no election or go to school where there are no schools; when such institutions exist, vast numbers of people are drawn into them, taking up the associated roles, behavioral scripts, and accounts.

Social Construction is a famous book. Nevertheless the ideas that Berger and Luckmann assembled were not much implemented in empirical research programs, at least in the US intellectual context. This is a striking outcome, given the range and seeming power of the ideas. Instead, as American sociology evolved in the 1960s and beyond, it sustained a would-be structural analysis, but marginalized, or individualized and psychologized, the attention to "lifeworlds."[2]

It is important to understand why constructionist ideas were marginalized, and sometimes aggressively excluded, in mainstream American sociological thought. Mainly, they cross a Red Line, by failing to emphasize the "free will" or agency attributed to individual actors, and to the organizations derived from these actors (including the US state), in institutionalized cultural doctrine (Meyer 2010).

1.2 The Red Line

A phenomenological orientation did not fit well with the new folk culture and social structure of the postwar period. That complex dramatically expanded the constitutional individualism of American culture, intensified in reaction to the disastrously failed statisms and corporatisms of European society, and the continuing threats of a cold war. In parallel, a more self-consciously professional and intendedly relevant social science reified much of the new culture, taking for granted many of its cultural assumptions, and accordingly becoming less interested in analyzing them. It was as if society was now, finally, a truly "real" system, made up of very real entities – especially individuals. With social and economic progress, humankind had finally transcended the arbitrary cultural confinements of a primitive past. Society was, now, stripped to its essentials, and the individuals in it were similarly hardwired purposive entities. (See Chapter 2 of this volume, "Society without Culture.") To depart from such conceptions, which were simultaneously academic theories and normative standards, was to cross a line. To disrespect the almost magical rights and powers of the (especially American) individual was a normative and intellectual violation, and often a violation of proper methodological standards. To properly understand social structures, one must understand the points of view of the "actors" within them. This idea was reasonable enough, but in practice it frequently led to the mistaken assumption that these points of view produce the social structure and changes in it. Historical and cultural forces then easily disappear in such analyses.

The glorification of the capacity of individual and organizational participants to modify their own worlds through action marginalized a more traditional analysis of human society as rooted in cultural meanings. A broad understanding of culture was reduced to its contemporary weakened forms. Culture came to mean mostly the set of goals and ideals animating the individual or organizational members of society. Survey research, along with aggregate ideas and definitions of culture, became more central. Culture became "tools" or "affordances" that people use (as in Swidler's [1986] influential analysis). Or to a lesser extent, culture could be the set of goals and ideals built into the polity – typically, the national state. The idea that people, their actions, and social structures are embedded in a larger set of meanings receded.

The liberalism of the period – in the broad historical sense – clearly seems causally implicated in these intellectual developments. Liberalism of one form or another was a dominant ideology of the postwar period. The liberal project reconstructed the institutional framework of society around a template of rationalized human actorhood, and the more recent neoliberal version intensified it (compare Ruggie 1982 and 1998). The new postwar individualism, the "society of organizations," expanded states, and a worldwide state system were outcomes in both theory and practice.

Social science rapidly shifted to treat these constructions as primordial actors in history, dropping an older standard cultural-institutionalism along the way. Individuals, given their normative centrality, were especially stressed. The fields of economics and psychology grew and gained policy centrality (Frank et al. 1995). Sociology shifted to emphasize social psychological processes. The field of anthropology destabilized. Overall, even history moved to focus on individuals – not just "great men" – rather than authorities and institutions. A taste for reductionism, as well as methodological individualism, became commonplace, and then dominant (see Chapters 6–8 of this volume). Much social theory, in other words, quickly became part of the contemporary cultural world, falling into society, rather than analyzing its foundational culture and structures.

The intensive emphasis on individuals and organizations as independent entities finally did provoke a reactive interest in the institutions that regulate systems involving these actors. Institutions began to reappear in social theory in the 1970s and 1980s. However, they were largely seen as "constraints" on the taken-for-granted social actors – a conceptualization far distant from Berger and Luckmann's cultural-institutional "worlds." Culture might appear as a few "rules" – for example, property rights or Westphalian sovereignty – thought to be essential for society as a largely economic or political game. Much purportedly institutionalist literature, in economics but also political science, was not actually much concerned with institutions, let alone with the broader meaning systems that they embody. Instead, it was about the ways in which coherent (and sometimes rational) actors are thought to build them, use them, resist them, and seek to change them. That was the primary interest.

The reification of actors ended up creating a considerable embarrassment for American sociology. Many of the sweeping social changes of the contemporary period are rooted in a changing cultural meaning system. Inattentive to this system, the field of sociology has produced limited analysis of the most striking social changes of the period. Analyses poorly account for the rise of a global environment movement that completely transcends local environmental problems. The discipline gives weak accounts of the whole raft of social changes around gender and the family system: worldwide increases in the status of women (including divorce and abortion rights), the recognition and legitimation of homosexuality, the legalization of the status of children, the liberations of sexual expression, current experiments with biological sex, and so on. The field deals poorly with the dramatic (and global) declines in the legitimacy of racial and ethnic and now national distinctions, with the dramatic rise of human rights ideologies. Most sociologies do not well explain the explosive rise in institutions of education at every level and in every country. They give feeble interpretations of global expansions in formal organization, elaborations of organizational structures, and demands for organizational transparency, social responsibility, and internal rectitude (Bromley and Meyer 2015). These institutional changes are not a primary interest.

In all these areas, descriptive empirical work routinely shows dramatic and often worldwide changes. Informal conversations constantly call attention to them. Explanatory models, however, are absent or primitive. Contemporary sociologists, for instance, certainly notice informally the extraordinary expansion of female participation in public society – many of them after all are women, who know they would not have been in the room a few decades ago. But if asked to explain the dramatic social change, few sociologists would have any convincing answer: even fewer would be able to coherently explain why the change is worldwide. Sociologists have focused upon changes within taken-for-granted cultural frames, not for the most part changes in the frames themselves.

1.3 The Neoinstitutional Perspective of This Book

The "sociological neoinstitutionalism" of this volume has focused on analyzing such changes. It treats the "actorhood" of modern individuals and organizations as itself constructed out of cultural materials – and treats contemporary institutional systems as working principally by creating and legitimating agentic actors with appropriate perspectives, motives, and agendas. The scholars who have developed this perspective have been less inclined to emphasize actors' use of institutions and more inclined to envision institutional forces as producing and using actors. By focusing on the evolving construction and reconstruction of the actors of modern society, institutionalists can better explain the dramatic social changes of the contemporary period – why these changes cut across social contexts and functional settings, and why they often become worldwide in character.

In this theoretical picture, the behavior of actors – the "action" itself – is as much a product of a script as the choice of an actor. The scripts are rooted, for instance, in ideologies of rights and human capital, and in highly simplified pictures of society (featuring an idealized polity, economy, family system, and religious order). Such ideologies certainly do depict contemporary actors as filled with choices and decisions. But much of this behavior is highly institutionalized, with the ideas about "action" in large part an overlay of "accounts" of activity (a "vocabulary of motives" [Mills 1940]). For example, the choices of contemporary young people to complete secondary school or attend college are generally understood to make good rational sense. Yet, many young people complete these steps without having decided to do so – they simply take it all for granted and follow along the conventionalized pathway. They are actors in a theatrical sense, not the senses employed in contemporary sociological thought. They may be rational (or intendedly rational) in some respects, but they are not, in the main, the actors imagined in much social theory. And because they are embedded in highly institutionalized and changing cultural scripts, an explosion in now-routinized "going to college" can become an astonishing worldwide script directing masses of young people in every country (Schofer and Meyer 2005).

There is no reason to suppose all these young persons are particularly irrational – indeed the script about education for both individual and collective progress is deeply institutionalized, and social and economic returns to education have been high. Rational or not, however, the question is whether and in what sense these people should be considered real actors as envisioned in much social theory. From an institutionalist point of view, their actorhood is itself a greatly expanded script in the modern order. And since actorhood is prominently a script, rationality becomes difficult (sometimes even impossible) to define.[3] More generally, if the core units making up the modern order are cultural constructions, rationality becomes a tautology.

Overall, the theoretical ideas presented in this book are distinct from more conventional lines of social theory along several axes. First, the conception of culture is much broader than an imagery of individual attitudes, whether about politics or gods. We include great areas of institutionalized doctrine as central cultural material: microeconomic theory, for instance, or scientific medicine as a set of principles, or psychological doctrines of individual empowerment – professional and pseudo-professional knowledges (in the sense of Foucault) of every sort. All sorts of schemes have cultural standing far over and above both social structures and individuals. They operate as frameworks for the creation and behavior of actors.

Second, the ideas here emphasize the cultural elaborateness and dependence of the actor identities. Far removed from any natural or functional aspects, the contemporary actor is a model – a highly theorized one, and hence ordinarily a very unrealistic one. This is why, in practically all contemporary societies, the ordinary individual person is seen as clearly "not good enough." Almost everywhere, a decade or more of carefully organized reconstruction through the medium of compulsory formal education is demanded. Even after all this forced socialization, people interact with a wide range of others – therapists, trainers, consultants – who bring a continuous supply of the ingredients for actorhood down to the inadequate individual. Similar huge consulting industries operate exoskeletally to sustain modern organizations and national states as actors. The expanded standards of actorhood produced and intensified in the whole postwar (liberal and neoliberal) period mean that every natural person can be seen as failed or inadequate, requiring much schooling and therapy. Every organization requires regulation and reform. Every national state is a partially or entirely failed state.

Thus, in institutional theories, disjunction between cultural models of actorhood and the practical capacities of modern social entities is a normal condition – a kind of moving equilibrium (Brunsson 1985, 1989). The rapidly expanding postwar world has not been held together by a dominant stabilizing organizational structure – its theories and ideologies imagine a world held together by capable and responsible actors. These theories usually have, as ideologies, a functional cast – this is a preferred intellectual form in a modern society that takes its pretenses seriously. But they achieve their functionalism by grossly expanded and unrealistic conceptions of who actors actually are and what they can do, creating the "decoupling" or loose coupling, of vision and empirical reality, emphasized in the institutionalist literature (Weick 1976; Meyer and Rowan 1977). Given the great gaps between models and practical possibilities, institutional theories tend to distance themselves from any assumed functionalism.

Third, as the previous point implies, the line of thought emphasizes continuous interpenetration between actors and changing cultural environments. New cultural schemes are directly incorporated: for officers of organizations, departments of states, and individual persons. For instance, as a business executive goes along, he or she is influenced not only by the MBA degree conferred years ago but also by the continuous evolution of business school ideologies in the current period. The actor, thus, is in continuous interdependence with the expanding cultural environment that built his or her original identity.

We do not present such theoretical ideas as a self-sufficient social theory. They differ in this metatheoretical respect from the many lines of social theory presented as putative closed or core systems (whether of power or interests or functions or communication). At the least, the ideas reflected in this book should be a corrective to much common theorizing, and we hope an addition to the corpus of well-established social theory. The line of thought offers hypotheses and empirical generalizations that go beyond those that are ordinarily considered. It presents a distinctive causal imagery, pursued in order to explain features of the social world not easily captured – or not even noticed – when thinking about social entities as if they are relatively natural ones, that is, having natures and lines of behavior mostly determined outside of, or prior to the effects of, the wider social world.[4]

1.4 Empirical Research

Because this is a book of social theory, it may inadvertently give a false impression of the overall line of thought. The line developed in close conjunction with empirical research focusing upon macrosocial forces and variations. Many scholars have been involved, and research bibliographies are lengthy.[5] The relevant research, emphasizing the contemporary cultural construction of actorhood, naturally focuses on those areas of social life where actorhood has been most highly culturally constructed – individualism, organizations, and national states. The postwar liberal order elaborated models of these entities, as social constructions: these models provided theories and ideologies of how social order could be structured in an explosively expanding global society. An early elaboration laid out multiple dimensions of research (Thomas et al. 1987). Chapter 4 of this volume presents a characterization and review of research through 2000. Here we will note some research topics, designs, and findings in main research areas, to illustrate the dialectic of research and theory.

The human individual: Postwar cultural developments, given the failure of corporatist and statist conceptions of society, have dramatically emphasized the capacity, rights, and authority of the individual. Early formulations of institutional theory drew upon some available studies in this area and proposed others (e.g., Meyer 1977). Some early empirical research examined the dramatic and worldwide expansion in rights attributed to children (Boli-Bennett and Meyer 1978) and women (Ramirez 1987). An interest in the elaboration and shaping of individuality naturally motivated research attention to the worldwide expansion of education at all levels. Early on it became clear that the education focused on the development of people as expanded human actors, rather than on efforts to train people to fit into structures of social roles (e.g., vocational ones) (Ramirez and Meyer 1980). Research showed that mass primary education had become almost universal in the world independent of local social resources or needs (Meyer et al. 1977, 1992; Ramirez and Boli 1987). Studies of over-time development of tertiary education tracked the enormous global expansion of university enrollments to their current level, perhaps two-fifths of current cohorts – again with only loose connection to social roles such as jobs (Schofer and Meyer 2005; Kamens 2012; Baker 2014). Further, it became clear that the dramatic expansion of education at every level was devoted to rather universalistic cultural ideas organized at the global level (Meyer et al. 1992; Frank and Gabler 2006). For example, the global Education-for-All movement depicted education as a human right that all proper actors should support anywhere (Chabbott 2009). The central points of these studies are precisely that education came to be focused on general models of actorhood, and that these models took on force worldwide. The proper human individual actor is defined worldwide in a surprisingly homogeneous way.

These points were deepened with empirical studies of the explosive expansion in world-defined human rights – transcending older models of the rights of the national citizen (Elliott 2007, 2011, 2014). Such studies tracked how human rights treaties emerged and were ratified almost everywhere – even by the worst actual violators in the world. The sorts of individual assigned these rights expanded greatly – women, children, immigrants, minorities, indigenous people, handicapped people, old people, and so on. And the nature of human rights, as defined in these sweeping cultural assertions, changed over time too: modern human rights empower the human as actor – they do not simply state entitlements. Contemporary humans have the old civil, political, and social rights; they now also have sweeping rights to assert their own cultures, religions, languages, and norms, and indeed to choose their own versions of gender.

The organization: The idea that organizations should themselves be seen as constructions of a rationalized culture developed in the 1970s, and was central to the rise of a range of institutional theories. In reaction to common pictures of organizations as natural, instrumental, and functional (see Scott 2003 for overview), Meyer and Rowan (1977, 1978) emphasized their dependence on wider cultural material, and thus their common arationality. The term "decoupling," used initially in Karl Weick's (1976) work, was emphasized to stress the integration of the organization with its environment, and the resultant loose internal integration (Bromley and Powell 2012). The line of thought had considerable influence in the rapidly expanding world of organizational research (Zucker 1977; DiMaggio and Powell 1983; Meyer and Scott 1983; Powell and DiMaggio 1991).

Institutional analyses, centrally, called attention to the dependence of organizations on common models – and, in particular, the idea of formal organization as a model. The concept of institutional isomorphism came to be central to the field: a picture of organizations, not as entirely adapted to local settings and functions, but as enactments of models of high formal rationalization, cutting across social sectors and countries, and expanding rapidly around the world. Studies showed that firms and government agencies and schools and hospitals are all built to conform to general models of their specific character (e.g., schools), but also models of the organization-as-actor in general. Naturally, decoupling is endemic in all these sorts of cases: practical adaptation may occur in practice, but it also becomes crucial to display proper actorhood – as a charity, or firm, or agency – in general. Thus many national states with very negative human rights records nevertheless signed on voluntarily to sweeping global human rights norms (Hafner-Burton et al. 2008). More and more of society came to be composed of similarly structured formal organizations – a "society of organizations," indeed (Coleman 1982; Bromley and Meyer 2015).

By the turn of the millennium, institutional theories had become central to the whole field of organizational research (Greenwood et al. 2008, 2017). Scholars now emphasize that contemporary organizations contrast sharply with older forms of formalization, such as classic bureaucracies – those that depended on the external sovereigns which they were to serve. In fact the older term "bureaucracy," with many negative connotations, was increasingly replaced by the more neutral term "organizations." These creatures are what Kruecken and Meier (2006) and Brunsson and Sahlin-Andersson (2000) call "organized actors," with choices and decisions of their own, over and above the controls of their nominal owners or sovereigns. They are understood to be engaged in rational purposive action – hence presupposing a great deal of imagined order in their environments. Strikingly, the model of social life as properly formalized around organizations, posturing and depicted as actors, has gone worldwide. Now it is found not only within practically all national states but also in the supra-national world beyond them (Bromley and Meyer 2015).

The national state in world society: Much of the early empirical research in the institutionalist vein concentrated on the striking fact that national states in the current world – supposedly and in part actually creatures of historical, ethnic, religious, and natural differences – were far more similar in structure and aspiration than common theories would predict. The idea that they are partly constructions of an increasingly integrated and rationalized world society strongly suggested itself as an explanation.

Ensuing studies in fact showed that formal state structures – constitutions for instance, but also agencies and policies – parallel each other (Boli 1987; Lee and Strang 2006, and many others). Ideologies of progress copy prestigious forms and change in homogenous ways (in the educational arena see Fiala 2006 and Fiala & Gordon Lanford 1987). Environmental policies copy forms worked out in professional networks or by prestigious polities (Frank et al. 2000; Hironaka 2014). Sweeping rules of accounting transparency rise to the fore and generate local adaptation (Drori et al. 2006; Jakobi 2013). Even ideologies of family life and gender relations flow along parallel (and Anglo-European) lines worldwide (Frank et al. 2010 studying the state regulation of sex).

World society: In contrast to legitimated individuals, organizations, and national states, the world as a whole is obviously not constructed as a social actor – it has been conspicuously stateless. Indeed, this feature is a main factor explaining the cultural elaborations of individuals and organizations and states as actors, making their own efforts at social order, social control, and progress. These constructed actors are accompanied by equally constructed cultural agents who operate as consulting "Others": putative agents of the collective good rather than narrower interests. Strong nation-states act in this way, with schemes of aid and support, but also with high-minded advice from experts and consultants of every sort. A huge industry of professional advisors has emerged, putting forth programs for the proper development of individuals, organizations, and states anywhere in the world (see Chapter 10, this volume).

To a striking extent the claimed authority of these "Others" is rooted in science or in an expanded range of professions (with their putative "best practices"). These authorities have displaced or supplanted religious ones. So, one line of research on world society has focused on the explosive expansion of science, a complex that has grown in numbers of people and activities, topical domains, global scope, and influence (Drori et al. 2003). A conspicuous domain has been the environment, now subject of elaborate scientific analysis spread around the world and providing urgent rationales for global collective action (Meyer et al. 1997; Frank et al. 2000; Ignatow 2007; Hironaka 2014). Environmental regimes and movements have been the focus of a good deal of institutional research, studying for instance the spread of arrangements for environmental impact assessment or the global spread of national parks.

Beyond science, a world proto-legal system has developed, emphasizing expanded doctrines of human rights, as noted earlier (Elliott 2007). A dense network of treaties and international organizations celebrates the expanded rights and capacities of all sorts of people – and the agency of the people to defend their rights. So there are rights asserted on a universal scale to education, health, welfare, and economic activity – and to culture, religion, and language. The conceptualization of rights also implies the capacity to act – the modern individual is seen as carrying authority to make the widest variety of choices in political, economic, social, cultural, religious, and familial life. The rights are asserted as applying to all humans – they go beyond traditional citizenship rights. Obviously, practice is very far from the asserted rights: the point is that the whole postwar period constructed an enormously expanded vision of a world society, not that this vision was put into practice. The expanded vision has had great impact on the formation of states, individuals, organizations, and people's "movements" of all sorts – this is the point of neo-institutional theory.

Contemporary world society has also been infused with models of the good society itself, around democratic ideals and norms of political, social, and economic transparency. This is a development that has been studied by many lines of scholarship, including the line represented in this book (e.g., by Drori et al. 2006, 2009, and Jakobi 2013). Models of democracy and open and free markets abound and take on much authority – they have, obviously, diffused around the world (Simmons et al. 2008, as well as Huntington 1991 among many others). The contribution of institutional theory has been to emphasize how a shared world cultural frame facilitates what may appear to be voluntaristic diffusion (Strang and Meyer 1993; Lee and Strang 2006; Simmons et al. 2008).

The strength of liberal models of individual and society clearly reflects the conditions of the postwar period, and the dominance of liberal societies in the world order. As this authority and dominance declines, so may the extraordinarily expansive visions the models contain: anti-liberal reactions seem to be increasing in the most recent period. We discuss future prospects in Chapter 12, considering

Introduction: Cultural Institutionalism 17

implications for world society but also for the forms of social theory appropriate for it.

1.5 Outline of the Book

The chapters of this volume were written within this research context. Following this Introduction (which constitutes Part 1 of the book), the chapters of Part 2 address basic theoretical issues in this one neoinstitutional line of work. Chapter 2, "Society without Culture," sets up the volume. Published in 1988, the paper focused upon the marginalization of the concept of culture in social theory. Chapter 3, "Institutions, Institutional Effects, Institutionalism," from 1991, sought to provide clarification of the basic ideas and definitions involved in the concept of institution, a term that has been employed in a wide variety of ways. Chapter 4, from 2002, provided a survey of the arguments across the main empirical areas of the research program, up to that time. Chapter 5 provides current reflections on these articles. We emphasize how much contemporary social science still imagines a "society without culture," and still works with conceptions of institutions that have an intellectually conservative quality.

The chapters of Part 3 discuss levels of analysis: the differences between and relations among individual, structural, and institutional or collective lines of argument. A central feature of institutional arguments is precisely their focus on causal processes at macrosocial levels. Chapter 6, from 2011, develops our conception of this fundamental issue, drawing not only upon sociological research – including the field's long discussion of Weber's "Protestant Ethic thesis" – but also including clarifications suggested by philosophers. Chapter 7 is a companion piece, providing a wide range of empirical examples of how insistence on individualistic thinking – including "methodological individualism," or the contemporary ideological emphasis on the human individual as a natural actor – has hindered the explanation of macrosocial outcomes. The chapter presents examples from European economic history, modern and postmodern economic development, and globalization. Chapter 8 provides current reflections on these articles, including ones stimulated by criticisms from would-be reductionists. We emphasize how and why many social scientists – those for whom modern ideology is grounding theory – still show discomfort with a pragmatic approach to multilevel theorizing, one that would include more collective and historical ways of thinking.

Part 4 presents chapters on the nature and construction of the "actors" of contemporary society – individuals, organizations, and states. Chapter 9 (from 2000) offers arguments about how the modern (European, now global) cultural system constructs the modern actor as an authorized agent for various interests. Seeing modern actorhood in this way helps greatly in explaining a number of otherwise anomalous or little-analyzed features of these entities. Chapter 10 (from 2009) discusses how the institutionalism of this volume has been used to understand the rise, nature, and impact of the world order – that is, international and transnational order – as itself a society. Chapter 11 provides current reflections on these articles, noting (among other observations) the remarkably unrealistic qualities attributed to individuals, organizations, and states in much contemporary social science.

Part 5 (Chapter 12) provides a capstone piece for this volume. It applies the line of social theory by analyzing the cultural frameworks that shaped social activity in three historical phases of the postwar period. We refer to the phase of embedded liberalism (Ruggie 1982), intensifying into neoliberalism, and then a recent emergent period, seemingly a post-liberal one. In so doing we seek to further illustrate how one might give broad cultural frameworks – institutionalized "meaning systems" – their due.

Notes

1. John Meyer played a leading role, with many collaborators (especially W. Richard Scott, but also Brian Rowan, Michael Hannan, Francisco Ramirez, John Boli, George Thomas, and others who are acknowledged in the various chapters here). Later many others contributed variously. See Chapter 4 for a depiction of the first twenty-five years.
2. This sundering was both reflected in and reinforced by the ongoing institutional and professional separation of sociology and cultural anthropology. Within sociology it was reflected in the treatment of "comparative sociology" as a separate subfield. These developments allowed and even encouraged inattention to history and comparison – and hence culture.
3. As now acknowledged by some "rational choice" theorists (e.g., Elster 2015: conclusion).

4. In saying this we by no means deny biology, psychology, and social psychology, in their attempt to isolate shapings that originate outside of the institutional and cultural order. (Consider the extraordinary corpus of behavioral biology assembled now by Sapolsky 2017.) Instead, we are criticizing the positing of natural tendencies, or the mere assumption of them, without empirical warrant. And we are criticizing the failure to consider the possible social construction of social entities, or the cultural shaping of their identities, or the scripting of lines of behavior for the entities. Any future real social science will have to be a multilevel one. (See Chapters 6–8 infra; also Sapolsky 2017 and Hacking 1999: ch. 1.)
5. Some bibliographies of studies at national and global levels: Boli et al. 2009, Meyer 2010; at organizational levels, Greenwood et al. 2008 and 2017.

References

Baker, D. P. (2014). *The Schooled Society: The Educational Transformation of Global Culture*, Stanford, CA: Stanford University Press.

Berger, P. (1963). *Invitation to Sociology*, New York, NY: Doubleday.

Berger, P. & T. Luckmann (1966). *The Social Construction of Reality*, New York, NY: Doubleday.

Boli, J. (1987). Human Rights or State Expansion? In G. Thomas, J. Meyer, F. Ramirez, & J. Boli. eds., *Institutional Structure*. Newbury Park, CA: SAGE, pp. 133–49.

Boli, J., S. Gallo-Cruz, & M. Mathias (2009). *World Society-World Polity Theory Bibliography*, Atlanta, GA: Department of Sociology, Emory University.

Boli-Bennett, J. & J. W. Meyer (1978). The Ideology of Childhood and the State: Rules Distinguishing Children in National Constitutions, 1870–1970. *American Sociological Review*, 43(6), 797–812.

Bromley, P. & J. W. Meyer (2015). *Hyper-Organization: Global Organizational Expansion*, Oxford: Oxford University Press.

Bromley, P. & W. W. Powell (2012). From Smoke and Mirrors to Walking the Talk: Decoupling in the Contemporary World. *The Academy of Management Annals*, 6(1), 483–530.

Brunsson, N. (1985). *The Irrational Organization*, Chichester: Wiley.

Brunsson, N. (1989). *The Organization of Hypocrisy*, Chichester: Wiley.

Brunsson, N. & K. Sahlin-Andersson (2000). Constructing Organizations: The Example of Public Sector Reform. *Organization Studies*, 21(4), 721–46.

Camic, C. (1986). The Matter of Habit. *American Journal of Sociology*, 91 (5), 1039–87.

Chabbott, C. (2003). *Constructing Education for Development*, New York, NY: Routledge.

Coleman, J. S. (1982). *The Asymmetric Society*, Syracuse, NY: Syracuse University Press.

DiMaggio, P. & W. W. Powell (1983). The Iron Cage Revisited: Institutional Isomorphism and Collective Rationality in Organizational Fields. *American Sociological Review*, 48(2), 147–60.

Drori, G., Y. Suk Jang, & J. W. Meyer (2006). Sources of Rationalized Governance: Cross-National Longitudinal Analyses, 1985–2002. *Administrative Science Quarterly*, 51(2), 205–29.

Drori, G., J. W. Meyer, & H. Hwang (2009). Global Organization: Rationalization and Actorhood as Dominant Scripts. *Research in the Sociology of Organizations*, 27, 17–43.

Drori, G., J. W. Meyer, F. O. Ramirez, & E. Schofer (2003). *Science and the Modern World Polity: Institutionalization and Globalization*, Stanford, CA: Stanford University Press.

Durkheim, E. (1969). Individualism and the Intellectuals. *Political Studies*, 17(1), 14–30.

Eisenstadt, S. N. (1966). *Modernization: Protest and Change*, Upper Saddle River, NJ: Prentice Hall.

Eisenstadt, S. N. (1996). *Japanese Civilization: A Comparative View*, Chicago, IL: University of Chicago Press.

Elliott, M. (2007). Human Rights and the Triumph of the Individual in World Culture. *Cultural Sociology*, 1(3), 353–63.

Elliott, M. (2011). The Institutional Expansion of Human Rights, 1863–2003: A Comprehensive Dataset of International Instruments. *Journal of Peace Research*, 48(4), 537–46.

Elliott, M. (2014). The Institutionalization of Human Rights and its Discontents: A World Cultural Perspective. *Cultural Sociology*, 8(4), 407–25.

Elster, J. (2015). *Explaining Social Behavior*, 2nd ed. Cambridge: Cambridge University Press.

Fiala, R. (2006). Educational Ideology and the School Curriculum. In A. Benavot & C. Braslavsky, eds., *School Knowledge in Comparative and Historical Perspective*. Dordrecht: Springer, pp. 15–34.

Fiala, R. & A. G. Lanford (1987). Educational Ideology and the World Educational Revolution. *Comparative Education Review*, 31(3), 315–32.

Frank, D. J., B. J. Camp, & S. A. Boutcher (2010). Worldwide Trends in the Criminal Regulation of Sex, 1945 to 2005. *American Sociological Review*, 75(6), 867–93.

Frank, D. J. & J. Gabler (2006). *Reconstructing the University: Worldwide Shifts in Academia in the 20th Century*, Stanford, CA: Stanford University Press.

Frank, D. J., A. M. Hironaka, & E. Schofer (2000). The Nation State and the Natural Environment, 1900–1995. *American Sociological Review*, 65(1), 96–116.

Frank, D. J., J. W. Meyer, & D. Miyahara (1995). The Individualist Polity and the Centrality of Professionalized Psychology. *American Sociological Review*, 60(3), 360–77.

Greenwood, R., C. Oliver, T. Lawrence, & R. Meyer, eds. (2017). *Sage Handbook of Organizational Institutionalism*, 2nd ed. Thousand Oaks, CA: SAGE.

Greenwood, R., C. Oliver, R. Suddaby, & K. Sahlin-Andersson, eds. (2008). *Sage Handbook of Organizational Institutionalism*, Los Angeles, CA: SAGE.

Hacking, I. (1999). *The Social Construction of What?* Cambridge, MA: Harvard University Press.

Hafner-Burton, E., K. Tsutsui, & J. W. Meyer (2008). International Human Rights Law and the Politics of Legitimation: Repressive States and Human Rights Treaties. *International Sociology*, 23(1), 115–41.

Hironaka, A. (2014). *Greening the Globe: World Society and Environmental Change*, New York, NY: Cambridge University Press.

Huntington, S. L. (1991). *The Third Wave: Democratization in the Late Twentieth Century*, Norman, OK: University of Oklahoma Press.

Ignatow, G. (2007). *Transnational Identity Politics and the Environment*, Lanham, MD: Lexington Books.

Jakobi, A. (2013). *Common Goods and Evils? The Formation of Global Crime Governance*, Oxford: Oxford University Press.

Kamens, D. H. (2012). *Beyond the Nation-State: The Reconstruction of Nationhood and Citizenship*, Bingley: Emerald Publishing.

Kruecken, G. & F. Meier (2006). Turning the University into an Organized Actor. In G. S. Drori, J. W. Meyer, & H. Hwang, eds., *Globalization and Organization*. Oxford: Oxford University Press, pp. 241–57.

Lee, C. K. & D. Strang (2006). The International Diffusion of Public-Sector Downsizing. *International Organization*, 60(4), 883–909.

Lipset, S. M. (1990). *Continental Divide: The Values and Institutions of the United States and Canada*, New York, NY: Routledge.

Meyer, J. W. (1977). The Effects of Education as an Institution. *American Journal of Sociology*, 83(1), 55–77.

Meyer, J. W. (2010). World Society, Institutional Theories, and the Actor. *Annual Review of Sociology*, 36(1), 1–20.

Meyer, J. W., D. Frank, A. Hironaka, E. Schofer, & N. Tuma (1997). The Structuring of a World Environmental Regime, 1870–1990. *International Organization*, 51(4), 623–51.

Meyer, J. W., D. Kamens, & A. Benavot, with Y. Cha, & S. Wong (1992). *School Knowledge for the Masses: World Models and National Curricula in the Twentieth Century*, London: Falmer.

Meyer, J. W., F. Ramirez, R. Rubinson, & J. Boli-Bennett (1977). The World Educational Revolution, 1950–1970. *Sociology of Education*, 50(4), 242–58.

Meyer, J. W., F. Ramirez, & Y. Soysal (1992). World Expansion of Mass Education, 1870–1970. *Sociology of Education*, 65(2), 128–49.

Meyer, J. W. & B. Rowan (1977). Institutionalized Organizations: Formal Structure as Myth and Ceremony. *American Journal of Sociology*, 83(2), 340–63.

Meyer, J. W. & B. Rowan (1978). The Structure of Educational Organizations. In M. W. Meyer, ed., *Environments and Organizations*. San Francisco, CA: Jossey-Bass, pp. 78–109.

Meyer, J. W. & W. R. Scott (1983). *Organizational Environments: Ritual and Rationality*, Beverly Hills, CA: SAGE.

Mills, C. W. (1940). Situated Actions and Vocabularies of Motive. *American Sociological Review*, 5(6), 904–13.

Parsons, T. (1966). *Societies: Evolutionary and Comparative Perspectives*, Englewood Cliffs, NJ: Prentice-Hall.

Parsons, T. (1971). *The System of Modern Societies*, Englewood Cliffs, NJ: Prentice-Hall.

Powell, W. & P. DiMaggio, eds. (1991). *The New Institutionalism in Organizational Analysis*, Chicago, IL: University of Chicago Press.

Ramirez, F. (1987). The Political Construction of Rape. In G. Thomas, J. Meyer, J. Boli, & F. Ramirez, eds., *Institutional Structure: Constituting State, Society, and the Individual*. Newbury Park, CA: SAGE, pp. 261–78.

Ramirez, F. & J. Boli (1987). The Political Construction of Mass Schooling: European Origins and Worldwide Institutionalization. *Sociology of Education*, 60(1), 2–17.

Ramirez, F. & J. W. Meyer (1980). Comparative Education: The Social Construction of the Modern World System. *Annual Review of Sociology*, 6, 369–99.

Ruggie, J. G. (1982). International Regimes, Transactions, and Change: Embedded Liberalism in the Post-War Economic Order. *International Organization*, 36(2), 379–415.

Ruggie, J. G. (1998). Globalization and the Embedded Liberalism Compromise: The End of an Era? In W. Streeck, ed., *Internationale Wirtschaft, Nationale Demokratie*. Frankfurt: Campus, pp. 79–98.

Sapolsky, R. (2017). *Behave: The Biology of Humans at our Best and Worst*, New York, NY: Penguin Press.
Schneider, L. & A. Silverman (2012). *Global Sociology: Introducing Five Contemporary Societies*, New York, NY: McGraw-Hill Education.
Schofer, E. & J. W. Meyer (2005). The World-Wide Expansion of Higher Education in the Twentieth Century. *American Sociological Review*, 70 (6), 898–920.
Scott, W. R. (2003). *Organizations: Rational, Natural, and Open Systems*, Upper Saddle River, NJ: Prentice Hall.
Simmons, B., F. Dobbin, & G. Garrett (2008). *The Global Diffusion of Markets and Democracy*, New York, NY: Cambridge University Press.
Strang, D. & J. W. Meyer (1993). Institutional Conditions for Diffusion. *Theory and Society*, 22(4), 487–511.
Swidler, A. (1986). Culture in Action: Symbols and Strategies. *American Sociological Review*, 51(2), 273–86.
Thomas, G., J. W. Meyer, F. Ramirez, & J. Boli (1987). *Institutional Structure: Constituting State, Society, and the Individual*, Beverly Hills, CA: SAGE.
Weick, K. (1976). Educational Organizations as Loosely Coupled Systems. *Administrative Science Quarterly*, 21(1), 1–19.
Wright, G. (1954). The Heritage of Contemporary France. In T. Cole, ed., *European Political Systems*. New York, NY: Alfred A. Knopf, pp. 593–698.
Zucker, L. (1977). The Role of Institutionalization in Cultural Persistence. *American Sociological Review*, 42(5), 726–43.

PART II

Institutional Theory: Its Role in Modern Social Analysis

2 | *Society without Culture:*
A Nineteenth-century Legacy (1988)

J. MEYER

Social scientists tend to look at the nineteenth century in terms of the social scientific categories constructed then. We also look at our own century mainly in terms of nineteenth-century categories. This is sometimes criticized and almost always emulated (for examples of both, see Tilly 1984). Thus, we have the notion of *society* as some sort of social system and somewhat separate from it the *state* as an organization with properties of purposive rationality. Society is made up of interdependent institutions, most notably an economy, but also a political system linking society to the state, and such institutions as the family, associational and community arrangements that reproduce society. The whole system is seen as a differentiated but interdependent one – a direct extension of a division of labor which is often used as a model or metaphor for the whole system. The world as a whole is an interstate system with some additional peripheries (the nineteenth-century idea is used for this, but not the terms, which would now seem racist or excessively evolutionary).

In using nineteenth-century images of the differentiated modern society, we still employ the two main variants, which differ in political imagery: "the division of labor" on the center, with the implication of mainly lateral distinctions along with a functional stratification system; from the left, "the class structure" with an implication of more vertical inequality that is functional for elites. Nineteenth-century issues about whether a society (or its more rationalistic and modern parts and its future) should be seen mainly as made up of a dominant economy or whether a wider range of institutional aspects are coequal still remain with us.

Beneath its classes and institutions, the nineteenth-century analyses had society made up of more elemental particles, which are still with us. Most prominently, there are *individuals* (citizens, workers, owners, buyers, sellers, voters, and so on): sometimes, as in English and American liberal thought, these are highly bounded individuals; while in German theory they are embedded in natural communities. In either case, these individuals are assembled in interest groups, occupational groups, firms, and so on, which also act as basic units of society. Society is made up of not only such units but their relations with each other of exchange, dominance, and solidarity.

2.1 Missing Elements

We get an idea of the nineteenth-century achievement and of the limitations of its analysis (and our own) by seeing what aspects of human social life are left out. What structures are seen as alien (properties of other kinds of societies, or of the past, but not the modern present)? What are seen as threatening or diabolic? What are utopian?

The most obvious weakened element in the nineteenth-century analysis of modern society is *culture*. The special field of anthropology is built around the analysis of more traditional societies as held in place by entrenched cultures, with their no-longer-elemental units immersed in a cake of custom built by history, transcendental authority, and natural evolution: there was to be no counterpart for the nineteenth-century present, nor for our own. Modern society was, for better or worse, a rationalistically analyzed and analyzable structure of particles and relations and in a larger sense functional interdependencies. Similarly, the intellectual analysis of the historical past contained substantial nonanalytic components stressing thematic meaning and cultural spirits, but in the nineteenth-century present and future of the social scientists, this was seen as becoming absorbed in reified social structure and social actions.

It will refine our point, that the theorists saw the nineteenth century as destroying culture in a wave of rationalistic institution building, to note the poles at which this is untrue. First, the nineteenth-century analysis well recognized its society's dependence on human cultural conceptions of nature: science and technology were seen as great cultural achievements of enormous, and sometimes diabolic, impact. The great optimism and pessimism about the scientific project lives on in our own analyses, and thus the acknowledgment that modern societies rely on cultural interpretations of nature just as much as traditional ones do. The difference was and is that scientific culture was believed to be objectively true.

Second, the nineteenth-century analyses certainly emphasized their societal dependence on cultural rules about transcendental and moral meanings, just as with traditional societies. Perhaps religion would and should die out, but there was much understanding of the need for transcendental meaning and values and much searching for them in nature, history, evolution, logic, and other deep structures. The Adam Smith who wrote the *Wealth of Nations* also wrote the *Theory of Moral Sentiments* – one can find the same dualisms in the post-Victorian creators of the new psychologies.

Third, the nineteenth-century analyses retained much awareness of the expressive aspects of human culture and their importance in their own society. Analyses rooting so much of society in individual consciousness and action tended to give much importance to the expression of individual sentiment and perception in such arts as music, literature, and painting. There was certainly no tendency to denigrate the subjective; indeed, there was, and is, much optimism and fear about its prospects.

What then was missing from the more complete analysis of culture that the same analysts would give to a society seen as more traditional? Missing was an analysis of modern human society itself as a cultural system, with its institutions and functions as cultural products and with its individual and associational elements as culturally constructed. The nineteenth century achieved an analysis of modern society as a real (positive) functioning system, made up of analyzable parts and relations operating under real requirements and constraints: a rationalized and rationalizable project. At one boundary there was nature (linked through cultural analysis); at another, unifying and universal moral visions (again reached through culture), and the primordial (mostly individual) internal components on which the system rested would carry meanings of their own. But society itself was a real system, not a cultural invention. One can speak of this as the invention of society without culture, and it certainly still lives as such in our own economic, political, psychological, and sociological analysis. Or one can, as some conservatives did, see it as the destruction of culture (or tradition, or community).

The vision seems widely shared, though with tonal variations. Some analyses have it that the modern society is progressive and ultimately equalitarian, while others view it as catastrophic and/or ultimately repressive and stratified. But they shared the vision that it was real, not a revised set of myths. Human society as culture was being destroyed, for better or worse, by rationalization and the emergence of real entities.

Even now, it is hard for most social science analyses to have it the other way. It is hard to see the new elements – the individual, the association, the firm, and other rationalized bureaucracy – as simply new cultural rules, no more natural or real than the old ones. Most analyses still have them bursting out of older (read cultural) constraints, as some sort of newer and more efficient and more natural entities: as unfettered forces. It is hard to see the new arrangements of economic, political, and familial life as cultural theory more than forces emergent from real society. It is especially hard to see the division of labor and the new class structure as cultural inventions in contrast to emergent elements.

There is an obvious reason for this theoretical distortion. The cultural transformations building up to and including the nineteenth century had undercut the older cultural authorities of the Western system in the name of new ideologies legitimated in terms of science and rationality. The culture of the new system was to become rulelike *because it was true*. Acknowledging that it might become true because it had been made rulelike was inconsistent with its premises. The "absolutism" of the nineteenth-century analysis of society, and its denial of itself as a culture, lay in this conception of society as a naturally self-legitimating system.

If one is, then, to step back and examine nineteenth-century society or our own as a system of cultural rules, one is led at once to the following crucial point. The cultural definitions and legitimations of society and social process in these modern arrangements are mainly made up of social scientific doctrines and their kin. For this reason, the social scientists – seeing them as natural and true – may not see their cultural power. But once stated, the point is relatively evident: modern economic arrangements, in both exchange and command economies, are organized under social scientific theory as are modern states and polities, as are modern educational systems and family arrangements, and so on. The doctrines involved are built into the professional knowledge as well as the legal and administrative authorities making up and altering these rules of the game. It is difficult to think of major social policy issues (for example, child abuse, the status of minorities, the improvement of education structures, and control of production organizations) that are not organized around social scientific principles of one sort or another functioning as culture.

2.2 The Ambiguous Conception of the State

Nowhere is the intellectual problem created by models of modern society without culture greater than in the nineteenth-century (and our own) conception of the state. The rise and intensification of the state system, and the organizational expansion of particular states, were the central phenomena given much attention. But the attempt to leave out the cultural aspects of the state, and to focus on what was seen as real, led to enduring problems. If one takes the state to be only a real organizational unit, made up out of power and tax revenue and compelling conformity through chains of command, a great deal is left out. Internally, it becomes difficult to explain the rise of nationalism, of democratic pressure, of interest group mobilization, and of individual citizenship rights. The well-recognized importance of legal arrangements and the law also becomes problematic, if the state is simply the head or coordinating structure of the modern social organism. Externally, the extraordinary reciprocities built into the wider interstate system become difficult to explain, and one must resort to the most entangling balance-of-power reasoning to explain one of the most enduring features of Western history.

But the organizational or realistic version of the definition of the state had, and continues to have, much power (for example, many of the papers in Evans et al. 1985; and in Tilly 1975; see also Wallerstein 1980). The alternative – to define the state as a legal and cultural project – has seemed much too idealistic: exactly the sort of normative and conceptual idealism the nineteenth-century discovery of society was to unmask.

Major research problems are left. If we define the state organizationally, those that have been intuitively the strongest in modern history (the Dutch, the British, and the American) seem hopelessly loose and weak; and some historically weaker ones (for example, Prussia, Sweden, France, or contemporary Third World states) are defined as strong because they have more organizational articulation. Internally, the organizational definition of the state has led to endless scholarly searches looking for the supposed coherence in policy and structure and the efficacy in producing organizational conformity that organizational theories require. Even the best cases – eighteenth-century Prussia or eighteenth- and nineteenth-century France – defeat the scholar: everywhere the search for coherent organizational structure finds weakness, entrenched rights, and so on.

The problem lies with the fact that the modern nation-state is so preeminently a cultural phenomenon – at the center lies a collection of claims to purpose, sovereignty, coordinative capability, representation of a nation and its citizens, and technical competence. The social scientific analysts deemphasize this aspect of the state perhaps because they are so much part of (or alternatively substitute for) it. There are many discussions in the social scientific literature on the relation of the social sciences to the state as organization – are they advisors, clients, sycophants, and so on? But if the state is defined in the larger sense as a cultural project in rationalization for progress, there is no question but that the social scientific ideologies – the individualistic models of psychologists and economists, the organizational models of sociologists and psychologists, and so on – are clearly components. Indeed, one could usefully argue that the social scientific analyses rose to greatest prominence where the *state* was strongest but the *state organization* was weaker: here the social scientific analyses become models of the proper social organization in the same sense that the state organization may provide the model in more highly bureaucratized contexts.

The consciousness that the state is a cultural entity tends to become absorbed, except in cases when the state's existence is entirely problematic. There is the fear of the state run amok – the totalitarian state – in which case the analysts indeed perceive the charismatic or cultural character of the enterprise. And when the state breaks down – or in the case of newly independent societies, does not yet exist – we are aware of the cultural character of the nationalist aspirations for it. What is missing is the idea that the dreams and myths that become apparent in such instances are also a continuing, evolving, and lively part of the state when the organizational aspect *is* in place. Ignoring this leaves analyses inattentive to the extraordinary tendency of modern states – modeled on quite general and worldwide evolving myths – to take on isomorphic qualities.

2.3 Organization

The consciousness that there is something beyond bureaucratic structure to the state is never completely eliminated, given the diffuse authority, the sovereignty claims, and the legal immersion of the modern Western state. The analysts, fashionably "realistic," hesitate to use such terms as culture, but certainly recognize elements of it in law and ideology. With other organizations, however, modern realism tends to take over more completely. Bureaucratic organizations are real assemblies of real offices and authority links; only in the recent period do the main social scientific analyses emphasize organizational dependence on and interpenetration of wider legitimating cultural rules. There is great faith in and fear of the possibilities of rational organizational structure, which perhaps inevitably makes up an iron cage for modern life (DiMaggio and Powell 1983); each step forward in the construction of the bureaucratic society is given great technical attention, as if a new machine were developing. This machine image is the enduring one, and in generation after generation of researchers and commentators the discovery that organization is not really like that comes as a surprise. The mythic and cultural aspects of rationality, as opposed to the mechanistic ones, come only into the margins of the social scientific consciousness and thus turn up more as surprising findings than as established theories and doctrines.

The same holds for other aspects of the organizational structure and modern societies. The faith in the existence as real entities of classes, interest groups, and other elements of the division of labor – a term of enduring significance and reification in social scientific thought – is a continuing feature. The hubris of the nineteenth century lay in the conceit that society was coming into existence as a real analyzable and plannable structure of parts and relationships, no longer at the mercy of the irrational gods and pervasive culture. This hubris, best vested and articulated in social scientific thought, itself makes up much of the culture and ideology of the system.

As a culture, rationality (or culturelessness) has had a good deal of coherence and continuity. But the inconsistency involved has been a constantly problematic element for the social sciences. Everywhere they look for the ideologically necessary "real structure," but find myth-laden uncertainty. The searches for the rational voter, consumer, worker, and producer lead to small correlations, as do those for the determinate organizational structure and for the clearly bounded, coherently structured, and densely informed interest and class groups. There has, for instance, been a chronic search for the real social classes throughout the history of empirical sociology. The metarules of class, written into constitutional and party arrangements and legal justifications, are clearly present as a culture, even in the Third World peripheries, but turn out to be rather decoupled from definite individual and group consciousness and action: small findings have to be trumpeted as proofs of large theoretical realities.

2.4 Individuals

The grounding element in most nineteenth-century analyses of society was (and remains) the individual, though other possible entities such as families, communities, or occupational groups were attempted in some visions. More liberal systems have continuously been dominant, and so individualistic analyses of society won out. A great deal of theory and discovery of the real and fundamental properties of the individual went on and has continued to the present. Contemporary individuals are still seen as very real entities and the fundamental units of society, but they have many more attributed properties of personality, motivation, and perception than did the individuals conceptualized in eighteenth- and nineteenth-century science and political order. Discovering and proving the bounded coherence of the economic, political, and psychological person has been a major enterprise in the institutionalization of modern models of society. The faith that individuals are real and coherent entities remains and is cultural and legal doctrine practically everywhere – but it has continuously posed major research problems for the social sciences. Great research traditions arise over the continuous discoveries that people are less coherent and rational actors and decisionmakers and theoreticians of themselves than theory requires: each round of discoveries is followed by a new generation of more complex theories discovering human individuality (including order and rationality) beneath the apparent disorder.

The sacredness of the individual, in modern systems, is so great that even the social scientific analysts tend to recognize cultural elements in it – though efforts to treat it as natural in language or biology remain. But the implications of the idea that individuality is a legal and religious and cultural myth structure much more than a natural social reality still remain poorly developed. We have, following the nineteenth-century thinkers, much analysis of the human as individual ego and actor; we have little analysis of this same human as *other*, imbued with cultural respect for its own individuality and that of others.

2.5 Research Problems

It seems necessary to try out many more social scientific models of modern society conceiving it as made up of the cultural rules of rationality, of individual-level social realism, and of the recipes for rational organization, including the state. We can understand better the spread of nineteenth-century social order around the world if we see it as an ideological system rather than only as a mixture of money and power. We can understand the ritual character of its institutions, and their peculiar and problematic relation to practice, if we think in terms of the myths that support the ritualization of rationality in so many ways.

A highly comparative perspective seems necessary. If one argues that modern states, organizations, interests, and individuals have a cultural character, cultural variation across time and space seems a crucial aspect of empirical work.

Beyond this, analyses of the evolution of the Western system as a cultural project seem urgently needed. How do the justifications and claimed functions of individuals, organizations, and states expand and spread over time? How are they integrated in various evolving models of the collectivity?

Finally, in examining the internal structure and evolution of Western systems, greater attention is needed to the collective and cultural aspects of the entities and functions involved. Crucial aspects of the state, organizational structures, interest groups, and the individual are the theories of how these are legitimate contributors to and components of the collective good. Modern history is thick with such justifications, and their availability is a central resource enabling the expansion and solidification of the associated structures. Models of change that treat the availability of legitimating rules for emergent social entities as a resource are needed, to parallel those we already have that follow the nineteenth-century theories rooting all of society in the power and resources of preexistent entities.

References

DiMaggio, P. J. & W. Powell. (1983). The Iron Cage Revisited: Institutional Isomorphism and Collective Rationality in Organizational Fields. *American Sociological Review*, 48(2), 147–60.

Evans, P., D. Rueschmeyer, & T. Skocpol, eds. (1985). *Bringing the State Back In*, Cambridge: Cambridge University Press.

Tilly, C. (1984). *Big Structures, Large Processes, Huge Comparisons*, New York, NY: Russell Sage Foundation.

Tilly, C., ed. (1975). *The Formation of National States in Western Europe*, Princeton, NJ: Princeton University Press.

Wallerstein, Immanuel. (1980). Mercantilism and the Consolidation of the European World-Economy, 1600–1750. Vol. II of *The Modern World System*. New York, NY: Academic Press.

3 Institutions, Institutional Effects, and Institutionalism (1991)

R. JEPPERSON[*]

Institution and institutionalization are core concepts of general sociology. Across the social sciences, scholars reach for these terms to connote, in one fashion or another, the presence of authoritative rules or binding organization. As I write, for example, the university where I work is holding a series of symposia on institutional racism. This series presumably differs from one that might be held on racism – or so at least its announcements suggest. The symposia seem to concentrate more on historical, organizational, and structural features of racism – institutional racism – features distinct from the race-related orientations and preferences of individuals.

This usage conforms with what may be the core denotation of *institution* in general sociology, that is, an institution as an organized, established, procedure.[1] These special procedures are often represented as the constituent rules of society (the "rules of the game"). They are then experienced and analyzable as external to the consciousness of individuals (Berger, Berger, and Kellner 1973: 11). This most general denotation may help us understand why some scholars have even identified sociology with the study of institutions. Durkheim did so, for example, calling sociology "the science of institutions" (e.g., [1901] 1950:1x). And one commentator on Weber suggests that "the theory of institutions is the sociological counterpart of the theory of competition in economics" (Lachmann 1971:68).

But the import and centrality of the concept of institution (and of its related terms) have not guaranteed clear and thoughtful usage. Some

---

[*] (a) See Chapter 5 note 1 for two important critical remarks about this chapter. (b) Citations for "this volume" in the text point to other chapters in the book in which this chapter first appeared, namely: W. W. Powell & P. J. DiMaggio, eds., *The New Institutionalism in Organizational Analysis*, Chicago: University of Chicago Press (1991).

scholars invoke *institution* simply to refer to particularly large, or important, associations. Others seem to identify institutions with environmental effects. And some simply equate the term with "cultural" effects, or with historical ones.[2]

This conceptual variety and vagueness is striking. It is also troubling, given the recent emergence of various "new institutionalisms" across the social sciences: in political science (e.g., March and Olsen 1984), in economics (Langlois 1986), in psychology (Farr and Moscovici 1984), and now in organizational analysis. Before such institutionalisms themselves become institutionalized – reified as distinct "theoretical strategies," codified in textbooks, and taken as given by practitioners – we had better take stock. In this spirit, this chapter is largely concerned with the conceptualization of institutions, institutional effects, and institutionalism. My intentions are twofold. First, I intend to describe a core structure within the semantic field of institutional terms. I recommend that we employ exclusively these core meanings and avoid a number of current conceptualizations, many of which serve only to confound institutional terms with other concepts or build untested empirical claims into our definitions. Second, by employing this clarification, I attempt to specify the distinguishing features of institutionalism as a line of theory.

In brief, I argue that institutionalization best denotes a distinct social property or state (and I attempt to specify this property), and that institutions should not be specifically identified, as they often are, with either cultural elements or a type of environmental effect (Sections 3.1 and 3.2 below). It then becomes possible to represent institutionalization as a particular set of social reproductive processes, while simultaneously avoiding the opposition of institutionalization and "change" (Section 3.3). And it becomes possible to represent institutionalism in an entirely straightforward way, as arguments featuring higher-order constraints imposed by socially constructed realities, and to distinguish it from other lines of argument (Sections 3.4 and 3.5).

While this chapter concentrates on basic conceptualization, it is decidedly substantive in its aspirations. I hope to provide materials of immediate utility for communicating about, organizing, and advancing substantive arguments. (Concepts without propositions do not constitute theory, as Homans properly reminded Parsons, but propositions linking ill-formed concepts also can represent much wasted effort.) My examples and applications are drawn from organizational analysis, but the basic conceptual issues are entirely general ones.[3]

3.1 Institutions and Institutionalization

I begin with examples of objects commonly thought to represent institutions. Consider the following list:

marriage	academic tenure
sexism	presidency
the contract	the vacation
wage labor	attending college
the handshake	the corporation
insurance	the motel
formal organization	the academic discipline
the army	voting

First note some differences between these objects. Some can be referred to as organizations, others not. Some may seem more "cultural," others more "structural." But the objects share important commonalities that encourage us to group them together. All are variously "production systems" (Fararo and Skvorctz 1986), or "enabling structures," or social "programs," or performance scripts. Each of these metaphors connotes stable designs for chronically repeated activity sequences. This basic imagery is at the core of sociological uses.[4]

We can tighten our conceptualization of institutional terms considerably by pursuing these metaphors. *Institution* represents a social order or pattern that has attained a certain state or property; *institutionalization* denotes the process of such attainment.[5] By *order* or *pattern*, I refer, as is conventional, to standardized interaction sequences. An institution is then a social pattern that reveals a particular reproduction process. When departures from the pattern are counteracted in a regulated fashion, by repetitively activated, socially constructed, controls – that is, by some set of rewards and sanctions – we refer to a pattern as institutionalized.[6] Put another way: institutions are those social patterns that, when chronically reproduced, owe their survival to relatively self-activating social processes. Their persistence is not dependent, notably, upon recurrent collective mobilization, mobilization repetitively reengineered and reactivated in order to secure the reproduction of a pattern. That is, institutions are not reproduced by "action," in this strict sense of collective intervention in a social convention. Rather, routine reproductive procedures support and sustain the pattern, furthering its reproduction – unless collective action blocks, or environmental shock disrupts, the reproductive process.

This qualification ("unless ... ") is important. The discussion so far might suggest that institutionalization is either equivalent to, or a form of, stability or survival. But this identification is inaccurate. If one holds a pattern to be institutionalized, one points to the presence of ongoing reproductive processes whereby "departures from normal forms of action defined by the [institutional] design tend to be counteracted" through routines (Fararo and Skvoretz 1986:224). But whether these processes actually succeed, and ensure the pattern's survival, is an entirely separate matter. For example, in certain conditions, high institutionalization can make a structure more vulnerable to environmental shock (from internal or external environments). Tocqueville's analysis of the "Old Regime and the French Revolution" provides a classic example: the French state was highly institutionalized, but in a way that made it highly vulnerable to environmental change (it was a "house of cards," in Tocqueville's phrasing) (Tocqueville [1856] 1955).

Consider again the above entries in the list of putative institutions. We consider voting to be an institutionalized social pattern in (say) the United States, while not in (say) Haiti. We do so in large part because voting in the United States is embedded in a host of supporting and reproducing practices and is not highly dependent (as it is in Haiti) on repeated political intervention for its employment. Similarly, the academic discipline is an institution within the modern university system because it is linked to other similarly institutional practices that, taken together, constitute the university system. These institutional practices require, again, relatively little "action" – repetitive mobilization and intervention – for their sustenance. More on the differences between institutionalization and "action" in a moment.

These examples remind us additionally that institutionalization is a relative property: we decide whether to consider an object to be an institution depending upon analytical context. The examples just above suggest one dimension of this general relativity: whether a practice is an institution is, (1), relative to particular contexts. But we can extend and formalize this relativity a bit more.

Within any system having multiple levels or orders of organization, (2), primary levels of organization can operate as institutions relative to secondary levels of organization. A microcomputer's basic operating system appears as an institution relative to its word-processing program (especially to a software engineer). In collectivities, constitutional procedures may appear institutional relative to practices of formal organization, and the latter practices institutional relative to unorganized social practices.

Further, whether an object is an institution is, (3), relative to a particular dimension of a relationship. In certain respects, Yale University is more institution to New Haven than to most other communities (it is a prominent fixture of the local environment); yet in other respects, Yale is less an institution in New Haven than elsewhere (Paul DiMaggio notes, only half kidding, that the prestige of an Ivy League university seems to equal the square root of the distance from it). Parents are more institutions to their own children, than to other kids, as taken-for-granted realities; yet children may contest their own parents' authority more than that of others' parents.

Finally, whether an object is an institution is, (4), relative to centrality. In systems, cores are institutions relative to peripheries. The regime of international politico-economic coordination is more an external, objective, constraint for Ghana than for the IMF. An association can be more an institution – more a fixed feature of an external environment – for a nonmember than for a member.

The details and dimensions are here less important than the general point – that the same term, "in a different reference" (MacIver 1931:16), may, or may not, denote an institution. Whether we consider an object an institution depends upon what we are considering to be our analytical problem.

3.1.1 How Do Institutions Operate?

Institutions are not just constraint structures; all institutions simultaneously empower and control. Institutions present a constraint/freedom duality (Fararo and Skvoretz 1986): they are vehicles for activity within constraints (thus the imagery of "production systems" suggested by Fararo and Skvoretz). All institutions are frameworks of programs or rules establishing identities and activity scripts for such identities.[7] For example, the formal organization, considered as an institution (March and Simon 1958:2–4; Stinchcombe 1973), is a packaged social technology, with accompanying rules and instructions for its incorporation and employment in a social setting. Institutions thus embody "programmed actions" (Berger and Luckmann 1966:75) or "common responses to situations" (Mead [1934] 1972:263). Institutionalized programs then produce expectational bonds or "reciprocal expectations of predictability" (Field 1979:59). Put informally: institutions operate primarily by affecting persons' prospective bets about the collective environment and collective activity.[8]

Through their effects on expectations, institutions become taken for granted, in some fashion. The qualifier ("in some fashion") is a crucial one: while most discussions directly associate institutionalization with "taken-for-grantedness" (e.g., Zucker 1983), this phenomenological concept is an ambiguous and underanalyzed one. Taken-for-granted objects are those that are treated as exterior and objective constraints (see, e.g., Berger and Luckmann 1966; Zucker 1983). But such facticity can take on a number of quite different forms. First, taken-for-grantedness is distinct from comprehension, as is well recognized (e.g., Berger and Luckmann 1966:60): a pattern may be treated as exterior, objective, constraining, whether or not persons feel they understand the pattern well. But also, and less recognized, taken-for-grantedness is distinct from conscious awareness: one may take for granted some pattern because one does not perceive it, or think about it; alternatively, one may subject the pattern to substantial scrutiny, but still take it for granted – if in a quite different fashion – as an external objective constraint. Further, taken-for-grantedness is distinct from evaluation: one may subject a pattern to positive, negative, or no evaluation, and in each case (differently) take it for granted.[9]

When analysts refer to institutions as taken for granted, they may have a more specific idea in mind. They are suggesting that institutions are those standardized activity sequences that have taken-for-granted rationales, that is, in sociological parlance, some common social "account" of their existence and purpose. Persons may not well comprehend an institution, but they typically have ready access to some functional or historical account of why the practice exists. They also have an expectation that further explication is available, should they require it. Institutions are taken for granted, then, in the sense that they are both treated as relative fixtures in a social environment and explicated (accounted for) as functional elements of that environment.[10]

3.1.2 To What Should Institutionalization Be Opposed?

It may further clarify our understanding of what institutionalization is if we consider what it is not. If a social object is not institutionalized, to what analytical class might it be said to belong?

Since institutionalization is a property of an order, it can be opposed, in the first instance, to the absence of order – in effect, to social entropy. But beyond this rather trivial contrast (and secondly), institutionalization can also be distinguished from the absence of reproductive processes. For example, we may find some social patterns that are the recurrent products of elementary social behavior (as pictured by Homans, or in contemporary biosociology). We may wish to consider some generic prestige or esteem processes, or common social patterns that emerge in cases of institutional breakdown, as examples (Homans 1961: ch. 16). In addition, some social patterns are repeated or persistent unintended consequences of social interaction, rather than chronically reproduced patterns. For example, consider the repetitive operation of some general sociological regularity, like the "social distancing" processes driving some patterns of housing segregation. In these cases, we may find a persisting social pattern, but it is not secured through the self-activating reproduction processes characteristic of institutions.

Third, institutionalization can be distinguished from other forms of reproduction. For example, we may wish to consider deep socialization (e.g., internalization) as a process distinct from institutionalization and as an alternative medium for the reproduction of social patterns. (It would be useful to have a typology of main social reproduction forms.) Here I wish to concentrate on just one contrast: between institutionalization and "action," as I have defined it above, as two different reproduction forms. A social pattern is reproduced through action if persons repeatedly (re)mobilize and (re)intervene in historical process to secure its persistence. In some Latin American countries, democracy is sustained (when it is sustained) by action in this sense, rather than by the institutional processes that largely promote it in (say) the United Kingdom. "Action" is a much weaker form of reproduction than institutionalization, because it faces all the "logic of collective action" problems well established in the literature (e.g., Olson 1965).

Similarly, when Dahrendorf speaks of the "institutionalization of class conflict" (1964:267 ff.), he is arguing that class action is supplanted: that the political interaction between classes proceeds largely without recurrent attempted interventions by organized classes into social processes and, additionally, that "class conflict" may be sustained in the absence of persisting class subcultures or class consciousness. (Whether he is right or wrong in so arguing is, here, irrelevant.) Class relations become less immediately political, since they become naturalized as a stable feature of constraining environment – they become institutionalized.

This institutionalization/action contrast is a central one. If one participates conventionally in a highly institutionalized social pattern, one does not take action, that is, intervene in a sequence, make a statement. If shaking hands is an institutionalized form of greeting, one takes action only by refusing to offer one's hand. If attending college has become an institutionalized stage of the life course, a young person takes action more by forgoing college than by enrolling in it. The point is a general one: one enacts institutions; one takes action by departing from them, not by participating in them.

To summarize so far, without attempting a tight definition: institutions are socially constructed, routine-reproduced (ceteris paribus), program or rule systems. They operate as relative fixtures of constraining environments and are accompanied by taken-for-granted accounts. This description accords with the metaphors repeatedly invoked in discussions – metaphors of frameworks or rules. These imageries capture simultaneous contextual empowerment and constraint, and taken-for-grantedness.

3.1.3 Examples of Arguably Less Productive Conceptualizations of Institutional Terms

I have argued that institutionalization is best represented as a particular state, or property, of a social pattern. I now need to distinguish this conceptualization, briefly, from other current depictions.

Some analysts render institutionalization as a "property" idea, as I do here, but associate it with the properties of legitimacy, or formal organization, or contextuality. Each of these associations seems misguided. Legitimacy may be an outcome of institutionalization, or it may contribute to it, but illegitimate elements can clearly become institutionalized (organized crime, political corruption, fraud, etc.).[11] Similarly, while we may wish to consider formal organization as an institution, or argue that formal organization can carry or generate institutions (e.g., Zucker 1987), or that some organizations have become institutions (the Red Cross), it is arbitrary to identify institutionalization with formal organization. We have good reason to consider voting and marriage to be institutions, for example, and they are not formal organizations.

Further, while some analysts equate contextual or environmental effects with institutional ones, they are analytically quite distinct. All institutional effects have contextual qualities, as we have seen (the quality of external, objective, constraint), but not all contextual effects are institutional ones.[12] Many contextual effects are aggregative in character, for example, rather than institutional. We may consider a number of international market effects on national economies as being contextual effects; while such markets have institutional foundations, we typically do not consider their effects as immediately or proximately institutional.

Context invokes a spatial contrast: external, widespread, or global, versus local. Some analysts use institutionalization not to invoke context but to delimit a particular level of analysis, most often a macro level. *Macro*, like contextual, can specify a wide span of both time and space, or alternatively – in what I think is a tighter usage – it can invoke an hierarchic comparison: more highly organized versus less highly organized.[13] In any case, identification of institution with any one level of analysis is also misleading. Some institutional effects are not macro-organized – for example, some of the "interaction rituals" captured by Goffman. These patterns may be widespread and therefore have contextual qualities, but they are institutionalized at submacro orders of organization. (More on these issues in a later section.)[14]

A third category of definitions differentiates institutions by associating them with particular social domains or controls. In organizational analysis, especially, many commentators associate institutions in one way or another with "culture," that is, with normative effects, ideas, conceptions, "preconscious understandings," myths, ritual, ideology, theories, or accounts. This conceptualization greatly confuses discussion and development of institutional arguments because any of the various social control structures can be more, or less, institutionalized; no one in itself encapsulates institutionalization. "Culture" – typically represented as those forms of "consciousness" with socially coordinating effects – may be more or less institutionalized. (For example, one might consider single parenting as a significant cultural pattern, but still not wish to represent it, at least yet, as a highly institutionalized one.) All institutions embody social rationales or accounts, but this is no reason to identify institutions with the class of rationales or accounts. It may be that analysts tend to equate institutionalization with culture for a historical reason: in the modern nation-states, much institutionalization is carried by cultural rules (as argued, e.g., in Meyer, Boli, and Thomas 1987).[15] But institutionalization is better reserved as an abstract property that can characterize many forms of social coordination.[16]

3.2 Forms and Degrees of Institutionalization

3.2.1 Forms of Institutionalization

One can delimit three primary carriers of institutionalization: formal organization, regimes, and culture. Perhaps most discussion has concentrated on institutional effects emanating from formal organization, for example, studies of the effects of work organization on individual conformity (Kohn 1969).

There are then two primary types of informally organized institutionalization. The first I denote by the term *regimes*, referring to institutionalization in some central authority system – that is, in explicitly codified rules and sanctions – without primary embodiment in a formal organizational apparatus. A legal or constitutional system can operate as a regime in this sense, but so can, for example, a profession (or for that matter, a criminal syndicate). With regimes, expectations focus upon monitoring and sanctioning by some form of a differentiated, collective, "center."[17]

Institutionalization can also be carried by "culture": here simply those rules, procedures, and goals without primary representation in formal organization, and without monitoring and sanctioning by some "central" authority. These rules are, rather, customary or conventional in character. Institutionalizing in culture produces expectations about the properties, orientations, and behavior of individuals, as constraining "others" (Mead) in the social environment.

In saying that institutions can be carried in different ways, I have distinguished between different types of rule or control structures (organization, regime, culture).[18] Institutions can certainly have a complex embodiment: in both regime and culture, for example (citizenship). But we need some such distinctions for a number of reasons. First, they force us to keep separate institutionalization, as a property, from particular types of rule or control structures. Also, institutions having different primary carriers (e.g., the handshake in "culture") may operate in different fashions. Further, we may wish to distinguish collectivities, or historical periods, by their relative reliance on the differing modes of institutionalization. For example, consider the claim that the history of the modern Western world is driven particularly by institutions "devolving from a dominant universalist historical culture" (Meyer, Boli, and Thomas 1987:27).

3.2.2 Degrees of Institutionalization

Can we generate a rough metric of institutionalization? For example, how might we compare the relative institutionalization of the following institutions in contemporary American society: the liberal state, racial discrimination, the corporation, sexism?[19] This topic represents a persistent weak point in institutional discussion, and I do little to remedy the problem here, beyond delimiting the issue.[20]

We can pull together some clues about how to proceed from the literature. Goffman's "total" institutions are entirely encompassing structures, highly sequestered from environments and tightly integrating various aspects of life around a singular plan (Goffman 1961). Berger and Luckmann provide more general imagery when they suggest that total institutionalization is, archetypically, liturgy – the total absence of "action." All "problems" are common; all "solutions" socially constructed and reified; all expectations common and publicly hegemonic (Berger and Luckmann 1966:80).[21] With total institutionalization, "the only distinctive contribution an individual can make is in the skill and style of performance" (Shibutani 1986:16).

This imagery suggests that one can perhaps best conceive of degrees of institutionalization in terms of relative vulnerability to social intervention. An institution is highly institutionalized if it presents a near insuperable collective action threshold, a formidable collective action problem to be confronted before affording intervention in and thwarting of reproductive processes.

A given institution is less likely to be vulnerable to intervention if it is more embedded in a framework of institutions. It is more embedded if it has been long in place (so that other practices have adapted to it) or more centrally located within a framework (so that it is deeply situated). It is more embedded if it is integrated within a framework by unifying accounts based in common principles and rules. Further, the greater the linkage of this institution to constraints conceived to be socially exogenous – namely, to either socially exogenous (transcendental) moral authority or presumed laws of nature – the less vulnerability to intervention.[22]

The degree of institutionalization is also dependent on the form of taken-for-grantedness. If members of a collectivity take for granted an institution because they are unaware of it and thus do not question it, or because any propensity to question has halted due to elimination of alternative institutions or principles (e.g., by delegitimating them through reference to natural or spiritual law), the institution will be decidedly less vulnerable to challenge and intervention, and will be more likely to remain institutionalized.[23]

3.3 Institutional Change

There are a number of distinct types and processes of institutional change. Remembering the principle that every entry is an exit from someplace else, we can distinguish four major types of institutional change: institutional formation, institutional development, deinstitutionalization, and reinstitutionalization.[24]

Institutional formation is an exit from social entropy, or from nonreproductive behavioral patterns, or from reproductive patterns based upon "action." Examples of these three exits, respectively, might be the institutionalization of the self, as it is differentiated from nature and the gods (e.g., in the Greek period [Snell 1960]), of sexuality (as discussed by Foucault 1978 or Elias 1978), and of class conflict (Dahrendorf 1964).

Institutional development (or elaboration) represents institutional continuation rather than an exit – a change within an institutional form. An example might be the expansion of citizenship, as charted by Marshall (1964).

Deinstitutionalization represents an exit from institutionalization, toward reproduction through recurrent action, or nonreproductive patterns, or social entropy. The crescive deinstitutionalizations of gender, or of community corporate structures, as central socio-organizational vehicles, are examples.

Reinstitutionalization represents exit from one institutionalization, and entry into another institutional form, organized around different principles or rules. The long-term transformation of religion in Western societies, captured in discussions of secularization, is an example of the reinstitutionalization of a persisting social force.

There are a number of distinct ways in which institutions, once established, can change (i.e., develop, become deinstitutionalized, be reinstitutionalized) (see generally the discussion in Eisenstadt 1968: 418–20). Institutions can develop contradictions with their environments (as pictured in ecological thinking), with other institutions (as pictured by Marx), or with elementary social behavior (as pictured by Homans 1961: ch. 16; see also Friedland and Alford, this volume). These contradictions, or, separately, exogenous environmental shocks, can force institutional change by blocking the activation of reproductive procedures or by thwarting the successful completion of reproductive procedures, thus modifying or destroying the institution. Institutions can embody endogenous change as well: for example, procedural rationality, as a social institution itself, drives social change by routinizing it.

3.4 Institutional Effects and Institutionalism

Institutional effects are those that feature institutions as causes. The imagined institutional effects may be upon institutions, as dependent variables (e.g., the effects of the state on science), or upon dependent variables that are not in themselves represented as institutions (e.g., the effects of changes in the educational system upon consumer choices). One can thus identify two major classes of institutional effects.

Institutional *explanations* are those featuring institutional effects, or that weight institutional effects highly relative to other effects, or that isolate institutionally caused features of an analytical object. Institutional *theories* then are those that feature institutional explanations. *Institutionalism* is a theoretical strategy that features institutional theories and seeks to develop and apply them.

It may be best to try to capture institutionalism by contrasting it with other lines of theory. One way to differentiate sociological arguments is by noting the degree to which they represent units as socially constructed, and by the levels of analysis most commonly employed in their causal propositions. The "levels" dimension distinguishes roughly between methodologically structuralist and individualist imageries; the "constructedness" dimension distinguishes between phenomenological and realist conceptions of causal units and processes. These two dimensions define a simple table of lines of theory (see the figure below).[25] Institutionalism invokes institutions as causes, so it necessarily emphasizes both high social construction and higher-order effects. In the catchphrases employed here, institutionalism thus tends to be both "phenomenological" and "structuralist." I first discuss the two dimensions abstractly and then explicate each cell of the figure with examples; I provide fullest development of the institutionalism cell.

Highly socially constructed units are opposed to putatively natural or non-contextual ones. That is, high constructedness denotes that the social objects under investigation are thought to be complex social products, reflecting context-specific rules and interactions. In low-construction (here, "realist") imagery, units may enter into social relations that influence their behavior, but the units themselves are socially pregiven, autochthonous.[26] In high-construction (here, "phenomenological") imagery, the units' existence is itself a framework-specific social creation – in phenomenological parlance, units are "constituted." These units may then be separately influenced by social ties as well.[27] In high-construction imagery, one cannot isolate subunit "foundations" of social organization; one rather seeks deep or core rules. The causal imageries are quite distinct: a natural base, a social superstructure, in realist lines; a nested system of social programs, in

Degree to Which Units Socially Constructed	Featured Level of Analysis	
	Low Order (Individualist)	High Order (Structuralist)
High Construction (Phenomenological)	1 "Org. Culture"; symbolic interaction	2 Institutionalism
Low Construction (Realist)	3 Actor &/or functional reduction attempts; neo–classical econ.; behavioral psych.; most neoinstitutional econ.; some network theory	4 Social ecology; resource dependence; some network theory

Figure 3.1 Lines of theory in organizational analysis

phenomenological ones. This fundamental difference is not captured by conventional (and questionable) idealist/materialist or structure/agency distinctions.[28]

By levels of analysis, the second dimension, I refer to the levels of social organization most commonly featured in causal propositions, namely, higher versus lower orders of organization. This dimension taps differences over how social influence or construction processes take place. Methodologically individualist lines try to invoke only low orders of social organization in their explanations and thus seek single-level explanations; they give relatively micro-orders causal primacy over more macro-orders of organization in this fashion. Structuralist lines allow for independent and unmediated effects of multiple orders of organization, and often, though not necessarily, see higher orders as having greater causal potency than lower orders.[29]

The figure can be put to quite general use, but here its cells present examples from organizational analysis. Consider the cell entries as ideal-typical tendencies. The lines of theory represented in cell 3, for example – low-low: individualist/realist – attempt to reduce organizational properties directly to primitively social units (low construction), linked primarily by interactions within a single, usually low, order of organization. With low values on both dimensions, the cell entries, not surprisingly, tend to come from outside of sociology – these lines of argument, at the limit (e.g., in the neoclassical theory of the firm) admit neither social content nor structure. So firms in this line of argument are represented as units showing little social construction (at the limit, as "black boxes"), affected primarily by each other (homogeneous units), and linked by causal processes operating through low orders of organization (at the limit, through markets conceived as aggregative containers, without much structure).[30]

The lines of argument in cell 4 (higher levels, low construction: structuralist/realist) differ from cell 3 primarily by injecting additional, and higher, orders of organization into their causal imageries. In these lines, firms may be the organizational counterpart to "fruit flies" – that is, largely natural entities – but they face environments having substantial structure and heterogeneity (e.g., multiple types of resource and selection constraint, represented at different orders of organization – as in resource dependence and ecological ideas). Interactional ties can be networks linking heterogeneous units (e.g., firms to individuals or states as well as to other firms).

The lines of thought in cell 1 differ from those in cell 3 in a separate way. In these individualist/phenomenological lines of argument, rather than adding levels and considering higher-order causal effects, cell 1 ideas depart from the "black box" imageries. Firms here can be histories, or cultures. In phenomenologically inspired social psychologies, for example – as in the ideas of Weick (1969), or in "organizational culture" research – the entities linked to one another are highly constructed: for example, identities or roles with complex local histories and specificity. In the "levels" dimension, however, the cell 1 ideas run parallel to those in cell 3. Causal imagery typically invokes single rather than multilevel analysis, and the primary causal forces invoked seem to operate at a relatively local level, linking a fairly homogeneous set of units (e.g., local negotiation of identities, or effects of past organizational culture upon the present one).

Cell 2 represents institutionalism (high-high: structuralist/phenomenological), departing from the reduction attempts of cell 3 along both dimensions. In institutionalist imagery, firms can be, among other things, embodied cultural theories of organizing (March and Simon 1958:2–4; Stinchcombe 1973; Meyer and Rowan 1977). Some examples of institutionalism may help clarify its characteristics. I start with some examples from outside of organizational analysis and then suggest some from within.

In historical sociology, institutionalism is apparent in the recently reinvigorated exploration of the formation and development of capitalism, individualism, and democracy. For example, arguments that individualism emerges as part of collective political and religious frameworks (and in part from the substantive contents of Christian doctrine), rather than from aggregations of persons' reactions to micro-level and immediate social experiences, are characteristically institutionalist ones. So are arguments that hold Christendom to be a driving force in the development of Western capitalism, not just by "pacifying" social relations by providing some normative framework (Mann 1986), but by constructing and stimulating economic relations through specific institutionalized cultural tenets (Meyer 1988). Institutionalist arguments are apparent in those depictions of "modernization" as the incorporation of an ideological package of institutions and accounts rather than a threshold effect of accumulated experiences and reactions (Inkeles and Smith 1974). In social psychology, Swanson, Goffman, and Berger and Luckmann all develop institutionalist lines in emphasizing the ways in which variation in collectivity types can constitute different forms of self (e.g., Swanson 1986: Goffman 1974; Berger, Berger, and Kellner 1973). Distinct institutionalist arguments are also apparent in the study of institutions themselves, such as education or the family. Note the argument that education affects society not only indirectly through socialization or credentialing of individuals, but also directly through the (higher-order and social construction) effects of education on other institutions, for example, through the creation of an educated society, theories of personnel, and a "scientized polity" (Habermas 1970; also see Meyer 1977).

This volume provides a number of examples of institutionalist argumentation in organizational analysis. The institutionalist emphasis on constructedness and high-order effects is apparent in its recurrent stress upon the dependence of formal organizing on special institutional conditions (e.g., Stinchcombe 1965; Meyer and Rowan 1977); in arguments about the incorporation of organizational practices from environments rather than the intraorganizational generation of such practices (Tolbert and Zucker 1983); in institutionalist emphasis upon the import of social as well as ecological ties between organizations (e.g., DiMaggio and Powell, this volume; perhaps also White 1981); in the argument that differences in firms across nation-states may represent instances of broader forms of organizing specific to types of polities (Jepperson and Meyer, this volume); in the suggestion that while contemporary societies may be full of organizations, and that while formal organization may be an institution within them, these societies are not best considered to be "societies of organizations" (ibid).

These institutionalist arguments generally not only stress the structuring quality of rules or frameworks, but also attribute causal import to the particular substantive contents of the rules invoked – frames are not just formal structures. Fararo and Skvoretz usefully distinguish institutional from network theory by indicating that institutional arguments are structural ones that also "[preserve] the content of social action and interaction"; "social relations are content-filled control structures" (Fararo and Skvoretz 1986:242, 230). For example, we can observe the emphasis placed upon the social history of elements; in practice, this can amount to invoking lagged dependent variables as causes. In addition, emphasis on construction entails attention to social reflexivity as itself an independent source of social structuration, that is, the operation of publicly prominent social analysis of and discourse about social processes, as, in itself, a potential structuring force.[31] In this dimension (degree of constructedness), institutionalist arguments then differ markedly from those that posit units with largely autonomous and naturally emanating experiences, reflections, choices, preferences, actions – both by calling the autonomy and inevitable emanation into question and, independently, by questioning and restricting the causal potency of these non- (or less-) constructed elements. Neither actor nor activity is thought to be primordial; there is then little tendency to consider either as foundational of social structure. Rules or frames are the basic elements of social structure, in institutionalist imagery, rather than some class of asocial subunits.

In its emphasis on multilevel causal connections and on high or macroorder effects, institutionalism differs from arguments that rely primarily on aggregative processes (e.g., the collective as largely an additive outcome of microlevel states), on "demographic" depictions of structure (structural features as reflecting relative proportions of sets of subunits [Stinchcombe 1968: ch. 3]), and on causal models that largely feature single-level explanations (e.g., microlevel outcomes associated with microlevel causes). The higher-order effects can operate in a contextual or environmental manner, or as a strict collective effect, that is, as in the effects of a "center" or core of a system, represented as a higher order of organization, on a periphery of the system.

3.5 Institutionalism and Actors

This discussion has attempted to explicate the distinctive character of institutionalism in organizational analysis and to link these properties to a general institutionalism in social science. Note I have not attempted to assess the relative merits or explanatory success of institutionalism versus the other lines of argument represented in Figure 3.1 (though I have suggested some distinctions that should have immediate utility for evaluating the logical status of various arguments). Nor have I attempted to assess the scope relations of the various lines, that is, to determine whether the lines of theory directly compete, or have different explananda, or reveal any complementarities. At the very least, however, the above discussion should raise strong suspicions about common oppositions of institutional and "actor," or "interest," arguments. Such a contrast may confound a number of quite distinct issues.

Consider institutional and "rational-choice" arguments; they are often said to exist in sharp opposition. But note that self-proclaimed rational-choice arguments often feature institutional constraints (in connection with opportunity costs) as central causes (Friedman and Hechter 1988; Elster 1986), and institutional arguments often invoke adaptive responses to change in institutional conditions (see Scott, this volume). Do these two lines of argument truly amount to competing paradigms? Alternatively, they might represent competing ways to invoke institutional effects, or reflect disagreements about proper microfoundations of macroeffects, to mention just two alternatives. The literature is unclear.

Some issues seem straightforward. Institutionalism, like any set of causal arguments, must be capable of providing "microtranslation" (Collins 1981) of its propositions, that is, samples of the lower-level processes embodied in higher-order effects (in effect, statements about activities or behaviors of persons). Some institutionalist lines of argument – particularly the early institutionalism of, for example, Durkheim, or those institutionalist arguments advanced by Parsons, or the primitive institutionalism of "culture and personality" studies – largely neglected microtranslation, or failed the microtranslation test (e.g., the childhood socialization arguments of the early culture/personality studies). But the new institutionalisms seem no less capable of providing microtranslations than noninstitutionalist arguments, though they may provide different ones. Institutionalism may not advance conventional arguments about "actors" or "action" (more on this in a moment), but such conventions by no means define the totality of legitimate causal arguments.[32] Similarly, successful influence attempts by a delimited "actor," carrying a specific "interest," represent only one category of possible social change explanations, and successful change arguments need not be limited to it. Institutionalism also contributes a distinctive set of ideas to the class of change arguments (e.g., the idea of institutional contradiction, in Marx, or in Friedland and Alford, this volume). (See the conspectus of institutionalist causal mechanisms provided by Scott, this volume.)

The conceptualization suggested in Section 1, above, opposed institutionalization, in part, to "action" – in the specific sense there defined – but not to actors. Institutional arguments need not be directly contrasted with actor and interest accounts; rather, they represent, in part, a distinctive line of argument about actors and interests. Institutional accounts argue, as discussed above, that actors cannot be represented as foundational elements of social structure.[33] They suggest, typically, that actors and interests are highly institutional in their origins and operation and, moreover, that in modern polity forms they are often constructed institutions themselves (as, e.g., in Jepperson and Meyer, this volume). Institutionalism suggests that social systems vary in the extent to which "action" is carried by actors, in the canonical sense of autonomous rational egoists, operating in private capacities. In modern systems much action is conducted by authorized collective agents of one sort or another. Systems also can vary in how much "action" they sustain, and in the degree to which social reproduction is dependent upon action, relative, for example, to institutional processes.

Action references often become the social-theoretic analogue to the economist's automatic (and nonexplanatory) invocation of preferences and utility. In response, institutionalism has tended to "defocalize" actors (DiMaggio 1988) purposefully, because undue focus on actors has seemed to impair the production of sociology. But this discussion is not yet well developed by either those in or outside of institutionalism, so debate on these matters has been shallow.

3.6 Reprise

Institutions and institutional effects are core to general sociology rather than peripheral to or competitive with it. Institutional effects should not be narrowly associated with explanations of stability or thought to be irrelevant to change; institutions can be powerful sources of both stability and change. And while institutionalization can be opposed, in part, to "action," it is not well distinguished from actor or interest effects.

There are ironies here. Perhaps the discussion of both institutions and action has remained insufficiently developed due to institutional processes. American sociology's long-standing reification of action (Münch 1986), rooted in the larger institutional matrix of American society, has promoted the taken-for-grantedness of action and has simultaneously hindered scholarly perception of institutional effects.

Acknowledgments

This chapter reflects the author's discussion or correspondence with Elaine Backman, Randall Collins, Carol Conell, Walter W. Powell, John W. Meyer, David Strang, and Morris Zelditch, Jr. It also draws on written comments provided by Carol Conell, Paul J. DiMaggio, and Francisco Ramirez on an earlier version. More specific acknowledgments are provided in the text.

Notes

1. MacIver 1931:15–17 distinguished sharply between an association, as an organized group, and an institution, as an organized procedure.
2. See Eisenstadt 1968 for a catalog of uses of the term, Znaniecki 1945 for a rich historical discussion of institutional thinking, and Scott 1987b for an overview of the use of the concept in organizational analysis.
3. This chapter draws on a large number of works, but especially upon Fararo and Skvoretz 1986; Zucker 1983; and Meyer, Boli, and Thomas 1987. Also, Sartori 1984 and Cohen 1980: ch. 7 provide powerful and complementary insights on the requisites of good conceptualization – insights this chapter attempts to employ.
4. This imagery is reflected in the work of a great variety of social theorists, including Mead [1934] 1972:261ff., Parsons 1951, Gerth and Mills 1953, Berger and Luckmann 1966, Durkheim [1901] 1950, Davis 1949, Hayek 1973, Goffman 1974, Buckley 1967, Eisenstadt 1968, March and Olsen 1984, Douglas 1986, MacIver 1931, Giddens 1984:375 and 1982:10, Bierstedt 1970:320, Shibutani 1986:16, and Stinchcombe 1986:904–5.
5. Here I follow Zucker 1983 in representing the terms as process and property variables, though I do not follow her in the details of conceptualization.
6. I have freely adapted a characterization provided by Fararo and Skvoretz 1986. I have also drawn upon Przeworski and Sprague 1971. I should add that institutions are not equivalent to norms. Many theorists have distinguished norms from institutions by making the latter, but not the former, self-policing. See, e.g., Schotter 1981:10–12; also Parsons, e.g., Parsons and Shils 1951:20: a norm is institutionalized, according to Parsons, *if* it is rewarded and sanctioned.
7. "Institutionalized situations with their moral and practical arrangements create individuals' obligations and powers, create activities" (Stinchcombe 1986a:905).

8. For examples of many additional, parallel, formulations, see Berger and Luckmann 1966:60 (institutions embody "what everybody knows," "recipe knowledge"); Lachmann 1971:13 (they are "orientation maps" of the future actions of others); and Parsons (institutions produce agreement on specific courses of action that a situation demands).
9. It seems especially arbitrary to associate institutions (as current discussions often do) with absence of thought or with positive evaluation. This practice smuggles untested empirical claims into our conceptualization and then impairs theoretic debate. For example, both Mary Douglas and Lévi-Strauss seem to associate institutions with absence of thought (with "unthink") (Douglas 1986; Lévi-Strauss 1966). So modern societies, revealing greater discourse about social practices, are presumably less institutionalized than nonmodern (e.g., tribal) ones. (Tribal systems for Lévi-Strauss are "cold" cultures, with their social institutions enmeshed with nature and without the endogenous contradictions generating change.) Contrast Stinchcombe, who argues that modern societies have both greater reflexivity and greater institutional self-replicating capacity (1968:115). We need to treat such differences as substantive theoretical ones, to be adjudicated empirically, rather than eliding them by treating them definitionally.
10. Comments by Francisco Ramirez, on a previous version of this chapter, stimulated this paragraph. He provides an excellent example, discussing the pre–Vatican II mass (quoted with permission): "No one would dispute its institutional character. The mass was always enacted, never the product of collective action. The mass was celebrated in Latin; the sequence of events was rigidly prescribed. Each event had a name. What the priest had to do in enacting a given event was set forth in a written script; what the undifferentiated others had to do in reaction (stand, kneel, bless yourself) was also carefully prescribed. The only variable was the content of the sermon (now called a homily) and whether the script was sung.... From an alien perspective a zombie-like production. But without attributing a high degree of comprehension to the participants (not everyone took a course in liturgy or even knew that the color of the vestments used in a given day had precise symbolic meaning), just about every participant could tell you that the mass was about worshiping God and that you were supposed to go to mass on Sundays and other days of obligation. The participants were not merely going through standardized interaction sequences without having some shared story-line as to what the practice was all about."
11. Walter Buckley is compelling in his insistence upon distinguishing institutionalization from legitimation: some "social problems," he

says, "are so pervasive, stable, and difficult to root out precisely because they are 'institutionalized.' That is, they involve complex interpersonal, and often highly organized, networks of expectations, communications, normative interpretations, interests, and beliefs, embedded in the same sociocultural matrix as are 'legitimized' structures" (1967:161, also 145, 129–30).

12. That is, contextual effects often refer to effects of the proportional distribution of individuals across groups within a collectivity, or to the rates of interaction between individuals in different social locations. See, for example, Przeworski 1974. For examples of such arguments, see Blau 1977.
13. *Macro* can refer to spatial extensiveness or large numbers, but also to a high order of organization within a structure having multiple orders of organization (a high order being a complex of lower orders: chapters are in part complexes of paragraphs, which are themselves organizations of sentences). Thus *macro* can refer to effects of a collective or system "center," relative to a periphery, as well as to global (extensive) effects upon a locality. The two usages are often conflated.
14. Note the ambiguous usage of *environment* in the organizational literature. Sometimes the term invokes context imagery (e.g., fields of organizations), other times macro (hierarchic ordering) imagery (e.g., references to law), sometimes both (e.g., "the institutional environment"). This is confusing.
15. A number of authors, including those just cited, may in fact confound these historical arguments with conceptual ones. This conflation was certainly a core impairment of Parsons' theorizing.
16. It is difficult to categorize and evaluate Stinchcombe's discussion of institutionalization – roughly, the process of binding power to a value (1968, esp. pp. 181–88). For him, an institution is best considered a structure in which powerful people are committed to some value (p. 107), or those values and norms that have high correlations with power. This imagery is evocative, but I do not find it sufficient for conceptual purposes, for two reasons: the imagery ties institution too closely to two relatively unstable concepts (power and value); it also directs one to focus unduly on formally organized institutions (as in Stinchcombe's own examples). In a recent book review, Stinchcombe employs a conceptualization much closer to the one recommended here (1986a).
17. *Center* in the sense of Shils 1975 or Eisenstadt 1968, not in a geographic sense.
18. These distinctions are not meant to represent different levels of analysis or organization.

19. One cannot properly engage in holistic comparison of institutionalization; the question "What is the relative institutionalization of the contemporary United Kingdom and France?", as historical particulars, does not lend itself to pursuit. It seems more legitimate (and in principle productive) to compare the relative institutionalization of institutions within collectivities, or types of institutions across societies, or of analytical types of social orders. One can compare, for example, the degree to which types of political regimes are institutionalized across comparable societies (as many often do; Huntington 1968 is largely on this topic). Or one can try to compare the relative institutionalization of various "nonmodern" (e.g., tribal, feudal) versus "modern" (i.e., the rationalized, rich, individualist) types of societies.
20. Most treatment of this topic in the literature has been implicit or, if explicit, informal and cursory. Parsons 1982 discusses the issue en passant and informally; Eisenstadt 1968 does so as well. Meyer, Boli, and Thomas 1987 provide a provocative but one-paragraph discussion. Huntington 1968 provides an extended treatment of degrees of political institutionalization. He associates greater institutionalization with greater adaptiveness, complexity, differentiation, insulation, and unification. He also provides some operationalization of these ideas, for comparing the institutionalization of governmental regimes. Welfling 1973 uses Huntington's work in an empirical study of the institutionalization of African party systems. Huntington's ideas may have broader utility, but they would seem to require greater tightening and generality. Wuthnow 1987: ch. 8 discusses the institutionalization of science in the seventeenth century and associates this institutionalization with organizational autonomy, procurement of a resource base, development of an internal system of communication and organization, and external legitimation. Shefter and Ginsberg 1985 provides an insightful, but entirely informal, discussion of the "institutionalization of the Reagan regime," associating institutionalization with a secure resource coalition, successful performance, agenda control, a legitimating ideology, and policies benefiting supporters. (However, they tend to confound institutionalization with survival, as do many treatments.)
21. Compare: "When everything is institutionalized, no history or other storage devices are necessary: 'The institution tells all'" (Schotter 1981: 139).
22. Compare Mary Douglas (1986:46ff., I paraphrase): a convention is institutionalized if any question about it receives an answer discussing the nature of the universe.
23. Meyer, Boli, and Thomas 1987:37 discuss the elimination of alternatives.

24. DiMaggio 1988a provides a similar listing.
25. In working out this figure, I have drawn upon conversations with John W. Meyer.
26. I am unhappy with the label "realist," but have no better alternative at hand. "Realism" has taken on the connotations I wish to suggest. There are actually two distinct forms of realism. The first, a naturalistic realism, exemplified in rational-choice-type arguments, sees units as having high social autonomy and represents them as primordial building blocks of social structure. The second, social structural realism, sees units as highly constrained by the positions they occupy within networks of statuses and roles (e.g., White, Boorman, and Breiger 1976). But these latter arguments remain a variant of realism because they do not see the units themselves (or the networks) as outcomes of social construction or constitution processes. They see the networks as representing "concrete" patterns of interactions (a common word, indicative of realist imagery); the units linked by these infrastructural networks are exogenous to the theory.
27. Phenomenological arguments allow for two distinct types of institutional effects: institutions can act as rules or instructions generating and defining social objects; they can independently operate as regulators of social processes. Compare Fararo and Skvoretz 1986:243.
28. Thus this "constructedness" dimension should not be conceived as representing differences on "where to draw the exogeneity/endogeneity line" or on where to stop trying to explain. The dimension captures far more substantial differences: differences over what the exogeneity is. In "realist" lines, the exogenous domain (of explanatory variables) is nonsocial – composed of asocial psychological states, or givens of nature (see Langlois 1986: ch. 10 on the aspirations for exogeneity in general equilibrium theory). "Phenomenological" arguments differ by calling into empirical question the supposed nonsocial character of the realist's exogenous variables, and thus by greatly restricting the range of nonsocial exogenous variables. In phenomenological arguments, the exogenous variables driving social endogenous variables can also be social ones – but represented at a different level of social organization, or reflecting some different dimension of sociality, than the endogenous social variables.
29. Structuralism denies that a microtranslation (Collins 1981) of a structural effect is equivalent to a set of macro-organized variables linked by an intervening microrelationship (and thus would deny Coleman's 1986 treatment of structural effects). The difference between this methodological structuralism and individualism thus centers on the

number and proper treatment of composition effects in social orders. (For a rare polemic in favor of methodological structuralism, see Mayhew 1980.)
30. Neoinstitutional economics, as represented, e.g., by Williamson, begins to depart from cell 3 along the "constructedness" dimension, but remains largely within this cell.
31. Thus institutional propositions include (but are not limited to) "theories of theorization effects" (Bourdieu 1977: 178). For example, Pfeffer, in his organizational analysis text, following Zucker, gives a number of examples of institutional effects that occur because a process is viewed by organization members as institutionalized in formal structure (Pfeffer 1982: 241, 242, 244).
32. I need to reiterate that microtranslation must be distinguished sharply from micro-reduction. The capacity for such translation is a requirement for a causal theory, and a guard again obfuscation: reduction, in contrast, represents perhaps an ultimate theoretic aspiration, but is not a requirement of theoretic adequacy. Further, providing microtranslations does not require provision of microfoundations, if this term is taken literally. *Foundations* may be a misleading metaphor for social science. The foundations of a building can stand without a superstructure; in the social world, however, the typical "foundations" imagined do not have this free-standing capacity. This point is behind Marx's excoriation of the "Robinson Crusoe" reasoning in classical economies, and behind Durkheim's reminder that there would be no modern "individual" without the (collective) "cult" of individualism.
33. It goes without saying that persons are the only ontological elements of social structure – unless one follows Hegel, of course. But this is a matter entirely separate from the epistemological and methodological issues we are discussing.

References

Berger, P., B. Berger, & H. Kellner. (1973). *The Homeless Mind: Modernization and Consciousness*, New York, NY: Random House.

Berger, P. & T. Luckmann. (1966). *The Social Construction of Reality*, Garden City, NY: Doubleday.

Bierstedt, R. (1970). *The Social Order*, 3rd edn, New York, NY: McGraw-Hill.

Blau, P. M. (1977). *Inequality and Heterogeneity*, New York, NY: Free Press.

Bourdieu, P. (1977). *Outline of a Theory of Practice*, Cambridge: Cambridge University Press.

Buckley, W. (1967). *Sociology and Modern Systems Theory*, Englewood Cliffs, NJ: Prentice-Hall.

Cohen, B. P. (1980). *Developing Sociological Knowledge: Theory and Method*, Englewood Cliffs, NJ: Prentice-Hall.

Coleman, J. S. (1986). Micro Foundations and Macrosocial Theory. In S. Lindenberg, J. Coleman, & S. Nowak, eds., *Approaches to Social Theory*. New York, NY: Russell Sage Foundation, pp. 345–63

Collins, R. (1981). On the Microfoundations of Macrosociology. *American Journal of Sociology*, 86(5), 984–1014.

Dahrendorf, R. (1964). *Class and Class Conflict in Industrial Society*, Stanford, CA: Stanford University Press.

Davis, K. (1949). *Human Society*, New York, NY: Macmillan.

DiMaggio, P. J. (1988). Interest and Agency in Institutional Theory. In L. Zucker, ed., *Institutional Patterns and Organizations*. Cambridge, MA: Ballinger, pp. 3–22

Douglas, M. (1986). *How Institutions Think*, Syracuse, NY: Syracuse University Press.

Durkheim, E. [1901] (1950). *The Rules of Sociological Method*, Glencoe, IL: Free Press.

Eisenstadt, S.N. (1968). Social Institutions: The Concept. In D. L. Spears, ed., Vol. XIV of *International Encyclopedia of the Social Sciences*. New York, NY: Macmillan, pp. 409–21.

Elias, N. (1978). *The Civilizing Process*, New York, NY: Urizen Books.

Elster, J. (1986). Introduction. In J. Elster, ed., *Rational Choice*. New York, NY: New York University Press, pp. 1–33.

Fararo, T. J. & J. Skvoretz. (1986). Action and Institution, Network and Function: The Cybernetic Concept of Social Structure. *Sociological Forum*, 1, 219–50.

Farr, R. M. & S. Moscovici, eds. (1984). *Social Representations*, Cambridge: Cambridge University Press.

Field, A. J. (1979). On the Explanation of Rules Using Rational Choice Models. *Journal of Economic Issues*, 13(1), 49–72.

Foucault, M. (1978). *The History of Sexuality*, New York, NY: Pantheon.

Friedman, D. & M. Hechter. (1988). The Contribution of Rational Choice Theory to Macrosociological Research. Meetings of the American Sociological Association.

Gerth, H. & C. W. Mills. (1953). *Character and Social Structure: The Psychology of Social Institutions*, New York, NY: Harcourt, Brace, and World.

Giddens, A. (1982). *Sociology*, New York, NY: Harcourt Brace Jovanovich.

Giddens, A. (1984). *The Constitution of Society*, Berkeley, CA: University of California Press.

Goffman, E. (1961). *Asylums: Essays on the Social Situation of Mental Patients and Other Inmates*, New York, NY: Doubleday.

Goffman, E. (1974). *Frame Analysis*, Cambridge, MA: Harvard University Press.

Habermas, J. (1970). *Toward a Rational Society*, Boston, MA: Beacon Press.

Hayek, F. A. (1973). Rules and Order. Vol. I of *Law, Legislation, and Liberty*. London: Routledge and Kegan Paul.

Homans, G. C. (1961). *Social Behavior: Its Elementary Forms*, New York, NY: Harcourt Brace Jovanovich.

Huntington, S. P. (1968). *Political Order in Changing Societies*, New Haven, CT: Yale University Press.

Inkeles, A. & D. H. Smith. (1974). *Becoming Modern: Individual Change in Six Developing Countries*, Cambridge, MA: Harvard University Press.

Kohn, M. L. (1969). *Class and Conformity*, Homewood, IL: Dorsey Press.

Lachmann, L.M. (1971). *The Legacy of Max Weber*, Berkeley, CA: Glendessary Press.

Langlois, R. N., ed. (1986). *Economics as Process: Essays in the New Institutional Economics*, Cambridge, MA: Cambridge University Press.

Levi-Strauss, C. (1966). *The Savage Mind*, London: Weidenfeld & Nicolson.

MacIver, R. M. (1931). *Society; Its Structure and Changes*, New York, NY: Ray Long and Richard R. Smith, Inc.

Mann, M. (1986). A History of Power from the Beginning to AD 1760. Vol. I of *The Sources of Social Power*. Cambridge, MA: Cambridge University Press.

March, J. G. & J. P. Olsen. (1984.) The New Institutionalism: Organizational Factors in Political Life. *American Political Science Review*, 78(September), 734–49.

March, J. G. & H. Simon. (1958). *Organizations*, New York, NY: John Wiley & Sons.

Marshall, T. H. (1964). *Class, Citizenship, and Social Development*, Garden City, NY: Doubleday.

Mayhew, B. H. (1980). Structuralism versus Individualism. *Social Forces*, 59 (2, 3), 335–75, 627–48.

Mead, G. H. [1934] (1972). *Mind, Self, and Society*, Chicago, IL: University of Chicago Press.

Meyer, J. W. (1977). The Effects of Education as an Institution. *American Journal of Sociology*, 83(1), 55–77.

Meyer, J. W. (1988.) Conceptions of Christendom: Notes on the Distinctiveness of the West. In M. Kohn, ed., *Cross-National Research in Sociology*. Newbury Park, CA: Sage, pp. 395–413.

Meyer, J. W., J. Boli, & G. M. Thomas. (1987). Ontology and Rationalization in the Western Cultural Account. In G. M. Thomas, J. W. Meyer, F. O. Ramirez, & J. Boli, eds., *Institutional Structure*. Beverly Hills, CA: Sage Publications.

Meyer, J. W. & B. Rowan. (1977). Institutionalized Organizations: Formal Structure as Myth and Ceremony. *American Journal of Sociology*, 83(2), 340–63.

Münch, R. (1986). The American Creed in Sociological Theory: Exchange, Negotiated Order, Accommodated Individuals, and Contingency. *Sociological Theory*, 4(1), 41–60.

Olson, M. (1965). *The Logic of Collective Action*, Cambridge, MA: Harvard University Press.

Parsons, T. (1982). *Talcott Parsons on Institutions and Social Evolution: Selected Writings*, ed. by L. H. Mayhew. Chicago, IL: University of Chicago Press.

Parsons, T. & E. A. Shils, eds. (1951). *Towards a General Theory of Action*, Cambridge, MA: Harvard University Press.

Pfeffer, J. (1982). *Organizations and Organization Theory*, Boston, MA: Pitman.

Przeworski, A. (1974). Contextual Models of Political Behavior. *Political Methodology*, 1(1), 27–61.

Przeworski, A. & J. Sprague. (1971). Concepts in Search of Explicit Formulation: A Study in Measurement. *Midwest Journal of Political Science*, 15(2), 183–218.

Sartori, G. (1984). Guidelines for Concept Analysis. In G. Sartori, ed., *Social Science Concepts: A Systematic Analysis*. Beverly Hills, CA: Sage Publications, pp. 15–85.

Schotter, A. (1981). *The Economic Theory of Social Institutions*, Cambridge: Cambridge University Press.

Scott, W. R. (1987a). *Organizations: Rational, Natural, and Open Systems*, 2nd edn, Englewood Cliffs, NJ: Prentice-Hall.

Scott, W. R. (1987b). The Adolescence of Institutional Theory. *Administrative Science Quarterly*, 32(4), 493–511.

Shefter, M. & B. Ginsberg. (1985). Institutionalizing the Reagan Regime. Annual meetings of the American Political Science Association.

Shibutani, T. (1986). *Social Processes: An Introduction to Sociology*, Berkeley, CA: University of California Press.

Shils, E. (1975). *Center and Periphery*, Chicago, IL: University of Chicago Press.

Snell, B. (1960). *The Discovery of the Mind*, New York, NY: Harper and Row.

Stinchcombe, A. L. (1965). Social Structures and Organizations. In J. G. March, ed., *Handbook of Organizations*. Chicago, IL: Rand McNally, pp. 142–93.

Stinchcombe, A. L. (1968.) *Constructing Social Theories*. New York, NY: Harcourt, Brace & World.

Stinchcombe, A. L. (1973). Formal Organization. In N. J. Smelser, ed., *Sociology: An Introduction*. New York, NY: Wiley, pp. 23–65.

Stinchcombe, A. L. (1986). Milieu and Structure Updated. *Theory and Society*, 15(6), 901–13.

Swanson, G. (1986). Phobias and Related Symptoms: Some Social Sources. *Sociological Forum*, 1(1), 103–30.

Tocqueville, A. [1856] (1955). *The Old Regime and the French Revolution*, Garden City, NY: Doubleday.

Tolbert, P. S. & L. G. Zucker. (1983). Institutional Sources of Change in the Formal Structure of Organizations: The Diffusion of Civil Service Reform, 1880–1935. *Administrative Science Quarterly*, 28(1), 22–39.

Weick, K. E. (1969). *The Social Psychology of Organizing*, Reading, MA: Addison-Wesley.

Welfling, M. B. (1973). *Political Institutionalization: A Comparative Analysis of African Political Systems*, Beverly Hills, CA: Sage Publications.

White, H. (1981). Where Do Markets Come From? *American Journal of Sociology*, 87(3), 517–47.

White, H. C., S. A. Boorman, & R. L. Breiger. (1976). Social Structure from Multiple Networks. I. Blockmodels of Roles and Positions. *American Journal of Sociology*, 81(4), 730–80.

Wuthnow, R. (1987). *Meaning and Moral Order: Explorations in Cultural Analysis*, Berkeley, CA: University of California Press.

Znaniecki, F. (1945). Social Organization and Institutions. In G. Gurvitch & W. E. Moore, eds., *Twentieth Century Sociology*. New York, NY: Philosophical Library, pp. 172–217.

Zucker, L. G. (1983). Organizations as Institutions. In S. B. Bacharach, ed., Vol. II of *Research in the Sociology of Organizations*. Greenwich, CT: JAI Press, pp. 1–47.

Zucker, L. G. (1986). Production of Trust: Institutional Sources of Economic Structure, 1840–1920. In B. M. Staw & L. L. Cummings, eds., Vol. VIII of *Research in Organizational Behavior*. Greenwich, CT: JAI Press, pp. 53–111.

Zucker, L. G. (1987). Institutional Theories of Organization. *Annual Review of Sociology*, 13, 443–64.

4 | *The Development and Application of Sociological Neoinstitutionalism (2002)*

R. JEPPERSON*

4.1 Introduction

Sociological neoinstitutionalism is one of the most broad-ranging "theoretical research programs" (TRPs) in contemporary sociology and one of the most empirically developed forms of institutional analysis. This program, centered around the work of John W. Meyer and his collaborators (but now extending beyond this group), has produced an integrated and extensive body of research about the nation-states, individuals, and organizational structures of modern society. The central concern of this institutionalism is the embeddedness of social structures and social "actors" in broad-scale contexts of meaning: more specifically, the consequences of European and later world culture for social organization (Meyer, Boli, and Thomas 1987:31).

This institutionalism originated in a set of theoretical papers in the 1970s by Meyer, and in concurrent research in the sociology of education, where the program has remained central. The program expanded into full-blown research efforts concerning organizations, the world system, and individual identity. Applications continue to proliferate. For instance, this institutionalism now supports one of the most extensive lines of research on current "globalization" – for example, John Boli and George Thomas' work on the extraordinary recent increase in international non-governmental organizations (Boli and Thomas 1997) – as well as new efforts on collective

---

* This chapter draws upon recent conversations or correspondence with John Boli, John Meyer, Thomas Risse, Evan Schofer, Marc Ventresca, and Morris Zelditch, and upon comments from this volume's editors. Meyer endured multiple queries about the research program during the preparation of this chapter, and Boli provided repeated commentary. The author appreciates the support of the Robert Schuman Center for Advanced Studies, European University Institute, Florence, Italy.

identity, sexuality, law, and for that matter even accounting. These efforts are now found across the sociological community at many of its major research sites.

This chapter surveys and analyzes the development of this TRP. It explicates its intellectual core, surveys its inter-related applications in different substantive domains, and analyzes the growth of these applications over time (including the role of exchanges with other lines of theory and research in this growth).[1] The primary concern is how this institutionalism has been used to generate substantive insights – that is, both new observations and new explanations of the social world.[2]

4.2 Intellectual Context

Meyer worked out a number of the core theoretical ideas by 1970.[3] A set of fundamental papers, developing and consolidating main ideas, appeared in print between 1977 and 1980: on the "effects of education as an institution" (Meyer 1977), on "institutionalized organizations" (with Brian Rowan [Meyer and Rowan 1977]), and on "the world polity and the authority of the nation-state" (Meyer 1980).[4]

In developing his ideas, Meyer was reacting to the enduring individualism of American sociology, the manifest empirical difficulties of its associated "action" and "socialization" theories (including Talcott Parsons' variant, emphasizing action guided by internalized norms), and the persistent attempt by much American social theory especially to analyze modern society as a "society without culture" (Meyer 1988).[5] Asked to characterize the development of his thinking, in an interview in *Sozusagen* (a students' publication of the Bielefeld department of sociology), Meyer indicates that he did not think of society as fundamentally constituted by "actors," or of people or structures as primarily actors (Krücken 2000). He " ... took less seriously the actorhood of individuals than American sociologists would normally do" (ibid:58): "I did not think individuals were the fundamental units of society, nor did I think they were tightly organized 'hard-wired' structures. I thought society was made up of knowledge and culture" (Meyer 1999b). Accordingly, in his work (the interview continues), Meyer tried to reconceptualize the sociology of education to "give it a less individualistic picture. It is less a matter of socializing raw individuals, but more about labeling, credentialing, and creating categories – more institutional in a word .... In organization theory, I did the same, and also in my work on the nation state, which I see as structures embedded in a broader meaning system and less as autonomous actors" (Meyer in Krücken 2000:58).

By seeing society as institutionalized "knowledge and culture," Meyer (then others) works from an analytical imagery as basic as the actor-and-interest imagery of more conventional sociology: namely, the "construction" of structures and actors within broad institutional frameworks, and the cultural "scripting" of much activity within these frameworks. By focusing upon the broad institutional frameworks of society (including world society), sociological neoinstitutionalism then *defocalizes* "actors" *on purpose*. The whole point of this TRP is to find out what can be gained by seeing actors (and interests and structures and activity) as in many respects derivative from institutions and culture. This idea is pursued in order to envision features of the social world not easily captured – or not captured at all – when focusing upon actors (Meyer and Jepperson 2000).

A clear research agenda has followed from this intellectual thrust. There is a background historical argument about the evolution of modern society within the institutional matrices and cultural schemas provided by Christendom (see Meyer 1989; Meyer, Boli, and Thomas 1987; Meyer and Jepperson 2000). There is an additional background argument about the long-term reconstruction of modern society around a world system of national states, the latter units constituted as societies of organizations and of citizen-individuals. The three main research clusters of the program then follow directly. National states are seen as embedded in a world polity and culture, and the common cultural contents and trends of these states are sought. Organizations are seen as embedded in national (and increasingly world) institutional environments, and their externally-institutionalized features are sought. People are seen as enacting elaborate doctrines of individualism, rather than acting in some more generic fashion; these doctrines have both world cultural sources and distinctive national variations, and both are studied. In each research area, many basic features of the entities examined – national states, organizations, individuals – are shown to be constructions of institutionalized cultural environments, rather than being "hardwired" and pregiven outside the social system.

4.3 Two Background Theoretical Arguments: An Introduction via the Sociology of Education

4.3.1 Questioning the Role of the "Socialization" in Producing and Reproducing Social Order

The American sociology of education of the 1950s and '60s – and American sociology generally – tended to assume a picture of society as made up of and produced by highly socialized individuals, the educational system then central in the reproduction of society in large part via its socializing activities. But empirical studies presented anomalies for this theoretical picture. Notably, many studies showed small "socializing" effects of American colleges on student attitudes, and only small differences in these effects across colleges, despite the big differences among colleges. Studies of medical schools found it difficult to isolate much "socialization," but did incidentally pick up dramatic shifts from medical students thinking of themselves as merely students to thinking of themselves as doctors.

In reflecting upon these results, and in conducting research on student college and occupational choices (e.g., Meyer 1970a), Meyer and colleagues developed the following interpretation (reflected in Meyer 1970a, 1972, 1977 and Kamens 1977). Seen as institutions, what schools do primarily is produce graduates and bestow the identity "graduate." If the social status and role of graduates in society is largely the same – as is the case in egalitarian American society, but not in many more status-stratified European ones – then the schools will largely have similar effects on individuals, because individuals are enacting a largely singular identity. (In Germany, in contrast, there are more differentiated categories of "graduate," and hence different identities [and attitudes] for individuals to enact.)[6] Relatedly, medical schools confer the identity "doctor": medical students learn they are doctors and people in the social environment learn this too, and these are large effects. David Kamens added the fundamental observation that schools develop formal structures that dramatize their advertised effects on students (Kamens 1977). For example, colleges emphasize their selectivity, or their "residential education," or their putatively rigorous requirements. In so doing schools "create and validate myths" concerning both the college experience and "the intrinsic qualities that their graduates possess" (Kamens 1977:208).

Two basic theoretical points are reflected here. First, the truly fundamental "socialization" is the construction and certification (the "chartering") of identities (Meyer 1970c), and this particular socialization can occur without any especially deep or common inculcation of values or attitudes (or knowledge, for that matter). Second, the "socialization" is as much of *others* in the social environment as of those directly involved in an institution: for instance, the medical profession teaches others about the identity "doctor" as well as medical students; colleges teach others about their graduates. In a word, the socialization is "diffuse" as well as direct (Meyer 1970c).

In making these arguments, this institutionalism was one of a number of lines of thought emerging in opposition to Talcott Parsons' and Robert Merton's emphasis on the internalization of "norms" as the foundation of social order. Instead, the "phenomenological" counterargument (shared by and developed within this institutionalism) was more cognitive and collective in character, in two respects. First, the fundamental "socialization" according to phenomenological sociology is the learning of broad collective representations of society – pictures of what society is and how it works – and the acceptance of these pictures as social facts. Peter Berger and Thomas Luckmann referred to learning "recipe knowledge" about the social system, and about being inculcated into a "symbolic universe" (1967); Meyer referred to learning about "symbols" (like the general symbol "school"), or to learning basic "myths" (i.e., broad cultural accounts) of society (Meyer 1970b, 1977). People learn highly abstract and symbolic accounts of society more than detailed empirical information; hence this learning coincides with people's well-known low levels of actual information about their social environment, even about matters of substantial import to them (such as schooling or job markets or marriage networks).

Second, the causality of social rules and "myths," argued Meyer, inheres "not in the fact that individuals believe them, but in the fact that they 'know' everyone else does ... " (Meyer 1977:75). That is, the truly fundamental beliefs for reproducing a social order are people's beliefs about *others'* behavior and beliefs; the basic "myths" of society operate primarily by establishing beliefs about what others think and expectations about how others will behave. Further, in this phenomenological line of argument, social order depends more upon the degree to which the basic myths of the system are taken-for-granted – accepted as realities, grounded in common expectations – than upon personal belief in them (Meyer 1977:65, Meyer 1970b).[7] In clarifying this point (and a number of related ones), Morris Zelditch distinguished between the *validation* of myths versus the *endorsement* of them (Zelditch 1984; Zelditch and Walker 1984): social order, contra Parsons and Merton, depends more on the degree of validation of collective reality – the pragmatic acceptance of rules and accounts as in place and binding – than upon the endorsement of it. This point has remained fundamental to institutionalism as it has developed.

4.3.2 Elaborating the Nature and Effects of Institutionalization

In the 1970s, scholars in the sociology of education were considering how education worked to "reproduce" societies over time. Addressing this issue, Meyer developed the argument that the educational system embodies a "theory of knowledge and personnel" of society, as well as socializing individuals and channeling them to social positions. That is, it is a primary institutional location for consolidating the knowledge system of society, and for defining and legitimating the specific identities of both elites and democratic citizens (Meyer 1972, 1977). Changes in educational curricula end up "restructur[ing] whole populations" by creating new categories of authoritative knowledge and then entirely new roles (new professions, new elites, new ideas about citizenship) (Meyer 1977:55). "Not only new types of persons but also new competencies are authoritatively created" by education as an evolving institution (ibid: 56). For example, the field of demography was codified within the education system, subsequently chartering and producing demographers, and eventually enabling and encouraging population control policies (Barrett 1995; Barrett and Frank 1999). In a formula, "institutionalized demography creates demographers, and makes demographic control reasonable,"[8] that is, legitimate and conventional.

Note that the causal connections posited in this example are *collective-level* and *cultural* in nature – they feature processes occurring within and between institutions (within the educational system, broadly considered, and between the educational system, professions, and the state). These processes are of course produced via the behavior of people, *but* (in this example): (1) the people implicated are various educators and scholars and state elites, hence occupants of highly institutionally constructed roles, operating more in their cultural and professional capacities – that is, as *agents* of the cultural system – than as generic individual "actors" bearing only simple or private interests. Also, (2) the causal linkages involved in these collective processes are far removed from the aggregation of simple social behavior, or from individual socialization and its aggregate effects, or even from the social network processes presented in educational stratification arguments. Attention to collective-level and cultural processes is the main distinguishing feature of this institutionalism, as we'll see.

4.4 Organizations in Institutional Environments[9]

4.4.1 Background: *Questioning the Integration and Boundedness of Organizations*

The institutionalist contribution to organizational analysis followed directly from the 1970s research on school organizations,[10] as well as from research on evaluation processes in organizations by W. R. Scott and Sanford Dornbusch (Dornbusch and Scott 1975), and from Scott's research on health care organizations. Meyer and Brian Rowan (1977) argued that schools survive in the first instance not because of tight organizational controls – or because of any particular effectiveness in schooling – but because of conformity with highly institutionalized categories and myths in the broader society (the basic idea of what a school is, or what mathematics is, or what "2nd grade" is). The emergent institutionalist idea was that these features might be general characteristics of organizations, at least far more so than generally acknowledged. Sociological neoinstitutionalism was "but one of several theories that developed in reaction to prevailing conceptions of organizations as bounded, relatively autonomous, rational actors" (Scott and Meyer 1994:1). As in other application areas, the institutionalist effort was to question the assumed naturalness of organizations, seeing them instead as "(a) connected to and (b) constructed by wide social environments" (Meyer and Scott 1992:1), as opposed to being prior realities external to the cultural system (Meyer, Boli, and Thomas 1987:22).

4.4.2 Three Core Ideas about Formal Organizing

In developing this line of argument, a starting idea was that the *building blocks* for formal organization were institutionally constructed and were "littered around the societal landscape" (Meyer and Rowan 1977:345). More specifically, the ongoing "rationalization"[11] of social life creates new organizational elements, and new social nodes around which formal organizations can form. Meyer and Rowan gave the following examples: the development of psychology certifies new professionals and creates new specialized agencies and departments; the expansion of professional research stimulates R&D units within organizations; the movement of sexuality into the public sphere new therapies and their associated organizations (ibid:344). This rationalization has been a continuing process: "A wider range of purposes and activities becomes legitimate grounds for organizing: child care; leisure activities and recreation; even finding a compatible marriage partner" (Scott and Meyer 1994:114).[12]

A second core idea, also in Meyer and Rowan (1977), was that "the formal structures of many organizations in postindustrial society ... dramatically reflect the myths of their institutional environments instead of the demands of their work activities" (p. 341). By "formal structure" the authors referred to a "blueprint for activities," including the table of organization and an organization's explicit goals and policies (p. 342). Formal structure is in many respects "ceremonial" in function: it often demonstrates adherence with currently predominant myths (i.e., cultural models) – including, in postindustrial environments, myths of rationality. Such adherence "signals rationality" to internal and external groups, and hence can enhance internal and external legitimacy, access to resources, and ultimately organizational survival (pp. 352–353, 355; also Scott and Meyer 1994:115).

Third, Meyer and Rowan (and then Meyer and Scott) stressed one particular structural consequence of the linkage of organizational elements to broad institutional structures. This linkage produces organizational forms that are often "sprawling" – loosely integrated and variously "decoupled." Formal structure and rules are often decoupled from actual activities; programs are often decoupled from organizational outcomes; internal organizational sectors are often decoupled from one another; and organizational decision-making activity is often decoupled from actual organizational action (e.g., Meyer 1983/

1992:239; Brunsson 1989). The decoupling of formal and informal activity was long observed in the organizational literature; this institutionalism now offered a more general explanation of it and made the observation central. "Stable organizing requires and results from external legitimation and may be quite consistent with a good deal of internal looseness" (Scott and Meyer 1994:2).

4.4.3 Different Types of Organizations

In contextualizing their arguments, Meyer and Rowan provided two reasons to think that institutional effects on organizations should be ubiquitous. First, they argued that the "rise of collectively organized society" had "eroded many market contexts," thus expanding the range of organizations subject directly to institutional forces (1977:354). Second, they added that even "[o]rganizations producing in markets that place great emphasis on efficiency build in units whose relation to production is obscure and whose efficiency is determined, not by true production functions, but by ceremonial definition" (ibid.:353).

Later, Scott (1987:126) and Scott and Meyer (1991:122–124) began to distinguish different sorts of institutional effects on organizations. In order to do so, they distinguished stronger and weaker "technical environments" from stronger and weaker "institutional environments": some organizations are subject to strong versions of both (utilities, banks), some weak versions of both (restaurants, health clubs), and some exist in one of two mixed patterns (e.g., general manufacturing organizations exist in a weaker institutional but stronger technical environment, while schools and mental health clinics exist in a weaker technical but stronger institutional environment). With this classification of environments at hand, Scott and Meyer, and independently Lynne Zucker, presented arguments about the conjoint effects of the varying environments on different sorts of organizations, concentrating upon variations in organizational structures and on patterns of success and failure (Scott and Meyer 1991; Zucker 1983, 1987).

4.4.4 An Elaboration: The Institutional Construction of the "Ground Rules of Economic Life"

These institutionalists insisted that even markets themselves are highly "institutionally constructed": thinking for example of all the legal, political, and social definitions involved in the coevolution of American society and the automobile market. This emphasis is not distinctive to this institutionalism but rather follows a general institutionalism going back to Max Weber. Recently this particular literature has begun to elaborate the idea of the institutional construction of "organizational fields," strategies, and doctrines (reviewed by Dobbin 1994a). First, scholars have pursued the "interdependence of state regulatory policies, organizational fields, and management strategies" (Scott 1995:99). In a formidable piece of research, Neil Fligstein studied the evolution of the largest American firms from the 1800s to the present (Fligstein 1990). Among other things, he found (in Frank Dobbin's admirable epitomization) that "the Sherman Antitrust Act of 1890 made mergers the favored business strategy at the dawn of the 20th century *and* popularized a new theory of the firm that reinforced horizontal integration. Then after World War II, the Celler-Kefauver Act, amending Sherman, made diversification the favored American business strategy *and* helped to popularize finance management and portfolio theory" (Dobbin 1995:280, emphasis added).

Dobbin has stressed the theoretical implication of this line of work: the economic environment, far from being generic or natural, is partly constituted and re-constituted by public policies and ideologies (Dobbin 1994b, 1995). Public policies alter "the ground rules of economic life" (ibid). New business strategies emerge under each policy regime, and eventually new theories emerge justifying the efficiency of the new strategies. Drawing upon his own historical and comparative research (Dobbin 1994b), Dobbin asks: "How did Americans arrive at the conclusion that rivalistic state mercantilism was the most effective means to growth? How did they come to believe that approach was wrong, and support cartels? How did they decide to crush cartels and enforce price competition?" (Dobbin 1995:282). Dobbin's answer (in brief) is that Americans altered earlier policies when the policies came into perceived conflict with institutionalized precepts of American democracy – especially the opposition to concentrated power. So, when new forms of concentrated power were perceived, reform efforts ensued and the rules of the game were eventually changed. After some further lag, economic doctrines adjusted to find the changed rules to be efficient (Dobbin 1995:301; 1994b). The institutionalist point: even the principles of rational organizing are themselves socially constructed and reconstructed.

4.4.5 Effects of Variation in Institutional Environments (1): Cross-National Variation

If formal organizing is interpenetrated with institutional environments, it follows that different institutional environments will construct different sorts of formal organizations. Most of the initial institutionalist research was US-centric, the primary exception being study of cross-national variation in educational organizations. In 1983 Meyer offered an explicit comparative framework, contrasting "statist," "corporatist," and "individualist" variants of modern institutional environments (and associating the historical trajectories of France, Germany, and the United States with these variants) (Meyer 1983b). He then linked this institutional variation to variation in the amounts, types, and structure of formal organizing, in a set of propositions. For example, Meyer argued that statist environments (such as France) are likely to suppress formal organizing relative to other environments, and to construct organizational structures that are simpler, more highly formalized, and sharply bounded (Meyer 1983b:276–277). Individualist environments (notably the United States) are likely to produce more formal organizing, with the organizations showing more formal structure, weaker boundaries, more functions, and (accordingly) less formal rationality than organizations elsewhere (ibid, pp. 275–276). Elaborating this analysis, Jepperson and Meyer (1991) drew upon the existing empirical literature on cross-national variation in organizations, and pointed out that this variation does appear to cluster by polity types. In an extensive research program on organizational variations in East Asia, Gary Hamilton and colleagues developed broadly parallel arguments. They found that the institutionalization of different models of authority powerfully affected the kinds of economic organizations that emerged in different countries (e.g., Hamilton and Biggart 1988; Orrù, Biggart, and Hamilton 1991). Despite the obvious import of this area of work, research on cross-national organizational variation within this institutionalism, testing and developing such ideas, has only recently begun to expand.[13]

4.4.6 Effects of Institutional Variation (2): Variation over Time

If formal organizing is interpenetrated with institutional environments, it also follows that changes in institutional environments will lead to changes in formal organizing. Here more work has been done – again, with most reference to the United States – organized around three sets of observations.

First, Meyer, Scott, and colleagues have focused upon the recent (post-1950s) and rapid institutional centralization in the United States (a centralization that remains "fragmented" in character when compared to the more statist systems). A correlate is that organizations are increasingly embedded in systems having a vertical structure, "with decisions about funding and goals more highly centralized and more formally structured today than in the past" (Scott and Meyer 1983/1992:150). One consequence is a *"trend toward societal sectorialization"*: the formation of "functionally differentiated sectors whose structures are vertically connected with lines stretching up to the central nation-state" (Scott and Meyer 1983/1992:150). Because of the continued fragmentation of this institutional environment (for instance, many governmental agencies at many levels, many professional authorities), administrative structures become more complex and elaborate (Scott and Meyer 1994:117 and Section 4.2). A consequence: many organizational systems are now "better viewed as loosely related collections of roles and units whose purposes and procedures come from a variety of external sources, not a unitary internal superior" (ibid:117).

Second, the ongoing rationalization of social structure around formal organizations – creating "societies of organizations" everywhere (Perrow 1991; Coleman 1974) – has also led to the *increasing standardization* of formal organizing. Organizations are now socially *depicted* as instances of formal organization rather than more specifically as schools or factories or hospitals (Meyer 1994a:44). "[O]ne can discuss proper organization without much mentioning the actual substantive activities the organization will do." Standardized management accompanies standardized organizations: "An older world in which schools were managed by educators, hospitals by doctors, railroads by railroad men now recedes into quaintness. All these things are now seen as organizations, and a worldwide discourse instructs on the conduct of organization" (ibid).

Third, the increasingly *expanded individualism* of contemporary societies "creates organizational work" (Scott and Meyer 1994:211 and Section 4.3). Organizations must deal with people carrying far more complex "educational, occupational, and psychological properties" (Scott and Meyer 1994:209). Existing organizations expand their structures to accommodate them: including, developing structures of "organizational citizenship," such as due process and grievance mechanisms and affirmative action (and programs of employee "development") (Dobbin et al. 1988). New categories of organizations arise to "create and modify individuals": new schooling, therapeutic, counseling, physical health, religious, and cultural organizations (Scott and Meyer 1994:211). Further, expanded individualism contributes to the *de-bureaucratization* of organizations: true bureaucracies and many tight systems of technical control (e.g., Taylorist ones) decline – so that over time, fewer people actually give and receive orders (ibid:212).

4.4.7 Linkages between Institutional Environments and Organizations

Meyer and Rowan (1977), Meyer, Scott, and Deal (1981), and Scott and Meyer (1983) discussed a wide range of processes linking institutional environments and organizations, although these were not especially highlighted or typologized. In 1983 Paul DiMaggio and Walter Powell presented such a typology in an influential analysis that helped to secure the standing of institutionalism as a main approach to organizational analysis (DiMaggio and Powell 1983).[14] Reviewing the literature, they asserted that "organizational isomorphism" – similarities of form and structure – can occur due to coercive processes (rooted in political control and in legitimacy-seeking), mimetic processes (rooted in the development of standard responses to uncertainty), and normative processes (rooted especially in professionalization). They then developed a number of propositions about organizational isomorphism and change, referring to these processes, and in addition discussed how these processes related to ones highlighted by other schools of organizational analysis. The typology has subsequently been generalized in a fundamental way by Scott (1995), in an analysis that has yet to take proper hold in the literature.[15]

David Strang and Meyer later added a general point specifically about the diffusion of organizational forms and practices: that the highly theorized nature of contemporary societies tends to heighten greatly the diffusion of organizational forms and practices (Strang and

Meyer 1993). Strang gives the example of the prominent, rapid, and highly theorized diffusion of (perceived) Japanese organizational practices in the US context (Strang 1994). Meyer and Scott discuss the earlier diffusion and conventionalization of modern personnel administration (Meyer and Scott 1992:1–2) in this connection.[16] In highly institutionalized (and theorized) environments, policies and programs tend to evolve and change in a highly "contextual" way. That is, reform ideas emerge and evolve within a dense (national, increasingly world) policy culture; local organizations sample from this culture in an often haphazard and decoupled fashion.[17]

Endnote. This institutionalism paints a picture of a "society of organizations," but not of autonomous and bounded ones: "Although organizations may have absorbed society, as Perrow claims, society has not less absorbed organizations" (Scott and Meyer 1994:4). In fact, this institutionalism has come to picture organizations as sufficiently interpenetrated with institutional environments, such that, analytically speaking, "organizations tend to disappear as distinct and bounded units" (Meyer and Rowan 1977:346).

4.5 Nation-States in a World Polity and Culture[18]

4.5.1 Background: Questioning "Modernization" – and the Hard Reality of States

Some of the same issues were eventually raised about states in the world system. In this research area, Meyer and Michael Hannan and their collaborators[19] in the 1970s were curious about the claims of a then highly conventionalized theory of societal "modernization." The research group was aware of a seemingly extreme gap between the strong claims of this literature, and a lack of serious evidence – in two senses. First, in scholarship, the empirical literature was very primitive, consisting largely of a cross-sectional (i.e., not longitudinal) correlational literature, plus scattered case studies. Second, in the world, scholars and advisors and elites from core-countries were encouraging more peripheral states to do things like expand education systems to mimic American or European ones – without basing such recommendations upon any plausible evidence. Hence both the research and the reality seemed highly ideological.

Thus motivated, the research group assembled available quantitative data on country characteristics in a "panel" format (that is, for many countries at regularly spaced time points) – such data had not been much assembled and analyzed, to the group's surprise – as well as coding additional cross-national material to create new measures.[20] As ideas and research designs consolidated, the group begin to focus upon direct institution-to-institution connections within the world system – that is, the specific inter-relations of political, educational, and economic structures and outcomes (ibid:5–6).[21]

The initial wave of research produced numerous findings (the studies were collected in Meyer and Hannan 1979), but the overall patterns of particular interest for institutionalism were the following. First, the research documented an "explosive expansion of national systems of education"; the sources of this expansion appeared "to lie outside the properties of particular countries and to reflect exigencies of global social organization whose logics and purposes are built into almost all states" (ibid:13–14). Second, in parallel fashion "[s]tates tend to expand their power and authority within society in all types of countries through the modern period" (ibid.:14). Third, in general, "[t]he world as a whole [during 1950–1970] shows increasing structural *similarities of form* among societies without, however, showing increasing *equalities of outcome* among societies" (ibid:15). The authors noted that this pattern may be "quite specific to a period of great economic expansion and extension of markets ... " and that "[a] period of sustained world-wide economic contraction or a long-term stabilization, might alter the picture considerably" (ibid:15).

To take a specific example, the studies of educational systems and curricula showed that both were changing substantially over time, but in a very similar way across countries: there was truly remarkable "isomorphism" (Meyer, Ramirez, and Boli-Bennett 1977; Ramirez and Rubinson 1979; Meyer and Ramirez 1981). This pattern presented a major anomaly (if initially a little-noticed one) for the sociology of education, which was functionalist[22] in its basic theoretical imagery. In a functionalist scheme, educational structures should have clear political or economic functions; hence, the large national economic and political variations of societies should be accompanied by big educational variations (since the educational and politico-economic variations should be adaptations to and facilitators of one another).

Empirically, however, this co-variation was not present: educational systems were more and more alike.

The interpretation that emerged, only fully consolidated after an extended period of work, was the following. It appeared that education was being constructed more for an imagined society than for real societies (at least in the post-WWII period of educational expansion). This argument reflects the general institutionalist idea that people in modern societies are constantly developing, redeveloping, and enacting *models* of society: modern social worlds are highly theorized, hence "imagined."[23] Further – a crucial point – while actual societies are very different, it appears that *imagined* societies are pretty much alike (at least for those countries with some connection to world institutions). So, the education seen as appropriate for world-imagined society is quite standardized: models of both imagined society and education appear to change over time at a (nearly) world level.[24] In fact, educational curricula are now explicitly organized around ideas of a global society and culture, and ideas of a globally standard individual (Meyer, Kamens, and Benavot 1992; McEneaney and Meyer 2000; Meyer and Ramirez 2000; Meyer 2000a).

4.5.2 A "World Polity" and World Culture As Well As a World Economy

During the same period, other scholars had also broached ideas of a broad "world system." Immanuel Wallerstein had initiated his pioneering historical studies of a world economy and stratification system (Wallerstein 1974), Charles Tilly and colleagues had initiated long-term studies of the development of European states (Tilly 1975), and a separate literature on economic "dependency" had posited effects of world network positioning on developmental paths. The distinctive institutionalist intervention, worked out in conjunction with the above-sketched research, was the argument that the world system was not limited to a world economy or geomilitary system. The world system also comprised a world "polity" and world culture – institutional features originating in Christendom. Further, Meyer and collaborators called particular attention to the specific configuration of the "modern world system": a "relatively unified cultural system and a densely linked economy [...] without a centralized political system" (Meyer and Hannan 1979:298; also Meyer, Boli, and Thomas 1981).

This configuration was highlighted as a cause of many features of modern social and political development, as we will see.

By 1980, pressing his theoretical line, Meyer wished to qualify and contextualize Wallerstein's account of the Western state system, primarily by reminding that the "Western state also developed in part as a project under the aegis of the now invisible universal Western Church and was legitimated by broad cultural mechanisms" (Thomas and Meyer 1984:470). "All the European societies in the modern period were deeply embedded, not only in a world commodity economy and system of exchange, but also in a constructed world collectivity – a society and a stateless polity ... " (Meyer 1981:899). In a review of Wallerstein's second volume of *The Modern World System*, Meyer argued that a number of features of the modern world could not be well accounted for without invoking this "wider cultural polity." To give the flavor of the argument:

The presence of this wider evolving culture provided a legitimating base for the unusual world Wallerstein writes about. It is a world in which long-distance exchange makes sense and can properly be incorporated and adapted to, in which such exchange can be extended to the furthest strange lands with which one has no direct political linkage, in which techniques are of general utility and can be copied, in which rationalized social structures and policies are not only competed with but quickly copied, in which the nominally ultimate state political authorities are legitimately seen as subordinate to wider purposes, in which these purposes are shared across units, and in which a shared orientation integrates disparate desiderata into a single value standard (monetarization) across units (international currency) (Meyer 1982:266).

4.5.3 The Embedding of Nation-States within a World Polity

The core ideas about a "wider cultural polity" were not deployed historically, however, but rather directed to the contemporary period. They were developed by Meyer in his paper on "the world polity and the authority of the nation-state" (Meyer 1980). Following the general institutionalist imagery, Meyer presented nation-states as "embedded in an exogenous, and more or less worldwide, rationalistic culture" (1999:123), a culture "located in many world institutions (in "interstate relations, lending agencies, world cultural elite definitions and organizations, transnational bodies" [Meyer 1980:117]). In particular, this culture was composed of "world definitions of the justifications, perspectives, purposes, and policies properly to be pursued by nation-state organizations" (ibid:120).[25]

Without invoking this world polity, Meyer argued, it seemed impossible to account for a number of basic features of the system of nation-states. First, its very existence: there is far more similarity in political forms in the world than one would expect if one attends primarily to the great differences in economic development and internal cultures.[26] And there is far more stability in forms than one would anticipate: the nation-state form has been a sticky one (Strang 1990).

Second, state structures and policy domains have continued to expand rapidly over time, and notably in formally similar ways across countries. More and more countries have more of the same ministries and the same broad policy programs. This "isomorphic expansion" has occurred even in the peripheries – if in a pronounced "decoupled" way in these zones. (Peripheral countries often adopt currently common ministries and plans, without implementing actual policies.)[27] All this standardization appears to develop within and be propelled by trans-country discourses and organizations – for example, in what have now been labeled as "epistemic communities" (scientific and professional), "advocacy networks," and international governmental and nongovernmental organizations.

4.5.4 The Long-Term Buildup of a "World Society" Carrying "Models" of Political Form and Responsibility

In reflecting upon the initial wave of research collected in Meyer and Hannan (1979), the authors noted a methodological limitation of their studies: that "[s]imple panel analyses of the relationships among features of national societies provide no information on larger system processes affecting *all* subunits. ... This takes us in the direction, not of causal comparative analysis (for we really have but one case evolving over time), but toward historical description and time series analysis" in order to "attempt to describe features of the whole system" over a longer period of time (ibid:12–13, 298). As research efforts continued, various scholars developed these research designs during the 1980s and 1990s.[28]

Some studies tracked the consolidation of the nation-state form itself: for instance, David Strang studied the decline in dependent and external territories in the world system, and showed that once units become sovereign states, they rarely exit that form (Strang 1990). Other scholars documented the consolidation of a basic formal model of a nation-state, seeing such a model reflected in formal applications for UN membership (McNeely 1995), in the development of standardized data systems across countries (ibid.), and in the development of more standard population censuses (Ventresca 1995). Increasing commonality in state activities and policies was clearly documented in various longitudinal research: commonality in (among other areas) science policies (Finnemore 1996b), welfare policies (Strang and Chang 1993), population control ideas (Barrett 1995), women's rights (Berkovitch 1999a, 1999b), environmental policy (Frank 1997; Meyer et al. 1997). Common changes in national membership and citizenship models was found as well: apparent in constitutional rights (Boli 1987a), and in the changing status accorded to women, ethnoracial minorities, sexual minorities, and labor migrants (e.g., Ramirez and Cha 1990; Bradley and Ramirez 1996; Frank and McEneaney 1999; Soysal 1994).

As this research consolidated, Meyer, John Boli, George Thomas, and Francisco Ramirez integrated the findings via a tightened theoretical argument, focusing upon the idea of a "world society," and specifically upon the idea that "[m]any features of the contemporary nation-state derive from *worldwide models* constructed and propagated through global cultural and associational processes" (Meyer et al. 1997:144–145, emphasis added). These processes have intensified in part due to the continuing "statelessness" of the world system, a background cause once again invoked (ibid:145). This configuration continues to generate an extensive transnational elaboration of collective agendas – within international organizations, scientific communities, and professions – agendas worked out for nation-state actors. Scientific, professional, and other international nongovernmental organizations have been institutionalized worldwide (documented and studied in Boli and Thomas 1997 and 1999), as have global consulting industries of various sorts, promoting recipes for economic, political, organizational, and individual development (Meyer 2000b). In this connection, Strang and Meyer argued that the culture of this world system provides substantial impetus for extensive diffusion of ideas, given its underlying assumptions of the ultimate similarity of societies and of common human actorhood (Strang and Meyer 1993).

Further, as nation-states try to act, while taking on increasingly elaborate forms and responsibilities, they come to depend more and more upon the increasingly elaborate consulting machineries, a dynamic that in turn generates more and more responsibilities (Meyer 2000b).[29]

In such a context, entire institutional complexes diffuse across the world system, leading to some striking departures from standard ideas about the adaptiveness of institutions. For instance: both the relative expansion of higher education within countries, and the relative development of scientific research organizations, show modest *negative* effects on countries' economic growth, at least in the short run (Meyer, Schofer, and Ramirez, forthcoming). This pattern has largely been neglected by social scientists because it has not made much sense when seen from dominant standpoints (including in this case neoclassical economics). The institutionalist interpretation, pursued in current research, is that countries tend to construct broad-spectrum higher education and science institutions, not ones tightly linked to economic development (ibid; also Schofer 1999). Accordingly, the presence of these institutions tends to be correlated with forms of world-cultural participation – for example, with the presence of human rights and environmental organizations – but negatively correlated with growth in the short term, probably due to the investment costs involved (Shenhav and Kamens 1991).

The theoretical idea is that conformity processes are also found at the level of entire institutional complexes within world society. Higher education and science appear to a kind of "turn-key" social technologies, imported into societies but in forms linked more to broad ideas about a progressive society rather than to narrower social objectives such as economic growth.

4.5.5 Transformative Processes

Some of the systemic processes at work may be transformative ones; institutionalists have called particular attention so far to three. First, it seems that the processes above are transforming the very nature of states. As "enactors of multiple dramas whose texts are written elsewhere," states increasingly are both expanded organizational forms, but also "sprawling, weakly integrated," fragmented ones (Meyer 1999:136–139, 1994a:51–53). This line of argument provides one theoretically principled account for now-common impressions of state decomposition or "disarticulation" (e.g., Smelser with Badie and Birnbaum 1994).

Second, in 1980 Meyer had argued that with the post-WWII buildup of the state, individuals had become more embedded in states, losing standing as autonomous actors (1980:132). However, with the intervening buildup of world society, there may be a trend-shift: Meyer and David Frank say that "the society to which the individual human belongs has also importantly globalized ... " (Frank and Meyer 2000). Earlier Yasemin Soysal had isolated the core issue: an emergent and partial move beyond the nation-state model, via a "reconfiguration of citizenship" from a model based upon nationhood to a more transnational one based upon personhood and human (rather than citizen) rights (Soysal 1994:137 and ch. 8). An emergent "post-national membership" – particularly apparent in Europe and surrounding issues of labor migration – "transgresses" the national order (ibid:159). This disruption is apparent in the rise of multicultural politics, in the loosening of citizenship restrictions and obligations (e.g., voting, military), and in expansion of multiple citizenship arrangements.

Third – an even longer-term transformation – as basic cultural models change, the evolution has produced new logics for the actors of the system, including states, social movements, foundations, and consultants. For example, David Frank argues that a new cultural account of the humanity–nature relationship, picturing humans as embedded in the natural world via a long evolutionary chain, has generated the two dominant types of environmental movements: one that defines nature as part of society to be managed, and one that defines nature as sacred and requiring protection (Frank 1997; Frank et al. 1999). Deborah Barrett argues that the current "neo-Malthusian" orientation in population policy is rooted in the evolution of theories representing population growth as a constraint upon economic growth (and in the displacement of earlier theories associating population growth with state power) (Barrett 1995; Barrett and Frank 1999).

4.5.6 Multiple Modernities and Their Logics: Seeing the Modern Polities as Organizing around Distinct Variants of a Common Cultural Model

In another distinct line of argument, Meyer and others have depicted the different modern polities as distinct variants of a common Western cultural model. In this effort, initial direction was provided by Guy Swanson's conspectus of different types of polities within early modern Europe (1967, 1971). In this analysis, Swanson distinguished polities depending upon their primary locations of collective authority and agency: in a state apparatus; in remnants of a feudal community; and in individuals pictured as having direct ties to god (Thomas and Meyer 1984:471). Attempting to generalize such ideas, Meyer sketched a typology of modern polity types, distinguishing between statist, corporatist, and individualist orders (loosely capturing France, Germany, and the United States in their broad historical trajectories) (Meyer 1983). This idea subsequently has received some elaboration and modification, and some empirical exploration (Jepperson and Meyer 1991; Jepperson 2000).[30]

It has been natural to argue that the different polity forms are responsible for a number of additional cross-national differences. For example, the arguments about the effects of varying polity-organization upon formal organizations, discussed above, have this character (i.e., Meyer 1983 and Jepperson and Meyer 1991). There have been other deployments of this sort. For instance, in a central book-length development using similar ideas, Yasemin Soysal showed that different types of European polities established different regimes for incorporating labor migrants into society (Soysal 1994). Similar arguments have been adduced for variations in constructions of family violence and child protection (e.g., that child or spouse abuse are less likely to emerge as public issues in more corporate polities [Meyer et al. 1988]), for cross-national variation in legal strategies (e.g., that statism and governmental centralization both appear to affect individual recourse to legal activity [Boyle 1998]), and for cross-national variation in voluntary associations (e.g., that different institutional orders construct different types of membership organizations and are more or less encouraging of individual participation in them [Schofer and Fourcade-Gourichas 2000]). Needless to say, these are just illustrative examples.[31]

In a powerful illustration and deepening of this line of argument, Frank Dobbin documented long-lasting historical effects of variations in basic political models (Dobbin 1994b, 1995). In his book on railroad development and industrial policy formation in the United States and Europe (esp. France), Dobbin shows that very different interpretations were given to railroad development in (statist) France and the (liberal) United States, despite surprisingly similar actual public sector involvements. Similar state activities were "concealed" as state actions in the United States while "revealed" and accentuated in France. The different interpretations were generated from the different pre-existing political cosmologies of France and the United States, and then the interpretations themselves were powerfully consequential (Dobbin shows) for the subsequent divergent development of industrial policies.

Endnote. The underlying institutionalist idea is that states too are interpenetrated with their institutional environments. They appear to be "at least as fraudulent as functional creatures as organizations, schools, and persons"[32] – a perspective at odds with the arch realism of much "theory of the state" in sociology and political science.

4.6 Individual Identity within Individualism[33]

4.6.1 *Background Argument: The Political Reconstruction of Society around Individualism*

Much of the development of national polities has been "channeled into an intensification of individualism, rather than taking other forms, so that it is easy to view the secularization and elaboration of individualism as a main theme in Western history" (Meyer 1986b:200). Institutionalism emphasizes that this individualism is an evolving public theory: a public political theory (citizenship), a public economic theory (markets), a public religious and cultural theory (the soul, the private self) (Meyer 1986b:200). As such, doctrines of individualism are central to the basic Western cultural models of society.

The research on the "world educational revolution" mentioned above was pursued in part in its connection with the production of modern individuals (including, citizen-members of nation-states) (Meyer, Ramirez, and Boli-Bennett 1977; Meyer, Ramirez, and Soysal 1992). John Boli's book on the emergence of mass schooling in Sweden is precisely about the institutionalization of schooling as the dominant approach to childrearing (and individual formation) (Boli 1989), as were Francisco Ramirez's and Boli's related surveys of comparative-historical material about the relations of states and schools

(Ramirez and Boli 1987a) and of available comparative data on the development of schooling systems (Ramirez and Boli 1987b). Boli showed in detail that the "social imperative" of mass schooling developed before the urban and industrial take-off of the 1860s and 1870s. Instead it was rooted in an earlier-developing Europe-wide social movement, in which European states, both competing with and imitating one another, attempted to construct nations of citizen-individuals (Boli 1989).[34]

4.6.2 Individualism as a Collective-Level Construction and Individual-Level Enactment

Standard ideas about the development of individualism have pictured it as an outcome of social-psychological, especially experiential, processes. For example, scholars have often depicted individualism as an outcome of people's reactions to their experience of markets or cities or industrial work. The causal imagery, often implicit, is one of people experiencing a market system individually, reacting to it largely individually (or maybe with others in households or local communities), and then through their aggregate reactions eventually producing a large-scale cultural commonality – individualism.

This picture has been almost axiomatic for many scholars. For example, in their survey-based study of the development of "individual modernity" in developing countries, Alex Inkeles and David Smith argued that "exposure to modern institutions produces modern persons," focusing in particular upon exposure to modern factories (Inkeles and Smith 1974:307). Presumably if enough people are exposed long enough, an individualist ("modernized") context is produced: that is, via an individual-level experiential process, and via aggregation of the common individual effects. Many other studies shared this imagery. However, the evidence produced by these same studies did not well support such interpretations. For instance, in the Inkeles and Smith data the best predictors of an individual's relative "modernity"[35] were his education level, then nationality, then mass media exposure – all reflecting highly ideological forces. To Inkeles and Smith's apparent surprise, other variables, including those better capturing people's social experience – for example, years of factory work, occupation, urban vs. rural origins, family background – were far less salient.

In response to such empirical patterns, Meyer offered a reinterpretation of individualism, featuring (once again) collective-level processes (Meyer 1986a, 1986b, 1990). In this alternative imagery, individualism is "*not* centrally the product of human persons organizing their experience for themselves," but rather in the first instance a doctrine worked out by "various bodies of professional officials – religious ideologues, their secular counterparts (for example, psychologists, teachers, lawyers, and administrators) – and by other institutions of the modern state" (Meyer 1986a:212, emphasis added). People are then aggressively tutored in such doctrine (in families, schools, the polity) and come to enact it as part of their basic identity. In this account, a different set of causal processes is featured: collective-level scripting together with individual enactment. From this account it would follow that the relative "modernity" of people (for instance) would vary depending more upon a person's relative immersion in the ideologies of individualism – in the education system, for instance – than upon their actual social experience. And this is what empirical research tends to show (Meyer 1990; Jepperson 1992).

In such arguments, Meyer and other institutionalists were not so much reacting to specific research programs but more to a general analytical imagery: the almost automatic rendering of societal outcomes in individual-level terms. For instance, James Coleman seemed to insist that the effect of Protestantism upon European society must be theorized as an aggregation of the changed behaviors of individuals re-socialized by Protestant churches and sects (Coleman 1986).[36] Sociological institutionalists depart from both the methodological individualism and from the specific substantive sociological claim. Instead, they would argue that Protestantism in the first instance modified collectively dominant models of society.[37] In so doing it also reworked the identity and status of the individual in these models, giving the individual dramatically enhanced metaphysical and public centrality. Over time individuals began to enact this new expanded identity, tutored by church, legal, and pedagogic scripts. This enactment can proceed concurrently with more experiential effects such as Max Weber's postulated "salvation anxiety," but may in fact be the more fundamental process involved in large-scale transformation. This argument is representative of the institutionalist challenge to individual-level processes and actor-centric explanation.

4.6.3 Construction of the Self Relative to an Institutionalized "Life Course"

In the same papers, Meyer argued that basic features of the self are as much affected by highly institutionalized scripts for assembling an individual identity than by any untutored, unscripted, "experiences" (Meyer 1986b:199). People "work out selves with a great deal of institutional support" (ibid). In particular, a distinctive personal identity is worked out relative to a highly standardized and institutionalized "life course": "carefully sequenced age-grade systems of childrearing, education, work, and retirement" (ibid:200). Much of a life is highly institutionally assembled and organized: for example, most middle-class people in the United States (for example) "know" that they will go to school, have a family and career and leisure, retire, and so on (ibid:207).

Because of this extensive structuring, Meyer hypothesizes, measures that tap people's subjective experience of the institutionalized life course – for instance, their consciousness of their education and occupation – will understandably show high prominence and high continuity over time. Other features of consciousness or personality closely linked to major life course statuses should also appear central and stable: for instance, cognitive competencies, values and tastes, knowledge, and perceived efficaciousness – qualities all linked to formal education. As a corollary, however, those aspects of subjectivity *less* directly tied to core life course statuses might be expected to show less stability over time: for instance, measurements of individual's needs for achievement or power or intimacy, or measures of self-esteem or self-control. Stability in these features of the subjective self may be suppressed, precisely because modern society "strips definite and fixed role-related content from the self, leaving it free to find motives, needs, expectations, and perceptions appropriate to the situation" (ibid, p. 209).

In such a context, Meyer adds, researchers can easily form impressions of a general "instability" of the self, but this is misleading. This impression is partly due to scholarly definition: that is, their conceptualization of the self as precisely those features of personal identity *not* institutionally and structurally stabilized (Meyer 1986b:208). "The whole mass of material connected to the rules of the life course tends to be excluded" from research definitions of the self, and, in fact, people generally "may use the term 'self' to capture only the transitory aspects of their identity" (ibid). The point: isolating cultural parameters of the self can help to account for otherwise anomalous features.

4.6.4 The Different Individualisms and Hence Different Individual Identities of the Modern Polities

The previous arguments were general arguments about individualism, and about individual identity within individualism. But this institutionalism also encourages one to look for variation: specifically variation in the kinds of individualism constructed in the different Western polities.

In initial formulations Meyer had distanced himself from "national character" (and related) ideas about cross-national variations in individual identity. For instance, reflecting upon the findings of *The Civic Culture*, Gabriel Almond and Sidney Verba's famous comparative study (1963), Meyer addressed the finding that people in Germany (in the late 1950s) tended to report a lower sense of political efficacy than individuals elsewhere. Meyer argued that this outcome as likely reflects features of the German political system than any uniquely German "characterological" deficiencies in ego-strength or self-esteem – that is, it is more likely that the German respondents were simply reporting the rather inefficacious status accorded to them, in the rather elitist and statist German democracy of the time (Meyer 1970b). The underlying idea, articulated later, is that modern nation-states are all "variously committed to individualism," but institutionalize different forms of it – forms that people learn to enact in their behavior and report in their talk (Frank, Meyer, and Miyahara 1995:362; Jepperson 1992). The United States represents a historically extreme form of individualism, given that it was originally constituted in an individualist and associational way (and fundamentally Protestant way) (Meyer 1983b, 1986a:214–15). In connection with this historical atypicality, in comparative studies Americans tend to get *high* scores in measures of self-direction and felt efficacy. In Meyer's argument, Americans respond this way more "because they think they are Americans, rather than because of any extraordinary individuation in their experience" – that is, because they are enacting the basic model of the American polity, a model that stresses individual agency and responsibility (Meyer 1990:54). The various European individualisms in contrast have all tended to embed the individual in more communal social structure of one sort or another (family, locality, other communities, the state). Accordingly, Meyer argues, one would expect Europeans relative to Americans to report less sense of autonomy and less felt social efficacy – which they in fact do in survey responses and interviews (Meyer 1986b:214; Jepperson 1992).

These institutionalist ideas have as yet only partly been pursued in research. Jepperson (1992) pursued and elaborated them some in a dissertation synthesizing available cross-national survey material, showing their utility in comprehending cross-national variation in individual attitudes and identities. Relatedly, David Frank, Meyer, and David Miyahara studied national variation in the size of the psychology profession worldwide, finding that the size of the profession (incorporating various controls) tended to covary roughly with the individualism of the polity (for example, Protestant countries were high) (Frank et al. 1995). This result accords with the idea that the greater the individualism of the polity, the greater the prominence of professionalized psychology – due to the greater public salience of issues of individual psychological identity in the more individualistic cultural settings.

4.6.5 *General Changes in Individual Identity as Individualism Has Evolved*

Meyer and others deployed the same basic ideas historically, to grasp some general West-wide changes in individual identity over time. "Individualism, like other central elements of Western doctrine, is continually being 'reconstructed'" (Meyer 1986a:212). Here less work has been done, but three ideas seem especially central.

First, the scope of individualism has continued to expand, both within and across societies – just as early Christian conceptualizations greatly expanded the number of morally relevant "souls" in the world. To reference just one line of research, Francisco Ramirez and colleagues have been innovative and persistent in tracking empirically the worldwide cultural reconstruction of women into citizen-individuals, focusing especially upon the movement of women into higher education – a movement long-in-coming but then rapid and nearly worldwide once initiated, even in countries (like some Islamic ones) that otherwise maintain high levels of gender segregation (Ramirez and Weiss 1979; Ramirez and Cha 1990; Bradley and Ramirez 1996).[38] Even more broadly, and obviously, ideas of basic "human rights" extend individuality (and a kind of world citizenship) to all humans (Boli and Thomas 1999b).[39]

A second general change: as more previously private issues and domains have become public over time, producing an expanded public domain across the modern nation-states, the private sphere has been correspondingly reconstructed. For instance, as sexuality has moved more into the public culture (and hence out of a more purely private realm), the private self is reconstituted. Over time, this private self is less sexed: more a "sexless figure for whom sexuality is a technique of proper linkage to the world, not an intrinsic element" (Meyer 1986a:224). In related research, David Frank and Elizabeth McEneaney studied changes in the legal regulation of sexuality. As individuals have replaced families as the basis of societies, sexuality has moved out of family control into a public sphere in which sexuality becomes a matter of public rights, and hence eventually less subject to legal control (Frank and McEneaney 1999).

Third, the long-term and ongoing deconstruction of previous corporate and collective identities (hypernationalisms, caste-like identities, family-based identities, collective religious identities), together with the concurrent buildup of equal personhood as a central public identity, are root causes of the "contemporary identity explosion" (Frank and Meyer 2000). The former process creates new available sources of personal identity (for instance, the taming of ethnicity in the United States creates newly available "symbolic ethnicity" for individuals). The second element creates a newly dominant node of identity to which all kinds of qualities and tastes can be attached. These ideas are being pursued in current institutionalist writing and research.

Endnote. This institutionalism casts individuals in the same light as modern society's other "actors": their actorhood is highly constructed and scripted. In this line of argument, basic features of individual identity have been reinterpreted as a consequence of collective-level cultural processes: in this case, the collective project of individualism.

4.7 Sociological Neoinstitutionalism as a Theoretical Research Program

4.7.1 Relations with Other Research Programs

Institutionalism has evolved as an integrated TRP, but with constant referencing of and "product differentiation" relative to other research programs. This attention has been somewhat unrequited, with institutionalism paying a bit more attention than it receives. This pattern is readily understandable, since institutionalism emerged in constant contrast to more dominant, and hence more secure and insular, actor-centric imageries. The specifics have varied by research areas, as follows.

Education. The applications in the sociology of education mentioned above were developed in close connection to an established literature on schooling effects, and they were intended to complement (and contextualize) the field's concentration upon the socialization of individuals and their "allocation" to positions in society. The integration of the intellectual results of institutionalism with those of other research programs has probably been richest and most basic in this area, and the TRP has been theoretically central within it (Meyer 1986c; Meyer and Ramirez 1981; Meyer and Ramirez 2000). It also has been a main carrier of the comparative and world-level research that has occurred in the field (Meyer and Ramirez, ibid), and it has been widely recognized for doing so.[40]

Organizations.[41] In organizational analysis, institutionalist applications evolved in a context dominated by realist, functionalist, and rationalist pictures: organizations as hardwired decision-making structures, functionally adapted to technical environments or powerful interests. In this area, the institutionalist intervention evolved concurrently with that of population ecology (with its related focus on organizational populations in environments). A productive exchange between these two programs has continued. For instance, ecologists have incorporated the idea that organizational populations might be constructed by institutional forces (Hannan and Freeman 1989), and they have tried to incorporate variation in legitimacy as one of the selection forces operating in environments (Carroll and Hannan 1989, an approach partly resisted by institutionalists in a direct interchange [Zucker 1989]). In contrast, less progress has been made in cleanly separating institutionalist arguments from more conventional "resource-dependence" ones, since institutionalism too invokes resource connections. Productive efforts, however, continue.[42] Little effort has been made to clarify the respective contributions and possible complementarities of institutionalist and rationalist (esp. "rational choice") arguments – the terms for doing so have not been well clarified, and the effort is hampered by mutual disinterest.[43] In programmatic statements, however, institutionalists have remained largely ecumenical, imagining that different imageries will make different contributions, and insisting mainly on the utility of maintaining a fully macroscopic and phenomenological perspective as well as others in the field (Scott 1995, passim; Meyer and Scott 1992:2–5).[44]

Given the arch realism of much organizational analysis, it has been common to typify institutionalism as an exaggerated culturalism: Charles Perrow groused that Meyer and Scott and others were "overboard with myth and symbols" – a characterization that some institutionalists played into (Perrow 1985).[45] The specifically *anthropological* meaning of "formal structure as myth and ceremony" was elided, as were Meyer and Scott's (and collaborators') broader structuralist and comparative efforts. Given this common characterization, it is surprising that sociological neoinstitutionalism has more recently been described by a recent review (rather hyperbolically) as "the leading perspective among organizational scholars in the U.S." (Mizruchi and Fein 1999:678), as well as being influential in Europe (Krücken and Hasse 1999). However, institutionalism has been established in this field in a truncated way.[46] There have been tendencies to focus narrowly upon the "mimetic isomorphism" isolated by DiMaggio and Powell (Mizruchi and Lein 1999), to treat institutionalism as having to do with narrowly symbolic issues or organizational culture, and to turn institutionalism into a modified actor/interest theory (featuring the interests of state or professional elites in producing organizational forms) – inducing Meyer, Scott, and Dobbin among others to demur.[47]

Nation-states. In this application area, there has been less integration, cross-fertilization, and attempted adjudication than within educational or organizational analysis. The institutionalist applications were developed in conjunction once again with an ecological perspective (represented by Michael Hannan). Meyer and Hannan initially reported that they could not easily find ways to adjudicate between institutional and ecological perspectives (Meyer and Hannan 1979:10–16); over time, Hannan moved away from world system studies, in part because the units in question (states) did not really appear to be under that much competitive selection pressure (at least of the stringent sort focused upon by population ecology). As institutionalist work evolved independently, a relationship to Wallerstein's world system program became more evident, a connection partly complementary and partly competitive in character. From the institutionalist standpoint, the emphasis on a world polity and culture was meant to provide contextualization for ideas of a world economy and stratification system. Perhaps for this reason, there has been more institutionalist reference to the Wallerstein-centered program than the reverse.[48]

Institutionalists were also partly trying to qualify other realist perspectives on states, those tending to see states as hard organizational structures largely in resource competition. (The opposition is presented most clearly in Thomas and Meyer 1984.) Initially realist-minded scholars did not much join the discussion, tending to ignore or downplay institutionalist efforts.[49] More recently, however, Charles Tilly has called attention to the importance of the "international modeling of state structures," drawing upon Meyer (1999) (Tilly 1999), and to the importance of cultural "scripting" more generally.[50] Also recently, the TRP has begun to show up in political science and international relations, traditionally redoubts of social science realism – if in a somewhat tamed form least disruptive of political science's theoretical categories.[51] However, the TRP is generating some substantive applications as well as merely commentary: in international relations, for example, Martha Finnemore has studied how international organizations tutor states (such as how UNESCO has scripted much science policy) (Finnemore 1996b); Peter Katzenstein and collaborators, drawing upon this institutionalism as well as other "constructivist" perspectives, have studied the consolidation of state identities and norms (Katzenstein 1996); and in a project coordinated by Alec Stone Sweet, Wayne Sandholtz, and Neil Fligstein, scholars draw in a routine way upon sociological neoinstitutionalism as one of their theoretical sources in studying the "institutionalization of Europe" (Stone Sweet, Sandholtz, and Fligstein, forthcoming).

Individualism. Research in this application area is highly scattered, and for that straightforward reason clear relations between research programs have not emerged. Meyer drew directly upon the extensive psychology-based literature on the life-course in developing his ideas about the self, and his formulations have in return been incorporated into the life-course literature. In contrast, a coherent interprogram discussion of individualism and the self has not yet formed: cultural and social historians, comparative social psychologists, anthropologists, and sociologists have been proceeding in a segmental way.

4.7.2 Contributions of the Program

The contributions of sociological neoinstitutionalism have been of three main sorts. First and foremost, like any truly basic analytical imagery, this institutionalism makes *new observations* possible – just as actor-centric imagery (its "rational choice" form) illuminated "collective action" (Olson 1965) and principal/agent relationships (Kiser 1999). Institutionalism too directs attention to different features of the social world, fundamental features that were otherwise unnoticed or disregarded. For instance, because of their focus upon possible effects of a broader world frame, institutionalists brought out the homogeneity in structure among nation-states. This homogeneity is striking, and remarkable given the great differences in country resources and cultures, but before institutionalism it had not been much problematized. In organizational analysis, institutionalists brought out the extraordinary world-spanning rationalization and standardization of organizational forms, as well as the transformation of organizational forms to accommodate the "expanded individuals" of contemporary society. Regarding individualism, institutionalists brought out (for example) the variation in professional psychology across countries, in its connection to differently constructed individualisms. In each of the application areas discussed above, the truly fundamental contribution of institutionalism has been to call attention to features of the social world that were largely *unobserved* before, let alone theorized.

Second, institutionalism also has offered *new explanations* – either about its new observations, or about established observations. For instance, sociology had long observed the ubiquitous decoupling of formal structures from informal arrangements and practical activity. The institutionalist literature gave this decoupling centrality and offered a more general explanation of it, linking it to conformity with institutionalized environments. Sociology had also obviously long observed the increasing individualism of modern society. Institutionalism offered new explanations, including the very basic argument that individualism was unlikely just an outcome of people's aggregated social experiences, but rather a collective doctrinal construction and individual enactment. Such ideas had certainly been voiced before – a root source is Emile Durkheim's discussion of the modern "cult of the individual" (Collins 1992: Ch. 2) – but the institutionalist interventions have isolated the core analytical issues much more clearly.

Third, the concentration upon institutionalized cultural models enables this institutionalism to produce *reflexive contributions*, by endogenizing features of social science in its explanations. For instance, institutionalism offers not only a distinctive set of observations and explanations about modern educational systems. It also offers a theory of the sociology of education itself: namely, how this field has largely accepted the cultural myths of education, its research agenda then historically rather narrowly organized around the ways in which educational realities fail to live up to these myths. Or how the literature on social stratification has similarly been organized around broader cultural myths of individualism and egalitarianism (focusing resolutely on specific forms of individual inequality and missing more organizational forms of it as well as overly backgrounding the extraordinary egalitarian dynamic of the contemporary period) (Meyer 1994b). Or how the literature on "international relations" has sustained its arch realism about states only by constantly redefining its turf so as to maintain a narrow focus on continuing forms of interstate conflict and disorder in the system, editing out a broader world polity and culture (Jepperson, Wendt, and Katzenstein 1996).

In principle, the contributions of sociological neoinstitutionalism should be complementary with insights generated by other basic analytical imageries. However, the whole issue of complementarity is rarely taken up, given sociology's sect-like segmentation and propensity to reify theories.

4.7.3 The Main Source of the Program's Contributions

Actor-centric imagery, as in James Coleman's most basic explication (Coleman 1986), "backgrounds" context and the historical construction of actors in a context, and foregrounds (1) largely taken-for-granted actors in their interest-driven choices and strategic interactions, and (2) the aggregations of these choices, or the outcomes of their strategic interaction games. The various utilitarian, exchange, and (many) network sociologies all build upon this basic imagery, if in differing ways.

In contrast, if one foregrounds cultural institutionalization, the picture of modern actors – organizations, states, individuals – as tightly integrated, highly bounded, autonomously acting entities, hardwired outside of society, is problematized. In fact, as empirically observed, these entities appear to be open, interpenetrated with institutional environments, and hence loosely coupled and varying in particular construction. Because of these qualities, actors from this institutionalism's standpoint are seen as rather derivative, for analytical purposes. For instance, if actors are highly open, rather than tightly bounded, they are then subject to many context effects: ranging from the initial contextual construction of modal actor identities, to the collective scripting of activity for identities, to actors' ongoing dependence upon consultation with "others" for managing identities and making (already highly scripted) choices. These context effects accordingly occupy institutionalist attention.

The task of causal analysis for this institutionalism is then different. It becomes the study of the construction and institutionalization of the cultural model that both defines identities *and* scripts the main lines of activity for identities. Thus, the modeling and enactment processes that transmit and reproduce these scripts are focalized, and the choice processes that occur within highly institutionalized frames and identities become of secondary interest. For example, the institutionalist interest is more in why and where markets are created, rather than market behavior, and why (and where) elections exist, rather than why people vote the way they do.[52] Similarly, the institutionalist interest is more in the non-choice (the taken-for-granted routine) of going to college for most middle-class American high school students, and less in the choice of which college to attend. There is fundamental interest in how contemporary individuals believe (and often pretend) they are making unscripted and autonomous choices – and in how researchers go along with the pretense – when more usually people are enacting models and scripts of broad collective construction and reach.

One upshot of institutionalist research is that modern actors only exist with a lot of institutional scaffolding and support; but then with this support they are not really actors in the senses often imagined. The "middle-class students" just mentioned (or their parents) can talk with much more elaboration and clarity than their forebears (or than, say, peasants). But much of their talk (as well as their menus of choice) is highly scripted and institutionally organized. They are thus more actor-like in some respects, but arguably less actors (than their forebears, or peasants) in other respects. In any case they are not plausibly the exaggerated actors marching around the metatheory of actor-centric social science. The bite of this institutionalism is its exposure of the hypocrisies of modern actorhood – and its related insistence that one needs to do anthropology about modern "actors" as much as about peasants (Meyer and Jepperson 2000).

While de-focalizing actors in order to problematize them, *people* and *activity* are nevertheless thoroughly invoked in institutionalist arguments. But the people who are invoked are not usually actors, and the activity invoked is not usually action – at least in the sense of generic humans engaging in highly informed, reflective, deliberative, and autonomous choice-making in pursuit of relatively private interests.[53] Instead the people invoked in this institutionalism are usually ones operating as *agents* of the collectivity (like professionals or state elites or advocates), formulating or carrying broad collective projects. Or, they are "*others*," in G.H. Mead's sense – that is, social responders and consultants, asserting the basic expectations and standard practices of society (Meyer 1994a, 1996). Collective agency and othering provide the primary microfoundations for this institutionalism.

4.7.4 Evolution and "Growth" of the Program

Pattern of Growth. Seen in ecological terms, the program gives the impression of pursuing a highly stable specialist strategy – in this respect like other basic imageries such as rational choice or population ecology (although unlike rational choice it has no pretense of being a self-sufficient or all-purpose imagery). In Joseph Berger and Morris Zelditch's terms (Berger and Zelditch 1998), the pattern of growth has been the "proliferation" of substantive applications over the domains defined by the main socially constructed "actors" of modern society – organizations, states, individuals. In each domain, as we've seen, the same basic logic is applied: the formation of actor-structures within institutional environments. As we've also seen, the specific substantive applications were also motivated by empirical anomalies (or theory-empirics gaps) apparent in the research literature.

Sources of growth. The proliferation of the program has been propelled primarily by what Berger and Zelditch call a "substantive working strategy" and a "methodological working strategy" (ibid). The substantive strategy is the theoretical imagery discussed throughout. The methodological strategy has been to study historical and comparative variations among contexts – due to the highly contextual nature of the core theoretical ideas. Institutionalists have especially sought to study the basic cultural models of social systems, and their effects; this concentration follows from the basic argument that the actors and "others" in modern social environments are constantly elaborating and taking up models for organizing and acting. Such studies have been fostered by a set of research designs in what someone half-seriously labeled "quantitative macro phenomenology"; these have been worked out by Meyer and colleagues (like Mike Hannan, Dick Scott, and Nancy Tuma), and deployed in many doctoral dissertations especially. These designs have often involved finding comparative or historical quantitative data – or materials that can be coded as counts – and using standard techniques of statistical inference, although often employed in exploratory and interpretive ways that cannot be described here.[54]

Over time research designs have become more diverse. Quantitative analyses have diversified beyond regression-based strategies, following the field. And the program has become less exclusively based in quantitative designs, especially with greater comparative historical work (for example, by Boli, Dobbin, Soysal, and others). Evidence and measurement strategies have continued to broaden, to include coding of (for example) yearbooks of international organizations (for study of the buildup of world culture [Boli and Thomas 1997]), college curricula (for study of changes in the knowledge system [David Frank, in preparation]), history and civics texts (for study of changing collective identities [Frank et al. 2000; Soysal 1998]), and conferences and discourse of international nongovernmental organizations (about women, environment, science) since the nineteenth century (for study of changing cultural models) (Boli and Thomas 1999).

In connection with these developments, the inferential strategies for showing institutional effects have become more direct. In initial research institutionalists sought mainly to demonstrate the existence of unexpected isomorphisms and decouplings, and then secondarily to infer, indirectly, the existence of institutionalization as a cause of them. This was an "inputed effects" strategy (Schneiberg and Clemens, forthcoming): the *absence* of standard (for example, organizational) correlations was taken as indirect evidence of the *presence* of institutional forces. In analysis of educational organizations, this inferential strategy worked well, since readers were informally quite familiar with the institutional classifications involved (grade-levels, standard curricula, etc.). In analysis of nation-states, the absence of major economic effects (say, on some feature of political structure) plus the presence of isomorphism, plus some evidence on world society processes, were used to infer institutionalization.

As research has expanded, there have been more direct demonstrations of institutional effects. For example, the research on the effects of "world society" contain a number of such more direct studies of the effects of change at the institutional level: David Frank et al. 1999 on changes in constructions of the environment, and their effects; Deborah Barrett on changes in ideology about population growth and control, and their effects (Barrett 1995; Barrett and Frank 1999); Nitza Berkovitch (1999a, 199b) on changes in doctrines about the identity and status of women, and their effects. (Boli 1999 summarizes some of this research.)

It seems fair to say that the research fertility of the program does *not* appear to be based in any of the following possible sources of theoretical innovation and growth. There are no special methodological tools or claims. There is no special theoretical formalization. There is no special epistemology or logic of explanation – beyond an insistence on multilevel analysis and hence an unwillingness to go along with the very special epistemology of methodological individualism. There is no exotic topical concentration: the program has generated applications in the historically core domains of sociology, and has published in standard general outlets. The fertility and distinctiveness of the program is based almost exclusively in its different theoretical imagery, and in the aggressive empirical deployment of this imagery in different domains using a set of similar research designs. Almost all energy has been put into identifying and exploring interesting substantive issues, new sources of data, and different possible explanations, with metatheoretic issues (for good or for ill) largely put aside.[55]

4.8 Conclusion

In its research fertility, theoretic integration, and continued expansion, sociological neoinstitutionalism seems a very substantial success.

However, institutionalism has been less successful in receiving full acknowledgement of these achievements, at least as yet. Two factors appear to account for this interesting disjunction. First, one should not underestimate a standard factor: the highly segmental ecology of the field sustains intellectual diversity but also produces little encouragement for actual interchange or recognition (or for that matter, for broad reading – there is often little incentive to know about others' work, even though the myth of mutual awareness and interest is maintained).

Second, probing a bit more deeply, the intellectual culture of American sociology is still predominantly individualist and realist in construction, and institutionalism maximally deviates by being both structuralist and phenomenological. Due to this deviance, it predictably has received feigned and real incomprehension – for instance, easy labeling as a dispensable concern for myth and symbols, or for other "superstructural" fluff. (Some neoinstitutionalist writings have played into these characterizations.) The fundamental institutionalist concern with the basic matrices of modern society is thereby elided. In this way, this institutionalism as yet is not firmly conventionalized as a line of truly basic social theory.[56]

However, the segmental ecology and intellectual culture of sociology have also facilitated institutionalism, internally – as one line of truly basic social theory. The worldwide social scientific reification of actorhood continues to give sociological institutionalism a lot of space – to defocalize actorhood – and produces far fewer near-competitors, and far less real criticism, than should be present. In this space, this institutionalism continues to "proliferate" as what Lakatos called a "progressive TRP," both expanding and deepening its research applications.

Notes

1. There are few treatments of sociological neoinstitutionalism as an integrated TRP. Krücken and Hasse (1999) is a monograph in German reviewing sociological neoinstitutionalism generally, starting with organizational analysis. The most important general theoretical statement is Meyer, Boli, and Thomas (1987). A consideration of conceptual issues is offered in Jepperson 1991. Other reviews concentrate upon parts of the program. DiMaggio and Powell (1991) concentrate upon organizational analysis. A book-length survey of the

whole range of neoinstitutionalist ideas and research in organizational analysis is provided by Scott (1995).

2. The scope of this chapter is intentionally restricted in the following ways: (1) The chapter limits itself to the sociological neoinstitutionalism associated especially with John Meyer, and does not attempt to provide an overview of the various institutionalisms present in sociological theory. Scott (1995) and DiMaggio and Powell (1991) provide more general overviews, as does Hall and Taylor (1996) for political science. It is probably safe to say that the sociological neoinstitutionalism surveyed in this chapter has been the version most developed as a "theoretical research program" in the specific sense analyzed by Berger and Zelditch (1998). (2) Within this restricted focus, there is particular attention to Meyer's work, for straightforward reasons: many of the core ideas and innovations in the program come from his individual work or from his collaboration with colleagues (such as Michael Hannan and W.R. Scott) and with students and ex-students. (3) Due to this volume's focus, and to space constraints, this review concentrates upon expositing the development of ideas within the research program. While it refers constantly to the program's empirical studies, it is not able to convey them with proper vividness and detail. Nor is it able to offer a critical evaluation of the program.

3. For instance, an unpublished memo on "institutionalization" bears that date (Meyer 1970b; ideas discussed with Morris Zelditch, Jr., among others), as does Meyer's article offering an institutional reinterpretation of the nature of "socialization" in schools (Meyer 1970c, to be discussed).

4. In a concurrent development, Lynne Zucker's "The Role of Institutionalization in Cultural Persistence" (1977) demonstrated experimentally that presenting a situation as an institutionalized formal organization has substantial effects upon individuals' expectations and behavior. (Zucker had studied at Stanford and had worked with a number of the sociologists and social psychologists there.)

5. Meyer was taking off most immediately from the general interest in contextual and structural thinking prominent at Columbia University in the 1960s, as well as from phenomenological ideas then developing in the sociological environment (including ethnomethodology, Peter Berger's [and Berger and Luckmann's] work, Erving Goffman's social psychology). These ideas were emerging partly in response to Talcott Parsons' and Robert Merton's focus upon norms, internalization, and socialization – a focus increasingly seen as excessive and empirically

problematic. Meyer was also influenced directly by Daniel Bell (viz., Bell's general macrohistorical concerns), and by Paul Lazarsfeld (viz., Lazarsfeld's concern for multilevel analysis). Meyer was a lecturer in a program led by Bell, and was a research assistant for Lazarsfeld.

6. In Germany, the educational system has been far more differentiated by types of schools, with the different tracks associated with different occupations and social status. Hence in Germany the identity "graduate" has not been a singular one: people have received one of a number of different identities from their participation in a particular segment of the educational system.
7. "Even Weber's idea that institutions require *legitimacy* can be reinterpreted to mean not that people must approve of them or like them, but that they must acknowledge that they are actually binding – that they do actually organize social responses to the actor" (Meyer 1970b).
8. Meyer, personal communication, July 2000.
9. Meyer and W. Richard Scott offer their own narrative of the emergence and development of this institutionalism in organizational analysis (Meyer and Scott 1992:1–17) – an account adhered to here. See Scott 1995 for an extended (book-length) and definitive treatment. See also Strang 1994 for a particularly effective characterization of the elaboration of research ideas in this area, as well as DiMaggio and Powell 1991 (esp. good on intellectual context), Zucker 1987 (for many substantive examples), and Dobbin 1994a (esp. good on phenomenological aspects of the program).
10. By Meyer, Elizabeth Cohen, Terrence Deal, and Brian Rowan, among others.
11. The idea, originating in Max Weber's work, that European (later, world) society reflects the following fundamental cultural and institutional dynamic: (1) continuing efforts to systematize social life around standardized rules and around schemes that explicitly differentiate and then seek to link means and ends; (2) the ongoing reconstruction of all social organization – both social activities and social actors, including the nation-state itself as an actor – as means for the pursuit of collective purposes, these purposes themselves subject to increasing systematization (Meyer, Boli, and Thomas 1987:24; Scott and Meyer 1994:3). More concretely, " ... through rationalization, authority is structured as a formal legal order increasingly bureaucratized; exchange is governed by rules of rational calculation and bookkeeping, rules constituting a market, ... [including] such related processes as monetarization, commercialization, and bureaucratic planning; cultural accounts increasingly reduce society to

the smallest rational units – the individual, but also beyond to genes and quarks" (Meyer, Boli, and Thomas 1987:25).
12. Institutionalists have mostly focused upon the contemporary expansions of formal organizing and their institutional sources. Scott and Meyer stated in 1994 that they have not tried to offer a "general macrosociological model of long-term organizational change" (1994:8), and neither they nor others in the immediate literature have pursued this task. Fligstein (1990) is a partial exception.
13. Some appears in Scott and Christensen 1995.
14. As did their edited volume, Powell and DiMaggio 1991.
15. Organizations respond to environments via three logics, Scott suggests: instrumentality, appropriateness, and orthodoxy (Scott 1995:35 and ch. 3). Instrumentality is based in expedience (awareness of possible legal sanctions, for example); appropriateness is based in social obligation (awareness of moral norms, for example); orthodoxy is based in taken-for-grantedness (perceived conceptual correctness, for example). This typology would seem to have quite general utility for social theory.
16. That is, modern personnel administration developed as a broad ideological movement, and eventually was "institutionalized as standard operating procedure – defined sometimes in law, but often in custom, professional ideologies, and doctrines of proper organizational management – and thus appears in many contexts. These procedures flow from organization to organization, sector to sector, and even country to country, as a collection of culturally defined categories and procedures, and as institutionalized packages supported by a variety of processes. Ultimately, they are taken-for-granted by individuals and organizations as the right way to do things" (Meyer and Scott 1992:1–2).
17. For this reason, "reform" waves sweep through organizational systems – "management by objectives," Japanese quality control ideas, "new math" in schools – but with haphazard, seemingly unpredictable, patterns of actual adoption in practices over various local settings (Meyer 1983a). The likelihood of implementation at any location is often hard to predict from local conditions and interest alignments.
18. For fuller reviews of this application area, see especially: Meyer et al. 1997; Meyer 1999a; Meyer 2000b.
19. The collaborators included John Boli[-Bennett], Christopher Chase-Dunn, Jacques Delacroix, Jeanne Gobalet, François Nielsen, Francisco Ramirez, Richard Rubinson, George Thomas, and Jane Weiss.
20. For example, features of national constitutions, "information load of exported products," number of cabinet posts in governments (Meyer and Hannan 1979:6).

21. Surprisingly, few studies had done this. Most available studies had pursued relationships among individuals, or among groups, within one or more societies, rather than studying macrosociological connections directly (Meyer and Hannan 1979:4–5).
22. As used here, "functionalism" does not refer to any specific theory, such as the "structural-functionalism" of classical anthropology or Parsons. Rather it refers to a general imagery: that of a highly bounded and tightly-coupled social "system," with its structures existing, or having the form that they do, because they are tightly adapted to and facilitative of one another. In the sociology of education, functionalist ideas tend to represent educational structures as filling various needs or requirements (or legitimating requirements) of stratification systems, or (in the neomarxian variant) of specific social classes (Meyer 1986c). From methodological discussions it has become clear that functional imagery is empirically and logically suspect, but that functional arguments of a more narrow-gauged sort, meeting certain analytical requirements, may be legitimate in some cases (Stinchcombe 1968; Elster 1983: ch. 2).
23. The language of "imagined society" was imported into the research program later, borrowed from Anderson (1991).
24. One striking example: UNESCO codified the tripartite (6/3/3) categorization of school grade levels to simplify and regularize data collection. This data collection scheme was then implemented as actual organizational structure in many school systems in the world.
25. Later Meyer referred more fully to "a set of models defining the nature, purpose, resources, technologies, control and sovereignty of the proper nation-state" (1999a:123).
26. That is, how is it that in spite of "the differentiating power of the world economy, the state system expands?" (1980:115). Relatedly, the legitimacy of other political forms, such as ethnic or religious polities, or polities based solely in economic associations, has weakened (ibid:120).
27. For instance, emphasis on national planning is especially common in *less*-developed countries. Further, sometimes planning cannot realistically be accomplished in these settings, but elites may nevertheless load up constitutions with currently dominant principles and programs – even if these are not to be enacted in practice (Meyer et al. 1997: 155).
28. Reviewed especially in Meyer 1999a and Meyer et al. 1997.
29. Writing about these "scripts" for nation-states, Francisco Ramirez adds that "[m]uch of what is articulated is advisory and much of the advice is sufficiently abstract to allow for cross-national variation in

interpretation and implementation. However, it would be difficult to explain the growing isomorphism among nation-states were one not to postulate the common models or blueprints that guide their formation" (Ramirez 2000).

30. However, as with organizational analysis, the macrohistorical side of sociological institutionalism has received less development than one would expect.
31. Jepperson 2000 provides more.
32. Meyer, personal communication, August 2000.
33. See Meyer 1986a for a partial overview of ideas in this research area.
34. Further, in an attempt to study the consolidation and institutionalization of standard life-stages of an individual – core to the construction of a standard individualist identity – Boli studied the incorporation of ideas about child protection and development into the political and ideological systems of many societies. He did so in part by coding references to children in the political constitutions of nation-states, using these references as indicators of the consolidation of a transnational ideology of childhood and individuality (Boli and Meyer 1978).
35. In this project, "individual modernity" referred to a syndrome of "attitudes, values, and dispositions to act," especially "a thrust toward more instrumental kinds of attitudes and behavior" (Inkeles and Smith 1974: 301, 291). The syndrome included an ideal of informed participant citizenship, an efficacious self-image, values of independence and autonomy, and openness to new experience and ideas (ibid).
36. In Coleman's version, a change in the social context (the Protestant Reformation movements) re-socializes individuals, who then behave differently (reflecting "salvation anxiety" and then greater economizing), and then, in aggregate, produce a further change in the context (eventually a more marketized social system) (Coleman 1986). Coleman seems to insist that the effects of Protestantism must take this form, or that the *major* effect of Protestantism would necessarily take this form, or that one must in any case theorize Protestantism in this form. Each of these claims seems arbitrary and quite problematic. For instance, the institutionalist explanation sketch is an entirely plausible alternative, in many respects a much more plausible one, yet it does not take the Coleman-prescribed form. (See Collins 1980 for a more collective-level reading of Weber's argument.) However, in principle the institutionalist explanation sketch could be either complementary to or competitive with the Coleman sketch. The point is that this is an empirical matter, not a matter for methodological fiat.

37. In this picture, in changing the dominant theory of collective purpose and progress, Protestantism reworked both the roles and the objectives of priests and lawyers and state elites, who, operating as agents of the changed theory, changed various rules of the societal game. (For example, rich people could subsequently use their money as capital investment, rather than having to buy status and protection.)
38. Ramirez and colleagues have also focused upon the expansion of women's suffrage in the world system, studying how a highly contested issue became a taken-for-granted feature of political life. (They find that between 1870 and 1940, the extension of voting rights to women is related to domestic features of countries: for instance, the degree of "Westernization" of, and strength of women's organizations within, a country. However, after this period, such factors appear much less important; instead, external factors seem to be at work: the policies of other countries in a region and in the world at large [Ramirez, Soysal, and Shanahan 1997; Ramirez 2000 for review].)
39. ... and to some degree, to non-humans: conceptions of "animal rights" accord a kind of individuality, and quasi- social membership, to a widening range of "charismatic fauna" (for instance, whales).
40. For instance, in 1995 Meyer was recognized for lifetime contributions to the sociology of education by the section on education of the American Sociological Association.
41. For the characterization of this section I draw especially upon discussion with Marc Ventresca.
42. Lynne Zucker has offered thoughts about how to sort out institutionalist versus other resource-dependence claims (Zucker 1987, 1991); Scott addresses the matter as well (1995).
43. For instance, Peter Abell provides an entirely standard and essentially uncomprehending rationalist account of neoinstitutionalism, then relegating institutionalism to mopping up residual variance after rationalists provide a baseline explanation (Abell 1995). Zucker points out that institutionalist claims are often set out again rather global rationalist *perspectives* rather than specific arguments; she concludes, understandably but perhaps hastily, that clean tests are not possible (Zucker 1987:457). Scott (1995:138–40) provides some necessary distinctions.
44. Dick Scott's long-standing ecumenical perspective has been particularly important and influential, the perspective in and of itself a major intellectual contribution (Scott 1987, 1995).
45. Although Perrow also applauded Meyer and Rowan's piece on the "structure of educational organizations" (1978), and lauded Powell

and DiMaggio's edited volume on the new institutionalism in organizational analysis.
46. I draw especially upon discussions with Marc Ventresca in this characterization.
47. Meyer and Scott 1992; Dobbin 1994a. For instance: "... professionals and state bureaucrats are as much creatures as creators of the ideologies they enact. And the models provided by dominant organizations in sectors or organizational fields may become institutionalized as theories, quite independent of the distribution of advantages created by this institutionalization" (Meyer and Scott 1992:3). They say further that it is not obvious "what interests or powers have driven all sorts of rationalistic functions – personnel structures, accounting arrangements, planning departments – into massive numbers of organizations of the world" (Scott and Meyer 1994:5).
48. In his review of world system studies, Christopher Chase-Dunn (who originally worked on the Meyer and Hannan–coordinated project) largely marginalized neoinstitutionalist efforts (Chase-Dunn 1989). Recently Wallerstein has acknowledged "world polity" ideas more openly, but has treated their applicability as limited largely to the current period of globalization (e.g., Wallerstein 1991).
49. For example, Charles Tilly's reviews of the field initially ignored institutionalist efforts (e.g., Tilly 1984, 1992). Theda Skocpol's initial reviews did acknowledge this institutionalism, but without giving it theoretical centrality (Skocpol 1985).
50. While extensively drawing upon neoinstitutionalist conclusions, Tilly also asks for more attention to "mechanisms" linking organizations and states to international models (Tilly 1999:407–409). See Meyer et al. 1997:157–62 for a more-than-usually extended discussion of specific linkages, at least a partial response to Tilly's line of questioning. Tilly 1997:Ch. 1 draws attention to variation in cultural "scripting," and calls for more attention to cultural effects generally.
51. So far, sociological neoinstitutionalism tends to be rendered within International Relations in a rather distorted way, as primarily being about "norms" and "socialization" – despite the fact that sociological neoinstitutionalism emerged *against* the emphasis on normative socialization found in Parsons and Robert Merton. Also, political scientists persist in criticizing the program for underplaying "agency" (here, actorhood), thereby ritually asserting their disciplinary identity (power, actors), and missing this institutionalism's intentional defocalizing of actors.
52. Thomas and Meyer point out relatedly that "[w]e have better studies of why people vote the way they do than of why there are elections, or of

market behavior rather than of why markets are created" (Thomas and Meyer 1984:462).
53. John Boli helped with this characterization of "action" (personal communication).
54. See Schneiberg and Clemens (forthcoming) as well as Meyer and Hannan 1979.
55. John Boli stressed this feature (personal communication).
56. Or even disregarded: for example, Randall Collins can leave the program out of his impressive overviews of sociology's intellectual capital (Collins 1988, 1994). A longer version of this paper provides a more elaborate "sociology of knowledge" of this institutionalism's intellectual position within sociology (Working Paper, Robert Schuman Centre for Advanced Studies, European University Institute, Florence Italy, 2001).

References

Abell, P. (1995). The New Institutionalism and Rational Choice Theory. In W. R. Scott & S. Christensen, eds., *The Institutional Construction of Organizations*. Thousand Oaks, CA: Sage, pp. 3–14

Almond, G. & S. Verba. (1963). *The Civic Culture*, Princeton, NJ: Princeton University Press.

Anderson, B. (1991). *Imagined Communities*, 2nd edn, London: Verso.

Barrett, D. (1995). *Reproducing Persons as a Global Concern: The Making of an Institution*. PhD dissertation, Stanford University.

Barrett, D. & D. Frank. (1999). Population Control for National Development: From World Discourse to National Policies. In J. Boli & G. M. Thomas, eds., *Constructing World Culture: International Nongovernmental Organizations Since 1875*. Stanford, CA: Stanford University Press, pp. 198–221.

Berger, J. & M. Zelditch, Jr. (1998). Theoretical Research Programs: A Reformulation. In *Status, Power, and Legitimacy*, by J. Berger & M. Zelditch Jr. New Brunswick, NJ: Transaction, pp. 71–93.

Berger, P. & T. Luckmann. (1967). *The Social Construction of Reality*, New York, NY: Doubleday.

Berkovitch, N. (1999a). The International Women's Movement: Transformations of Citizenship. In J. Boli & G. M. Thomas, eds., *Constructing World Culture: International Nongovernmental Organizations Since 1875*. Stanford, CA: Stanford University Press, pp. 100–26.

Berkovitch, N. (1999b). *From Motherhood to Citizenship*, Baltimore, MD: Johns Hopkins University Press.

Boli, J. (1987a). Human Rights or State Expansion? Cross-National Definitions of Constitutional Rights, 1870–1970. In *Institutional Structure: Constituting State, Society, and the Individual*, by G. Thomas, J. W. Meyer, F. O. Ramirez, & J. Boli. Newbury Park, CA: Sage, pp. 133–49.

Boli, J. (1987b). World Polity Sources of Expanding State Authority and Organization, 1870–1970. In *Institutional Structure: Constituting State, Society, and the Individual*, by G. Thomas, J. W. Meyer, F. O. Ramirez, & J. Boli. Newbury Park, CA: Sage, pp. 71–91.

Boli, J. (1989). *New Citizens for a New Society*, Elmsford, NY: Pergamon.

Boli, J. (1999). World Authority Structures and Legitimations. In J. Boli & G. M. Thomas, eds., *Constructing World Culture: International Nongovernmental Organizations Since 1875*. Stanford, CA: Stanford University Press, pp. 267–300.

Boli, J., F. Ramirez & J. W. Meyer. (1985). Explaining the Origins and Expansion of Mass Education. *Comparative Education Review*, 29(2), 145–68.

Boli, J. & G. M. Thomas. (1997). World Culture in the World Polity: A Century of International Non-Governmental Organization. *American Sociological Review*, 62(2), 171–90.

Boli, J. & G. M. Thomas, eds. (1999a). *Constructing World Culture: International Nongovernmental Organizations Since 1875*, Stanford, CA: Stanford University Press.

Boli, J. & G. M. Thomas. (1999b). INGOs and the Organization of World Culture. In J. Boli & G. M. Thomas, eds., *Constructing World Culture: International Nongovernmental Organizations Since 1875*. Stanford, CA: Stanford University Press, pp. 13–49.

Boli-Bennett, J. & J. W. Meyer. (1978). The Ideology of Childhood and the State. *American Sociological Review*, 43(6), 797–812.

Boyle, E. H. (1998). Political Frames and Legal Activity: Anti-Nuclear Power Litigation in Four Countries. *Law & Society Review*, 32(1), 141–74.

Bradley, K. & F. Ramirez. (1996). World Polity Promotion of Gender Parity: Women's Share of Higher Education, 1965–85. In A. M. Pallas, ed., Vol. XI of *Research in Sociology of Education and Socialization*, pp. 63–91.

Brunsson, N. (1989). *The Organization of Hypocrisy: Talk, Decisions, and Action in Organizations*, New York, NY: Wiley.

Carroll, G. R. & M. T. Hannan. (1989). Density Dependence in the Evolution of Populations of Newspaper Organizations. *American Sociological Review*, 54(4), 524–48.

Chase-Dunn, C. (1989). *Global Formation: Structures of the World Economy*, Cambridge: Basil Blackwell.

Coleman, J. S. (1974). *Power and the Structure of Society*, New York, NY: Norton.
Coleman, J. S. (1986). Social Theory, Social Research, and a Theory of Action. *American Journal of Sociology*, 91(6), 1309–35.
Coleman, J. S. (1988). *Theoretical Sociology*, Orlando, FL: Harcourt Brace Jovanovich, Inc.
Coleman, J. S. (1992). *Sociological Insight*, New York, NY: Oxford University Press.
Coleman, J. S. (1994). *Four Sociological Traditions*, New York, NY: Oxford University Press.
Collins, R. (1979). *The Credential Society: A Historical Sociology of Education and Stratification*, New York, NY: Academic Press.
Collins, R. (1980). Weber's Last Theory of Capitalism: A Systematization. *American Sociological Review*, 45(6), 925–42.
DiMaggio, P. & W. W. Powell. (1983). The Iron Cage Revisited: Institutional Isomorphism and Collective Rationality in Organizational Fields. *American Sociological Review*, 48(2), 147–60.
DiMaggio, P. & W. W. Powell. (1991). Introduction. In W. W. Powell & P. DiMaggio, eds., *The New Institutionalism in Organizational Analysis*. Chicago, IL: University of Chicago Press, pp. 1–40.
Dobbin, F. (1994a). Cultural Models of Organization: The Social Construction of Rational Organizing Principles. In D. Crane, ed., *The Sociology of Culture: Emerging Theoretical Perspectives*. Oxford: Basil Blackwell, pp. 117–42.
Dobbin, F. (1994b). *Forging Industrial Policy: The United States, Britain, and France in the Railway Age*, New York, NY: Cambridge University Press.
Dobbin, F. (1995). The Origins of Economic Principles: Railway Entrepreneurs and Public Policy in 19th-Century America. In W. R. Scott & S. Christensen, eds., *The Institutional Construction of Organizations*. Thousand Oaks, CA: Sage, pp. 277–301.
Dobbin, F., J. R. Sutton, J. W. Meyer, & W. R. Scott. (1993). Equal Opportunity Law and the Construction of Internal Labor Markets. *American Journal of Sociology*, 99(2), 396–427.
Dobbin, F., L. Edelman, J. W. Meyer, W. R. Scott, & A. Swidler. (1988). The Expansion of Due Process in Organizations. In L. G. Zucker, ed., *Institutional Patterns and Organizations: Culture and Environment*. Cambridge, MA: Ballinger, pp. 71–100.
Dornbusch, S. M. & W. R. Scott, with the assistance of B. C. Busching & J. D. Laing. (1975). *Evaluation and the Exercise of Authority*, San Francisco, CA: Jossey-Bass.
Elster, J. (1983). *Explaining Technical Change*, Cambridge: Cambridge University Press.

Finnemore, M. (1996a). Norms, Culture, and World Politics: Insights from Sociology's Institutionalism. *International Organization*, 50(2), 325–47.

Finnemore, M. (1996b). *National Interests in International Society*, Ithaca, NY: Cornell University Press.

Fligstein, N. (1990). *The Transformation of Corporate Control*, Cambridge, MA: Harvard University Press.

Frank, D. (1997). Science, Nature, and the Globalization of the Environment, 1870–1990. *Social Forces*, 76(2), 409–35.

Frank, D., A. Hironaka, J. Meyer, E. Schofer, & N. Tuma. (1999). The Rationalization and Organization of Nature in the World Culture. In J. Boli & G. M. Thomas, eds., *Constructing World Culture: International Nongovernmental Organizations Since 1875*. Stanford, CA: Stanford University Press, pp. 81–99.

Frank, D., A. Hironaka, & E. Schofer. (2000). The Nation-State and the Natural Environment over the Twentieth Century. *American Sociological Review*, 65(1), 96–116.

Frank, D. & E. McEneaney. (1999). The Individualization of Society and the Liberalization of State Policies on Same-Sex Sexual Relations, 1985–1995. *Social Forces*, 77(3), 911–44.

Frank, D. & J. W. Meyer. (2000). The Contemporary Identity Explosion: Individualizing Society in the Post-War Period. Unpublished paper, Harvard University.

Frank, D., J. W. Meyer, & D. Miyahara. (1995). The Individualist Polity and the Prevalence of Professionalized Psychology. *American Sociological Review*, 60(3), 360–77.

Frank, D., S. Wong, F. Ramirez, & J. W. Meyer. (2000). What Counts as History: A Cross-National and Longitudinal Study of University Curricula, 1895–1994. *Comparative Education Review*, 44(1), 29–53.

Hall, P. & R. Taylor. (1996). Political Science and the Three New Institutionalisms. *Political Studies*, 44(5), 952–73.

Hamilton, G. & N. W. Biggart. (1988). Market, Culture, and Authority: A Comparative Analysis of Management and Organization in the Far East. *American Journal of Sociology*, 94(Supplement), S52–S94.

Hannan, M. T. & J. Freeman. (1977). The Population Ecology of Organizations. *American Journal of Sociology*, 82(5), 929–64.

Hannan, M. T. & J. Freeman. (1989). *Organizational Ecology*, Cambridge, MA: Harvard University Press.

Inkeles, A. (1983). *Exploring Individual Modernity*, New York, NY: Columbia University Press.

Inkeles, A. & D. H. Smith. (1974). *Becoming Modern*, Cambridge, MA: Harvard University Press.

Jepperson, R. L. (1991). Institutions, Institutional Effects, and Institutionalism. In W. W. Powell & P. J. DiMaggio, eds., *The New Institutionalism in Organizational Analysis*. Chicago, IL: University of Chicago Press, pp. 143–63.

Jepperson, R. L. (1992). National Scripts: The Varying Construction of Individualism and Opinion Across the Modern Nation-States. PhD dissertation, Yale University.

Jepperson, R. L. (2000). Institutional Logics: The Constitutive Dimensions of the Modern Nation-State Polities. Working Paper RSC No. 2000/36, European University Institute, Florence, Italy.

Jepperson, R. L. & J. W. Meyer. (1991). The Public Order and the Construction of Formal Organizations. In W. W. Powell & P. J. DiMaggio, eds., *The New Institutionalism in Organizational Analysis*. Chicago, IL: University of Chicago Press., pp. 204–31.

Jepperson, R. L., A. Wendt, & P. Katzenstein. (1996). Norms, Identity, and Culture in National Security. In P. Katzenstein, ed., *The Culture of National Security*. New York, NY: Columbia University Press, pp. 33–78.

Kamens, D. H. (1977). Legitimating Myths and Educational Organization: The Relationship Between Organizational Ideology and Formal Structure. *American Sociological Review*, 42(2), 208–19.

Katzenstein, P. J., ed. (1996). *The Culture of National Security*, New York, NY: Columbia University Press.

Kiser, E. (1999). Comparing Varieties of Agency Theory in Economics, Political Science, and Sociology: An Illustration from State Policy Implementation. *Sociological Theory*, 17(2), 146–70.

Krücken, G. (2000). An Interview with John W. Meyer. *Sozusagen* (Dept. of Sociology, Bielefeld) 7:58–63.

Krücken, G. & R. Hasse. (1999). *Neo-Institutionalismus*, Bielefeld, Germany: Transcript Verlag.

McEneaney, E. & J. W. Meyer. (2000). The Content of the Curriculum: An Institutionalist Perspective. In M. Hallinan, ed., *Handbook of Sociology of Education*. New York, NY: Plenum, pp. 189–211.

McNeely, C. (1995). *Constructing the Nation-State*, Westport, CT: Greenwood.

McNeill, W. (1963). *The Rise of the West*, Chicago, IL: University of Chicago Press.

Meyer, J. W. (1965). Some Non-Value Effects of Colleges. Working Paper, BASR, Columbia University.

Meyer, J. W. (1970a). High School Effects on College Intentions. *American Journal of Sociology*, 76(1), 59–70.

Meyer, J. W. (1970b). "Institutionalization." Unpublished paper.

Meyer, J. W. (1970c). The Charter: Conditions of Diffuse Socialization in Schools. In W.R. Scott, ed., *Social Processes and Social Structures*. New York, NY: Holt, pp. 564–78.

Meyer, J. W. (1971a). Comparative Research on the Relationships Between Political and Educational Institutions. In M. Kirst & F. Wirt, eds., *Politics and Education*. Boston, MA: D. C. Heath.

Meyer, J. W. (1971b). Economic and Political Effects on National Educational Enrollment Patterns. *Comparative Education Review*, 15 (1), 28–43.

Meyer, J. W. (1972). The Effects of the Institutionalization of Colleges in Society. In K. Feldman, ed., *College & Student*. New York, NY: Pergamon, pp. 109–26.

Meyer, J. W. (1977). The Effects of Education as an Institution. *American Journal of Sociology*, 83(1), 55–77.

Meyer, J. W. (1978). Strategies for Further Research: Varieties of Environmental Variation. In M. Meyer, ed., *Environments and Organizations*. San Francisco, CA: Jossey-Bass, pp. 352–368.

Meyer, J. W. (1980). The World Polity and the Authority of the Nation-State. In A. Bergesen, ed., *Studies of the Modern World-System*. New York, NY: Academic Press, pp. 109–37.

Meyer, J. W. (1981). Review Essay: Kings or People. *American Journal of Sociology*, 86(4), 895–899.

Meyer, J. W. (1982). Political Structure and the World Economy. *Contemporary Sociology*, 11(3), 263–266.

Meyer, J. W. (1983a). Innovation and Knowledge Use in American Public Education. In *Organizational Environments*, by J. Meyer and W. R. Scott. Beverly Hills, CA: Sage, pp. 233–260.

Meyer, J. W. (1983b). Institutionalization and the Rationality of Formal Organizational Structure. In *Organizational Environments: Ritual and Rationality*, by J. W. Meyer, W. R. Scott, & associates. Beverly Hills, CA: Sage, pp. 261–282.

Meyer, J. W. (1986a). Myths of Socialization and Personality. In T. Heller, M. Sosna, & D. Wellbery, eds., *Reconstructing Individualism*. Stanford, CA: Stanford University Press, pp. 212–25.

Meyer, J. W. (1986b). The Self and the Life Course: Institutionalization and Its Effects. In A. Sorensen, F. Weinert, & L. Sherrod, eds., *Human Development and the Life Course*. Hillsdale, NJ: Erlbaum, pp. 199–216.

Meyer, J. W. (1986c). Types of Explanation in the Sociology of Education. In J. Richardson, ed., *Handbook of Theory and Research for the Sociology of Education*. Westport, CT: Greenwood Publishing, pp. 341–59.

Meyer, J. W. (1988). Society without Culture: A Nineteenth Century Legacy. In F. Ramirez, ed., *Rethinking the Nineteenth Century*. Greenwood, NY: Greenwood Publishing, pp. 193–201.

Meyer, J. W. (1989). Conceptions of Christendom: Notes on the Distinctiveness of the West. In M. Kohn, ed., *Cross-National Research in Sociology*. Newbury Park, CA: Sage, pp. 395–413.

Meyer, J. W. (1990). Individualism: Social Experience and Cultural Formulation. In J. Rodin, C. Schooler, & K. Schaie, eds., *Self-Directedness: Causes and Effects Throughout the Life Course*. Hillsdale, NJ: Erlbaum, pp. 51–8.

Meyer, J. W. (1992a). From Constructionism to Neo-institutionalism: Reflections on Berger and Luckmann. *Perspectives*, 15(2), 11–12. Washington, DC: American Sociological Association.

Meyer, J. W. (1992b). The Social Construction of Motives for Educational Expansion. In B. Fuller & R. Rubinson, eds., *The Political Construction of Education*. New York, NY: Praeger Publishers, pp. 225–38.

Meyer, J. W. (1994a). Rationalized Environments. In *Institutional Environments and Organizations*, by W. Richard Scott, J. W. Meyer, & others. Newbury Park, CA: Sage, pp. 28–54.

Meyer, J. W. (1994b). The Evolution of Modern Stratification Systems. In D. B. Grusky, ed., *Social Stratification in Sociological Perspective*. Boulder, CO: Westview Press, pp. 730–7.

Meyer, J. W. (1996). Otherhood: The Promulgation and Transmission of Ideas in the Modern Organizational Environment. In B. Czarniawska & G. Sevon, eds., *Translating Organizational Change*. Berlin: de Gruyter, pp. 241–52.

Meyer, J. W. (1999a). The Changing Cultural Content of the Nation-State: A World Society Perspective. In G. Steinimetz, ed., *State/Culture: State Formation after the Cultural Turn*. Ithaca, NY: Cornell University Press, pp. 123–43.

Meyer, J. W. (1999b). Memo to H. Fujita. Stanford University, September 1999.

Meyer, J. W. (2000a). Globalization and the Curriculum: Problems for Theory in the Sociology of Education. *The Journal of Educational Sociology*, 66, 79–95.

Meyer, J. W. (2000b). Globalization: Sources and Effects on National States and Societies. *International Sociology*, 15(2), 235–50.

Meyer, J. W., J. Boli, & G. M. Thomas. (1981). Rationalization and Ontology in the Evolving World System. Meetings of the Pacific Sociological Association.

Meyer, J. W., J. Boli, & G. M. Thomas. (1987). Ontology and Rationalization in the Western Cultural Account. In *Institutional*

Structure: Constituting State, Society, and the Individual, by G. M. Thomas, J. W. Meyer, F. O. Ramirez, & J. Boli. Newbury Park, CA: Sage, pp. 12–38.

Meyer, J. W., J. Boli, G. Thomas, & F. Ramirez. (1997). World Society and the Nation-State. *American Journal of Sociology*, 103(1), 144–81.

Meyer, J. W., J. Boli-Bennett, & C. Chase-Dunn. (1975). Convergence and Divergence in Development. *Annual Review of Sociology*, 1, 223–45.

Meyer, J. W., D. Frank, A. Hironaka, E. Schofer, & N. Tuma. (1997). The Structuring of a World Environmental Regime, 1870–1990. *International Organization*, 51(4), 623–51.

Meyer, J. W. & M. Hannan, eds. (1979a). *National Development and the World System*, Chicago, IL: University of Chicago Press.

Meyer, J. W. & M. Hannan. (1979b). Issues for Further Comparative Research. In J. W. Meyer & M. Hannan, eds., *National Development and the World System*. Chicago, IL: University of Chicago Press, pp. 297–308.

Meyer, J. W. & M. Hannan. (1979c). National Development in a Changing World System: An Overview. In J. W. Meyer & M. Hannan, eds., *National Development and the World System*. Chicago, IL: University of Chicago Press, pp. 3–16.

Meyer, J. W. & R. L. Jepperson. (2000). The "Actors" of Modern Society: The Cultural Construction of Social Agency. *Sociological Theory*, 18(1), 100–20.

Meyer, J. W., D. Kamens, & A. Benavot, with Y. Cha & S. Wong. (1992). *School Knowledge for the Masses: World Models and National Primary Curricular Categories in the Twentieth Century*, London: Falmer Press.

Meyer, J. W. & F. O. Ramirez. (1981). Comparative Education: Synthesis and Agenda. In J. Short, ed., *The State of Sociology*. Newbury Park, CA: Sage, pp. 215–38.

Meyer, J. W. & F. O. Ramirez. (2000). The World Institutionalization of Education. In J. Schriewer, ed., *Discourse Formation in Comparative Education*. Frankfurt: Peter Lang Publishers, pp. 111–32.

Meyer, J. W., F. O. Ramirez, R. Rubinson, & J. Boli-Bennett. (1977). The World Educational Revolution, 1950–1970. *Sociology of Education*, 50(4), 242–58.

Meyer, J. W., F. O. Ramirez, & Y. Soysal. (1992). World Expansion of Mass Education, 1870–1970. *Sociology of Education*, 65(2), 128–49.

Meyer, J. W., F. O. Ramirez, H. Walker, S. O'Connor, & N. Langton. (1988). The State and the Institutionalization of Relations Between Women and Children. In S. M. Dornbusch & M. Stroeber, eds.,

Feminism, Children, and the New Families. New York, NY: Guilford Press, pp. 147–58.
Meyer, J. W. & B. Rowan. (1977). Institutionalized Organizations: Formal Structure as Myth and Ceremony. *American Journal of Sociology,* 83(2), 340–63.
Meyer, J. W. & B. Rowan. (1978). The Structure of Educational Organizations. In M.W. Meyer, ed., *Environments and Organizations.* San Francisco, CA: Jossey-Bass, pp. 78–109.
Meyer, J. W. & R. Rubinson. (1975). Education and Political Development. *Review of Research in Education,* 3(1), 134–62.
Meyer, J. W., E. Schofer, & F. O. Ramirez. Forthcoming. The Effects of Science on National Economic Development, 1970–90. *American Sociological Review.*
Meyer, J. W. & W. R. Scott. (1983a). Centralization and the Legitimacy Problems of Local Government. In *Organizational Environments,* by J. Meyer & W. R. Scott. Beverly Hills, CA: Sage, pp. 199–215.
Meyer, J. W. & W. R. Scott. (1983b). *Organizational Environments: Ritual and Rationality,* Beverly Hills, CA: Sage.
Meyer, J. W. & W. R. Scott. (1992). Preface to the Updated Edition. In *Organizational Environments,* updated edition, by J. W. Meyer & W. R. Scott. Newbury Park, CA: Sage, pp. 1–6.
Meyer, J. W., W. R. Scott, & T. E. Deal. (1981). Institutional and Technical Sources of Organizational Structure: Explaining the Structure of Educational Organizations. In H. D. Stein, ed., *Organization and the Human Services.* Philadelphia, PA: Temple University Press, pp. 157–78.
Mizruchi, M. S. & L. C. Fein. (1999). The Social Construction of Organizational Knowledge: A Study of the Uses of Coercive, Mimetic, and Normative Isomorphism. *Administrative Science Quarterly,* 44(4), 653–83.
Olson, M. (1965). *The Logic of Collective Action,* New York, NY: Schocken Books.
Orrù, M., N. W. Biggart, & G. G. Hamilton. (1991). Organizational Isomorphism in East Asia. In W. W. Powell & P. J. DiMaggio, eds., *The New Institutionalism in Organizational Analysis.* Chicago, IL: University of Chicago Press, pp. 361–89.
Perrow, C. (1985). Review Essay: Overboard with Myth and Symbols. *American Journal of Sociology,* 91(1), 151–5.
Perrow, C. (1986). *Complex Organizations: A Critical Essay,* 3rd edn, New York, NY: Random House.
Perrow, C. (1991). A Society of Organizations. *Theory and Society,* 20(6), 725–62.

Powell, W. W. & P. J. DiMaggio, eds. (1991). *The New Institutionalism in Organizational Analysis*, Chicago, IL: University of Chicago Press.

Ramirez, F. O. (2000). Women in Science/Women and Science: Liberal and Radical Perspectives. Unpublished paper, Stanford University, October 2000.

Ramirez, F. O. & J. Boli. (1987a). On the Union of States and Schools. In *Institutional Structure*, by G. M. Thomas, J. W. Meyer, F. O. Ramirez, & J. Boli. Newbury Park, CA: Sage, pp. 173–97.

Ramirez, F. O. & J. Boli. (1987b). The Political Construction of Mass Schooling: European Origins and Worldwide Institutionalization. *Sociology of Education*, 60(1), 2–17.

Ramirez, F. O. & J. Boli. (1987c). Global Patterns of Educational Institutionalization. In *Institutional Structure*, by G. M. Thomas, J. W. Meyer, F. O. Ramirez, & J. Boli. Newbury Park, CA: Sage, pp. 150–72.

Ramirez, F. O. & Y. Cha. (1990). Citizenship and Gender: Western Educational Developments in Comparative Perspective. In *Research in Sociology of Education and Socialization*, Vol. IX, pp. 153–74.

Ramirez, F. O. & J. W. Meyer. (1980). Comparative Education: The Social Construction of the Modern World System. *Annual Review of Sociology*, 6, 369–99.

Ramirez, F. O. & R. Rubinson. (1979). Creating Members: The Political Incorporation and Expansion of Public Education. In J. W. Meyer & M. T. Hannan, eds., *National Development and the World System*. Chicago, IL: University of Chicago Press, pp. 72–84.

Ramirez, F. O., Y. Soysal, & S. Shanahan. (1997). The Changing Logic of Political Citizenship: Cross-National Acquisition of Women's Suffrage Rights, 1890 to 1990. *American Sociological Review*, 62 (5), 735–45.

Ramirez, F. O. & J. Weiss. (1979). The Political Incorporation of Women. In J. Meyer & M. Hannan, eds., *National Development and the World System*. Chicago, IL: University of Chicago Press, pp. 238–49.

Schneiberg, M. & E. S. Clemens. Forthcoming. The Typical Tools for the Job: Research Strategies in Institutional Analysis. In W. W. Powell & D. L. Jones, eds., *How Institutions Change*. Chicago, IL: University of Chicago Press.

Schofer, E. (1999). Science Associations in the International Sphere, 1875–1990: The Rationalization of Science and the Scientization of Society. In J. Boli & G. M. Thomas, eds., *Constructing World Culture: International Nongovernmental Organizations Since 1875 World Polity Formation since 1875*. Stanford, CA: Stanford University Press, pp. 249–66.

Schofer, E. & M. Fourcade-Gourinchas. (1999). State Structures and Voluntary Associations. Annual meeting of the American Sociological Association.
Scott, W. R. (1983/1992). Introduction: From Technology to Environment. In *Organizational Environments*, updated edition, by J. W. Meyer and W. R. Scott. Newbury Park, CA: Sage, pp. 13–17.
Scott, W. R. (1987). *Organizations: Rational, Natural and Open Systems*, 2nd edn, Englewood Cliffs, NJ: Prentice-Hall.
Scott, W. R. (1995). *Institutions and Organizations*, Thousand Oaks, CA: Sage.
Scott, W. R. & S. Christensen. (1995). *The Institutional Construction of Organizations*, Thousand Oaks, CA: Sage.
Scott, W. R. & J. W. Meyer. (1983/1992). The Organization of Societal Sectors. In *Organizational Environments: Ritual and Rationality*, updated edition, by J. W. Meyer & W. R. Scott. Newbury Park, CA: Sage, pp. 129–53.
Scott, W. R. & J. W. Meyer. (1991). The Organization of Societal Sectors: Propositions and Early Evidence. In W. W. Powell & P. J. DiMaggio, eds., *The New Institutionalism in Organizational Analysis*. Chicago, IL: University of Chicago Press, pp. 108–42.
Scott, W. R., J. W. Meyer, & associates. (1994). *Institutional Environments and Organizations*, Thousand Oaks, CA: Sage.
Shenhav, Y. & D. H. Kamens. (1991). The "Costs" of Institutional Isomorphism: Science in Non-Western Countries. *Studies of Science*, 21 (3), 527–45.
Skocpol, T. (1985). Bringing the State Back In. In P. B. Evans, D. Rueschemeyer, & T. Skocpol, eds., *Bringing the State Back In*. Cambridge: Cambridge University Press, pp. 3–37.
Smelser, N., with B. Badie & P. Birnbaum. (1994). The Sociology of the State Revisited. In N. Smelser, ed., *Sociology*. Oxford: Blackwell, pp. 59–75.
Soysal, Y. (1998). Identity and Transnationalization in German School Textbooks. *Bulletin of Concerned Asian Scholars*, 30(2), 53–61.
Soysal, Y. N. (1994). *The Limits of Citizenship*, Chicago, IL: University of Chicago Press.
Stinchcombe, A. (1968). *Constructing Social Theories*, New York, NY: Harcourt, Brace, & World.
Stone Sweet, A., W. Sandholtz, & N. Fligstein, eds. Forthcoming. *The Institutionalization of Europe*, Oxford: Oxford University Press.
Strang, D. (1990). From Dependency to Sovereignty: An Event History Analysis of Decolonization, 1870–1987. *American Sociological Review*, 55(6), 846–60.
Strang, D. (1994). Institutional Accounts as a Form of Structural Analysis. *Current Perspectives in Social Theory*, Supplement 1, 151–74.

Strang, D. & P. Chang. (1993). The International Labor Organization and the Welfare State: Institutional Effects on National Welfare Spending, 1960–1980. *International Organization,* 47(2), 235–62.

Strang, D. & J. W. Meyer. (1993). Institutional Conditions for Diffusion. *Theory and Society,* 22(4), 487–511.

Sutton, J., F. Dobbin, J. Meyer, & W. R. Scott. (1994). Legalization of the Workplace. *American Journal of Sociology,* 99(4), 944–71.

Swanson, G. (1967). *Religion and Regime,* Ann Arbor, MI: University of Michigan Press.

Swanson, G. (1971). An Organizational Analysis of Collectivities. *American Sociological Review,* 36(4), 607–24.

Thomas, G. M. & J. W. Meyer. (1984). The Expansion of the State. *Annual Review of Sociology,* 10, 461–82.

Thomas, G. M., J. W. Meyer, F. O. Ramirez, & J. Boli. (1987). *Institutional Structure: Constituting the State, Society, and the Individual,* Newbury Park, CA: Sage.

Tilly, C., ed. (1975). *The Formation of National States in Western Europe,* Princeton, NJ: Princeton University Press.

Tilly, C. (1984). *Big Structures, Large Processes, Huge Comparisons,* New York, NY: Russell Sage.

Tilly, C. (1992). *Coercion, Capital, and European States,* Cambridge: Basil Blackwell.

Tilly, C. (1997). *Roads from Past to Future,* Lanham, MD: Rowman and Littlefield.

Tilly, C. (1999). Epilogue: Now Where? In G. Steinmetz, ed., *State/Culture.* Ithaca, NY: Cornell University Press, pp. 407–19.

Ventresca, M. (1995). Counting People when People Count: Global Establishment of the Modern Population Census, 1820–1980. PhD dissertation. Stanford University, Department of Sociology.

Wallerstein, I. (1974). *Capitalist Agriculture and the Origins of the European World Economy.* Vol. I of *The Modern World-System.* New York, NY: Academic Press.

Wallerstein, I. (1991). *Geopolitics and Geoculture: Essays on the Changing World System,* Cambridge: Cambridge University Press.

Zelditch, M. Jr. (1984). Meaning, Conformity, and Control. *Journal of Mathematical Sociology,* 10(2), 183–90.

Zelditch, M. Jr. & H. A. Walker. (1984). Legitimacy and the Stability of Authority. In E. Lawler, ed., Vol. I of *Advances in Group Processes: Theory and Research.* Greenwich, CT: JAI, pp. 1–27.

Zucker, L. G. (1977). The Role of Institutionalization in Cultural Persistence. *American Sociological Review,* 42(5), 726–43.

Zucker, L. G. (1983). Organizations as Institutions. In S. Bacharach, ed., Vol. II of *Research in the Sociology of Organizations*. Greenwich, CT: JAI, pp. 1–47.
Zucker, L. G. (1987). Institutional Theories of Organization. *Annual Review of Sociology*, 13, 443–64.
Zucker, L. G. (1989). Combining Institutional Theory and Population Ecology: No Legitimacy, No History (Comment on Carroll-Hannan, 1989). *American Sociological Review*, 54(4), 542–45.
Zucker, L. G. (1991). The Role of Institutionalization in Cultural Persistence: Postscript. In W. W. Powell & P. J. DiMaggio, eds., *The New Institutionalism in Organizational Analysis*. Chicago, IL: University of Chicago Press, pp. 103–6.

5 | Reflections on Part II: Institutional Theory

R. JEPPERSON AND J. MEYER

The chapters in Part II provided overviews of the motivation and main theoretical ideas of the cultural institutionalism of this volume. Chapter 2 presented a short intellectual history of the peripheralization of the concept of culture in Anglo-American social theory. Chapter 3 provided clarification of the ideas of institution, institutionalization, and institutionalism.[1] Chapter 4 surveyed the main ideas and empirical application of the line of thought during its first twenty-five years. Here we provide some current reflections occasioned by revisiting these chapters.

5.1 From Margin to Mainstream

Institutional theory arose to give an account of the framing – in good part cultural in character – of the society of high modernity in the world after 1945, and in the neoliberal period well established after 1990. If the various "old institutionalisms" had been about the social embeddedness of people, groups, and societies, the new world reconceptualized them all as more disembedded "actors." And the new institutional theories are about the construction and social control of these entities. Hwang and Colyvas (2011) show a dramatic increase in the use of the term "actor" in the social sciences throughout the whole period and view the shift as an important cultural reframing. But during the 1970s, the images and arguments of institutional theory lay at the edge of standard social scientific thinking about contemporary societies and the people and organizations that inhabit them. Institutional theory was something of an exotic or acquired taste.

Since that period, institutional theory has become more mainstream and central in fields like organizational theory (e.g., Greenwood et al. 2017). Its success reflects the intellectual work of many scholars, perhaps specifically the influence of empirical analyses calling attention to the great importance of wider environments in the creation of modern societies, organizations, and individual identities. But it also reflects the dramatic social changes of the past quarter century: the so-called neoliberal period that may now be coming to an end.

During this period, many of the fundamental cultural and organizational characteristics and trends of high modernity were greatly intensified and in some ways transformed under the impact of globalization. As partly foreseen by Daniel Bell (1973), and analyzed later by many others, societies around the world moved far beyond what was once seen as their bases in productive economic life and enlarged political control. Everywhere there was the expansion of what is called the "knowledge" society or economy, and concretely agriculture and industry give way to the "service sector" that so heavily depends on "knowledge." If modern society saw itself as something of a machine, the postmodern society extends this machine into the production of goods once considered evanescent: the term "hyper-organization" attempts to comprehend it (Bromley and Meyer 2015). Enormous ranges of expansive organization and occupation in the postmodern society clearly depend, not on immediate and visible functionality, but on abstract and universal definitions: in other words, on the cultural environment, institutionalized in the university and its scientific culture (Drori et al. 2003; Frank and Meyer 2007).

Accordingly, lines of thought that pay attention to the cultural environment have gained more centrality. At the same time, however, the conceptualization of culture in the social sciences generally remains a thin one, and there are strained attempts to see the protagonists of the new culture – even the most outlandish gurus promulgating recipes for personal, organizational, or national happiness – as creatures of organized power or productive functionality. Similarly, the great sociocultural movements that are so prominent throughout the periods remain poorly analyzed and explained, even as they reframe sexual and gender identities as liberated choices; redefine the natural environment as ecosystemic; and rationalize the social order as formal organization.

5.2 The Focus on "Actorhood" in Institutional Theory

In recent decades, social environments on a global scale have undergone cultural transformation, typified by scientific and educational explosions (Meyer et al. 1992; Drori et al. 2003; Schofer and Meyer

2005). As a result, the core ontological entities of society have gone through similar expansions: the postmodern individual, organization, and state are reconceived to have capacities far beyond those envisioned in the past. Neoliberal culture structures these participants as "actors." It also greatly expands the scripts that construct, empower, and constrain actorhood, hence the focus on "actorhood" in this volume's line of social theory.

An explosion of human rights norms, certified by global institutions, supports a greatly expanded notion of the individual (Elliott 2007 and elsewhere). The human being comes under reconstruction through many years of compulsory education (now seen as a global human right), and very large numbers gain standing as even more empowered actors by continuing to higher education (Schofer and Meyer 2005).

Collectivities are similarly restructured: groups become formal organizations, so traditional religious, educational, and medical arrangements are transformed into "non-profits" (Bromley and Meyer 2017). Formal organizations, in turn, expand into hyper-organization, building in multiple culturally defined missions (Bromley and Meyer 2015). Finally, in the neoliberal period there is the obvious transformation of the nation-states around the world: their mystique and charisma weaken, and their environmentally defined responsibilities as organizations expand so rapidly that a great many of them can be depicted as "failed states" – incompetent as actors and requiring further rationalizing reform (e.g., Fukuyama 2014).

Effective actorhood becomes the core cultural script of contemporary society, and in many realist analyses it is the only script, as everything in social life can be interpreted as resulting from interested actors choosing and carrying out purposive actions – in some economistic theories, self-interested ones. In modern social thought as well as modern cultural ideology, "action theories" are central, in which all of society is constituted by, and produced by, the decisions or choices of the actors involved.

Such realist lines of thought can incorporate some regulating social institutions that the actors in a system could construct and agree on. Perhaps economic actors agree to organize some property rights, and Westphalian state actors might agree on the principle of sovereignty (North and Thomas 1973; Krasner 1999). Rules so created might well act as serious constraints on actors, if properly enforced by organizational structures. Organizational power would be involved – otherwise the actors would feel free to cheat when it was advantageous to do so, and the rules would break down.

Realist lines of thought can go only so far, however, and are utterly inadequate to explain the sweeping social changes of the contemporary period. An associated individualistic model of culture further hinders social science.

5.3 Still the "Society without Culture"?

It is still commonplace to render something as more "cultural" if it lies beyond the boundaries of the instrumental and rational. An effective skill is less likely to be seen as cultural than an ineffective one. An expressive purpose is more cultural than an instrumental one. Or, in Swidler's usage, the toolkit of culture is more likely to appear under conditions of uncertainty (Swidler 1986).

From such points of view, increasingly developed over the post-Enlightenment centuries, modern rationalized society squeezes out culture and comes to look like a highly rational and instrumental machine – the main theme of Chapter 2. Culture is left as an irrational residue or a property of non-moderns. This perspective, dominant in the social sciences and also in common understanding, sees a host of traditional institutional arrangements, customs, and habits as coming under the purposive scrutiny of actors. Over time, activity comes to reflect decisions rather than habits, knowledge rather than superstition, and purposes rather than sentiments.

For every institutional sector of society, the same theoretic translations occur. Seen as non-embedded, economic customs and political power become rational and purposive actors and organizations. Religion reflects the needs and choices of individual actors. Science is disconnected from folk beliefs and traditions. In recent translations, ethnic attachments become choices of individual persons (Lieberson and Waters 1988). So do family relations, seen as constructions of putatively rational individual choices and preferences: sex and gender are increasingly choices of actors, and one can alter them.

From the perspective of institutional theory, the social changes of the contemporary period cannot plausibly be treated as if they were an escape of a newly enlightened humanity from superstition. More sensibly they represent the rise of a highly rationalized cultural system, developing over the past century and intensifying, as well as increasingly globalizing, during the post–World War II period.

5.4 Relative Absence of a Collective-level Picture of Culture

But there has been little room, in the dominant realist social science, for anything like a collective culture: conceptions and norms so established as to be taken for granted by actors. When the term "culture" is employed, in the main it does not refer to collective social realities. It refers rather to the attitudes and tastes of the actors who make up these realities. In other words, culture, now mostly killed off as a property of society, reappears as a property of the actors (often individual ones) who make up society. Thus we discover political cultures, or religious ones, through survey research, or through the analysis of voting patterns or of consumer choices. In the contemporary world, surveys and analyses of these sorts have become very common: survey research can be carried out almost everywhere, and the World Values Survey, Eurobarometer, or International Social Survey Program data systems span the globe (Jepperson 1992).

In contrast, a more macroscopic analysis sees the actors, as well as their identities and purposes, as constructions of wider cultural and organizational frames. The supermarket clerk, expecting money in return for apples, is playing a role rather than expressing eagerness for the money: elaborate justifications and interpretations of the role ricochet down through modern history. The apple–money exchange is, on the ground, far from contested or conflictual – as it was in more traditional marketplaces. It can be carried out with many gestures of friendliness. These are rituals, with elaborate cultural rationales surrounding and legitimating them. The customer and clerk are producing individual and collective good, not fighting over money: they may sincerely wish each other to "have a nice day." The exchange is so customary – and so institutionalized in broad systems – that from the point of view of both participants, the actor–action relationship is mainly tautological, not one involving much purposive calculation.

5.5 Actor and Choice Systems as Collective Culture

Such elaborate cultural embedding is routine, as the example illustrates. In order to have actors and to posture as actor, much cultural construction is necessary: rules of actorhood, shaping of people and groups into actors, and counsel and therapy for staying on script. And in order for rationalized action to become possible and scripted, much institutional work must happen: to create educational and professional systems by which choice can be tamed, to structure worlds of life and career that make calculation reasonable and often definitive, to construct great and stable markets now on a global scale, and to provide various sorts of governance for a global system of actors and actions.

From this point of view, the culture of the contemporary world is only incidentally some songs, peculiar tastes left over from a savage past, or a few values or purposes given legitimacy. It exists centrally in the rules that define the modern individual, organizational, and national actor, and set out purposes and criteria for these entities. Many of the rules originate in the natural sciences and even more are emanations of the social sciences and associated journalistic and professional cultures: economic theory is a central cultural discourse in the contemporary world, as are principles of human rights, equality, and empowerment. Related, great educational and occupational hierarchies specify which alternatives make sense and structure them in relation to each other. Culture, thus, lies in the great national tests – deliberately selected to be distant from real life – sorting out huge numbers of young people on a culturally defined scheme of aptitude (Ramirez, Schofer, and Meyer 2018). It lies in elaborate specification of requirements for entry into particular occupations and in the definition of the appropriate work for these.

The collective cultural rules are elaborated far beyond the actual capabilities of the people, organizations, and states involved, so there is a great deal of decoupling (Bromley and Powell 2012) and much outright failure and scandal. So in response, much of modern social structure is made up of what are called agents, not people and groups acting principally as self-interested actors. There is the massive expansion of the professions – occupations intended to serve the needs of principals of some sort. Whole institutional systems have arisen in education, medicine, psychological therapies, and similar aids. At the organizational level, there have been great expansions in consulting firms assisting organized actors in becoming better actors. At national and supra-national levels, great assemblies of nongovernmental and nonprofit enterprises have developed that ostentatiously avoid self-interested purposive action, instead promoting claims about the common good (Boli and Thomas 1999).

5.6 A Note on "Social Construction"

With this emphasis on the consequences of broad cultural frames and institutional orders, the line of thought of this book is – obviously – a "constructivist" or "constructionist" one. Chapter 1 noted that explanation invoking social construction has a long history in social science, even if the rhetoric of construction only became explicitly articulated in the 1960s (e.g., with Berger and Luckmann and beyond).

Now there are a number of explications about how "constructivist" explanations work. Chapters 6 and 7 provide our own.[2] From an expanding set we would also call attention to March and Olsen (1989), Hacking (1999), Roy (2001), Searle (2010), and Scott (2014); we would also go back to Berger (1963: Chs. 4–6), and Berger and Luckmann (1966).

Nonetheless, predictably there are periodic eruptions of protest that explanation via social construction is incoherent or unscientific. There is some warrant for this concern of course: there are volumes of loose talk invoking social construction, a counterpart to the volumes of loose "rational actor" talk. Both lines of thought can become essentialisms – in effect, everything, in all features, constructed; or everything, in all features, chosen with a simple directing interest. So, Hacking opens his book on social construction (just referenced) with a list of twenty-four entities that are said to be socially constructed, and he worries.

But then Hacking turns around and suggests some useful tightenings for constructivist arguments and offers constructivist explorations of issues concerning madness, child abuse, weapons research, and even "rocks" (i.e., science studies). And nowadays some sociology textbooks manage to invoke social construction in straightforward and seemingly unobjectionable ways (e.g., Kanagy and Kraybill [1999], discussing the "construction, objectification, internalization, and renovation" of the social world). "Social construction" is unavoidable in social science, and, if used analytically, it cannot be done without.[3]

5.7 Conclusion

The central ideas of institutional theory envision actors and actions as constructions reflecting highly institutionalized cultural patterns. Of course, with institutionalization, these constructions come to be perceived as natural and obvious – that is what institutionalization allows.

Rational choice systems are themselves cultural constructions (with biopsychological inputs, of course). They too come to be seen as natural over time.

In recent decades, social change has been so rapid and apparent that it has been hard to avoid seeing the changing cultural frames behind the putatively realist social order. The expansion of attributed individual rights and capacities, the explosion in the construction of rationalized organizations, and the enormous rationalization and taming of models of the national state, all show rapidly evolving cultural principles behind their construction: it is all incompletely concealed by institutionalization. So, in empirical research and in social theory, cultural-institutional theories continue to survive, and indeed prosper. We return to this theme in the concluding Chapter 12. But we also consider there the implications of increasing attacks on the whole expansive culture of the postwar world – and especially its neoliberal triumphalism. There are increasing direct attacks on the empowered individualism of the period, on global economic structuration, and on the putative destruction of family and community by expansive rationalized formal organization. As new cultural frames arise contesting the dominant liberal schemes, we can anticipate institutionally produced changes in what the realists thought was the solid rock of interested actorhood.

Notes

1. (From R. J.) I wish to call attention to two issues with Chapter 3: (1) The list of purported institutions on an early page conflated institutions and conventions – a major blunder. Institutions are typically reproducing *complexes* of rules, roles, and routines. Conventions do not have this denotation. So, in the list, the handshake is not an institution (obviously). Some of the other entries would be institutions, or not, depending upon specific usage. (2) The discussion of "carriers" of institutionalization is desultory at best, and the idea of institutionalization in culture risks tautology. Scott (2014: 95–104) shares useful material that could provide the basis for a better conceptualization of institutional carriers.
2. See also Jepperson, Wendt, and Katzenstein (1996) for application to the field of international relations.
3. For a good example of how social construction arguments become standard and are deployed without heavy breathing, consider a description from the publisher's website of William Roy's *Making Societies: The Historical Construction of Our World* (Roy 2001):

"Leading the reader through examples drawn from around the world, the author shows how these categories [time, space, race, gender, class] are social constructions; historically formed, ideologically loaded, and subject to change."

References

Bell, D. (1973). *The Coming of Post-Industrial Society: A Venture in Social Forecasting*, New York, NY: Basic Books.

Berger, P. (1963). *Invitation to Sociology: A Humanistic Perspective*, Garden City, NY: Doubleday.

Berger, P. & T. Luckmann (1966). *The Social Construction of Reality*, Garden City, NY: Anchor.

Boli, J. & G. Thomas, eds. (1999). *Constructing World Culture: International Nongovernmental Organizations since 1875*, Stanford, CA: Stanford University Press.

Bromley, P. & J. W. Meyer (2015). *Hyper-Organization: Global Organizational Expansion*, Oxford: Oxford University Press.

Bromley, P. & J. W. Meyer (2017). "They Are All Organizations": The Cultural Roots of Blurring between the Nonprofit, Business, and Government Sectors. *Administration & Society*, 49(7), 939–66.

Bromley, P. & W. W. Powell (2012). From Smoke and Mirrors to Walking the Talk: The Causes and Consequences of Decoupling in the Contemporary World. *Academy of Management Annals*, 6(1), 483–530.

Drori, G., J. W. Meyer, F. Ramirez, & E. Schofer (2003). *Science in the Modern World Polity*, Stanford, CA: Stanford University Press.

Elliott, M. (2007). Human Rights and the Triumph of the Individual in World Culture. *Cultural Sociology*, 1(3), 353–63.

Frank, D. & J. W. Meyer (2007). University Expansion and the Knowledge Society. *Theory and Society*, 36(4), 287–311.

Fukuyama, F. (2014). *Political Order and Political Decay: From the Industrial Revolution to the Globalization of Democracy*, New York, NY: Farrar, Straus, and Giroux.

Greenwood, R., C. Oliver, T. Lawrence, & R. Meyer, eds. (2017). *The SAGE Handbook of Organizational Institutionalism*, 2nd ed. Thousand Oaks, CA: SAGE.

Hacking, I. (1999). *The Social Construction of What?* Cambridge, MA: Harvard University Press.

Hwang, H. & J. Colyvas (2011). Problematizing Actors and Institutions in Institutional Work. *Journal of Management Inquiry*, 20(1), 62–66.

Jepperson, R. (1992). National Scripts: The Varying Construction of Individualism and Opinion across the Modern Nation-States. PhD dissertation, Yale University.

Jepperson, R., A. Wendt, & P. Katzenstein (1996). Norms, Identity, and Culture in National Security. In P. Katzenstein, ed., *Culture and National Security*. New York, NY: Columbia University Press, pp. 33–78.

Kanagy, C. & D. Kraybill (1999). *The Riddles of Human Society*, Thousand Oaks, CA: Pine Forge Press.

Krasner, S. (1999). *Sovereignty: Organized Hypocrisy*, Princeton, NJ: Princeton University Press.

Lieberson, S. & M. Waters (1988). *From Many Strands: Ethnic and Racial Groups in Contemporary America*, New York, NY: Russell Sage Foundation.

March, J. & J. Olsen (1989). *Rediscovering Institutions: The Organizational Basis of Politics*, New York, NY: Free Press.

Meyer, J. W. (1996). Otherhood: The Promulgation and Transmission of Ideas in the Modern Organizational Environment. In B. Czarniawska and G. Sevón eds., *Translating Organizational Change*. Berlin: De Gruyter, pp. 241–52.

Meyer, J. W., F. Ramirez, & Y. Soysal (1992). World Expansion of Mass Education, 1870–1970. *Sociology of Education*, 65(2), 128–49.

North, D. & R. Thomas (1973). *The Rise of the Western World: A New Economic History*, Cambridge: Cambridge University Press.

Ramirez, F. O., E. Schofer, & J. W. Meyer (2018). International Tests, National Assessments, and Educational Development, 1970–2012. *Comparative Education Review*, 62(3), 344–64.

Roy, W. (2001). *Making Societies: The Historical Construction of Our World*, Thousand Oaks, CA: Pine Forge Press.

Schofer, E. & J. W. Meyer (2005). The World-Wide Expansion of Higher Education in the Twentieth Century. *American Sociological Review*, 70(6), 898–920.

Scott, W. R. (2014). *Institutions and Organizations*, 4th ed. Los Angeles, CA: SAGE.

Searle, J. (2010). *Making the Social World*, Oxford: Oxford University Press.

Swidler, A. (1986). Culture in Action: Symbols and Strategies. *American Sociological Review*, 51(2), 273–86.

PART III

The Institutional Level of Analysis

6 | Multiple Levels of Analysis and the Limitations of Methodological Individualisms (2011)

R. JEPPERSON AND J. MEYER[*]

This article discusses relations among the multiple levels of analysis present in macrosociological explanation – i.e., relations of individual, structural, and institutional processes. It also criticizes the doctrinal insistence upon single-level individualistic explanation found in some prominent contemporary sociological theory. For illustrative material the article returns to intellectual uses of Weber's "Protestant Ethic thesis," showing how an artificial version has been employed as a kind of proof text for the alleged scientific necessity of individualist explanation. Our alternative exposition renders the discussion of Protestantism and capitalism in an explicitly multilevel way, distinguishing possible individual-level, social-organizational, and institutional linkages. The causal processes involved are distinct ones, with the more structural and institutional forms neither captured nor attainable by individual-level thinking. We argue more generally that "methodological individualisms" confuse issues of explanation with issues about microfoundations. This persistent intellectual conflation may be rooted in the broader folk models of liberal individualism.

6.1 Introduction

Sociology is partly constituted by ideas of "emergent properties" and multiple levels of analysis. These ideas have been discussed throughout the history of the discipline. We refer to the expansive literatures on "social facts," structural effects, micro- and macro-levels, and structures and agents – epitomized in reviews (e.g., Alexander and Giesen

---

[*] We have benefited from comments provided by Albert Bergesen, John Boli, Marion Fourcade, David Frank, Kyriakos Kontopoulos, Peter Meyer, Francisco Ramirez, Evan Schofer, Ann Swidler, and anonymous reviewers. We also draw upon past conversations with Shmuel Eisenstadt, Edgar Kiser, and Morris Zelditch Jr.

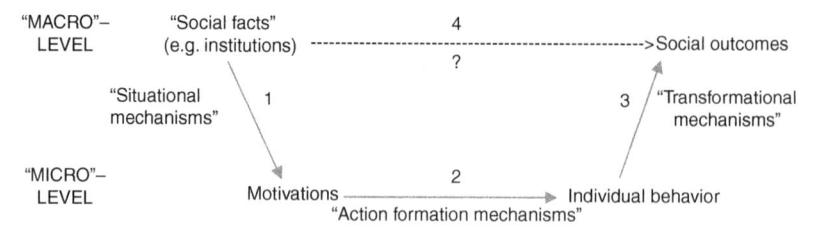

```
"MACRO"–      "Social facts"           4
 LEVEL        (e.g. institutions) ---------------------------->Social outcomes
                                       ?
              "Situational   \ 1                    3  / "Transformational
              mechanisms"     \                       /    mechanisms"
                               \                     /
"MICRO"–                        \          2        /
 LEVEL                      Motivations ----------> Individual behavior
                                "Action formation mechanisms"
```

Figure 6.1 Boudon-Coleman diagram
(After Coleman [1986a, 1986b] and Hedström and Swedberg [1998])

1987; Blau 1974; Knorr-Cetina 1981; Mayntz 2003; Münch and Smelser 1987; Turner and Boyns 2002) and reflected upon by philosophers (e.g., Bhargava 1992; Bunge 1996; Fodor 1997; Garfinkel 1981; Kincaid 1996; Little 2007).

Yet substantial ambiguity still surrounds the central analytical issue that motivates this article. The issue, in a phrase, is: "Is there such a thing as macro-macro causation?" (Little 2007:362). Spelled out: Are there fully macroscopic explanations – explanations linking one "macro-" property to another macro-property – that are separate from explanations that link one macro-property to another via micro-causal pathways? If so, what is the nature of the difference?

The issue is illustrated recently by the familiar "Boudon-Coleman diagram" (Bunge's [1996] label, reflecting Boudon [1981]). In Figure 6.1, does the direct macro-macro link – arrow 4 – represent a distinctive and legitimate set of causal linkages? Or is that arrow a stand-in to be dispensed with when a macro-to-micro-to-macro pathway – arrows 1, 2, and 3 – is provided?

Coleman himself sometimes diagrams a direct macro-to-macro connection, but then drops it to focus upon the macro-to-micro-to-macro pathway. The relationship of the direct macro-to-macro arrow to the individualistic pathway is not discussed (see especially Coleman 1987). A related treatment by Hartmut Esser on "explanatory sociology" (Esser 1994) also includes a direct macro-to-macro arrow. Sociology is multilevel, Esser says, but causation occurs only at the bottom. What this means is left unexplained. In contrast, Hedström and Swedberg in an oft-cited treatment do not include any macro-level connection in their Boudon-Coleman variant (Hedström and Swedberg 1998:21ff). System-level properties are linked exclusively via the micro-pathway.

Given the centrality of the issue for sociology as a discipline, the murkiness regarding the direct macro-level linkage is striking. Many discussions acknowledge that a direct macro-macro connection is empirically present in some sense. But rarely does one find a clear sense of what that means, or a clear treatment of the differences – if any – between the different pathways pictured in the Boudon-Coleman diagram. If anything, the methodological individualism offered by Hedström and Swedberg has become a kind of default interpretation.

The main overviews of the "macro-micro connection," cited above, do not directly address this core issue by working with actual sociological explanations – they typically are philosophical in character. Sawyer (2002:219) in a review can then indict sociologists for failing to provide a clear account of structural causation. Philosophers, in turn, can claim that the discussion remains confused (Zahle 2007:334–36) and that the whole issue requires "fresh thinking" (Little 2007:344). (Treatments that do partly address the specific issue using substantive examples include Collins [1981, 1988], Hannan [1992], Kontopoulos [1993], Münch [1987], and Stinchcombe [1991].)

We address the central theoretical lacuna in this article. We attempt to provide a clear exposition of multilevel explanation with substantive examples, showing that macro-level causal pathways are distinct from micro-level ones. We seek to provide specification and illustration of structural levels of analysis, of the nature of the causal arguments at these levels, and of the relations of more structural (and institutional) levels to the individual level of analysis. In so doing we also provide a rebuttal to a fundamental element of methodological individualism: the idea that more structural arguments are at best merely "explanation sketches," or temporary stand-ins for a later proper individualist analysis.

We take up a discursive opportunity provided by Coleman (e.g., 1987, 1990, and elsewhere) and his intellectual colleagues. We refer to Coleman's use of Figure 6.1 to render Weber's "Protestant Ethic thesis" ([1904/1905] 1996) as a proof text for individualistic explanation. We criticize this usage, and offer an alternative *multilevel* schema for summarizing the substantive historical discussion of Weber's topic – the connections between Protestantism and capitalist development.

Our effort begins with Eisenstadt's reminder that the Reformation involved broad changes in entire systems of *rules* and entire sets of *roles*, as well as changes in motivations (Eisenstadt 1965, 1968b). That is, for this explanatory problem, it is entirely reasonable to hypothesize that changed religious ideas affected individual economic goals, and subsequently changed whole economies. (The famous individual-level argument.) But changed religious rules and roles also altered the social organization of economic life – via a distinct set of causal processes. And, at an institutional level, the changed religious institutions and cosmologies of a whole society altered the entire set of rules governing economic life – another distinct set. That is, causal processes at multiple levels appear to have independent explanatory import.

We argue that methodological individualisms avoid or deny multiple levels of analysis because they confuse explanation with attention to the microfoundations of social life. Of course all causal social processes work through the behaviors and ideas of individual persons – this "ontological truism" (Watkins 1952) is a basic premise of all post-Hegelian naturalist social science. But this premise (sometimes called "ontological individualism") in no way necessitates an explanatory (or "methodological") individualism. (See Bhargava [1992], Bunge [1996], Fodor [1997], Kincaid [1996], and Sawyer [2002] for this point.)

Developing this idea, we also build upon the related principle, stressed by Stinchcombe and reinforced by Sawyer, that the levels of analysis featured in a sociological explanation should be an empirical rather than doctrinal matter (Sawyer 2002; Stinchcombe 1991). For some explanatory issues individual-level explanations will be central. But for others they may be ineffective or irrelevant. Here are eight reasons that have appeared in the literature, presented to motivate the discussion that follows. (1) The presence of purposive self-interested actors in a social situation does not indicate that an explanatory model limited to such actors will be sufficient (since studying the "lower-level" composition of any structure does not guarantee explanation) (Bunge 1996:241–81). (2) "Higher-level" explanations (more structural, more macroscopic) are sometimes better than lower-level ones – or the only potential explanations available (Mayhew 1980; Sawyer 2002:23). (3) In many cases a social process, precisely because it represents "organized complexity," may have individual-level "realizations" that are too heterogeneous or complex to theorize (Fodor 1997; Goldstein 1973; Simon 1962; Stinchcombe 1991). (4) In any case, structural arguments remain possible even when individualist ones are not available

(Sawyer 2002:220). In addition, (5) an undue focus on lower-level mechanisms can bring in causally irrelevant material (Sawyer 2003:215). Further, (6) many social explanations do not require much attention to (for example) psychological states (Goldstein 1973). And (7) many structural arguments do not assume or require any particular or special theory of agency or subjectivity in the first instance (Hannan 1992; Sawyer 2002). Finally, (8) in some instances a focus upon lower-level mechanisms may be an outright waste of time, if one is truly interested in explanation (Stinchcombe 1991).

6.2 Recent Methodological Individualisms

Nonetheless in recent years doctrinal methodological individualisms have become more codified and conventional. A wide range of arguments in sociology focus on the aggregation of the behavior of persons or collectivities conceived as bounded and purposive "actors," or upon the strategic interaction of putative actors. As Kincaid (1996) notes: "Much contemporary social science makes methodological individualism its official methodology" (1996:7).

The intended scope of the newer individualistic imageries is expansive. For Coleman, for instance, a primary objective is to develop explanations of "the macro-level of system behavior," of "institutional structure," and of "historical phenomena often large in scale" (Coleman 1990:1–26; Coleman and Fararo 1992:x, xvi). Sometimes the newer individualistic imagery is represented in an ecumenical fashion, as only one of a set of various complementary-and-competing theoretic imageries (e.g., Coleman and Fararo 1992; Fararo 1992). Different imageries generate distinct arguments to be adjudicated (or integrated) via empirical analysis.

In other formulations, however, the representation of individualist theorizing is more exclusivist and doctrinal. In these cases methodological individualism is presented as an all-purpose and self-sufficient matrix for social theory. The posture is "microchauvinist" (Turner and Boyns 2002), present to varying degrees in, for example, the work of Abell (1997), Coleman (1990), Elster (1989), Hechter (1989), and Hedström and Swedberg (1998). Here the claim is that social scientific explanation must reason through causal processes that reach to the presumed bottom-line of the person, conceived as a sharply defined purposive "actor." As Michael Hannan notes, "many [sociologists] assume without reflection that sociological theories that do not direct explicit attention to natural persons are inherently flawed" (Hannan 1992:127). A philosopher of social science has suggested that many social scientists now treat methodological individualism as a "categorical imperative," "unconditionally binding for all social scientists, because it is based on certain self-evident truths about society" (Udehn 2002:501).

In stark contrast, recent empirical discussions of macrosocial outcomes – such as long-term economic development in the historical West or in the contemporary world – have been patently "multilevel" in character, employing various structural and institutional arguments as well as individual-level ones. In the literature on Anglo-European modernization, for example, explanatory ideas have expanded to consider broad institutional frameworks over long time periods (Baechler et al. [1988] and Engerman [2000] provide overviews). Scholars have been *driven* to develop various structural and institutional arguments – as well as individual-level ones – out of pragmatic explanatory necessity. Most of the structural hypotheses they have had to employ cannot realistically be converted into any individualist form. A whole range of useful hypotheses could not even be considered if one insisted upon employing individualist imagery in an exclusive way.

Consider the history of the "Weber thesis" itself. In the actual historical discussion of socioeconomic development in the modern world, Weber's thesis was entirely absorbed in broader analyses of institutional conditions for development. There are the Roman legal ideas transmitted through the Church and propelling political and organizational rationalization (Anderson 1974; Berman 1983). There is the long-term Christian demystification of nature (Eisenstadt 1999; Huff 2003), supported by a highly rationalized monasticism (Collins 1986, 1999; Werner 1988). There is the extraordinary intellectual and technological dynamism of the Medieval period, once conceived as dark and static (Landes 1998; Mokyr 1992; White 1978). There are the institutional sources of the states system within Christendom, and the effects of that competitive system on economic development (Mann 1986; Strayer 1973; Tilly 1990; Wallerstein 1974). Then there are all sorts of ecological factors (the physical layout of Europe, the Baltic and Atlantic economies) that fostered accumulation (Jones 1981; Landes 1998; McNeill 1974; Pomeranz 2000) and weakened the controls of traditions (allowing the success of both Protestant heresy and proto-capitalist trading systems).

In these substantive lines of thought, the textbook Protestant ethic thesis is unrecognizable. Current discussions of European development present a broad series of institutional forces operating at a macro-sociological level, supporting some structures (the mobilized and competitive national state) and cultural models (rationalized society, moral individualism), and weakening others (feudal aristocracy, the direction of resources into the Church). In fact, as a substantive argument, the narrow thesis was absorbed quite early, starting with Weber's own work. As Collins (1980) emphasizes, by the time Weber gave his lectures on "General Economic History" in 1919–1920, the Protestant ethic thesis as we know it played a minor role. The legal and institutional changes aided by the Reformation were given great importance. But the social psychological effects of Calvinism were given a much more circumscribed place (see Weber [1923] 1950:365ff).

Nonetheless, the thesis survived and evolved in the last century as a meta-theoretical instrument rather than a substantive theory of development. It provided a compelling story of how prior institutional changes, possibly triggering an intriguing psychological process, might have produced great historical change. Accordingly, one finds a long and continuing intellectual history of breathtaking claims like those of David McClelland, in *The Achieving Society*, suggesting that "[t]he Protestant Reformation might have led to earlier independence and mastery training, which led to greater Achievement [need for achievement], which in turn led to the rise of modern capitalism" (1967:47).

6.3 The Boudon-Coleman Diagram and Associated Thinking

Coleman and others, picking up this individualistic narrative, employed the Protestant ethic thesis in an influential tutorial for sociological explanation (Coleman 1986a, 1986b, 1987, 1990). Others have made similar efforts: Boudon (1981), Hartmut Esser (1994), Hernes (1976, 1989), Wippler (1978), Wippler and Lindenberg (1987), and Zetterberg (1965, 1993). In each case, an individualistic explanatory scheme is offered, and Weber's more structural and institutional arguments are set aside.

Figure 6.2 shows the way in which the Protestant ethic thesis is presented by Coleman. We insert the labels of types of "mechanisms"

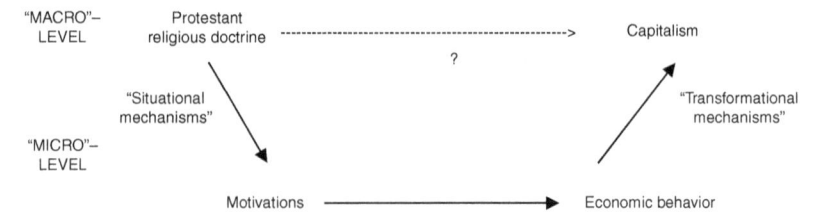

```
"MACRO"-      Protestant
  LEVEL    religious doctrine  ------------------------------->  Capitalism
                                            ?
            "Situational"                              "Transformational
            mechanisms"                                  mechanisms"
"MICRO"-
  LEVEL
                    Motivations  ───────────────▶  Economic behavior
```

Figure 6.2 Typical reconstruction of Weber's "Protestant ethic thesis" (After Coleman 1986 and Hedström and Swedberg 1998)

suggested by Hedström and Swedberg (1998:21–22; cf. Esser 1994). The figure presents a very simple explanatory structure. Causal relations between historical and institutional structures occur primarily or exclusively through micro-processes: that is, through similar situational effects on a large number of individuals, who then generate new lines of action, together transforming society. Coleman et al. do not use the scheme to grapple with substantive arguments about Protestantism or the rise of the modern economy – there is no reference to the substantive literature. Instead, they are advocating a certain style of explanation, and arguing (to varying degrees) that it should have something close to monopoly status.

Coleman's initial discussions accompanying his schema indicated that causal effects can occur at multiple levels of analysis (1986a, 1986b, 1987). Coleman mentioned examples of hypothesized collective effects, referring to work by Hannan and Freeman (1986) on organizational change and by Skocpol and Orloff (1986) on welfare states (Coleman 1986b:355ff). Coleman raised some questions about these collective-level arguments but he did not rule them out. Instead, Coleman indicated that his own primary interest was to develop a better "theory of transitions" between the level of behavior of individual actors and the level of social system behavior (Coleman and Fararo 1992:ix; cf. Coleman 1987).

At other points, however, Coleman's treatment slides into a more doctrinal individualism. In his fuller treatment, Coleman (1990) dispenses with any exclusively system-level interconnections (i.e., the macro-to-macro arrow). The examples of possible collective effects are dropped. Here Coleman is disposed to claim that "the central theoretical problem in sociology is the transition from the level of the individual to a macro level" (1986b:347). He also suggests that macro-level propositions are temporary stand-ins for individual-level explanations (1990:20).

With these latter arguments the "macro-micro-macro" sketch became interpretable as an all-purpose form of explanation. Hedström and Swedberg (1998) seem to present the schema in just this way. Wippler and Lindenberg (1987) have made similar arguments. Here is Hedström and Swedberg's treatment:

> [P]roper explanations of change and variation at the macro level entails showing how macro states at one point in time influence the behavior of individual actors, and how these actions generate new macro states at a later time. That is, instead of analyzing relationships between phenomena exclusively on the macro level, *one should always try* to establish how macro-level events or conditions affect the individual (Step 1), how *the individual* assimilates the impact of these macro-level events (Step 2), and *how a number of individuals*, through their actions and interactions, generate macro-level outcomes (Step 3). (1998:21–22, emphases added)

> [They add a footnote that says:] The logic of Coleman's argument also suggests that *any kind of continuous social action can be conceptualized as a long chain of successive macro-micro-macro transformations* ... the analytical point is precisely to explain this cumulative social action of a large number of macro-micro-macro transitions. (1998:22, emphases added)

This conceptualization reflects the exclusivist form of methodological individualism that we critically highlight.

6.4 Multiple Levels of Analysis in Sociological Explanation

If one insists upon individualist formulations, whole sets of social processes will not be considered for possible hypotheses. To make this point we reconstruct the substantive discussion of Protestantism and capitalism in an explicitly multilevel way. Beyond the individual level, we note distinct sets of causal processes working through social-organizational arrangements, and then processes occurring at a very macrosociological, or institutional, level.

6.4.1 Levels of Analysis

"Levels of analysis" in scientific explanation typically refer to sets of causal processes, each representing different degrees of organizational complexity (hence the idiom of "levels of organization" and "levels of complexity"). This is the conceptualization present in the physical sciences (e.g., Anderson 1972; Gell-Mann 1994; Wilson 1998), and in the philosophy of science (e.g., Bunge 1996; Sawyer 2002; Simon 1962; Thomson 2003:89–100; cf. Kontopoulos 1993 for the social sciences). Philosophers and scientists refer to quantum-level processes, molecular-level ones, cellular ones, and so on through ecological processes and beyond – the ontology of the sciences is "hierarchical" (Anderson 1972; Simon 1962). "Higher-level" processes are currently stable "emergent" configurations of lower-level ones; these configurations then themselves can have causal powers (Bunge 1996:241–81; Thomson 2003:89–100).

Herbert Simon referred to a continuation of such levels into the "architecture of complexity" of the social world (Simon 1962): a hierarchy of levels of organization ranging from social-psychological processes and "elementary social behavior" (Homans 1961) through various social-organizational processes, to cultural-organizational ("institutional") complexes. This social architecture is bounded on the "lower" side by the psychological and biological processes seen as subsocial ones.

In the multilevel exposition here we distinguish between three different sets of causal processes: individual-level ones, social-organizational ones, and institutional ones.[1] For example, when scholars think about economic development they consider individual-level processes, such as the possibility that societies may develop more rapidly because their individual persons are socialized as educated and more productive actors. They also consider social-organizational ones, such as Wallerstein's ideas about how particular trade dependencies may affect development opportunities (Wallerstein 1974). Other potentially relevant processes may be more institutional in character, as when expanded education legitimates and thus fosters technical and social rationalization, sometimes eventuating in economic development (Meyer 1977).

Furthermore, there are consequential interactions among processes operating at different levels. For instance, the individual-level effect of education depends on institutional rules giving credentialing advantages to educated persons (Collins 1979; Meyer 1977). The effects of schooling and other socialization efforts are likely to be weak in social contexts that do not support or legitimate the new values. Instruction in

Multiple Levels of Analysis and the Limitations 149

knowledge and values is likely to be more effective if the possession of the new knowledge or values is required in valued roles in society. In any case, the causally operative levels must be decided via substantive and empirical adjudication, not dictated by theoretical precommitments.

6.4.2 Individual-Level Explanation

One can categorize the main "individual-level" processes invoked by social scientists as follows:

- strictly individual-level, subsocial, processes, that is, those considered to be primarily biological and psychological in origin and organization;
- social-psychological processes (processes in which both intrapsychic and social mechanisms are inextricably engaged, such as in personality formation);
- "elementary social behavior" in the sense of Homans (1961) (e.g., interaction in small groups), or Schelling (e.g., in his "tipping" models of residential segregation, invoking so-called simple social processes involving very little social organization [Schelling 1971]);
- organizationally rudimentary exchange relations, "simple" group dynamics, "collective behavior" (e.g., crowd dynamics), and "simple" forms of strategic interaction (such as those captured by game theory).[2]

In Weber's *Protestant Ethic* there were two main individual-level arguments. The "salvation anxiety" argument – the idea that Calvinist predestination produced uncertainty and compelled self-discipline and hard work – is the individual-level proposition that has been especially attractive to meta-theoretical users of Weber. Yet this idea has not fared well in substantive discussion (Parkin 1982:45; Poggi 1983:47). Contemporary empirical social science is critical of the kind of psychology involved in the "salvation anxiety" proposition. It turns out that fear is often a poor motivator of complex behavior (e.g., ceasing to smoke, driving safely, avoiding drugs), and it is difficult to imagine that people can be frightened into long-run capitalist behavior.

In his own work, Weber emphasized a second more general individual-level dynamic. "Psychological impulses originating in religious belief ... [give] direction to the individual's everyday way of life and [prompt] him to adhere to it" (Weber in Bendix 1960:63–64).

Protestant sects, especially Calvinism (he thought), extended a more "rational mode of life" outside of monastic circles – in effect, bringing religious discipline to the masses (Weber [1923] 1950:365; see Collins 1980; Gorski 2003). Religious strictures encouraged the "rationalization of the conduct of life in general" (Weber [1923] 1950:354). Over time, more individuals became responsive to economic discipline and economic motivation. This second more general formulation ended up as the main individual-level component in Weber's broader explanatory framework (Collins 1980). The "world historical transformation" – the development of economic rationalism – "was *not* the product of Puritanism; rather, Puritanism was a late development that reinforced tendencies that had distinguished European society for a long time past" (Bendix 1960:71–72).

Thus Weber's individual-level arguments were highly contextualized – in contrast to the impression given by the Boudon-Coleman sketches. More recent empirical research has taken the same direction. Researchers are increasingly aware that each part of the causal sequence of Figure 6.2 requires special conditions. Without strong institutionalized support for transformed individual outcomes: (1) The socializing effects of Protestantism on individual attitudes are not likely to be strong. (2) Whatever attitudes may be changed are unlikely to be stable over decades. Personality characteristics are known to be unstable over long periods. (3) Any changed attitudes are unlikely to lead to changed behavior, absent strongly supportive conditions. Changed workplace behavior requires strong structural support. (4) Finally, changed individual attitudes or behavior are unlikely to aggregate into shifts in the institutional structure of society. Weber himself stressed repeatedly that strong desires for profit characterize many societies without producing anything like capitalism (e.g., Weber [1920] 1996:17ff).

This necessary contextualization presents a problem for those who would privilege individual-level explanations. For Figure 6.2's sequence to be credible, it must be embedded in a society that legitimates Protestant beliefs, that continually reinforces them in individuals, that facilitates their implementation in capitalist action, and that validates capitalist action (formerly stigmatized, as in most societies) as producing the collective good. But if all this supportive social structure is in place, one must consider whether it has effects of its own, quite over and above any effects on individual motives. And if all this supportive structure exists for capitalist activity, why would this activity depend on the private fears and hopes of individuals?

We are not criticizing individual-level explanation per se. For example, for the topic at hand, David Landes' recent rendition of an individual-level hypothesis seems plausible: that Protestantism eventually "encouraged the appearance in numbers of a personality type that had been exceptional and adventitious before," a "new kind of businessman" that was an important ingredient in the expansion of the new manufacturing enterprises (Landes 1998:178, 175). We are only criticizing the exclusive insistence upon individual-level formulations.

6.4.3 Explanation in Terms of Social-Organizational Processes

Sociologists distinguish two "structural" levels of analysis above the individual or elementary social level. One is social-organizational, the other more institutional.[3] Social-organizational processes refer to the causal influences attributed to (for example) hierarchic, network, market, and ecological formations. In each case, specific structural features are the properties of interest: for instance, Simmel's idea that triadic structures generate distinctive dynamics wherever found. Contemporary exemplars are Granovetter (1973) on effects of weak versus strong network ties, Burt (1982) on effects of "structural holes," White (1970, 1992) on dynamics of "vacancy chains," and ecological ideas emphasizing the effects of properties of competitive niches upon organizational survival (Hannan and Freeman 1989). Sociologists also invoke a number of "emergent" and more collective social-organizational properties that have a cultural character: group values, typified social positions (roles), prestige patterns, emotional dynamics, interaction rituals, organizational cultures.

Weber's main social-organizational idea about Protestantism has to do with the formation of a new collective actor (Poggi 1983). Protestantism facilitated the transformation of a preexisting collective actor – the urban commercial estate – into the legitimated burgher class of entrepreneurs. Protestantism enhanced the class solidarity among Protestant burghers, by providing a religiously based class morale. In addition, rising commercial classes embraced Protestantism for purposes of political and economic legitimation (Bendix 1960:49–82;

Parkin 1982:60–62). Networks of the new collective actors could expand, facilitated by common ideology and the trust generated by shared community (Parkin 1982:60–62; also Mann 1986).

In a more structural imagery, the capitalist is produced less by the inner motives of some individuals than by an evolving religious and political structure that defines a new role or collective actor. The new structures give prestige and legitimacy to the role, and set it in effective relation to other structures, including the state, the religious system, property ownership, and the family system. Quite apart from any motivational effects, the Reformation certainly modified roles and organizational structures throughout society. It weakened the legitimacy of many important roles, and dramatically strengthened others. In the religious arena, the authority of state elites was expanded, and the old roles undercut – priests and bishops were subordinated, and the authority of the cathedral and monastery and papacy destroyed. The religious autonomy of the individual, and of the church as an association of individuals, was enhanced. Politically, landowners and aristocrats were weakened, and the rationalized state greatly empowered. Economically the old roles of the pariah bankers and merchants were undermined, along with the whole complex of landowner–serf relations. The authority and legitimacy of free individuals functioning in markets were greatly strengthened.

Structural explanations, in other words, give accounts of how changed distributions of social values and opportunities occur – in this case supported by dramatic religious changes. Much less causation is located in individual personality or actorhood, and structural arguments do not typically rely upon strong (and empirically questionable) assumptions about the competence, coherence, and boundedness of persons. It is one thing to be a capitalist if that implies the social role of pariah or alien or thief – perhaps some very distinctive values and orientations are necessary, requiring much socialization (religious or otherwise). It is quite another thing to be admired as a capitalist carrier of progress, and quite routine motives may suffice to encourage individuals to want to be recognized as successful. One does not need to assume very much about values or personality to understand that young persons in the 1990s might have seen investment banking as an attractive career.

6.4.4 Explanation in Terms of Institutional Processes

The structural imagery in American sociology often features networks, typically with limited cultural meaning and few supra-individual properties. A recent example is provided by Padgett and McLean (2006), who represent social context by "multiple-network architectures" (2006:1468). People are treated as "cross-domain composites of roles" (2006:1469). This kind of reasoning has been very productive. However, it does not capture the actual imagery about roles used in substantive macrosociological explanation. For instance, the destruction of the "priest," and of the magical values attached to formerly stigmatized roles of the entrepreneur or the usurer, are imperfectly captured by pure network imagery. These roles embody dramatic cultural meanings – grand social models and ideologies extending across time and space. They involve cosmologies as well: metaphysical claims about the nature of humans, the physical world, and the moral world.

Historically, sociology has pulled together conceptions of phenomena at this level of analysis using the concept "institution" (Berger and Luckmann 1967; Buckley 1967; Eisenstadt 1968a). Institutions are chronically reproducing complexes of routines, rules, roles, and meanings. They have organizational aspects – structures of authority and responsibility, often integrated in something like control systems. They also have cultural aspects – generalized models formulating and justifying rules, built up into systems of thought and analysis (legal models, political models, religious models, knowledge systems, professional discourses). Instances of institutional structures such as the Catholic Church, national state, monetary system, constitutional legal system, limited-liability corporation, scientific academy, and research university exemplify both organizational and cultural dimensions.

Sociologists propose distinctive causal processes at the institutional level. For instance, substantive treatments of the Reformation (by Weber and others) routinely feature institutional-level arguments. We call attention to five such arguments in the literature (cf. Eisenstadt's early reviews [1965, 1968b] and Gorski's recent complementary discussion [2005]).

Reconstruction of polity and community: The Reformation obviously weakened the roles and ideas linking society in a liturgical manner, via the Church and a nominally hierarchical social order (Eisenstadt 1965, 1968b; Walzer 1965; Zaret 1989). It led to the collapse of the ideal of imperial unity as well (McNeill 1963).

Instead, the eventual Reformation settlements ended up strengthening new ideas of corporate territorial "societies" independent of the Church (McNeil 1963; Parsons 1977). Moreover, the main institutional innovation of Protestantism – the sect – represented a new model of polity and community.[4] This model constituted individuals as empowered agents, responsible for bridging the gap between spiritual ideals and mundane realities. People were supposed to throw off what Marx called "the idiocy of rural life" and to enact an entirely new identity, eventually producing the "cult of individualism" (Durkheim [1898] 1969) that we now naturalize.

Legitimating and reconstructing economic activity: By investing economizing with moral significance, Protestant ideology contributed to the collective legitimation of practical economic activity, and of profit and wealth. This line of argument was at the core of Weber's *Protestant Ethic*, but commentators have focused upon the more individualistic formulations. Private gain became a public good in the new cultural models. This change was a striking departure from the ideological stigmatization of commerce typical in agrarian societies and pronounced in Catholic natural law doctrines. Ideas of just price and just wage, for example, had left economic activity in a state of "intellectual, moral, and legal chaos" (Lüthy 1968:106). Protestant reform groups directly contributed to reformulations of ideas of covenant, contract, and natural law. Calvin himself worked on ideas for rationalizing capital and interest accounts (ibid:107). Banking was reenvisioned as part of an autonomous economic sphere, governed by its own distinctive economic calculus. Restrictions on entrepreneurs and corporations were eased. Eisenstadt talks about a general "incorporation of Protestant premises into law" in England, Scandinavia, the Netherlands, and (later) the United States, making eventually for more "flexible," "open," and "autonomous" institutions (Eisenstadt 1968b:12). Counter-Reformation zones, in contrast, tended to stifle the economic developments of the time (Lüthy 1968; Trevor-Roper 1967).

Legitimating the national state: The attack on the Church chartered the national state as the primary legitimate polity, and subsequently proto-national development efforts (Mann 1986:467ff; Parsons 1977; Wuthnow 1989). Calvinism appears to have provided new models of social discipline and executive administration, central in national state-building efforts in some zones of Europe (e.g., in the Netherlands and Prussia) (Gorski 2003).

Restructuring collective action: Protestant sects made new voluntarist organizational forms possible. The very idea of sect members running their own congregations allowed for ongoing experiments with new models of organized action (Thompson 1963; Walzer 1965). People no longer required clans or guilds to act collectively. In addition, Protestant cultural models gave concrete legitimacy to a wide range of collective projects for intendedly rational action in a mundane world – and not just economic ones. Protestant ideas "opened" up the world as a thoroughly objectified, profaned, manipulable field for purposeful "action" (Poggi 1983:70), while desacralizing older forms of authority and related traditions (Walzer 1965). Ideas about the potential for and obligation of social progress intensified. ("It was the Reformation that reestablished the ethical rigorism and instrumental activism of the Old Testament" [Münch 1994:183].) The idea that this progress could occur partly through the action of ordinary persons became far more prominent – after all, Protestantism greatly expanded the number of imagined empowered souls in the world. But notions of these kinds were put in place not by role or dispositional evolution, but by central authorities carrying broad theoretical discourses (e.g., the English, French, and American revolutionaries).

Legitimating science: The institutionalization of religious pluralism in Europe, after the settlements of the Religious Wars, indirectly contributed to the conventionalization of intellectual pluralism (McNeill 1963; Zaret 1989). In so doing the Reformation promoted "the [ideological] skepticism and refusal of authority that is at the heart of the scientific endeavor" (Landes 1998:179). Recent work has backed Weber's hypothesis that while "scientific progress and Protestantism must not at all be unquestioningly identified," Protestantism helped to "[place] science in the service of technology and economics" (Weber [1923] 1950:368; Merton 1970; cf. Mann 1986:471; Landes 1998:178ff). Hence Protestantism not only encouraged "high science" (Mann 1986:471), but promoted the gradual rise of science as a central modern institution engaged with every collective purpose (Drori et al. 2003).

In summary, the Reformation precipitated broad institutional changes in dominant models of individual and society. The consequences were not simply economic. And as institutional changes they had long histories in Western development – long preceding and long following the Reformation itself.

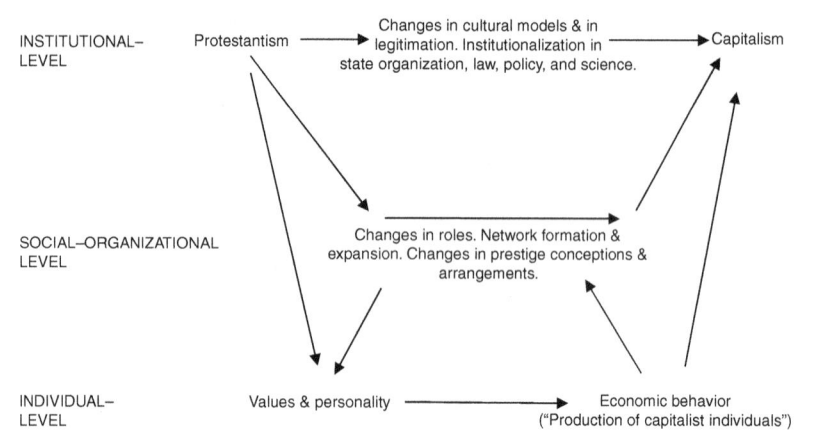

Figure 6.3 Possible pathways linking Protestantism and capitalism at different levels of analysis

6.4.5 Multilevel Analysis

The point of the above section was simply to call attention to lines of likely *distinctive causal influence*. We epitomize the discussion in Figure 6.3, which provides a multilevel alternative to Figure 6.2. We show causal pathways operating at three levels of analysis. If one reifies the Boudon-Coleman diagram – and the way of thinking associated with it – one is likely to fixate on possible causal processes such as the "Protestant ethic thesis." One might not seek out causal possibilities such as the social-organizational and institutional ones we have discussed (see Garfinkel 1981:164ff for the general analytical point). Yet discussion of the possible relations of Protestantism and capitalism would remain entirely superficial unless one does consider them.

6.5 The Conflation of Explanation and Microfoundations

The more doctrinal methodological individualists might persist in arguing that one should seek to convert the pathways of Figure 6.3 into those of Figure 6.2. Hedström and Swedberg (1998) seem to make this argument, in the passage quoted earlier. The idea that structural arguments are at best explanation sketches, to be resolved into and replaced by more adequate individual-level explanations, is now relatively commonplace. This idea depends upon three separate notions, two legitimate but one fallacious and invalidating. First, there is the (legitimate) requirement of adducing specific causal processes if one purports to offer a causal explanation. Second, there is the (legitimate) requirement of being able to illustrate micro-instantiations of any process (i.e., examples of the constituent people and activities involved). Third, there is the *alleged* necessity of formulating arguments exclusively in terms of micro-processes. This allegation reflects a conflation of issues of explanation with issues of microfoundations, as we now explain. (See Kincaid [1996:142–90] for extended development of this point; also Bhargava [1992] and Sawyer [2002].)

The distinction between microfoundations and explanation has great import across the sciences. Consider current theories of psychological depression for illustration. The availability of medications targeting neurotransmitters has given recent discussions a neurophysiological focus. However, analysts obviously consider multiple possible etiologies of depression, loosely differentiated by levels of analysis (and categorized as, e.g., neurology, psychiatry, psychology, and family dynamics). The explanatory role of neurotransmitter balance can vary from central to entirely peripheral in these accounts. Perhaps some depressions can be attributed primarily to genetic or ontogenetic neurotransmitter imbalance. But in other proposed etiologies, neurotransmitters may be envisioned only as carrying microfoundations, without having explanatory centrality. For instance, it has been proposed that some depressive syndromes are adaptive responses to trauma among less "resilient" individuals (Kessler 1997). It has been proposed that women may inhabit more depressogenic social networks than men (Kessler and McLeod 1984). It has been proposed that some depressive syndromes are culturally scripted personality styles (an allegation about Central Europe, for instance [e.g., Kurzweil 1989, Townsend 1978]). These etiologies invoke different levels of causation. In each of these putative etiologies, neurotransmitters will of course be present and operative – and hence causally implicated from an ontological standpoint – but they will have greatly varying explanatory relevance.

This example is representative of countless others across the sciences, wherein microfoundations must be distinguished from explanation. In social science, *the "microfoundations" of social-organizational and institutional causal pathways are not equivalent to causal arguments at the level of individuals conceived as actors*. For example, the microcomposition of a truly collective-institutional process is not equivalent to one of Coleman's macro-micro-macro explanations.

To drive home this point for sociology, one can consider the different "micro-samples" that make up different causal processes. A micro-sample refers to the constituent people and activities isolated in a specific setting and time (we adapt language from Collins [1981, 1988]). The micro-samples of any social process, suggests Collins, can be imagined as "filmstrips" – that is, what specific scenes might one film in an attempt to capture some imagined social process? The scenes (people and activities) that one would film in order to capture an institutional process are different from what one would film to capture a social-organizational process or – most relevant here – an individual-level one. Any of the possible processes connecting Protestantism and capitalism at the different levels could be filmed – with sufficient creativity, of course – and in that sense one would capture "micro-samples" in time and space. But the scenes, players, and activities would be quite different for each level of analysis.

The filmstrips (micro-samples) of an hypothesized process working through individual actors might in fact capture some version of Coleman's macro-micro-macro sequence – for example, Landes' (1998) version mentioned earlier. (Different religion, different socialization, different identity, different aggregated behaviors reshaping community.) But the filmstrips of an institutional-level process – its micro-samples – would *not* capture a Protestant ethic process or any other process at the level of the person seen as an individual actor aggregating with others, or interacting in a strategic game. For instance, if one considers Lüthy's (1968) account of changed banking laws – an institutional story – the micro-samples would be drawn from legal guilds and court ministries, featuring legal and religious professionals enacting highly institutionalized roles rather than functioning as individual actors. One would be sampling how Protestant theory modified the collectively dominant model of society. Priests and lawyers and state elites, operating as carriers of the changed model, worked to change various rules of the social game. They worked to legitimate usury, for instance. Among other consequences, rich people eventually became more likely to use their money to engage in capital investment, rather than to buy status and protection.

Of course collective processes are produced and reproduced by persons' behaviors (the "ontological truism"). But the "microfoundations" of many collective processes do not involve a mass of similar individuals, operating as choosing actors, affected by a situation, taking new actions, and changing society via some aggregation or assembly. One would not be able to work a truly collective process into such a framework: the micro-realizations of institutional processes are likely to be multiple and heterogeneous – since institutions are chronically reproduced *complexes* of disparate rules, roles, routines, and meanings.

Put another way: individual-level causal pathways capture effects produced by relatively unorganized people. Here causation is generated by their subsocial or elementary social characteristics. In contrast, more structural imageries capture causation generated by more and more collective and complexly organized activities. In social-organizational imageries, for example, the featured causal influences might be those generated by (say) relatively durably organized networks of social roles, or group cultural and religious commitments. These patterns will have distinct micro-instantiations, having to do with (for instance) the opportunities or communications available to people (or other units). But the causality lies with the effects of the role networks themselves, not with variations in the unit-level properties. Similarly, in more institutional imagery, the featured causal influences are those generated by broad complexes of organization and meaning. The micro-instantiations might have to do with (for instance) complementary sets of role enactments, or with enactments of broad ideological scripts. But the causality emerges from the complex organization of roles, routines, and meanings that we call institutional structure – and not from variations in role enactments or in the individuals involved.

The recent emphasis on "mechanisms" has obscured these necessary distinctions. It is not only that the term is used in many different ways (Gerring [2007] finds nine definitions; Mahoney [2001] finds 24). The problem is more deeply rooted. First, the discourse about mechanisms conflates the idea of causal process in general – a causal pathway or "chain" – with the idea of the lower (or lowest-relevant-level) causal processes within a multilevel system. Second, some analysts conflate microfoundations with causality in general (Hedström and Swedberg [1998] seem to do this, as does Little [2007:358] in his recent philosophical review).

The conflations ensure the elision of the core analytical distinction illustrated by this article. That distinction, to summarize, is the following. Two macro-properties can be connected via a micro-level causal pathway, as the Boudon-Coleman diagram depicts. But two macro-properties may also be connected via distinct macro-level causal pathways – or distinct meso-pathways – as our outline of Weber's topic has shown (and as Figure 6.3 depicts). In the latter cases, one may go on to seek micro-foundations *if* it is analytically useful to do so – Stinchcombe's (1991) original point. The recent literature on mechanisms misses this fundamental distinction, and hence avoids the theoretical task of attending to the multiple levels of analysis involved in sociological explanation.

6.6 Postscript

We have emphasized the intellectual costs of assigning privileged status to individualist explanation, using interpretations of Weber's Protestant ethic as our focus. Any levels essentialism, micro *or* macro, will distort and impoverish social science.

From a scientific standpoint, pure "atomism" and pure "holism" are both fictions (Bunge 2000:396). All the sciences must attend both to composition and to emergent systemic properties, and only some of the latter result from aggregation (Bunge 1996:256, 241–81; Thomson 2003:89–100). The physical sciences during the contemporary period have experienced a robust development of multilevel theorizing, displacing doctrinal atomisms – doctrinal holisms (such as vitalism in biology) having been displaced much earlier (Bunge 2000:384; also Gell-Mann 1994; Wilson 1998).

It is worth reflecting, then, why social scientists in the modern period have recurrently returned, often with a good deal of passion and even moralism, to micro-reductionist themes. (In contrast, "macrochauvinisms" have faded, remaining only in weakened forms in some Continental circles.)

Social science has never been far removed from underlying folk and policy models – national models into the late twentieth century and more global ones now (Münch 1986, 1994, 2001). In the Anglo-American context, methodological individualism has reemerged repeatedly as a kind of revitalization movement – "bringing men back in" and the like – offering for some scholars a great simplification that might finally lead to a proper and pure social science. Many analysts of social science have detected a constitutive individualism in especially American social science (Bunge 1996:241–63; Hawthorn 1987; Levine 1995; Münch 1986, 2001; Sawyer 2003:221ff; Udehn 2002; Varenne 1984; Zahle 2007:319ff). Liberal and especially American cultural models of society notoriously dramatize and valorize purposive individual action. In the contemporary period these models have intensified and rapidly globalized, weakening notions of states and communities as primordial collective actors, and driving the "cult of individualism" to heights Durkheim could never have envisioned (Durkheim [1898] 1969). Now there are strong folk and professional visions of a whole world of equal, free, educated individuals making all the choices that drive a global economy, polity, society, and cultural system. The individual, now, is the one certain ontological element left in social life. It is no wonder that social science reifies these visions.

In this reification, a powerful preference for "rock bottom" accounts is created (Watkins's phrase [1957]). Images of modal individuals aggregating in plebiscitary or market-like ways are highly conventionalized, and provide a cultural matrix – in effect, a set of defaults – for social scientific explanation. It is natural to formulate explanations that feature plebiscitary and market-like aggregations of individuals, imagined as modal citizens or consumers, and to focus upon the psychological states of such individuals. (Varenne [1984] has made this argument about American "anthropological conversations," and Münch [2001] has discussed the [different] matrix of German social theory.) Even the most individualistically inclined social scientists are of course aware of institutions and culture. However, it may seem natural to neglect such forces in professional work, or to think that such forces cannot be measured or theorized, or to assume that individual-level analyses will implicitly capture them.

There is a broader epistemological issue here. There is an underlying tension within modernity's ideological system between its romance of human agency (Sawyer 2003:221ff) and its scientific project. The scientific telos leads necessarily toward biological, ecological, structural, and cultural causation and hence to displacement of action theories. But a culture that descriptively and normatively stresses decisions and decision-based "actions" will tend to support isomorphic professional models, whatever violence to reality such models may do (Brunsson 1985; Kahneman et al. 1982). Such models have in fact proliferated wherever dramas centered on empowered actors are central – today the world of interstate relations, of inter-organizational relations, and the market world of relations among persons seen as actors.

The most rapidly developing contemporary industries are those that prop up the individual as actor – educators, therapists, consultants, and professional advisors. Similarly expanded industries service the other more derivative actors of the modern system – the rationalized organization, the expanded service-oriented state. So exaggerated intellectual individualisms become possible because of extraordinarily elaborated institutional structures – ones that methodological individualisms would disregard, at substantial cost to the project of social science.

Notes

1. The terms "macro," "micro," and (sometimes) "meso" make it easy to conflate complexity with scale – that is, spatial size or extension in time. But scale and complexity are analytically independent dimensions. In social science one might refer to the "collective level" (for example, the polity) of, say, families – a fairly "micro" unit in scalar terms. One might also refer to a "micro-level" (perhaps specific commodity chains) of the world system, a "macro" scalar unit. Here, we focus on levels of causal processes differentiated by complexity – the fundamental denotation in the philosophy of science.
2. The example of game theory shows that aggregation of behaviors is not always an element in more individual-level and "elementary social" imagery (as Coleman stressed [1987]). For instance, a game theoretic model of "class conflict," such as in Przeworski and Wallerstein (1982), employs economic classes as units. Their interaction does not primarily affect society via aggregation. Yet the core model is a bargaining game between two stylized unitary actors, hence a relatively "simple" social interaction in the technical sense just defined.
3. The boundaries between the three "levels" necessarily blur. Social-organizational ideas blur on the one side with individual and elementary social ones. For instance, ideas about social movements blur with ideas of "collective behavior," the latter having a more individualist

cast. Ideas of organizational and professional cultures blur with ideas about cultures having longer and more institutional histories.
4. We are indebted to Ann Swidler for this point.

References

Abell, P. (1997). Homo Sociologicus: Do We Need Him/Her? In S. P. Turner, ed., *Social Theory and Sociology*. Hoboken, NJ: Wiley Blackwell, pp. 229–34.

Alexander, J. C. & B. Giesen. (1987). From Reduction to Linkage: The Long View of the Micro-Macro Link. In J. C. Alexander, et al., eds., *The Micro-Macro Link*. Berkeley, CA: University of California Press, pp. 1–44.

Anderson, P. (1974). *Lineages of the Absolutist State*, London: New Left Books.

Anderson, P. W. (1972). More Is Different. *Science, New Series*, 177(4047), 393–6.

Baechler, J., J. A. Hall, & M. Mann, eds. (1988). *Europe and the Rise of Capitalism*, Oxford: Basil Blackwell.

Bendix, R. (1960). *Max Weber: An Intellectual Portrait*, Garden City, NY: Anchor.

Berger, P. L. & T. Luckmann. (1967). *The Social Construction of Reality*, Garden City, NY: Anchor.

Berman, H. J. (1983). *Law and Revolution: The Formation of the Western Legal Tradition*, Cambridge, MA: Harvard University Press.

Bhargava, R. (1992). *Individualism in Social Science*, New York, NY: Oxford University Press.

Blau, P. M. (1974). Parameters of Social Structure. *American Sociological Review*, 39(5), 615–35.

Boudon, R. (1981). *The Logic of Social Action*, London: Routledge and Kegan Paul.

Brunsson, N. (1985). *The Irrational Organization*, Chichester: Wiley.

Buckley, W. (1967). *Sociology and Modern Systems Theory*, Englewood Cliffs, NJ: Prentice Hall.

Bunge, M. (1996). *Finding Philosophy in Social Science*, New Haven, CT: Yale University Press.

Bunge, M. (2000). Ten Modes of Individualism – None of Which Works – And Their Alternatives. *Philosophy of the Social Sciences*, 30(3), 384–406.

Burt, R. (1982). *Toward a Structural Theory of Action*, New York, NY: Academic Press.

Coleman, J. S. (1986a). Social Theory, Social Research, and a Theory of Action. *American Journal of Sociology*, 91(6), 1309–35.

Coleman, J. S. (1986b). Micro Foundations and Macrosocial Theory. In S. Lindenberg, J. S. Coleman, & S. Nowak, eds., *Approaches to Social Theory*. New York, NY: Russell Sage Foundation, pp. 345–63.

Coleman, J. S. (1987). Microfoundations and Macrosocial Behavior. In J. C. Alexander, B. Giesen, R. Münch, & N. J. Smelser, eds., *The Micro-Macro Link*. Berkeley, CA: University of California Press, pp. 153–73.

Coleman, J. S. (1990). *Foundations of Social Theory*, Cambridge, MA: Harvard University Press.

Coleman, J. S. & T. J. Fararo. (1992). Introduction. In J. S. Coleman & T. J. Fararo, eds., *Rational Choice Theory*. Newbury Park, CA: Sage, pp. ix–xxii.

Collins, R. (1979). *The Credential Society*, New York, NY: Academic Press.

Collins, R. (1980). Weber's Last Theory of Capitalism: A Systematization. *American Sociological Review*, 45(6), 925–42.

Collins, R. (1981). The Microfoundations of Macrosociology. *American Journal of Sociology*, 86(5), 984–1014.

Collins, R. (1986). *Weberian Sociological Theory*, Cambridge: Cambridge University Press.

Collins, R. (1988). *Theoretical Sociology*, San Diego, CA: Harcourt Brace Jovanovich.

Collins, R. (1999). *Macrohistory*, Palo Alto, CA: Stanford University Press.

Drori, G., J. W. Meyer, F. O. Ramirez, & E. Schofer. (2003). *Science in the Modern World Polity*, Palo Alto, CA: Stanford University Press.

Durkheim, E. [1898] 1969. Individualism and the Intellectuals. *Political Studies* 17, 14–30.

Eisenstadt, Shmuel N. 1965. Transformation of Social, Political, and Cultural Orders in Modernization. *American Sociological Review*, 30(5), 659–73.

Eisenstadt, Shmuel N. (1968a). Social Institutions: The Concept. In D. L. Sills, ed., *International Encyclopedia of the Social Sciences*, Vol. XIV. New York, NY: Macmillan, pp. 409–21

Eisenstadt, Shmuel N. (1968b). The Protestant Ethic Thesis in an Analytical and Comparative Framework. In S. N. Eisenstadt, ed., *The Protestant Ethic and Modernization*. New York, NY: Basic Books, pp. 3–45.

Eisenstadt, Shmuel N. (1999). *Fundamentalism, Sectarianism, and Revolution*, Cambridge: Cambridge University Press.

Elster, J. (1989). *Nuts and Bolts for the Social Sciences*, Cambridge: Cambridge University Press.

Engerman, S. L. (2000). Max Weber as Economist and Economic Historian. In S. Turner, ed., *The Cambridge Companion to Weber*. Cambridge: Cambridge University Press, pp. 256–71.

Esser, H. (1994). Explanatory Sociology. *Soziologie*, 3, 177–90.

Fararo, T. (1992). *The Meaning of General Theoretical Sociology*, Cambridge: Cambridge University Press.
Fodor, J. (1997). Special Sciences: Still Autonomous After All These Years. *Philosophical Perspectives*, 11, 149–63.
Garfinkel, A. (1981). *Forms of Explanation*, New Haven, CT: Yale University Press.
Gell-Mann, M. (1994). *The Quark and the Jaguar*, New York, NY: W.H. Freeman.
Gerring, J. (2007). The Mechanismic Worldview: Thinking Inside the Box. *British Journal of Political Science*, 38, 161–79.
Goldstein, L. J. (1973). The Inadequacy of the Principle of Methodological Individualism. In J. O'Neill, ed., *Modes of Individualism and Collectivism*. London: Heinemann, pp. 264–76.
Gorski, P. S. (2003). *The Disciplinary Revolution*, Chicago, IL: University of Chicago Press.
Gorski, P. S. (2005). The Little Divergence: The Protestant Reformation and Economic Hegemony in Early Modern Europe. In W. H. Swatos, Jr. & L. Kaelber, eds., *The Protestant Ethic Turns 100*. Boulder, CO: Paradigm Publishers, pp. 165–90.
Granovetter, M. (1973). The Strength of Weak Ties. *American Journal of Sociology*, 78(6), 1360–80.
Hannan, M. (1992). Rationality and Robustness in Multilevel Systems. In J. S. Coleman & T. J. Fararo, eds., *Rational Choice Theory*. Newbury Park, CA: Sage Publications, pp. 120–36.
Hannan, M. & J. Freeman. (1986). The Ecology of Organizations: Structural Inertia and Organizational Change. In S. Lindenberg, J. S. Coleman & S. Nowak, eds., *Approaches to Social Theory*. New York, NY.
Hannan, M. & J. Freeman. (1989). *Organizational Ecology*, Cambridge, MA: Harvard University Press.
Hawthorn, G. (1987). *Enlightenment and Despair: A History of Social Theory*, Cambridge: Cambridge University Press.
Hechter, M. (1989). Rational Choice Foundations of Social Order. In J. H. Turner, ed., *Theory-Building in Sociology*. Newbury Park, CA: Sage, pp. 60–81.
Hedström, P. & R. Swedberg. (1998). Social Mechanisms: An Introductory Essay. In P. Hedström & R. Swedberg, eds., *Social Mechanisms*. Cambridge: Cambridge University Press, pp. 1–31.
Hernes, G. (1976). Structural Change in Social Processes. *American Journal of Sociology*, 82(3), 513–54.
Hernes, G. (1989). The Logic of the Protestant Ethic. *Journal of Rationality and Society*, 1, 122–61.

Homans, G. (1961). *Social Behavior: Its Elementary Forms*, New York, NY: Harcourt, Brace and World.
Huff, T. (2003). *The Rise of Early Modern Science*, 2nd edn, Cambridge: Cambridge University Press.
Jones, E. L. (1981). *The European Miracle*, New York, NY: Cambridge University Press.
Kahneman, D., P. Slovic, & A. Tversky. (1982). *Judgment Under Uncertainty*, New York, NY: Cambridge University Press.
Kessler, R. (1997). The Effects of Stressful Life Events on Depression. *Annual Review of Psychology*, 48(1), 191–214.
Kessler, R. & J. McLeod. (1984). Sex Differences in Vulnerability to Undesirable Life Events. *American Sociological Review*, 49(5), 620–31.
Kincaid, H. (1996). *Philosophical Foundations of the Social Sciences*, Cambridge: Cambridge University Press.
Knorr-Cetina, K. (1981). The Micro-Sociological Challenge of Macro-Sociology: Towards a Reconstruction of Social Theory and Methodology. In K. Knorr-Cetina & A. V. Cicourel, eds., *Advances in Social Theory and Methodology*. Boston, MA: Routledge & Kegan Paul, pp. 1–48.
Kontopoulos, K. M. (1993). *The Logics of Social Structure*, Cambridge: Cambridge University Press.
Kurzweil, E. (1989). *The Freudians: A Comparative Perspective*, New Haven, CT: Yale University Press.
Landes, D. S. (1998). *The Wealth and Poverty of Nations*, New York, NY: Norton.
Levine, D. N. (1995). *Visions of the Sociological Tradition*, Chicago, IL: University of Chicago Press.
Little, D. (2007). Levels of the Social. In S. P. Turner & M. W. Risjord, eds., *Philosophy of Anthropology and Sociology*. Amsterdam: Elsevier, pp. 343–72.
Lüthy, Herbert. (1968). Once Again: Calvinism and Capitalism. In S. N. Eisenstadt, ed., *The Protestant Ethic and Modernization*. New York, NY: Basic Books.
Mahoney, J. (2001). Beyond Correlational Analysis: Recent Innovations in Theory and Method. *Sociological Forum*, 16(3), 575–93.
Mann, M. (1986). A History of Power from the Beginning to AD 1760. Vol. I of *The Sources of Social Power*. Cambridge: Cambridge University Press.
Mayhew, B. H. (1980). Structuralism Versus Individualism. *Social Forces*, 59 (2), 335–75, 627–48.
Mayntz, R. (2003). Mechanisms in the Analysis of Social Macro-Phenomena. *Philosophy of the Social Sciences*, 34(2), 237–59.
McClelland, D. (1967). *The Achieving Society*, New York, NY: Free Press.

McNeill, W. (1963). *The Rise of the West*, Chicago, IL: University of Chicago Press.
McNeill, W. (1974). *The Shape of European History*, New York, NY: Oxford University Press.
Merton, R. K. (1970). *Science, Technology & Society in Seventeenth-Century England*, New York, NY: Howard Fertig.
Meyer, J. W. (1977). The Effects of Education as an Institution. *American Journal of Sociology*, 83(1), 55–77.
Mokyr, J. (1992). *The Lever of Riches*, Oxford: Oxford University Press.
Münch, R. (1986). The American Creed in Sociological Theory: Exchange, Negotiated Order, Accommodated Individualism, and Contingency. *Sociological Theory*, 4(1), 41–60.
Münch, R. (1987). The Interpenetration of Microinteraction and Macrostructures in a Complex and Contingent Institutional Order. In J. C. Alexander, et al., eds., *The Micro-Macro Link*. Berkeley, CA: University of California Press, pp. 319–36.
Münch, R. (1994). *Sociological Theory: From the 1850s to the 1920s*, Chicago, IL: Nelson-Hall.
Münch, R. (2001). *The Ethics of Modernity*, London: Rowman and Littlefield.
Münch, R. & N. J. Smelser. (1987). Relating the Micro and Macro. In J. C. Alexander, et al., eds., *The Micro-Macro Link*. Berkeley, CA: University of California Press, pp. 356-88.
Padgett, J. F. & P. D. McLean. (2006). Organizational Invention and Elite Transformation: The Birth of Partnership Systems in Renaissance Florence. *American Journal of Sociology*, 111(5), 1463–568.
Parkin, F. (1982). *Max Weber*, London: Routledge.
Parsons, T. (1977). *The Evolution of Societies*, Englewood Cliffs, NJ: Prentice Hall.
Poggi, G. (1983). *Calvinism and the Capitalist Spirit*, Amherst, MA: University of Massachusetts Press.
Pomeranz, K. (2000). *The Great Divergence*, Princeton, NJ: Princeton University Press.
Przeworski, A. & M. Wallerstein. (1982). The Structure of Class Conflict in Democratic and Capitalist Societies. *American Political Science Review*, 76(2), 215–38.
Sawyer, R. K. (2002). Durkheim's Dilemma: Toward a Sociology of Emergence. *Sociological Theory*, 20(2), 227–47.
Sawyer, R. K. (2003). Nonreductive Individualism Part II: Social Causation. *Philosophy of the Social Sciences*, 33(2), 203–24.
Schelling, T. (1971). Dynamic Models of Segregation. *Journal of Mathematical Sociology*, 1(2), 143–86.

Simon, H. (1962). The Architecture of Complexity. *Proceedings of the American Philosophical Society*, 106(6), 467–82.
Skocpol, T. & A. S. Orloff. (1986). Explaining the Origins of Welfare States: A Comparison of Britain and the United States, 1880s–1920s. In S. Lindenberg, J. S. Coleman, & S. Nowak, eds., *Approaches to Social Theory*. New York, NY: Russell Sage Foundation, pp. 229–58.
Stinchcombe, A. (1991). The Conditions of Fruitfulness of Theorizing About Mechanisms in Social Science. *Philosophy of the Social Sciences*, 21(3), 367–88.
Strayer, J. (1973). *The Medieval Origins of the Modern State*, Princeton, NJ: Princeton University Press.
Thompson, E. P. (1963). *The Making of the English Working Class*, New York, NY: Pantheon Books.
Thomson, G. (2003). *On Philosophy*, Toronto: Wadsworth.
Tilly, C. (1990). *Coercion, Capital, and European States*, Cambridge, MA: Blackwell.
Townsend, J. M. (1978). *Cultural Conceptions and Mental Illness: A Comparison of Germany and the U.S.*, Chicago, IL: University of Chicago Press.
Trevor-Roper, H. R. (1967). *Religion, the Reformation and Social Change*, London: Macmillan.
Turner, J. H. & D. E. Boyns. (2002). The Return of Grand Theory. In J. H. Turner, ed., *Handbook of Sociological Theory*. New York, NY: Plenum Publishers, pp. 353–78.
Udehn, L. (2002). The Changing Face of Methodological Individualism. *Annual Review of Sociology*, 28(1), 479–507.
Varenne, H. (1984). Collective Representation in American Anthropological Conversations: Individual and Culture. *Current Anthropology*, 25(3), 281–300.
Wallerstein, I. (1974). Capitalist Agriculture and the Origins of the European World-Economy in the Sixteenth Century. Vol. I of *The Modern World System*. New York, NY: Academic Press.
Walzer, M. (1965). *The Revolution of the Saints*, Cambridge, MA: Harvard University Press.
Watkins, J. W. N. (1952). The Principle of Methodological Individualism. *British Journal of the Philosophy of Science*, 3(10), 186–89.
Watkins, J. W. N. (1957). Historical Explanation in the Social Sciences. *British Journal for the Philosophy of Science*, 8(30), 104–17.
Weber, M. [1904/1905] 1996. *The Protestant Ethic and the Spirit of Capitalism*, Los Angeles, CA: Roxbury.

Weber, M. [1920] 1996. Max Weber's Introduction to the Sociology of Religion (1920). In M. Weber, *The Protestant Ethic and the Spirit of Capitalism*. Los Angeles, CA: Roxbury, pp. 13–31.

Weber, M. [1923] 1950. *General Economic History*, Glencoe, IL: Free Press.

Werner, K. F. (1988). Political and Social Structures of the West. In J. Baechler, J. A. Hall & M. Mann, eds., *Europe and the Rise of Capitalism*. Oxford: Basil Blackwell, pp. 169–84.

White, H. (1970). *Chains of Opportunity*, Cambridge: Harvard University Press.

White, H. (1992). *Identity and Control*, Princeton, NJ: Princeton University Press.

White, L., Jr. (1978). *Medieval Religion and Technology*, Berkeley, CA: University of California Press.

Wilson, E. O. (1998). *Consilience*, New York, NY: Knopf.

Wippler, R. (1978). The Structural-Individualistic Approach in Dutch Sociology. *Netherlands Journal of Sociology*, 14, 135–55.

Wippler, R. & S. Lindenberg. (1987). Collective Phenomena and Rational Choice. In J. C. Alexander, B. Giesen, R. Münch, & N. J. Smelser, eds., *The Micro-Macro Link*. Berkeley, CA: University of California Press.

Wuthnow, R. (1989). *Communities of Discourse*, Cambridge, MA: Harvard University Press.

Zahle, J. (2007). Holism and Supervenience. In S. P. Turner & M. W. Risjord, eds., *Philosophy of Anthropology and Sociology*. Amsterdam: Elsevier, pp. 311–42.

Zaret, D. (1989). Religion and the Rise of Liberal-Democratic Ideology in 17th-Century England. *American Sociological Review*, 54(2), 163–79.

Zetterberg, H. L. (1965). *On Theory and Verification in Sociology*, 3rd edn, Totowa, NJ: Bedminster Press.

Zetterberg, H. L. (1993). Rationalism and Capitalism: Max Weber. Ch. 2 of the web publication, *European Proponents of Sociology Prior to World War*, zetterberg.org.

7 The Limiting Effects of Analytical Individualism:

Examples from Macrosocial Change (2007)

R. JEPPERSON AND J. MEYER[*]

Real explanatory discussion, in historical and comparative research, has moved in broad and contextualizing directions, far removed from the formalisms of a doctrinal individualism. It necessarily relies upon social-organizational and institutional argumentation, as well as on individual-level ideas. Hence real theory, operative in actual intended explanations, tends to be sharply decoupled from theory in the more normative and scientist sense.

In this section, we illustrate the limitations imposed by doctrinal individualism. As a transition, we begin with conceptualizations of European religious culture. We then give examples from discussions of European economic development, European modernity in general, postindustrial development, and world development and globalization. The intellectual limitations we are concerned with are notably: (a) an exaggerated emphasis upon individual-level causal formulations (often implausible ones); (b) failure to consider processes operating at other levels, including especially the most institutional and cultural levels; and (c) failure to consider interactions between more institutional and more individual-level processes.

7.1 Conceptualizing European Religious Culture in General

We note is passing, first, that the prominent but artificial Protestant Ethic thesis directed attention away from the substantive literature on

---

[*] This chapter continues and extends with empirical examples the discussion in the previous chapter. It is an excerpt (pp. 281–299) from "Analytical Individualism and the Explanation of Macrosocial Change," originally published in *On Capitalism*, ed. by V. Nee and R. Swedberg (Stanford University Press, 2007), pp. 273–304. We have benefited from comments from Al Bergesen, David Frank, Peter Meyer, Francisco Ramirez, Ann Swidler, and the participants at the 2004 conference that provided the basis for the above book.

Protestantism and its historical context. This literature, beginning with Weber himself, considered more institutional-level roles of Protestantism (e.g., Butterfield 1950, 1979; McNeill 1963; Walzer 1965; Merton 1973; more recently Fulbrook 1983; Zaret 1985; Wuthnow 1987; Gorski 2003). In this literature, Protestantism is represented (if in various ways) as a phase in a long-term process of European rationalization of social structures in terms of models of nature as lawful, and of society as a modifiable system, with a strong individual as its bottom-line element. Thus, far beyond the narrow economistic individual depicted in the Protestant Ethic thesis, the ideological movements surrounding the Reformation built expanded models of nature (thus science) and of the human collective society (thus the national state) and set individuals in legitimated relation to both.

Second, the Protestant Ethic thesis has also deflected theoretical attention from the broader effects, including collective ideological effects, of Christianity itself. For instance, there are the ways that Christian models of society promoted (in comparative perspective) "the destruction of the extended family" – the "religious institutionalization of equality was the foundation upon which an autonomous bourgeoisie developed in the cities of western Europe" (Bendix 1960: 417; cf. Collins 1980, Goody 1983). There are the ways that Christianity constantly "promoted moral and social improvement" (Mann 1986: 398), one of the sources of the oft-noted "rational restlessness" (Weber) or "activism" (Eisenstadt 1987: 11–13) of European civilization. There are the ways that Christian religious orders developed ideologies of economic rationalization (Collins 1986, 1999; Werner 1988). Points such as these have been well established in scholarly literatures, as the citations to central figures suggest. However, such points, despite their substantive centrality, have not much entered into the dominant meta-theoretical discourses about European development.

The reason is that the narrow Protestant Ethic thesis conceptualized religion, anachronistically, as a set of beliefs held by individual persons, not as a fundamental culture and organizational system of a European polity. This approach, by no means incidentally, treats religion in the preferred format of modern individualistic ideology. Looking through the wrong end of a historical telescope, it tends almost entirely to miss the institutional centrality of historical Christendom.

In this connection, and as background for the sections that follow, we wish to delineate three very basic changes in Western cultural models within Christendom. These changes help to capture long-term patterns in institutional development – patterns that have been sustained, as we will indicate, in the contemporary period. We refer to the evolution and institutionalization of a cultural model that envisions a *rationalized and progressive society*, made up of *empowered individuals*, and functioning in a *lawful nature* (cf. Eisenstadt 1999: 51–67).

Thus, one development involves the cultural-institutional shift toward what we now call individualism. In the cultural models of Christendom, intensified with Protestantism but antedating it, individual persons acting in a real world are placed at the center of things and are to be valued and empowered by themselves, others, and authorities. This feature is deeply institutionalized. For instance, it is located in principles of individual citizenship, which have an early origin, as Weber stressed (Bendix 1960; Bendix 1964; Collins 1980). In the contemporary period, these cultural principles are reformulated in broadened ideas of human rights (Ramirez and Meyer 2002). The underlying principles have been carried in sweeping social, cultural, and religious movements and lodged in legal and doctrinal systems (Meyer and Jepperson 2000; Frank and Meyer 2002). These movements have been relatively independent from economic developments, and the logic of capitalism has not been an especially important causal factor.

A second long-term cultural-institutional dynamic is the shift in models of collective society from liturgical to systemic (Duby 1980). Like the individual, society is envisioned as capable of improvement – it can and should progress, via rational strategies of action in a world that can be analyzed as lawful. This picture of society has a transcendent character, revealed for instance in the modern universalist assumption that development can occur anywhere. Through many transformations in Western history, from the Renaissance, Reformation, and Enlightenment down to contemporary development theories, an increasingly detailed analysis of society itself has been produced. In this analysis, society's components are desacralized (individuals aside) and seen as properly under systemic control.

A third change is indeed the long-term shift in conceptions of nature from fallen and disorderly and arbitrary to analyzable and lawful. The modern authority of science reflects a long-term outcome of this set of assumptions (Butterfield 1950; Huff 1995; Drori et al. 2003).

Integrating these components is the underlying principle of rationalization, taking three forms.[1] First, one can discern tightening organization of the Western European cultural ontology around its three primary elements: individual, society, and nature. Second, one can discern the ongoing elaboration of each element: expanded ideas (and constructions) of the individual; expanded ideas (and "structuration") of society; expanded ideas of (and technological interaction with) nature. Third, one can discern the ongoing systematization of the relations among the main elements – what is ordinarily meant by the term rationalization. So, in the evolving cultural model, the hard-wired individual and the systemic society can be linked together (and linked with nature) in elaborately rationalized structures. Society and individual are not fundamentally at odds. The proper individual can be integrated into the good society under the laws of nature, in ways that violate the integrity of none of these elements. This project naturally requires and justifies enormously expanded and differentiated organizational structures, to pursue technical relations with nature, and social ones between individual and society (cf. Giddens 1986 on "structuration"). In this project, a great many social structures of the pre-modern world are weakened and delegitimated (most prominently those linked to the old Church), and a great many new rationalized and differentiated ones are created (such as rationalized corporate organizations). We wish to invoke this evolving cultural-institutional framework in the sections that follow.

7.2 Accounting for European Economic History

For a long time, accounts of European economic development have been constrained by doctrinal individualism, taking the specific form of economism. Various analysts have detected an (Adam) "Smithian" imagery in the literature, a representation of European economic development as if it were the story of the liberation of a natural exchange system. (Marx famously complained about this tendency, of course.) Remarkable as it may seem, it is still probably accurate to say that the European economic system (and hence "capitalism" itself) has been taken for granted to some degree – and hence under-theorized. For instance, when the economic historian E. L. Jones reviewed the literature in 1980, he "found little directly on the rise of the market except in the oldest literature" (Jones 1981: 243). When Robert Brenner reviewed neo-Marxian work on capitalism, including the first volume of Wallerstein's *The Modern World System*, he found "neo-Smithians" who implicitly assumed that "capitalism was there before it emerged" (Macfarlane 1988: 191 epitomizing Brenner 1977). When Michael Mann completed his more recent synthesis of the historical literature, he observed that prominent neoclassical accounts (by North and Thomas, for instance) seemed to "assume the existence of a market in the first place" (Mann 1986: 411).

Jones pointed out that the explanandum for European economic development was obviously "much more than the usual conception of an economic process" (Jones 1981: 238), involving structural changes normally held constant by economists (see North 1981: 57). Struggling with this issue earlier, Weber complained numerous times about what we would now call the naturalizing of capitalism. For instance, he criticized the tendency to see the "impulse to acquisition, pursuit of gain, of money, of the greatest possible amount of money" as the key to the European economic story: These have in themselves "nothing to do with capitalism. ... It should be taught in the kindergarten of cultural history that this naïve idea of capitalism must be given up once and for all" (Weber [1920] 1996: 17).

For Weber, the essence of modern "rationalized" capitalism as an economic system was the expansion of production by the method of market-oriented "enterprise." When he tried to delineate this rationalized capitalism specifically, however, Weber found he had to describe an elaborate institutional complex of production arrangements, legal arrangements, markets, and financial structures (see Bendix 1960: esp. 53–54). Moreover, he had a hard time distinguishing these defining characteristics from their preconditions – that is, it was hard to isolate an economy, in any narrowly defined sense (Stinchcombe 2004: 429–431; also Bendix 1960). So, although Weber talked about "capitalism," following Marxian precedent, in practice his actual explanandum was a broad institutional system, including a normative order.[2] For instance, Weber reminded that capitalism may "even be identical with the restraint, or at least a rational tempering" of "unlimited greed for gain" (Weber [1920] 1996: 17). As a broadly defined institutional (and normative) system, this capitalism embodied an ideology of collective progress, one that entailed far more than mere support for individual accumulation. The legitimation of enterprise authority, and of freedom of contracting, was central to the expansion and stabilization of capitalism. This legitimation was provided by an

The Limiting Effects of Analytical Individualism 175

ideology of economic and social progress that, as we have discussed, was bound up with the system (Stinchcombe 2004; Hirschman 1977).[3]

As later scholars problematized the European economic system, they have also followed Weber (consciously or not) in reconceptualizing the issue of explaining it. This move has occurred along two axes. First, causal reasoning has become broader and more systemic: More and more dimensions of institutional structure have been seen as centrally involved in the historical development. Second, causal forces have been conceived to operate over longer periods. We consider these points in turn.

First, in reasoning at the institutional level, one focuses upon broad organizational and cultural systems rather than more narrowly defined causal structures, such as shifts in the motives of some businessmen or the development of a few new technologies.[4] Because the explanandum, European development, is itself an institutional (and normative) system, broad political, religious, and cultural forces are likely to be intertwined with it. The evolution of Douglass North's work is illustrative. As North came to stress, "[t]he simple fact is that a dynamic theory of institutional change limited to the strictly neoclassical constraint of individualistic, rational purposive activity would never allow us to explain most secular [economic] change" (North 1981: 58). A proper account of the economic "rise of the West" seemed to require, he argued, a whole set of interrelated arguments: in his language, a theory of demographic change, a theory of the growth in the stock of knowledge, and a theory of institutions (including property rights, the state, and ideology) (1981: 7). The details are not what is relevant here; the point is that the historical record motivated a move far beyond any standard economism. It is interesting to note that this move in a way recapitulates Weber's earlier investigations. For Weber, broad processes of political and cultural rationalization – as reflected in the development of the bureaucratic and representative state and of a more universalist economic ethic – became main causes of European economic development (see Collins's reconstruction [1980]). Both North and Weber were drawn from the details of production and exchange into delineations of broad sociocultural systems that give value and meaning to some activities and withdraw them from others. Their efforts are representative of current substantive discussion.

Second, the time frame for causal analysis has lengthened greatly. Ideas about a dramatic "industrial revolution" are no longer dominant in the substantive literature. For instance, in Mann's explicit discussion of possible formulations, the European economic explanandum becomes "an extraordinarily long and almost continuous process [of economic development] lasting from before AD 1000 to 1800" and beyond (Mann 1988: 9; cf. Jones 1987: xx–xxi, Cameron 1989, Maddison 2001).

These two shifts in the substantive discussion – both causal broadening and lengthening – have redirected attention to Christendom as a cultural and institutional complex. For some time one would not have heard about Christendom in theoretical talk about European "modernization." From the point of view of intendedly hardboiled European history, the history of the Church and of religion in general was properly located in a separate academic field. A modern scholar could be quite conversant with European history and know almost nothing about the religious component. From the point of view of analytical individualism, Christendom is too broad a construct, operating over too long a time frame. Broad institutional frameworks were to be bracketed (as too macrosociological) or were somehow seen as ineffable (as too cultural or "ideal").

However, in Mann's reconstruction – to stay with what must be the high point of recent substantive work – Christendom as a cultural-institutional framework operates as a cause in a number of fundamental institutional-level ways. For example, in Mann's account, Christendom created a "minimal society," with some "normative order" and (relative) "pacification." Early on, it institutionalized and legitimated effective local possession of autonomous economic resources and allowed goods to be commodities of exchange (Mann 1986: 406–407). Christian doctrine was a source of constant social (including economic) rationalization efforts. Complementary work by Collins stresses that Christendom's monastic orders (as in Asia) served as an initial "leading edge" of economic "breakout" from the existing coercive-agrarian economies; they were the initial commercial nodes and development engines (Collins 1986, 1999).

It is striking to note that current economic historians have featured long-term institutional-level processes too, in ways that have been missed. Economic theory tells economic historians that the engine of growth is economically useful knowledge (DeLong, forthcoming). This premise has directed their attention to knowledge systems, and then recently to science as a set of socially enabling institutions (Mokyr

2002). For example, Joel Mokyr says that economic historians, despite their differences, have one central agreement about European economic development: "Europeans knew more" – they "learned rather greedily" and wanted to apply what they learned (Mokyr 1999). Jones, in a related conclusion, noted that Europe always seemed to have "a number of individuals whose creative talents were directed to improving the means of production" (Jones 1981: 228).

This application of economic theory leads in directions that move far away from analytically individualist economism. The processes, involving knowledge systems, are institutional-level. Invocation of knowledge systems goes beyond the institutional effects called attention to by North to include the broader rationalization projects of European culture: monastic orders, scientific societies, universities, educational systems. As we discuss in detail in the following, the consequences of such rationalization projects and knowledge systems also extend far beyond the economic, creating all sorts of feedback effects (e.g., through institutions like democracy).

Talk about knowledge systems produces "analytic narratives" in economic theory that are not primarily individual-level ones, despite ideological attempts to argue that they must be (e.g., by Bates et al. 1998). And the "mechanisms," in the substantive literature, are not limited to individual-level ones. Knowledge systems include great institutions like science, the university, a whole educational apparatus, and a host of highly organized professions. These structures have roles and legitimating principles extending far beyond the motives of individual persons (Drori et al. 2003).

These intellectual developments are insufficiently recognized in self-consciously theoretical domains, given the discursive dominance of analytical individualism. Analysts fail to follow the theoretical implications of their own work. For instance, Mokyr often defaults to locating innovation in individuals, not in systems that select innovations, a far more plausible starting place for explanation (1992, 2002).[5] Landes has been criticized for invoking "culture" (in Landes 1998) as a master explanation in rather undisciplined ways, often involving vague "attitudes." We argue that analytical individualism hinders more substantial theoretical syntheses. For instance, (economic historian) Landes does not draw upon (macrosociologist) Mann's work, or upon (macrosociologist) Collins' directly relevant discussions comparing Chinese, Japanese, and European "religious capitalisms" (Collins 1986, 1999) – let alone upon sociological theory more broadly considered.

One simple way to review the preceding discussion is to note that the theory associated with analytic individualism has become more narrowly economistic (and individualistic) over time, to an impressively formalized degree. However, the substantive discussion of Western economic expansion has become less and less economistic (cf. Cameron 1989: 9–16, Engerman 2000). It has seen the Western economy as itself a broadly institutional and cultural construction, full of meanings and legitimations as much as instrumental motivations, and as intertwined with and embedded in long-lived institutional frameworks.

7.3 European Modernity in General

A core theme of analytical individualism – with its picture of history as produced by hard-wired, autonomous, and purposive individual actors – is that private instrumental goals represent the central mechanism driving historical change. For the most part, this theme gives pride of place to material economic forces in interpreting history. As modern society and its individualistic culture have developed over recent periods, this line of thought has become more extreme and intensified as formalized economistic theory. However, in striking opposition, substantive historical analyses focusing on the rise of Europe have gone in the opposite direction, seeing European rationalization and development as taking place in many different institutional sectors.

Economism, of course, is embedded in the broader narrative of modernity: Much intellectual and popular discourse has treated the core of that history as fundamentally economic. Modernity is "capitalism." The societies are "capitalist societies" or "industrial societies" – identifying societies with economic characteristics is common practice. The familiar materialist narratives rendered economic rationalization as the primary driving force, with other forms of rationalization as defensive consequences. Powerful economic forces of rationalization destroy an older society, the story went. Ultimately, in defensive balancing through multitudes of protests, political and cultural and educational rationalization arises from attempts to control the economic forces (a central version is Polanyi [1944] 1957). Mechanisms like anomie, or relative deprivation, or other defensive processes, were advanced (as in mass society theories, which despite empirical failure retain their many lives in the current period). The narrative was often given an individualist flavor, as if heroic (or demonic) capitalists and authentic (or explosively irrational) laborers, as individuals, were at the center of historical causation.

Mann finds that dominant neoclassical economic theories still "[see] history as capitalism writ large" (Mann 1986: 534). When Braudel reflected upon his own corpus of work, and upon European history writ large, he criticized Weber and the entire ensuing literature for its "exaggeration of capitalism's role as promoter of the modern world" (Braudel 1977: 67). Debates about the "transition from feudalism to capitalism," or about "the industrial revolution," located very sharply in space and time, became distillations of European modernity itself. Even the path-breaking works by Wallerstein (1974) and Perry Anderson (1974) largely identify the modern world system with the economy (in Anderson's case, by stretching the concept of "mode of production" to the breaking point). Some exceedingly narrow accounts of modernity offer economic magic bullets of one sort or another: new ploughs or ships or property rights.

The economistic imagery has not held up well under examination. Contemporary substantive work no longer treats as obvious that industrial capitalism in material production was the special breakthrough to modernity in history. The originating history has been pushed back, repeatedly: from nineteenth-century industrialization back through capitalism, Protestantism, science, urbanization, commercialization, medieval Christendom, agricultural revolution, into an institutional-ecological matrix preceding 1000 (see Mann's characterization of the literature [Mann 1988: 11–12], which is broadly concurrent with that of Landes [1998], Cameron [1989], and Maddison [2001]).

In following the record back, it has become clear that dominant theoretical narratives, in so focusing upon economic rationalization, elided Weber's other main dimension of European development: the long-term reconstruction of institutional life around rationalized bureaucracy, law, science, and individualism. In fact, the historical literature discusses social rationalization across a very broad front, one by no means especially concentrated upon economic matters. In the political system, there is the rise and legitimation of the national state in Europe's earliest periods (Strayer 1973), in its later development (Wuthnow 1989; Toulmin

1992), and in our own time (Meyer et al. 1997). There is rationalized education, which expanded dramatically after the Reformation and continues to expand at even greater rates in recent decades (Boli 1989; Schofer and Meyer 2005). There is rationalization in the religious system itself, with the rise of modern organizational forms in both denominations and congregations (e.g., Chaves and Sutton 2004). There is science, a core institution of the modern system, sometimes linked to economic activity, but typically not. Despite fashionable contemporary theoretical attempts to see close links, the capitalists are not really behind Galileo's search for moons around Jupiter and in our own time are not particularly behind the search for life on these moons. Expanding dramatically after the Reformation, science only acquired strong economic linkages in the late nineteenth and twentieth centuries (Merton 1973; Mann 1986:471; Wuthnow 1987; Huff 1995). Even for our own time, theoretical and ideological literatures have greatly overstated the closeness of the linkages (Drori et al. 2003).

This situation is typical and reflects the defects of economistic analytical individualism. In analyzing science, education, or the rise of the (bureaucratic and democratic) state, theorists place heavy emphasis on the causal force of economic (or capitalist) development, just as they stress the putative services such institutions provide for the economy (or capitalist economy). The researchers who actually study the rise of these modern institutions do not generally find the theoretically assumed close linkages.[6] Researchers on educational expansion historically and in our own period, for example, were surprised to discover how weak the effects of economic development were (see Chabbott and Ramirez 2000 for a general review). In America and elsewhere, educational expansion preceded capitalist expansion. In the period since World War II, education expansion has been endemic, yet almost unrelated to economic conditions (Meyer et al. 1977; Meyer, Ramirez, and Soysal 1992). The same conclusions are reached by those who actually study scientific (or political) development. The rationalized institutions of modernity, in short, arise out of long-term institutional developments in European history.

Classical economisms rested on the assumption, best articulated by Marx and Engels, that only material production revealed a true developmental history (Marx and Engels [1845–46] 1978: e.g., 154–155). This assumption, brought to light and measured against the full historical record, has not remained plausible. European political, cultural, and economic development has seemed too much of a piece, one not expressible in terms of any magic independent variable. The most intensive recent examination of the causal issues involved in explaining European modernity has undoubtedly been Mann's (1979, 1986, 1988, 1993). In grappling with historical materials, Mann found that he was compelled to distinguish four independent engines driving historical development: economic, political, military, and ideological (an imagery partly captured in the title of Ernest Gellner's complementary effort *Plough, Sword, and Book* [Gellner 1990].) Further, Mann was unable to assign any general primacy among them: In one historical period, one driver seems the dominant "reorganizing, tracklaying force," at other times another one. Recall too that North, addressing economic outcomes only, was driven to invoke political and ideological histories, exogenous to his economic account.

Here we do not mean to endorse any particular formulation. We simply note that such substantive developments are not as theoretically prominent as they should be. When theory is so much at odds with substantive research, there are those who take the scientific position that reality must quickly be modified (currently, in a variety of neoliberal projects). We take the scientific view that perhaps modern analytical individualist theory is imperfect and needs much repair.

7.4 Later Modernity and Postindustrial Development

Interpretations of our own societies and times show the same conspicuous disjunctions between doctrinal theory and more substantive analysis. There is a continuing overstatement of the centrality of economic rationalization and a great underemphasis on political, administrative, educational, scientific, and medical rationalization. In analyzing rationalization, there is an over-emphasis on the differentiation of structures and underattention to continuing social construction: the expansion of contemporary individuality, the ongoing elaboration of contemporary society. In analyzing the "economy" itself, there is too little attention to the institutional or cultural embeddedness of its activities and structure.

Empirical assessments of long institutional trends find several interrelated strands, not just one. There is indeed the ongoing expansion of the exchange system and rationalization of it. There is of course more and more elaborate monetarization and market coordination and financial structuration: Money has truly become a more generalized medium of exchange. Along with these changes one finds an expansion in *conceptions* of the economy – the imagined economy enlarges greatly – a cultural and institutional form now extending to a global level.

There is also the expansion of a host of noneconomic institutions, structures, and social strata, the extraordinary expansion of noneconomic criteria in assessments of social life and its goals, and the astonishing capacity of modern people (for better or worse) to act collectively in completely noneconomic ways. Theoretical discourse has concentrated upon the first strand: The common assumption has been that the dominant institutional trends in later modernity have been economic. Dominant narratives have missed (or downplayed unrealistically) the second strand: the expanded polity and the expanded society – that is, the continuation of institutional processes discussed in the previous section. Here we indicate the main lacunae.

First, most basic, theoretical accounts still somehow leave out the expansion of sociopolitical controls over of the economy. All the contemporary "capitalisms" did truly become "political economies." With the rise of big government and the expansion of law, they are all more collectivist, in a sense more "communal," in Daniel Bell's formulation (Bell 1973). One forgets that Schumpeter and Polanyi were so struck by differences from the nineteenth century that they envisioned "the passing of the market economy," at least in the strict sense (Polanyi 1977). To them, the twentieth century primarily represented a massive growth in planning, what J. R. Hicks called the "administrative revolution" (Hicks 1969: chap. 10). In fact, in long-term perspective – and despite the current neoliberal period – "criteria of individual utility and profit maximization [have] become subordinated to broader conceptions of social welfare and community interest" (Bell 1973: 481). We would add that criteria of utility, both individual and collective, have been elaborated as well – there are many new forms of politically constructed value. Here, with Bell, we are referring to the expansion of explicitly conceived public goods and services: environmental protection, public health, individual health, education, and all sorts of media of self-expression.

Second, we engage in mental gymnastics to conceptualize our own society as if it were principally an economy in the old sense of commodity production (see Block 1990). This tendency involves an unfortunate equating of rationalization with monetarization, and monetarization with traditional meanings of the *economic*. However, most rationalization in the modern system, whether monetarized or not, is not traditionally economic in character (i.e., concerned with anything about commodity production or exchange). Most of it lies in rationalized educational arrangements (with their credentials and credits), medical arrangements (with their procedural definitions of care as a service, their elaborated professional and organizational forms), administrative structures in public and private life (with elaborate systems of authority and prestige), and so on. There is the rise of a whole set of institutions helping people manage a rationalized family life and, for that matter, a rationalized and elaborated life course (Meyer 1986; Meyer and Jepperson 2000). There is the now vast range of nonprofit organizations, principally engaged in the noneconomic rationalizations of the modern system, present in both national and world domains (Boli and Thomas 1999).

Within what is loosely called the economy itself the same processes of cultural elaboration and rationalization go on, little related to the logics of capitalism and the means of production. Modern firms have an astonishing array of management structures far removed from production and responding to political and cultural demands from the environment: safety people, environment people, legal officers, public relations people, accountants and economists, and so on and on. For none of these people can clear measures of economic productivity be established. All these managers, many trained in business schools with little hint of knowledge about or interest in productive forces, represent forms of rationalization very distant from what was once called, or thought of as, the economy.

Third, when rationalization involves monetarization – which it certainly often does – there is no reason to imagine that the money involved is a particularly economic commodity in the traditional sense of production and exchange. True, people are paid for something called *work* (a modern metaphor based in classic notions of labor), but think how far their activities depart from the archetypes of household or agricultural or industrial labor. People are paid, yes, but for activities that by only the greatest stretch can be called economic in any original sense – they are paid as schoolteachers, administrators, child care workers, medical personnel, counselors, and so on. Much of the money received in these activities is spent outside the commodity economy proper. A related observation can be made about profit. It is certainly a central mechanism (although with the expansion of government and non-profits, obviously not an exclusive one), but firms accumulate it by producing not only commodities but the most broadly imaginable human services.

The point is that money, in the modern system, is far removed from any narrowly defined economy. Parsons argued that money is a generalized medium of exchange; it would be better to say, now, that it has become a generalized medium of value. Marx wrote about the power of money in bourgeois society, imagining that this power reflected economic causation in history, and modern people tend to think that way, too. (When we see the university, for instance, as too greatly influenced by considerations of money, we assume without reflection that this means by economic power.) It would be better to parallel Marx's insight with the idea that bourgeois society also developed enormous power over money: Money has, in a way, been socially appropriated, transforming it. Money, originally a narrowly economic commodity, is used to value pastors, teachers, professors, therapists, child care providers, "sex workers," students of the moons of Jupiter, and the widest variety of administrators. It is also used to support the widest array of identity activities and choices of modern persons, generated by the extraordinary legitimation of ideas of expansive personhood and its expression (Frank and Meyer 2002).

Is the monetarized economy dominating society? Or does society dominate the economy? *Both* economization and sociopolitical embeddedness have occurred and are consequences of long-run institutional developments. An analysis that focuses only on one question (like conventional economic thinking) is an interesting ideological outcome of the evolving system, but not one to be taken very seriously in substance.

Fourth, the expansion of money, as interpreted via analytically individualist ideology, has produced a vast imagined economy and an unclearly delineated one. At the extreme, the economy is thought to be present wherever exchange of any utilities is to be found. With such extraordinary concept stretching, arbitrary conflations are quick to follow. For instance, one looks for utilities – say, in family interaction – and then assumes that price-like dynamics are operative and predominant. Or, one defines the economic in terms of monetarization, and then assumes, say, that market dynamics are present – because the economic is also often associated with markets. Work is monetarized and incomes attached to jobs do have some market-like dynamics. So then one speaks freely of "labor markets" and treats pay patterns as straightforward market outcomes (as in sociology's "functional theory of stratification" and in conventional microeconomic characterizations). Yet we know from empirical research that pay is not principally established in markets (e.g., Granovetter and Tilly 1988). Educational status, for instance – a central definer of both individual and occupational positions in the modern order – has principally nonmarket bases. Somehow we imagine that the factors affecting pay – say, those producing the large cross-national differences in how much top executives make – are deflections from some sort of true underlying market value. The problematic reification of markets is readily apparent.

With such expansive conceptualization, the properties of money or markets or utilities – or any rationalization – are projected onto one another, in a way that forecloses serious analysis. Economism becomes child's play. For instance, note the current popularity of the concept *capital*: We now have human, cultural, social, and political capitals, routinely invoked in serious literatures. Although it is empirically the case that various factors affect whether (or where) a child goes to college, calling them capital, and then treating college attendance as an economic profit center, is a gross distortion. The economistic parlance of "capital" has great attraction, however, because economics is imagined as somehow most fundamental.

The vast imagined economy is an element, ultimately, of analytical individualism. Social structures that have been highly rationalized – like labor allocation and pay structures – are treated as merely economic and then built around individual choices (choice of a job, a career, a school). These choices can then be reified and focused upon, with institutional context and construction backgrounded, at best. We extend this point in our concluding section.

7.5 World Development and Globalization

Recent attention has shifted from national to regional and world levels of social organization and development. The term *globalization* has become intensely fashionable, along with a sense that forces operating at the world level have taken on lives of their own. Much of the discussion follows the familiar patterns of earlier discourse analyzing national-level developments.

Thus, globalization is commonly taken to mean economic globalization and the spread of a world capitalism. The discussion misses the rapid modern construction of a world society that transcends economic linkages (Meyer 2002). Much of modern world globalization builds its institutions not around economic controls, but around political and cultural ones (following the disaster of World War II and the crises of the Cold War). Thus we have an explosively expanding world organizational system (Boli and Thomas 1999), a network of standardizing controls over national states (Meyer et al. 1997), huge world human rights and environmental mobilizations (Ramirez and Meyer 2003; Frank and Meyer 2002), and an exponentially growing world educational system built around common mass and elite institutions (Meyer and Ramirez 2000; Schofer and Meyer 2004). All of these institutional arrangements occur prior to, and relatively independently of, recent expansions in economic exchange. Many are actually sources of ongoing socioeconomic rationalization.

The world economy itself is a much more collectively oriented structure than we perceive: Its institutions are infused with ideas about world collective goods. Massive numbers of intergovernmental and nongovernmental associations pursue goals thought to benefit the world as a whole (Boli and Thomas 1999). Countries are routinely asked to change economic or environmental policies in the interests of the world rather than the country itself, and organizations like the World Bank proclaim and try to represent principles of ecology and of human rights.

We have, in short, a rapidly expanding global society, filled with all sorts of rationalized institutions. Nominally economic and noneconomic institutions clearly affect one another in all sorts of ways. For example, current world free-trade ideologies directly reflect ideas of the world as a single society. So do the forces that resist expanded world free trade – these groups too have a strikingly globalized character and act in terms of political and cultural norms that are now global in character. Oddly enough, both sides of the modern (and partly mock) globalization/antiglobalization battles pretend to agree with an entirely inadequate and traditional analysis. The globalization forces, in this primitive analysis, represent demonic (or virtuous) forces of world capitalism. The antiglobalization forces represent defensive or progressive (or irrational and reactionary) attempts by put-upon local communities beset by this capitalism – the old narrative, once again.

The whole analysis is distorted. It ignores the breadth of the global institutionalization process – the range of the institutional forces involved, and the extent to which they celebrate (in various and conflicting versions) models of a world society of free modern individuals. It also tends to ignore the extent to which these broader institutionalized cultural forces cause rather than simply reflect changed patterns of nominally economic relations. Faced with this expansive institutional system, producing rapid change everywhere in the world, theoretical analyses rooted in an economistic individualism have been bloodless. It is impossible to think seriously about all this change if it is seen merely in terms of economic globalization.

7.6 Conclusions and Reflections

In this paper, we presented the conventionalized Protestant Ethic thesis as an exemplar of a dominant intellectual culture of modern (especially American) social science – analytical individualism. Weber's narrow thesis, in the *Protestant Ethic*, has effectively been absorbed in a broad literature on Western rationalization. This rationalization covers many institutions, has long historical roots, and continues into our own time. It centrally involves the invention of stronger and stronger models of society as a social system. Even more centrally (at least in liberal forms), it involves the invention of stronger models of the individual as "actor" (Meyer and Jepperson 2000; Frank and Meyer 2002). In every institutional sector, processes of differentiation and rationalization have more and more tightly defined the goods of individual and society and created elaborate roles and organizational structures linking the two (and embedding both in a scientized Nature).

However, a prominent individualist theoretical discourse represents the social world as created and changed by something called "individuals," in quite a strong sense: This individual, in much Western theory, is the dramatic actor in history, and acquires this actorhood either through nature or through religious legitimation. This imagery is especially prominent in the liberal versions of Western ideology, which have been influential or dominant throughout the modern period. Corporatist or statist alternatives also focus on the individual (often more as imagined beneficiary than as creator of the social world), but to a lesser extent (see Jepperson 2002 for a typology and analysis). In recent decades, during which the individualist and reductionist aspects of the Weber thesis have been given special attention, liberalism has turned quite triumphant.

The tendency to see the individual as a very real (i.e., natural and materially focused) center for the social universe goes far beyond a decorative meta-theoretical individualism. It infuses (and, from an analytic point of view, distorts) the Western intellectual, social, and policy self-conceptions and analyses. We call anything rationalized "economic" and even more see anything monetarized as "economic." We root our explanations of these things in an individualist rhetoric, understating the extraordinary power of ideas (models, myths) of the collective good in modern social change. We become ideologues of the modern system's individualism, instead of analyzing this individualism and economism as something like a religious form.

The fact that contemporary social science operates within a vast and highly institutionalized system sustains individualist mythology. If they are so inclined, social scientists can simply take for granted the elaborate rationalization and institutionalization and then focus upon individual behaviors in investment, labor, innovation, management, and the like. One can rest content that such behaviors, construed as choices, somehow "ultimately" produce and reproduce the system. (One can likewise take for granted the role structure of organizations and institutions and treat people as merely typical individuals making decisions.) In fact, the more extensive and secure the institutionalization, the more that one can cultivate exclusively individualistic intellectual tastes. From a strictly scientific standpoint, the recurring causes of an institutionalized system are institutional reproduction routines, along with processes of institutional change (Jepperson 1991; Scott 2001). Yet this institutional reproduction (and change) may merely be set aside intellectually as somehow not truly fundamental. One can then imagine that all causation is merely individual action subject to constraints. Taking for granted an elaborate system, one can also imagine that no cultural dynamics are present: just raw individuals – more truly natural now, in emancipated modernity – making their choices.

Until very recently, this mythology has been constructed around ideas of national societies. In recent decades, these ideas have come undone and cultural models have begun to depict society as global in character. This evolution destabilizes some social scientific thinking and in a curious way repeats at a world level some of the intellectual and ideological trends of the earlier evolution of the liberal national state and society.

The rapidly integrating world we observe is a strikingly liberal system, because it has almost no capacity for a strong state (Meyer 2002). Its political forms are thus like those observed by Tocqueville in the stateless nineteenth-century America. One such form is extraordinarily intensified liberal individualism – notions of the strong, socialized, involved, participatory individual human actor. Thus we get, on both right and left, very strong emphases on the individual in the modern globalized world. On the right, one finds sweeping doctrines about property rights, individual values, individual educational achievement, due process, and so on. On the left, one finds equally sweeping doctrines about human rights in other (more welfare-related) senses. The ideological uses of individualism, in other words, remain very much alive, and we can predict that Protestant Ethic–like theses – in the most individualist and reductionist forms – will continue to be a kind of proof text, now of global individualism. We can also predict that the distortions in social scientific analysis produced by such emphases will continue to shadow our analyses of the globalized world.

Notes

1. Weber used the term *rationalization* broadly to denote a wide range of projects of systematization and ordering: in his words, of "economic life, of technique, of scientific research, of military training, of law and administration," and even of "mystical contemplation" (Weber [1920] 1996: 26). He saw "Occidental rationalism" as itself a distinctive culture, propelled by various religious, political, and intellectual movements, and then institutionalized in various structures (like states, sciences, and professions – the great rationalizers of modern societies) (Muench 1994: chap. 9).
2. Parsons goes as far as to argue that "'Capitalism' in the sense in which Weber means it, must be regarded not as a form of economic organization alone, but as the distinctive pattern of a whole society. Terminologically this agreed with other schools of thought, notably the Marxian, of which Weber was acutely conscious." Parsons says that Weber often uses the term to refer to the "total institutional order" (Parsons 1951: 79).
3. Stinchcombe argues that the belief that capitalism brings progress was a "latent precondition" of capitalism in Weber's analysis. He gives reasons for concurring with Weber (Stinchcombe 2004: 429–431).

4. It is telling that a recent overview of "modern economic theory and development" opens by stating that "[d]evelopment is no longer seen primarily as a process of capital accumulation but rather as a process of organizational change" (Hoff and Stiglitz 2000: 389).
5. Our comments here parallel Braudel's criticism of Schumpeter for treating the entrepreneur as a "sort of *deus ex machina*" (1977: 63). However, we note that Mokyr in recent statements invokes explicitly macrocultural ideas, referring to the importance of an "epistemological" distinctiveness of Western culture and of an "industrial enlightenment" preceding nineteenth-century industrialization (Mokyr 2002).
6. For instance, Weber concluded that "capitalism has not been a decisive factor in the promotion of that form of 'rationalization' of the law which has been peculiar to the Continental West ever since the rise of Romanist studies in the medieval universities" (Weber [1925] 1954: 318). Contemporary studies have supported this judgment (e.g., Berman 1983: 538ff).

References

Anderson, P. (1974). *Lineages of the Absolutist State*, London: New Left Books.

Bates, R., A. Greif, M. Levi, J. Rosenthal, & B. R. Weingast. (1998). *Analytic Narratives*, Princeton, NJ: Princeton University Press.

Bell, D. (1973). *The Coming of Post-Industrial Society*, New York, NY: Basic Books.

Bendix, R. (1960). *Max Weber: An Intellectual Portrait*, Garden City, NY: Anchor.

Bendix, R. (1964). *Nation-Building and Citizenship*, New York, NY: John Wiley & Sons.

Block, F. (1990). *Postindustrial Possibilities: A Critique of Economic Discourse*, Berkeley, CA: University of California Press.

Boli, J. (1989). *New Citizens for a New Society*, Elmsford, NY: Pergamon.

Boli, J. & G. Thomas, eds. (1999). *Constructing World Culture: International Nongovernmental Organizations since 1875*, Stanford, CA: Stanford University Press.

Braudel, F. (1977). *Afterthoughts on Material Civilization and Capitalism*, Baltimore, MD: Johns Hopkins University Press.

Brenner, R. (1977). The Origins of Capitalist Development: A Critique of Neo-Smithian Marxism. *New Left Review*, 104, 25–92.

Butterfield, H. (1950). *The Origins of Modern Science, 1300–1800*, London: G. Bell and Sons.

Cameron, R. (1989). *A Concise Economic History of the World*, Oxford: Oxford University Press.
Chabbott, C. & F. Ramirez. (2000). Development and Education. In M. Hallinan, ed., *Handbook of the Sociology of Education*. New York, NY: Plenum, pp. 163–87.
Chaves, M. & J. Sutton. (2004). Organizational Consolidation in American Protestant Denominations, 1870–1990. *Journal for the Scientific Study of Religion*, 43(1), 41–66.
Coleman, J. S. (1986). Social Theory, Social Research, and a Theory of Action. *American Journal of Sociology*, 91(6), 1309–35.
Coleman, J. S. (1990). *Foundations of Social Theory*, Cambridge, MA: Harvard University Press.
Collins, R. (1980). Weber's Last Theory of Capitalism: A Systematization. *American Sociological Review*, 45(6), 925–42.
Collins, R. (1986). *Weberian Sociological Theory*, Cambridge: Cambridge University Press.
Collins, R. (1999). *Macrohistory*, Stanford, CA: Stanford University Press.
DeLong, J. B. Forthcoming. What Do We Really Know about Economic Growth? In M. Boskin, ed., *Economic Growth*. Stanford, CA: Hoover Institution.
Drori, G., J. W. Meyer, F. O. Ramirez & E. Schofer. (2003). *Science in the Modern World Polity: Institutionalization and Globalization*, Palo Alto, CA: Stanford University Press.
Duby, G. (1980). *The Three Orders: Feudal Society Imagined*, Chicago, IL: University of Chicago Press.
Eisenstadt, S. N. (1987). Centre Formation and Protest Movements. In S. N. Eisenstadt, L. Roniger, & A. Seligman, eds., *Centre Formation, Protest Movements and Class Structure in Europe and the United States*. London: Frances Pinter, pp. 7–23.
Eisenstadt, S. N. (1999). *Fundamentalism, Sectarianism, and Revolution*, Cambridge: Cambridge University Press.
Engerman, S. L. (2000). Max Weber as Economist and Economic Historian. In S. Turner, ed., *The Cambridge Companion to Weber*. Cambridge, UK: Cambridge University Press, pp. 256–71.
Frank, D. & J. W. Meyer. (2002). The Contemporary Identity Explosion: Individualizing Society in the Post-War Period. *Sociological Theory*, 20(1), 86–105.
Fulbrook, M. (1983). *Piety and Politics*, Cambridge: Cambridge University Press.
Gellner, E. (1990). *Plough, Sword, and Book*, Chicago, IL: University of Chicago Press.

Giddens, A. (1986). *The Constitution of Society: Outline of a Theory of Structuration*, Berkeley, CA: University of California Press.

Goody, J. (1983). *The Development of the Family and Marriage in Europe*, Cambridge: Cambridge University Press.

Gorski, P. S. (2003). *The Disciplinary Revolution*, Chicago, IL: University of Chicago Press.

Granovetter, M. & C. Tilly. (1988). Inequality and Labor Processes. In N. Smelser, ed., *Handbook of Sociology*. Newbury Park, CA: Sage, pp. 175–221.

Hicks, J. (1969). *A Theory of Economic History*, Oxford: Oxford University Press.

Hirschman, A. (1977). *The Passions and the Interests*, Princeton, NJ: Princeton University Press.

Hoff, K. & J. E. Stiglitz. (2000). Modern Economic Theory and Development. In G. M. Meier & J. E. Stiglitz, eds., *Frontiers of Development Economics*. New York, NY: Oxford University Press, pp. 389–459.

Huff, T. (1995). *The Rise of Early Modern Science: Islam, China and the West*, Cambridge, UK: Cambridge University Press.

Jepperson, R. L. (1991). Institutions, Institutional Effects, and Institutionalism. In W. W. Powell & P. J. DiMaggio, eds., *The New Institutionalism in Organizational Analysis*. Chicago, IL: University of Chicago Press, pp. 143–63.

Jepperson, R. L. (2002). Political Modernities: Disentangling Two Underlying Dimensions of Institutional Differentiation. *Sociological Theory*, 20(1), 61–85.

Jones, E. L. (1981). *The European Miracle*, New York, NY: Cambridge University Press.

Jones, E. L. (1987). *The European Miracle*, 2nd edn, New York, NY: Cambridge University Press.

Landes, D. S. (1998). *The Wealth and Poverty of Nations*, New York, NY: W. W. Norton & Company.

Macfarlane, A. (1988). The Cradle of Capitalism: The Case of England. In J. Baechler, J. A. Hall, & M. Mann, eds., *Europe and the Rise of Capitalism*. Oxford: Basil Blackwell, pp. 185–203.

Maddison, A. (2001). *The World Economy: A Millennial Perspective*, Paris: Organization for Economic Cooperation and Development.

Mann, M. (1979). Idealism and Materialism in Sociological Theory. In J. W. Freiberg, ed., *Critical Sociology*. New York, NY: Irvington Publishers, pp. 97–120.

Mann, M. (1986). A History of Power from the Beginning to A.D. 1760. Vol. I of *The Sources of Social Power*. Cambridge: Cambridge University Press.

Mann, M. (1988). European Development: Approaching a Historical Explanation. In J. Baechler, J. A. Hall, & M. Mann, eds., *Europe and the Rise of Capitalism*. Oxford: Basil Blackwell, pp. 6–19.

Mann, M. (1993). The Rise of Classes and Nation States, 1760–1914. Vol. II of *The Sources of Social Power*. Cambridge: Cambridge University Press.

Marx, K. & F. Engels. [1845–46] 1978. The German Ideology. In R. C. Tucker, ed., *The Marx-Engels Reader*, 2nd edn. New York, NY: W. W. Norton & Company, pp. 146–200.

McNeill, W. (1963). *The Rise of the West*, Chicago, IL: University of Chicago Press.

Merton, R. (1973). *The Sociology of Science*, Chicago, IL: University of Chicago Press.

Meyer, J. W. (1986). The Self and the Life Course: Institutionalization and Its Effects. In A. Sorensen, F. Weinert, & L. Sherrod, eds., *Human Development and the Life Course*. Hillsdale, NJ: Erlbaum, pp. 199–216.

Meyer, J. W. (2002). Globalization, National Culture, and the Future of the World Polity. *Hong Kong Journal of Sociology*, 3, 1–18.

Meyer, J. W., J. Boli, G. Thomas, & F. Ramirez. (1997). World Society and the Nation-State. *American Journal of Sociology*, 103(1), 144–81.

Meyer, J. W. & R. L. Jepperson. (2000). The "Actors" of Modern Society: The Cultural Construction of Social Agency. *Sociological Theory*, 18(1), 100–20.

Meyer, J. W. & F. Ramirez. (2000). The World Institutionalization of Education. In J. Schriewer, ed., *Discourse Formation in Comparative Education*. Frankfurt: Peter Lang, pp. 111–32.

Meyer, J. W., F. Ramirez, R. Rubinson, & J. Boli-Bennett. (1977). The World Educational Revolution, 1950–1970. *Sociology of Education*, 50(4), 242–58.

Meyer, J. W., F. Ramirez, & Y. Soysal. (1992). World Expansion of Mass Education, 1870–1970. *Sociology of Education*, 65(2), 128–49.

Mokyr, J. (1992). *The Lever of Riches*, Oxford: Oxford University Press.

Mokyr, J. (1999). Eurocentricity Triumphant. *The American Historical Review*, 104(4), 1241–6.

Mokyr, J. (2002). *The Gifts of Athena*, Princeton, NJ: Princeton University Press.

Muench, R. (1994). *Sociological Theory: From the 1850s to the 1920s*, Chicago, IL: Nelson-Hall.

North, D. C. (1981). *Structure and Change in Economic History*, New York, NY: W. W. Norton & Company.

Parsons, T. (1937). *The Structure of Social Action*, New York, NY: McGraw-Hill.

Parsons, T. (1947). Introduction. In T. Parsons, ed., *Max Weber: The Theory of Social and Economic Organization*, New York, NY: Free Press, pp. 3–86.

Parsons, T. (1951). *The Social System*, New York, NY: Free Press.

Polanyi, K. [1944] 1957. *The Great Transformation*, Boston, MA: Beacon Press.

Polanyi, K. (1977). *The Livelihood of Man*, New York, NY: Academic Press.

Ramirez, F. & J. W. Meyer. (2003). Expansion and Impact of the World Human Rights Regime: Longitudinal and Cross-National Analyses over the Twentieth Century. National Science Foundation proposal (2002–2004).

Schofer, E. & J. W. Meyer. (2004). The Worldwide Expansion of Higher Education in the Twentieth Century. *American Sociological Review*, 70 (6), 898–920.

Scott, W. R. (2001). *Institutions and Organizations*, 2nd edn, Thousand Oaks, CA: Sage Publications.

Stinchcombe, A. (2004). The Preconditions of World Capitalism: Weber Updated. *The Journal of Political Philosophy*, 11(4), 411–36.

Strayer, J. (1973). *The Medieval Origins of the Modern State*, Princeton, NJ: Princeton University Press.

Toulmin, S. (1992). *Cosmopolis: The Hidden Agenda of Modernity*, Chicago, IL: The University of Chicago Press.

Wallerstein, I. (1974). Capitalist Agriculture and the Origins of the European World-Economy in the Sixteenth Century. Vol. I of *The Modern World System*. New York, NY: Academic Press.

Walzer, M. (1965). *The Revolution of the Saints*, Cambridge, MA: Harvard University Press.

Weber, M. [1904/5] 1996. *The Protestant Ethic and the Spirit of Capitalism*, Los Angeles, CA: Roxbury Publishing Company.

Weber, M. [1920] 1996. Max Weber's Introduction to the Sociology of Religion. In *The Protestant Ethic and the Spirit of Capitalism*. Los Angeles, CA: Roxbury Publishing Company, pp. 13–31.

Weber, M. [1923] 1950. *General Economic History*, Glencoe, IL: The Free Press.

Weber, M. [1920] 1996. *Max Weber on Law in Economy and Society*, Cambridge, MA: Harvard University Press.

Werner, K. F. (1988). Political and Social Structures of the West. In J. Baechler, J. A. Hall & M. Mann, eds., *Europe and the Rise of Capitalism*. Oxford: Basil Blackwell, pp. 169–84.

Wuthnow, R. (1987). *Meaning and Moral Order*, Berkeley, CA: University of California Press.

Wuthnow, R. (1989). *Communities of Discourse: Ideology and Social Structure in the Reformation, the Enlightenment, and European Socialism*, Cambridge, MA: Harvard University Press.

Zaret, D. (1985). *The Heavenly Contract*, Chicago, IL: University of Chicago Press.

8 Reflections on Part III: Levels of Analysis

R. JEPPERSON AND J. MEYER

The social sciences continue to struggle over the issue of "levels of analysis" – the ontological standing and causal relations of interdependent entities from the biological components of the person to world (or universal) society. Chapters 6 and 7 (a) provided a general treatment of the multiple levels of analysis involved in social theorizing, (b) provided an explicit conceptualization of more collective, including institutional, levels, (c) illustrated the importance of considering multiple levels of analysis in social explanations, and (d) discussed the explanatory costs of would-be reductionisms that insist upon theoretical or methodological individualism. Here we reflect upon this effort.

8.1 The Standard Philosophical and Scientific Conceptualization of Levels

In the relevant philosophical and scientific literatures, the conceptual issues concerning levels of analysis are largely settled and unexciting. Chapters 6 and 7 rely upon the standard philosophical and scientific literatures. The core idea is that "levels" denote degrees of complexity of structuring, in organization and meaning. (So in the physical world, an organism is more complexly organized than a molecule.) The different sciences have consolidated around a hierarchy of degrees of complexity – physics, chemistry, biology, with interstitial sciences. The hierarchy can be extended "upward" to include the human and social sciences.

This hierarchically organized system features "downward" as well as "upward" causation, in Donald Campbell's language (Campbell 1974). Higher levels of organization can operate causally upon their own substructures: "the distribution of lower-level events and substances" can be partially determined by higher-level properties (ibid: 180). For instance, "mothering style" in monkeys apparently has epigenetic effects on more than a thousand cortical genes (Sapolsky 2017: 221). In human evolution, mind and culture are "emergent" realities from biological evolution, and then both mind and culture have their own effects (on human sexuality, for instance [Gray and Garcia 2013:308 & passim]). People who might worry about "downward" causation are unlikely in substance to deny that culture (as, say, typical diet) can affect body, or that culture (as, say, dominant religion) can affect mind (as, say, individual beliefs or psychological states). We provide many examples of empirically established downward causation in Chapters 6 and 7, especially in the latter. Social causation – apparently causation in general – operates both up and down.

However, the issue is often seen asymmetrically in the social sciences (e.g., by Coleman 1986a, b): causation upward is seen as the choices of lower-level "actors" (often individuals), while causation downward is seen as external influence on these actors. The idea that the actors and choices themselves are changing social constructions is thereby excluded. That idea is core to our institutional analyses but is often seen as problematic – a scientific violation, and perhaps a normative one too – in much conventional social scientific analysis.

A chronic but needless confusion is generated by the fact that all levels of social structure work through the behavior of human persons – past or present – and produce their effects on the behavior of such persons. (The "ontological truism" labeled by Watkins [1952], discussed in Chapter 6.) The intellectual question is to determine analytically and empirically whether the behavior involved should be seen as a product of the individual, or rather of the larger structures in which that individual is embedded. Chapter 6 discusses this point extensively; Chapter 7 provides additional examples.

8.2 Levels of Analysis in the Social Sciences

By levels, the social sciences most often refer to the scale of the units under investigation. ("Macrosociology is about millions of people," said Stinchcombe [1985].) Scale and organizational complexity are often conflated. It would be better to treat them separately. After all, in the physical world, an organism is a far more complexly organized object than a star, despite the much greater scale of stars (Gribbin and Gribbin 1999). Most of the time social scientists can get away with conflating scale with complexity: in the social world, larger scale often goes along with more "structuration."

Many distinctions of "levels" could be made in principle, but in practice just a few basic ones are typically distinguished. The individual is most commonly emphasized: it seems straightforward to promulgate explanations of the way properties of the individual, say sex, affect other properties such as voting behavior. Often groups or communities or organizations are treated in the same way, as when Dobbin (2009) studies whether organizations with affirmative action programs are more likely to have improved environmental performance. Similarly, societies or nation-states can be the levels at which explanation is put forward: Are societies with presidential regimes more conflict-prone than those with parliamentary ones?

The levels are often treated as nested, though this is not really the case in social life. An individual woman may vote in two different countries and can participate in multiple organizations: she can directly reflect her membership in very large systems. Similarly, organizations like the World Wildlife Fund are involved in multiple countries, and link up to grand and scientized institutional models. These are instances of the interpenetration of levels, importantly underplayed in realist analyses and central to institutionalist ones.

Thus in principle units at mixed levels of analysis can be distinguished, and are in fact routine. One can distinguish unorganized racial or ethnic groups – they might be large in number (hence "macro"), but aggregates (so not complexly structured), but with shared culture (a collective property). But discussion of (say) Finns, wherever they are located, would typically reduce in practice to explanatory ideas about individual Finns, who may be seen as infused with cultural and biological characteristics. Ideas about an ethnic spirit or geist as a collective Finnish matter – or simply customs – are not much considered in contemporary social science. This disinterest embodies a fundamental mistake, since Finnish individuals and organizations are imbued with awareness of their Finnishness as they enter into social action.

In the same way, with globalization it is sometimes possible to discuss the human race as an entity about which explanatory propositions might be made. Again such discussion is quickly reduced to propositions about individual persons or organizations (including national states): in the absence of a world state, modern discussions of a world society are weak and arise rather late (Meyer and Risse 2018). The talk is often bloodless: perhaps genetics makes the individuals, especially the male ones, prone to war. Overall, the nature and standing of the individual person is elaborated in discussions of globalization; the nature and standing of world society is much less so.

In the social sciences levels of analysis are interpenetrated, rather than completely distinct. Nation-states are made up of individual people, and people, beyond being raw individuals, are members of nation-states. So explanations at one level may refer to causal processes at another. If a soldier shoots another soldier, it may have nothing to do with their individual properties or relations: it may simply be that two armies are at war, and thus it might be pointless to study causality as arising from the personalities involved. On the other hand, causal explanation of a societal process – say, a decline in a birth rate – may properly invoke little more than changes in the individuals involved (e.g., a rise in education produces women who prefer to have fewer children). The point here is that the content of an explanation must be worked out empirically, considering possible connections at multiple levels of analysis, sorting out which connections are present and substantial, and which are not.

8.3 The Evolution of Thinking about Levels of Analysis in Sociology

A *locus classicus* is the work of Durkheim, with his dramatic attempt to distinguish individual facts from the social facts on which he concentrated (Durkheim 1951), and with his awareness of the modern "cult of the individual" (Durkheim 1958, 1969). The suicide rate, he argued and observed, has different origins and properties than the individual suicides making it up. He made a dramatic issue out of the matter, setting himself in opposition to the psychology of Tarde and the aggregative analyses of collective behavior. Durkheim's point became an identity assertion among sociologists, as it reflected a centrally sociological vision – but it also had the property of deviance in a society that reified the individual person and found contextual effects to be almost shocking.

The development of quantitative research after World War II produced massive data sets on both individuals and the contexts in which these individuals functioned. A well-known paper by Robinson (1950) dramatized levels of analysis: it showed, à la Durkheim, extreme differences between the correlations of variables at the individual level, and the correlations between the same variables at more collective levels. To reduce the issue to absurdity, note that the correlation between individual education and entry into the US Congress is high, while the correlation between the average education in a state and number of congresspersons is very low.

Following on Robinson, a whole literature arose, dealing with what was seen as a conundrum – but what was also seen as central to a true sociology focusing on real social facts. Merton (1968), Barton (1961), and Lazarsfeld and Menzel (1961) produced work on the meaning of collective or aggregative measures. Shifting to analysis rather than measurement, many studies focused on forms of statistical analysis that employed both individual and collective properties in analyzing behavior. Contextual analysis, it was called: Blau (1960), Davis (1966; Davis et al. 1961), and others tried to relate forms of statistical analysis to types of arguments in social theory. But particular statistical forms do not match clearly with forms of substantive reasoning. The real impact was to legitimate the statistical examination of the effects of variations among groups on social and behavioral outcomes.[1]

More broadly, the whole discussion did encourage thinking about the effects of social structural variations on the behavior and orientations of individuals over and above properties of those individuals. For example, education may have positive effects on individual political participation, but participation might be lowered in contexts where everyone else has more education (Nie, Junn, and Stehlik-Barry 1996). Such effects had always seemed routine in both historical and qualitative literatures on social behavior but now could be explored more formally.

The research formulation allowed for two quite distinct theoretical interpretations. One was micro and realist, influenced by the individualism of contemporary culture. As a matter of principle, perhaps we should see contextual effects on behavior as always heavily mediated by properties of the individuals involved. In other words, true scientific analyses would push social effects far to the back of the explanatory models, which would elaborate more proximate mechanisms through which the effects occur (Hauser 1970). In research at the University of Michigan built on social psychological traditions, this idea was axiomatized as the "funnel" principle, reflecting a theoretically individualist conception of the individual in society (Campbell et al. 1960). This social psychological picture of society remains an implicit paradigm for many American sociologists.

But a second theoretical interpretation was this: We could imagine quite direct effects of contextual change or variation, if we see the individual identity as a role, or social construction. In this case, as the construction changes, behavior and attitudes might change, relatively independent of any elaborate developmental or choice process within the individual. For instance, if a business manager's main identity is as an MBA from Harvard, when the Harvard professors articulate an ideology of corporate social responsibility the manager might simply go along. This is the phenomenological picture of society within the individual (Berger 1963: Ch. 5), less well represented in both social theory and empirical work. We outlined how this line of argument works in Chapters 6 and 7.

8.4 Social Explanation in a Culturally Individualist Society

Chapters 6 and 7 emphasize how contemporary culture, both social scientific and general, has strong normative and cognitive preference for explanations operating at the level of the individual. Economy, polity, social relations, and culture are all treated, in contemporary ideology, as reflecting choices of, and variations in, people seen as individuals. With the great movements of liberalism and neoliberalism in contemporary world society, the tendency to see social processes as working through the choices of individual persons as distinct entities becomes very strong. The fields of economics and psychology have grown and gained policy centrality, the field of sociology emphasizes social psychological processes, and the field of anthropology is destabilized. Overall, even history focuses on society as made up of individuals, rather than authorities and institutions (Frank et al. 2010; Lerch et al. 2017). The taste for reductionism, as well as methodological individualism, is strong and is supported by much institutionalized ideology.

Those who focus upon institutions, then, must contend with the principle that contemporary institutions work through, or appear to work through, or are designed to work through, the behavior and choices of people conceived as individuals and conceiving of themselves as individuals. For example, the institutionalized theories of economic growth suppose that it is produced by individual choices in labor, capital, and technology, and increasingly by individual innovation and entrepreneurship.

In response, Chapters 6 and 7 emphasize that social science must consider multiple levels of analysis, rather than focusing on one individualist level – if it actually wishes to engage in explanation as opposed to dramatizing individual agency. The two papers do not call for privileging collective-level explanation. They acknowledge that sometimes the most appropriate explanations of social life will feature the individualistic explanations favored by social psychologists or game theorists or rational choice proponents – that is, explanations that feature social outcomes as reflecting aggregated individual changes or choices. Sometimes these ideas allow for sufficient explanations, but far less often than thought in the American intellectual context. The human sciences also need *subsocial* analysis, for that matter: that is, sociobiological explanations that isolate programming built in by biological evolution. Such explanations, if truly sober-minded and robust – as opposed to fanciful possibilities or ideological projections – are entirely compatible with institutional and collective forms of argument. After all, social behavior is obviously shaped at multiple levels. The progress of a student is clearly affected by individual genetics, biography, family, community, school, teacher, friends, and levels of analysis all the way up to global society. Some influences are quite direct, others indirect. Social science should be multilevel because social ontology is multilevel.

8.4.1 The Current Penchant for "Microfoundations"

An individualistic preoccupation is once again apparent in the renewed search for "microfoundations" of organizational and institutional processes. In Chapter 6 we emphasize the important differences among micro-explanation (or "reduction"), seeking microfoundations, and (following Randall Collins) providing "microtranslation" – that is, micro-samples of a "higher-level" process. The current search for microfoundations conflates these substantial differences.

The search has been successful in providing micro-samples of human behavior in a variety of organizational contexts (Boltansky and Thevenot 2006; Thornton et al. 2012; Haack et al. 2019). But in discovering foundations it is completely unsuccessful. The people and behavior analyzed are typically highly schooled creatures of the contemporary educational and organizational systems: carriers of a highly developed liberal culture. They are by no means causally autonomous generators of solely "upward causation." In the contemporary society, micro-social action has highly macrosocial sources.

There is another point, from Chapter 6, that we wish to re-emphasize. One might think that an institutionalist explanation must involve special microfoundations – for example, some distinctive set of assumptions about the human being, or about human beings in organizations. Making this point explicit should dispel the idea immediately. The cultural institutionalism of this volume doesn't depend upon any exotic assumptions about people. In fact the line of thought doesn't make its own claims about human nature or psychology – those claims are the province of other disciplines, after all. Usually, institutionalist arguments assume little more than people's pragmatic acceptance of roles or routines or cultural meanings. Some scholars may of course be interested in what employees or organizational actors are specifically doing, feeling, and thinking – they want the "micro-samples" of some collective process. (Randall Collins' "filmstrips," referenced in Chapter 6.) And when scholars have looked, the results are not exotic. Typically, such scholars have found that the micro-makeup of a collective process is heterogeneous: a congeries of, for example, conformity, intended strategic action, emotional expression, and biological drives. After all, biologists, psychologists, and social psychologists have not identified a unitary "logic" of social behavior. The point here is that the plausibility or success of institutionalist arguments in no way awaits new or distinctive findings about the micro-level of human action or interaction.

8.5 Conclusion

Social science's discomfort with multiple levels of analysis, and its limited willingness to consider the changing cultural frames underlying modern liberal-individualist society, explains the corresponding failure to comprehend the great socio-cultural movements of our period. Major changes, reflecting great shifts in underlying normative and cognitive models, are unpredicted and grossly underanalyzed: (a) the worldwide change in status of women, children, and gay-lesbian people; (b) the global educational explosion; (c) the worldwide rise of the professions; (d) the global expansion of democratic forms; (e) a global environment movement, independent of specific environmental problems; (f) the global expansion of rationalized organizational forms, and of emphasis on transparent organizational relationships (and stigmatization of "corruption"); (g) the shift of political organization in a populist and plebiscitary direction; (h) the decline of previously standard forms of family and community organization.

Most of these changes reflect waves of cultural development rather than simple aggregations of individual choices. Consider the expanded rights of children, gay-lesbian rights, the environmental movement, and the diffusion of direct democracy: in each of these cases, collective reinterpretation was dramatic. But efforts to theorize these changes are often distorted to highlight the individuals and their strategic choices.

The impairing consequences of a dogmatic individualism have also been apparent in those segments of social science that have a policy orientation or have migrated to professional schools, such as business schools. There one finds a stark tendency to depict the institutional order as merely a domain of manipulation of powerful individuals, with little attention to that order as a project with its own history and trajectory. As teaching and research take up policy foci, they almost inevitably emphasize the centrality of actors and action: decision, choice, and implementation. One does not train people in professional schools to be passive carriers of institutional traditions: the MBA is to be a carrier of divine providence, not a barnacle on its rump.

To understate, American sociology in particular clearly experiences a tension between dramatizing cultural preoccupations and engaging in social scientific work. As a central instance, the field takes very seriously the conception of society as made up of putatively equal individuals. This produces problematic causal analyses of why, in reality, inequalities continue, looking at the world not in explanatory terms (why time one moves to time two), but in normative ones (why time two is inadequate compared with a possible time three). So there are dozens of studies of why females are uncommon in the field of electrical engineering, very few studies of why they are increasingly there, and even fewer studies of the global cultural changes that now define this as an important problem.

Notes

1. Much later, technical issues (correcting standard errors for the grouping of data) were cleared up in a major statistical effort (Raudenbush and Bryk 2001).

References

Barton, A. (1961). *Organizational Measurement and Its Bearing on the Study of College Environments*, New York, NY: College Entrance Examination Board.
Berger, P. (1963). *Invitation to Sociology*, Garden City, NY: Doubleday.
Blau, P. (1960). Structural Effects. *American Sociological Review*, 25(2), 178–93.
Boltanski, L. & L. Thévenot (2006). *On Justification: Economies of Worth*, Princeton, NJ: Princeton University Press.
Campbell, A., P. E. Converse, W. Miller, & D. Stokes (1960). *The American Voter*, Chicago, IL: University of Chicago Press.
Campbell, D. T. (1974). Downward Causation in Hierarchically Organized Biological Systems. In F. J. Ayala & T. Dobzhansky, eds., *Studies in the Philosophy of Biology: Reduction and Related Problems*. London: Macmillan, pp. 179–86.
Coleman, J. S. (1986a). Micro Foundations and Macrosocial Theory. In S. Lindenberg, J. S. Coleman, & S. Nowak, eds., *Approaches to Social Theory*. New York, NY: Russell Sage Foundation, pp. 345–63.
Coleman, J. (1986b). Social Theory, Social Research, and a Theory of Action. *American Journal of Sociology*, 91(6), 1309–35.
Davis, J. A. (1966). The Campus as a Frog Pond: An Application of the Theory of Relative Deprivation to Career Decisions of College Men. *American Journal of Sociology*, 72(1), 17–31.
Davis, J., J. Spaeth, & C. Huson (1961). A Technique for Analyzing the Effects of Group Competition. *American Sociological Review*, 26(2), 215–25.
Dobbin, F. (2009). *Inventing Equal Opportunity*, Princeton, NJ: Princeton University Press.
Durkheim, E. (1958). *Professional Ethics and Civic Morals*, Glencoe, IL: Free Press.
Durkheim, E. (1951). *Suicide*, Glencoe, IL: Free Press.
Durkheim, E. (1969). Individualism and the Intellectuals. *Political Studies*, 17(1), 14–30.
Frank, D. J., B. J. Camp, & S. A. Boutcher (2010). Worldwide Trends in the Criminal Regulation of Sex, 1945 to 2005. *American Sociological Review*, 75(6), 867–93.

Gray, P. B. & J. R. Garcia (2013). *Evolution and Human Sexual Behavior*, Cambridge, MA: Harvard University Press.
Gribbin, J. & M. Gribbin (1999). *Almost Everyone's Guide to Science*, New Haven, CT: Yale University Press.
Haack, P., J. Sieweke, & L. Wessel, eds. (2019). *Microfoundations of Institutions*, Bingley: Emerald Publishing.
Hauser, R. (1970). Context and Consex: A Cautionary Tale. *American Journal of Sociology*, 75(4), 645–64.
Lazarsfeld, P. & H. Menzel (1961). On the Relation Between Individual and Collective Properties. In A. Etzioni, ed., *Complex Organizations*. New York, NY: Holt, Rinehart & Winston.
Lerch, J., P. Bromley, F. O. Ramirez, & J. W. Meyer (2017). The Rise of Individual Agency in Conceptions of Society: Textbooks, Worldwide, 1950–2011. *International Sociology*, 32(1), 38–60.
Merton, R. (1968). *Social Theory and Social Structure*, New York, NY: Free Press.
Meyer, J. W. & M. Risse (2018). Creation and Claims of a World Society. In S. Rangan, ed., *Capitalism Beyond Mutuality: Perspectives Integrating Philosophy and Social Science*. Oxford: Oxford University Press, pp. 25–57.
Nie, N., J. Junn, & K. Stehlik-Barry (1996). *Education and Democratic Citizenship in America*, Chicago, IL: University of Chicago Press.
Raudenbush, S. & A. Bryk. (2001). *Hierarchical Linear Models*, 2nd ed. Thousand Oaks, CA: SAGE.
Robinson, W. S. (1950). Ecological Correlations and the Behavior of Individuals. *American Sociological Review*, 98(1), 351–7.
Sapolsky, R. (2017). *Behave*, Cambridge, MA: Harvard University Press.
Stinchcombe, A. (1985). Macrosociology is About Millions of People. *Contemporary Sociology*, 14(5), 572–5.
Thornton, P., W. Ocasio, & M. Lounsbury (2012). *The Institutional Logics Perspective*, Oxford: Oxford University Press.
Watkins, J. W. N. (1952). The Principle of Methodological Individualism. *British Journal of the Philosophy of Science*, 3(10), 186–9.

PART IV

Institutions of Modernity and Postmodernity: The Construction of Actors

9 The "Actors" of Modern Society: The Cultural Construction of Social Agency (2000)

J. MEYER AND R. JEPPERSON[*]

Much social theory takes for granted the core conceit of modern culture, that modern actors – individuals, organizations, nation-states – are autochthonous and natural entities, no longer really embedded in culture. Accordingly, while there is much abstract metatheory about "actors" and their "agency," there is arguably little theory about the topic. This article offers direct arguments about how the modern (European, now global) cultural system constructs the modern actor as an authorized agent for various interests via an ongoing relocation into society of agency originally located in transcendental authority or in natural forces environing the social system. We see this authorized agentic capability as an essential feature of what modern theory and culture call an "actor," and one that, when analyzed, helps greatly in explaining a number of otherwise anomalous or little-analyzed features of modern individuals, organizations, and states. These features include their isomorphism and standardization, their internal decoupling, their extraordinarily complex structuration, and their capacity for prolific collective action.

9.1 Introduction

Modern culture depicts society as made up of "actors" – individuals and nation-states, together with the organizations derived from them.

---

[*] An original version of this article was prepared for a conference on institutional analysis at the University of Arizona, March 1996. We appreciate the support of the Institute for International Studies at Stanford University in its preparation and the comments of Al Bergesen, John Boli, Thomas Fararo, David Frank, Edgar Kiser, Walter W. Powell, Francisco Ramirez, Evan Schofer, participants in the Arizona conference, and anonymous reviewers. We also draw upon previous discussions with Shmuel Eisenstadt, Ann Swidler, and Morris Zelditch, Jr.

Much social science takes this depiction at face value, and takes for granted that analysis must start with these actors and their perspectives and actions. We refer for instance to elaborate interest-based theories so committed to assuming actorhood that they leave its actual properties unanalyzed. Modern actors are seen as autochthonous and natural entities, no longer really embedded in culture (Meyer 1988). Out of the unspecified core of actorhood emanate the utilities and preferences said to produce the entire social world. In the background of such analyses one sometimes finds mention of prior cultural rules – for example, a system of property rights in part culturally derived – but these rules are typically presented as preconditions, operating mainly at some earlier point in history. The modern social system at present is imagined to operate via fully realized and unfettered actors pursuing their goals (if under institutional "incentives" and "constraints," understood as background conditions).

This realist (as opposed to phenomenological) imagery[1] is so dominant and legitimated that it is taken as a kind of faith by scholars in most North American circles, and recently in many European ones as well. Standard culturalist imagery departs only somewhat from this vision. It often features a dramatic emphasis on human voluntarist interpretation and action (Alexander 1986; Sewell 1992), but it also provides little specification of what the modern agent is like. Such scholars add attention to "meanings," but often seem to assume, we think erroneously, that they arise out of the raw (untutored, unscripted) social experience of actors. In so doing, these scholars often underplay the highly constructed, scripted, and legitimated character of modern actorhood – despite their emphasis on culture.

Accordingly, there is more abstract metatheory about "actors" and their "agency" than substantive arguments about the topic. This characterization is arguably valid even if one takes into account European discussions, which have perhaps been more attentive to the constructed features of actorhood, and less prone to reify actors. In social theory generally, modern actorhood is routinely treated as a given condition or attainment – or even a universal telos of human or social nature. Assumptions about actorhood are now so taken for granted that social scientists use the term "actor" with little reflexivity to denote people or organized groups, as if such entities are by definition actors.

In this article, in contrast, we take seriously the idea that the modern "actor" is a historical and ongoing cultural construction, and that the particulars of this construction should help to account for a number of specific features of actorhood, including anomalous and unnoticed ones. We offer direct social theory taking up this topic. In doing so, we depend upon two main analytical departures.

First, we see the actorhood of individuals, organizations, and national states as an elaborate system of social *agency* that has a long and continuing religious and postreligious evolution.[2] Our main theme on this issue concerns the ongoing relocation into society of agency originally located in transcendental authority (gods) or in natural forces environing the social system. Over time these exogenous forces (e.g., godly powers) have been relocated as authority immanent within society itself, enlarging social agency, relocating authority from god to church, from church to state, from church and state to individual souls and later citizens. Recognizing the spiritual immanence of Western societies (as Durkheim did) will help us see the development of modern actorhood as more a cultural devolution – from god to society, on to individuals and organizations – than a natural evolution from less to more social complexity, or an aggregate product of interest-based struggles over naturally given goals.

Second, we call attention to the ways in which this cultural system constructs the modern actor as an *authorized agent* for various interests (including those of the self). This agentic construction, we will argue, accounts for much of the uniqueness of modern actorhood. Notably, participants in modern society enact in their identities substantial agency for broad collective purposes. Under the terms of a wider rationalized and universalistic culture, they are constructed as having the capacity and responsibility to act as an "other" to themselves, to each other, and indeed for the wider cultural frame itself (as with Mead's "generalized other"). We see this authorized agentic capability as an essential feature of what modern theory calls an "actor."

In Section 9.2 we sketch the continuously evolving cultural rules that construct, maintain, and elaborate actors. Section 9.3 analyzes the types of agency that the modern actor takes up. Section 9.4 locates the origins of this system of agency in the modern, especially liberal, polity. Section 9.5 then derives a number of propositions about common structural and dynamic features of modern individuals, states, and organizations – the similarities of the three types of actors itself both motivation and subject for our analysis. In this section we also present propositions about a number of structural features of modern society as a distinctive action system.

In undertaking this analysis we apply and elaborate one line of contemporary sociological theory, so-called sociological institutionalism (Thomas, Meyer, Ramirez, and Boli 1987). We purposefully employ the theoretical and empirical resources of this research program rather than attempting to synthesize or address other contemporary theoretical efforts.[3]

9.2 The Cultural Rules of Modern Actorhood

We first address the question: What are the cultural rules that constitute agentic actorhood in the first place and that subsequently structure it? We attempt to isolate and explicate rules of actorhood located within the modern Western cultural framework. (We do not attempt to offer an explanation of their origins or development, or a commentary upon such explanations.[4])

It is routinely noted (but as often forgotten) that the Western cultural framework reflects the development, expansion, and secularization of the principally religious models of Western Christendom, a sustained cultural evolution extending into the human rights movements of the contemporary period (Weber 1927; Parsons 1966; McNeill 1963; Eisenstadt 1986, 1987; Mann 1986; Hall 1986; Thomas et al. 1987; Meyer 1989). These models involve a sharp delineation of, and "axial tension" (Eisenstadt 1986) between, society and its natural and spiritual environments. This differentiation is historically associated with the distinctive ongoing "rationalization"[5] of cultural representations of nature, the spiritual domain, and society.

In the Western picture, humans have the capacity and responsibility to modify society and to intervene in lawful nature, in order to reduce discrepancies between mundane realities and transcendentally chartered goals (Eisenstadt 1986). Further, the resolution for this "axial tension" is to be this-worldly, attained through the joint transformation of society and the individual. Society is instrumentalized as a modifiable vehicle for salvation (later, progress and justice) (Bellah 1964; Thomas and Meyer 1984), but in the Western tradition it is the cultural project that is sacred, not some specific control structure in itself. The contrast with China in this respect, from an early historical period, is striking (Weber 1927; Needham 1954; Eisenstadt 1986, 1987).

The spiritual environment in the Western ontology is increasingly simplified and abstract over time, consolidated in a high god who is rendered eternal, lawful, and relatively noninvasive in both nature and society – and thus not what moderns would consider much of an actor. The natural environment in this ontology is represented as unified and lawful, and over time is purged of animist or spiritual forces; it is deadened, and again not filled with what moderns would call actors. The modern cultural dramatics of human actorhood – what Weber called the "rational restlessness" of the modern system – are in good part a precipitate or devolution of these distinctive cultural properties.

9.2.1 The Rationalization of Representations of Nature

In Western culture, nature is tamed and demystified through the extraordinary development, expansion, and authority of science. Nature is represented by elaborate lawfully defined entities set in imagined lawful relation to each other; the laws involved are held to be universally binding rather than culture-specific. More and more domains are incorporated over time into this cognitive system: psyches, elements of human society, the ecosystem, the forces of the history of the universe and its current physical operation, the evolution of life, species, and human language. Animist and spiritual forces are marginalized or purged, relative to other cultural ontologies (e.g., ancestor spirits disappear from nature). This process is a continuing one, and to this day one finds new rationalizations of previously opaque entities and relations: for instance, particularistic conceptions of life, the earth, and the human race are undercut by discoveries of life in rocks from Mars and far inside the earth, of new planets and stars, of more details of primate evolution, and so on. Or human behavior previously seen as arbitrary is given analysis in terms of psychological, medical, or environmental bases. To be sure, pseudo- and nonscientific spiritualisms and naturalisms remain as core elements of the cultural ontology (as we discuss below), but they are under constant encroachment and displacement by putatively scientific accounts, which then routinely receive public authoritativeness and standing.

This cultural development has been globalized to an astonishing degree, so that the "scientific outlook" has public authority in most parts of the world, with scientists attaining substantial public (even philosophic) standing in world culture. In most versions of high modernity, the scientific outlook in fact comes to define both rationality and the progressive society, with obviously enormous effects.

Responsible individual and social actors are to take scientific knowledge into account in their activities; in fact, doing so becomes, in an ever-broadening array of world regions, a desideratum of rational behavior (Inkeles and Smith 1974). Individual persons, including business and political leaders, may privately have little scientific knowledge or faith. Routinely they have idiosyncratic, syncretic, mixtures of beliefs, privately consulting all sorts of carriers of spiritual or mystical authority, medical functionaries far removed from scientific grounding, and so on. Scientists themselves declare religious beliefs, but these private belief systems are no longer adequate bases for the posture of proper rational modern actorhood. A competent defense in a trial court or a legislative hearing, or before the court of public opinion, must claim that one's actions were guided by the best scientific and professional advice: the claim that one acted under advice from a palm reader has little standing.[6]

The rationalization of the picture of nature creates some of the elements of modern actorhood. This rationalization creates a constantly expanding set of recognized entities with their functional interrelations and often associated legitimated "interests." New elements and functions are recognized, such as wetlands, species diversity, the functions of the rain forest, the declining whale population, scarce or dangerous metals, and so on. Some of these entities can be seen as having interests that require protection or recognition: one can now argue for the *rights* of whales, or of species in general, or even of geological forms (as in the Gaia movement). Shifting from functional analyses of nature to ideas about rights moves beyond simple scientific rationalization, and obviously adds moral elements. But the underlying rationalized scientific analysis is almost always a crucial component of these rights claims: It is much easier to argue for rights for whales if one also has an analysis of whales' sentient qualities or their crucial roles in an ecology.

New properties and interests are also discovered in aspects of human society that are represented as being rooted in nature. For instance, new natural properties of the individual, and thus potential rights, are conceived (e.g., self-esteem). New laws and functions defining society are articulated (economic and social development, the costs of dependency), producing definitions of new rights and interests. And new elements of social organization acquire analytic standing, producing organizations that may claim legitimate interests and rights (for women, ethnic groups, the physically limited, fetuses, and also such functionally defined groups as occupations and professions).

Thus the rationalization of nature and the rationalization of society are highly interpenetrated. Proper human activity and social organization must take into account the imagined lawful entities and relations in the natural environment (including the natural laws thought to govern human individuals and social organization, as proclaimed by the psychological and social sciences). But the enriched analysis of nature, in this broad sense, also provides agendas for expanded rational human activity: new analyses create a constant flow of new social problems and possibilities (see Schofer 1999).

Implicit in much realist theoretical imagery is the idea that the processes of rationalization of nature and society more or less inevitably produce the phenomenon of actorhood. For instance, differentiated individuals in a complex society are thought naturally to acquire individual consciousness and actorhood (Simmel, and many others). Differentiated structures in a complex environment are thought naturally to produce formal organizational actors through pressures for efficiency or stability (e.g., North and Thomas 1973). World or regional complexity, differentiation, and conflict are thought to produce naturally the nation-state as a rational actor (Tilly 1992; Wallerstein 1974).

Putting aside the particulars of such analyses, the underlying assumption seems fundamentally mistaken. The rationalization of nature does produce an expanded set of recognized entities and relations. In the social domain, these may be entities accorded with natural functions that have the character of social rights, but they are not yet actors. Whales may be accorded rights of a sort, and validated human actors may represent these rights (as we discuss below), but whales are not actors. Nor are the ethnic cultures displayed in museums, or fetuses, or interest groups not yet formally organized (e.g., labor or women in premodern societies). For an entity with recognized interests to be seen as a legitimate actor requires another step: the cultural construction of the capacity and authority to act for itself. We argue that in the modern system, this capacity comes from the wider cultural system, and can best be seen as the cultural devolution of originally spiritual agency.

9.2.2 The Rationalization of Representations of the Spiritual World, and the Rise of the Agentic Actor

As with the natural world, the spiritual one has been highly rationalized in the Western ontology. There has been a remarkably continuous unification, generalization, and taming of the spiritual domain and spiritual authority (a process discussed by both Durkheim and Weber; also by Bellah 1964; Collins 1982, chap. 2.; Eisenstadt 1986; Thomas et al. 1987). Spiritual forces have been progressively consolidated into a single high god, in a relatively linear religious evolution. In a strikingly stepwise way, god "takes leave of time and space" (Durkheim), and its anthropomorphic qualities decline. God does not so much die (contrary to Nietzsche), but is deadened in the sense of greatly reduced agency. This evolution continues in the contemporary period, with the reconstruction of god as basic principles (as evidenced, for instance, in much modern religious thought of the high culture sort, or in "the force" of *Star Wars*).

Further, in the modern Western ontology, there is an ongoing diminishment of the domain under direct transcendental-spiritual control. This domain becomes more truly transcendental over time, with the pullout of god from society. It is also highly rationalized, as in the ongoing and aggressive search for more common and universal principles of justice and morality (as in modern attempts to create and elaborate global conceptions of "human rights" and to implement them in legal systems [Boyle and Meyer 1998]).

With the increasing transcendence and inertness of god, agency and authority are relocated immanently in society's structures and rationales. Some agency is built into modern pictures of the agentic authority and responsibility of the state and other organizations; much devolves to the modern individual, who is empowered with more and more godlike authority and vision.

Social and individual actors thereby attain greater reality and standing, and more functions and responsibilities – they are now agents of higher principles, and hence highly legitimated in ways unique to modern Western culture. Elaborate schemas of socioeconomic development become the responsibilities and purposes of nation-states. These states are truly projects in ways far more elaborated than for other polities (Thomas and Meyer 1984). The status of the individual as responsible creature and carrier of purpose and the moral law is greatly enhanced (McNeill 1963; Hall 1986; Dumont 1986; Thomas et al. 1987). Individuals attain sacral standing across more and more dimensions: age, sex, race, ethnicity, sexuality, and physical limitations. Accordingly they enact both more self and more public standing than do people outside the modern system (Inkeles and Smith 1974; Jepperson 1992). Structured social organizations arise to pursue, with great legitimacy, validated individual and collective purposes and responsibilities. Whole societies are reconstructed around a network of historically distinctive rationalized purposive associations (Coleman 1973). Individuals and societies together are seen as the authorized centers and sources of all social action (hence the dominance of actor and action theories in social science). "Man" as actor – individuals, organizations, states – carries almost the entire responsibility for the now-sacralized human project, with gods, other spiritual forces, ancestors, or an animated nature drained of agency.

We should note that all this cultural development has been globalized to a very substantial (in fact, astonishing) degree in the period following World War II. First, both the cultural system and the associated roster of agentic actors have expanded on a nearly worldwide basis: The nation-state form, with individuals as citizens, and organizations as components, is found worldwide. Second, while there are attempts in Asia and the Islamic world to limit the spread of models originating in the West, a surprising feature of the modern system is how completely the Western models dominate world discourse about the rights of individuals, the responsibilities and sovereignty of the state, and the nature of preferred organizational forms. One can as yet find little impact of other huge civilizational forces (China, Islam) on the standardized rule structures found in those institutions, organizations, and associations operating on a world scale (see, e.g., Meyer, Boli, Thomas, and Ramirez 1997). Third, and most recently, the various formal "others" of this system – collectives representing sciences, professions, and rationalized world associations – explicitly deploy the expanded standards and putative truths as collective culture for the world, with substantial influence (Boli and Thomas 1999). In effect, Christendom had some modest attainments as a missionary movement, but has achieved vastly greater hegemony in its transformation into science, law, and rationalized education.

9.2.3 The Resulting Identity of "The Actor"

We have discussed what seem to be the essential cultural ingredients of modern actorhood. First, stemming from the rationalization of the realm of nature, and of aspects of humans and human society seen as of nature, one finds the natural human entity with valid and lawful functions and interests. This is the human individual or group that can be represented as behaving in terms of natural (scientifically expressible) laws. Second, devolving from rationalized spiritual authority, one finds the legitimated agent and carrier of authority, responsibility, and capacity to act in history. The integration of these two elements in a single imagined natural-and-spiritual entity is what moderns mean by the term "actor."

9.3 Features of the Agentic Actor

The constructed capacity for responsible agency is the core of modern actorhood. In this section we try to isolate the different sorts of agency that constitute modern actors. We distinguish agency for a self, for other actors, for entities that are not actors, and for principle (i.e., for cultural authority).

9.3.1 Agency for the Self

The modern actor is a mobilized agent for its self (or for other "principals," as we will discuss later). Modern culture creates an agentic individual managing goals thought to reside in a personality or life course (the "principal" for individuals); a sovereign state managing goals of a national society; and an organizational structure managing its legitimated interests.

The two cultural sources of this structure discussed above both introduce a great deal of standardization and scripting. A first aspect is widely recognized: modern cultural formulations defining individual, organizational, or state entities and interests are highly standardized, and evolve and expand in similar ways over time. For example, discourses of self-esteem, originally reflective of alternative lifestyles, over time transform into standard technology of the self, thereby elaborating it. The modern organization similarly has elaborated over time, with the expansion of accounting, personnel, information, planning, safety, and environmental elements. The modern state is agent for an expanding array of domains of national society, from economic or scientific development to education to individual health – with each domain itself conceived more expansively over time.

Most social theory has recognized one way or another that core social entities have been more elaborately constructed over time. The agentic aspect and its underlying spiritual devolution is less well recognized. Modern individuals, organizations, and nation-states, in becoming legitimated agents for their underlying interests, incorporate the highly standardizing responsibility to enact imagined moral and natural principles. The proper modern agentic individual, for instance, manages a life, carrying a responsibility not only to reflect self-interest but also the wider rationalized rules conferring agency. Helplessness, ignorance, and passivity may be very natural human properties, but they are not the properties of the proper effective agent. Modern agentic actors involve themselves in all sorts of efforts elaborating their agentic capabilities, efforts that often have only the most distant relation to their raw interests. Organizations, for example, develop improved information systems toward no immediate goal (Feldman and March 1981; Brunsson 1989), or management training programs stressing individual self-development and organizational culture (Scott and Meyer 1994). Nation-states clearly devote resources to the development of agentic capabilities that are little related to their actual political agendas: for example, science policy (Finnemore 1996a), or the elaboration and celebration of internal cultural features (e.g., Hobsbawm 1983; Anderson 1991).

9.3.2 Agency for Other Actors

Assisted by elaborate structures of otherhood, individuals and collectives take up available cultural technology for developing actorhood (Brunsson 1989). Thus mobilized in standardized and stylized ways, supported by a host of external cultural definitions and social structures, modern actors can easily shift from agency for the self to agency for other actors – from actorhood to otherhood – whether these other actors be states, organizations, or individuals.

In fact, a striking feature of the modern system is the extreme readiness with which its actor participants can act as agents for other actors. They can do this, with rapidity and facility, as employees and consultants, as friends and advisors, as voters and citizens. They can do it in exchange for resources, or as a free good to the world around them. And they do it much more often and more easily than do participants in less rationalized cultural systems. Ready opining, on the widest range of issues, is a notable feature of modern individuals and is distinctive to them (Lerner 1959; Inkeles and Smith 1974). Organizations display their successes on every occasion (rather than conceal them from their competitors, as in older and more typically rational behavioral forms); national states are eager to serve as models for the world around them with cascades of assistance programs, publicity, and displays before international organizations (Meyer et al. 1997).

Since individuals and organizations and nation-states incorporate an enormous amount of standardizing rationalized material, it becomes very easy for them to put their standardized agency at the service of other actors. Individuals in an instant can advise others of their true interests, or can participate in complete good faith as advisors and consultants to organizations that they might have known nothing about previously. And of course they can nearly instantaneously become, as voters, agents of the greater national collectivity. Modern organizations and states have similar and more powerful agentic capabilities, and can advise and collaborate in all sorts of collective activity: they also serve as agents of their own individual members or citizens.

9.3.3 Agency for Nonactor Entities

Modern actors also mobilize as agents for the imagined interests of nonactor entities recognized in the cultural system. For instance, individuals, organizations, and nation-states now mobilize their agency on behalf of the ecosystem, whales, trees, birds, plants, or species in general: that is, on behalf of nonactors. They similarly mobilize agency for imagined potential actors, such as fetuses, the unorganized poor, the unrecognized and unorganized groups of women or laboring classes, dying languages and cultures, and so on. The capacity to do so arises from the modern actor's imagined competence in applying natural and moral law, competence that can be put to the service of the widest variety of legitimated entities, whether the entities are themselves actors or not.

9.3.4 Agency for Principle (i.e., for Cultural Authority)

As we have discussed, the modern actor is in good part an agent operating under very general rules, and can serve as agent or consulting other for a wide variety of legitimated principals having recognized functions or interests: selves, other actor individuals or organizations, entities without actorhood. But one third-party principal is in practice always involved: in becoming an authorized agent (of the self, or of any other), the proper modern actor assumes responsibility to act as agent of the imagined natural and moral law. Otherwise the actor risks either incompetence or corruption.

At the extreme, agentic actors represent not any recognized entity or interest, but instead become purely agents of principle. This priestly stance is a most highly developed and respected role running through the modern system and carrying much authority in it. Thus moral and legal theorists pursue and develop abstract models independent of any practical interest, and are highly admired. Honored scientists attend to matters of presumed truth remote from any consequence: the moons of Jupiter (the matter that put Galileo in trouble once again receives attention); the origins of the universe, or of humankind, or language; attempted communication with putative intelligent life elsewhere. The authoritative voice of the sciences and professions stems from the posture of pure otherhood; that is, from their claim to speak for wider truths and standards, beyond any local situation or interests (Meyer 1994a).

Prevailing social theory has little to offer in explanation of the extraordinary prestige attached to agency for principle, and (as we discuss below) very poorly accounts for the social authority of the professions and professionals involved. The prestige and authority of this form of agency become explicable if we explicitly recognize the dependence of modern actorhood on a rationalized culture of natural and moral law. The carriers of this law can be seen as crucial authorities in the maintenance of actorhood. If fostering the actorhood of states, organizations, and individuals is a crucial desideratum in the modern system, the consultants who help actors do so are prized authorities (Brunsson 1989; Meyer 1994a).

9.4 The Linkage of Agentic Actorhood to the Modern, Especially Liberal, System

The agency system we are analyzing is very much a historical construction in the general sense already discussed: it arises from the religious and legal history of the West. It is also a construction in a more specific sense: its elaboration is tied to the liberal model of sociopolitical organization that has dominated the post–World War II epoch, with its emphasis on individual rather than diffuse corporate or state authority, on democratic forms and the market economy, and so on. The dominance of the United States during the period, and the collapse of Europe (and, relatedly, corporatism) at the beginning of the period, are obviously consequential historical factors.

The cultural model of the liberal system is Protestant and Anglo-American in origin but has been carried worldwide in the latter half of the twentieth century. Versions can be found throughout the global system and its organizations (e.g., the United Nations system, the World Bank). The liberal model legitimates an actor (a self or an interest) as an abstract, rather contentless, entity in social space. It also constructs a standardized agent who manages, elaborates, and standardizes that self, employing the latest cultural recipes: elaborate psychological theories for individuals (e.g., self-development [Frank, Meyer, and Miyahara 1995]), organizational theories for firms (participatory management, budgeting systems), development theories for nation-states (neoclassical economics [Biersteker 1992], science management [Finnemore 1996a], welfare policies [Strang and Chang 1993]). The liberal model is distinctive in foregrounding "action," creating extensive psychological, biological, and organizational theory about this action, and focusing upon proper agency arrangements and enactment.

Cultural devolutions other than this liberal form occurred within the broader Western tradition, producing different distributions of social agency. Some featured subunit actorhood much less. The varying devolutions reflect secularized versions of the different religious formations within Western Christendom (McNeill 1963; Jepperson and Meyer 1991). In these religious polities, and in the secularized formations that eventually built upon them, spiritual charisma could be distributed across three main locations: (a) in a central institutional complex (a monarchy, a high Church, a state); (b) in the community as an organic body (that is, in a sacralized matrix of relations [e.g., a system of corporate orders]); or (c) in spiritualized subunits (namely, individuals empowered as souls carrying responsibility for responsible action, whether individually or associationally).

Variations in the social construction of agentic actorhood follow. If a center arrogates spiritual authority and agency, organizations and individuals (and civil society) will tend to have less autonomous agentic standing. If instead relations are more sacralized, then both the center (for instance, a state) and subunits will tend to have less charismatic standing. In the more liberal forms that became dominant in the world polity after World War II, much more charisma was located in subunits (individuals and associations in civil society), producing the system of agentic actorhood under analysis here. In each case, godly authority and powers devolve into social organization, but find different institutionalization.

Consider for instance the more corporate Western traditions, like the Germanic and Scandinavian ones. Locating more authority and charisma in a social community as an organic body (i.e., in a relational system), they gave more substantive content to their constituent (more corporate) social entities: For instance, some organizations or corporate structures may be seen as having long-standing natural rights; theories of personality (and gender) feature more biological grounding (Jepperson 1992; Frank, Meyer, and Miyahara 1995). While this (extrasocial) content of the self (or interests) is expanded, the idea of agentic actorhood is less developed and less central.

Even in the current period, after much standardizing pressure, the more corporatist national variants of the modern system (Germany, Scandinavia, Westernized Japan) more overtly specify the tasks and functions that specific entities are naturally supposed to want and do. Such corporatist arrangements tend to trap entities in explicitly articulated role and hierarchic structures, and less in scripted agency – placing more emphasis on direct training, control, and discipline (Meyer 1983; Jepperson and Meyer 1991; Hofstede 1980; Laurent 1983). Insuring proper agency is a source of much uncertainty and anxiety, hence organizational theories are notoriously more power-oriented in Central Europe than in the Anglo-American tradition (Hofstede 1980; Laurent 1983; Crozier 1964). In contrast, the liberal system organizes more directly around agency: it is in a literal sense more an action system than a control structure (thus the notoriously loose, ill-defined, overlapping, and sprawling organizing structures of the liberal system [Meyer and Scott 1983]). Organizational theories vary accordingly, with their historically distinctive emphasis on informal, tacit, associational coordination, rather than control.

The individual in both these models is "embedded" in social organization, but in the more dominant liberal variant of the modern system, the individual is entrapped in standardized agency more than in explicit social control schemes. Correspondingly the modern (especially liberal) individual displays more standardized "public virtues" (Dahrendorf 1967) relative to nonmoderns, and relative to elaborated private qualities. This is the flattened selfhood but exaggerated actorhood – in our language, the agency profile – so noted for American individuality (classically by Tocqueville; and analyzed by Dahrendorf 1967; Varenne 1977; Thomas et al. 1987; Jepperson 1992).

9.5 Implications for Understanding Features of Modern Actorhood and Social Structure

More direct explanations of a number of features of contemporary social structure become possible if one begins with an analysis of an expanding system of social agency, with a system of constructed "actors" as its carrier. Unacknowledged agency dynamics permeate and shape modern social structure. "Actors" are agents for larger realities and larger imagined truths: they are in substantial part monads of a larger cultural project. Accordingly, they celebrate ideals of mobilized agency, and enter into the sweeping collective action that is distinctive to modern society. In this section we call attention first to features of modern actorhood that come into clearer relief once one attends to its agentic character. Then we bring to attention a number of features of collective authority and action that otherwise go unnoticed or are only arduously accounted for in conventional lines of argument.

9.5.1 The Structure of the Modern Actor

9.5.1.1 The tension between principal and agent within the actor – between legitimated self and agency for this self – generates consequential inconsistencies and contradictions (as in any principal-agent relationship), and occasions ongoing cultural evolution.

Many of the deepest contradictions of "interest" faced by modern actors are those between the interests of the underlying self and those of highly standardized and enacted agency. The underlying self has goals to pursue or interests to protect; the agent is charged to manage this interestedness effectively, but in tune with general principles and truths. This structure creates contradictions and tensions. For instance, the interests of the university as a raw actor[7] involve the production of education and research at low cost; in contrast, the goals of the university as agent are to have effective management control, the maximum number of expensive professors, and the complete array of prestigious programs. In parallel fashion, interests of the nation include socioeconomic development and the enhancement of individual welfare; in contrast, goals of the state as agent involve expensive structures and controls (e.g., the creation and expansion of decorative economic plans and policies, the maintenance of expensive universities) far removed from these objectives.

This same tension is dramatic for individuals, and is celebrated in classic psychological dualisms (I versus Me, long-run versus short-run interests) and in associated analytical conundra (weakness of the will, self-deception, altruism, attitudes versus behavior). Individuals follow their Id (or Inner Child, or whatever) and sacrifice agentic effectiveness, or they build up their agency in canonical ways, but then lose touch with their self. To escape highly standardized agency, actors search for new authenticities or for particularistic cultures in which to express their selves; more contradictions, and cultural evolutions, follow (e.g., therapists and consultants struggle to reconcile the demands of "the new organization" with the desiderata of personal growth).

Much cultural production arises around both the principal and agent elements of actorhood. In connection with the "principal," there are ideologies of self-development and expression for individuals, participatory and representational structures in organizational life, and rituals of authenticity in collective life (for example, democracy itself, or evolving ideologies of diversity). Cultural models of legitimate selfhood or interests continually evolve, reconceptualizing what natural motives and purposes are supposed to be: for example, editing (and taming) the imagined true nature of the nation and its heritages; socializing the true purposes of the organization; developing conceptions of the natural individual that are harmonious with responsible agency.

Models of agency become ever more encompassing as well: political and organizational theories of information, control, and coordination (and sometimes suppression of raw actorhood) become more elaborate; psychological models of self-management become more elaborate as well (and occupy a large share of American popular culture). Much professional work then goes into the improvement of the principal-agent linkage. As new stresses are discovered in individuals and organizations, there is further theorization and modification of the associated principal/agent technologies. All this production expands the structural complexity of the modern actor and also expands its reliance on consultation with a wide range of others. Models of the individual, the organization, and the state are all much more ramified, as is the structure of otherhood supporting the enactment of these more complex models.

9.5.1.2 The highly standardized and scripted nature of agency produces highly isomorphic actors.

Modern actors enact highly standardizing models for agency and scripts for activity, producing two notable sorts of isomorphism. First, modern agentic actors are highly isomorphic within actor types: people enact highly standardized individualism (Inkeles and Smith 1974; Inkeles 1983; Thomas et al. 1987; Jepperson 1992); organizations are highly (and increasingly) structurally similar (Hannan and Freeman 1989; Meyer and Rowan 1977; DiMaggio and Powell 1983); so are nation-states (see the reviews by Finnemore 1996b and Meyer et al. 1997). This phenomenon is most difficult to explain if these entities are seen as raw actors, since they vary so extremely in resources (100-to-1 in the case of states) and also in backgrounds and conditions.

For instance, the model of the effective modern individual is remarkably isomorphic everywhere, and people in fact come to talk and behave in similar ways when they enact these models (Inkeles and Smith 1974; Inkeles 1983). This is also true, and increasingly so, of organizations, so that management texts and consulting firms now flow rapidly into and across sectors and countries, and organizations have in fact become more isomorphic in their structures, procedures, and accounts (Meyer 1994a). Standardized models and recipes are widespread for nation-states too (e.g., UNESCO or World Bank models), and these entities have also become more isomorphic (McNeely 1995).

Second, the isomorphism of the different actor elements of the modern system is also remarkable: individuals, organizations, and states reveal strikingly similar agentic structures and dynamics – the motivation for this chapter. Despite the obvious substantive differences among individuals, groups, and states, the cultural reduction of all to the agent-actor identity produces great commonalities, commonalities that have been taken for granted in most theorizing. Agentic actors at any level are to form clear boundaries and purposes, effectively integrated sovereignty, coherent control systems, and rational technologies.

9.5.1.3 The standardization of agency also helps to account for the decoupling of structural elements of the modern actor.

Institutional lines of argument like ours have striking advantages in the explanation of the decoupling of structural elements of modern individuals and organizational actors. If these entities are in fact mobilized agents assembled within an expanding rationalistic culture, they are often laboring to enact high policies of the most elaborate and standardized forms. However, they are trying to do so with limited and highly variable resources under great local and variable constraints. Imagine, for instance, a Third World country trying to maintain a broadly legitimated stance toward women's rights in a traditional peasant economy (Berkovitch 1999). In such a situation decoupling can understandably be extreme.

For individuals, attitudes and opining will be disconnected from actual behavior (a renowned instance of decoupling that has seemed so problematic for conventional theories of personhood, yet seems such a fundamental and consequential characteristic). For organizations, decision-making discourse will be disconnected from decision making, and both from action (Brunsson 1989). Nation-state constitutional claims and policies are notoriously decoupled from local practices (Boli 1987). In all these cases, the efforts of a highly agentic actor, immersed in general principles of agency, are only loosely coupled to the structures of acting. Many specific decouplings and inconsistencies follow from this underlying structural feature.

One specific decoupling in modern individuals, insufficiently problematized, is revealed in the capacity of individuals to transition quickly from mundane experience into agency for high culture. Marx noted long ago that the Protestant revolutions transformed people into their own priests, and Tocqueville noted how the Americans he met could at a moment's notice posture as if they were advisors to the president. Such comportments seem endemic to the modern system, as when professors move from banal private experience to dispensing high cultural principles in their lectures, or when friends deploy the psychological wisdom of the ages to one another (independent of their own competencies). The agentic empowerment from the broader culture here seems obvious, especially in the liberal polities: the modern individual carries a little piece of ex-godly agency, and has a little role in society's mission to act in history. The properly agentic actor is always partly an agent of the broader historical telos of the modern system, and its postures reveal this telos.

9.5.1.4 The ongoing rationalization and expansion of social agency in modern culture greatly heightens the overall structuration of modern actors.

A most remarkable feature of modern actors, neglected or marginalized by most theorizing, is how complexly structured they are, and how much this structuration has increased over time, and continues to increase (Meyer 1994a). Nation-states, holding constant overall resources and basic functions, are much more elaborate than they were even a few decades ago: they have programs, ministries, and policies covering a much wider range of activities (see Finnemore [1996b] and Meyer et al. [1997] for general reviews; Barrett and Frank [1999] for population control policy; Berkovitch [1999] for policies on the status of women; Frank, Hironaka, Meyer, Schofer, and Tuma [1999] for the environment). Organizations too have tended toward structural elaboration, holding constant reasonable measures of size and technical complexity (Meyer 1994a; for specific examples, see Dobbin, Sutton, Meyer, and Scott [1993], Edelman [1990], Sutton, Dobbin, Meyer, and Scott [1994]). Older academics can easily remember a time when a university entailed the most modest personnel, accounting, legal, safety, environmental, medical, and counseling offices. The expansion in these structures is apparent in most world regions, and covers every sort of organized social sector. Similarly, the inclination of modern individuals everywhere to form plans and policies of an articulated kind seems clear, and their self-proclaimed dimensions and capacities, fueled by the agentic emphases of modern education, are now legion (Inkeles and Smith 1974; Inkeles 1983; Jepperson 1992; Meyer, Ramirez, and Soysal 1992).

To be sure, expanded structuration partly follows from increased complexity and scale in local activities and resources, as is conventionally theorized. But holding these factors constant, structuration also follows directly from the great cultural rationalization of domains that the agentic society, and hence its responsible actors, must take into account; that is, from the elaboration of the principals and principles of proper agency. The less capable student may now be diagnosed as dyslexic, and if so, s/he should do something about it, in proper agentic fashion. Correspondingly the agentic university and nation-state should provide otherhood for such students, and incorporate proper policies. Both individual and collective goods are thereby enhanced in this process. The changes represented would proceed much more haltingly (if at all) without the high legitimation involved.

9.5.2 The Society of Agentic Actors

A society of these standardized, decoupled, complexly structured agentic actors is necessarily a distinctive one, quite different from a society of raw actors imagined by some realist social theorists.

9.5.2.1 A society of agentic actors generates an elaborate social structure of othering activity, given that the modern actor (a) shifts routinely from agency for the self into otherhood for the widest variety of other actors, and (b) is remarkably receptive to othering.
(a) In an instant modern actors transform into others; they brim with rule-laden and intendedly thoughtful counsel for each other. This posturing is taken as natural both by them and their principals, with the obvious hypocrisies largely neglected and unproblematic. Modern individuals also stand ready to offer their services as agents for organized actors, as members (of organizations, of polities), and as consultants. A defining characteristic of the virtuous agentic actor is the capability to enter in good faith the structure of an organized actor, and to assume with little question its purposes. And of course modern individuals comport themselves as advisory others to whole nation-states, in their identities as citizens: they are filled with putative disinterested and relevant opinion. Relatedly, modern organizations and states assume agency responsibilities for the individuals within them, making advice available on the widest variety of topics (from mental health to childrearing).

A "desire for prestige" seems patently inadequate to account for all this enactment of otherhood, given that it is so obviously an institutional construction. Nor is straightforward self-interest sufficient, since much othering is at odds with the more obvious actor interests. For instance, modern actors will take time from their own pursuits to advise and instruct others in general truths, or even to reveal the grounds for their successes to their competitors. This is an inexplicable phenomenon absent attention to the generalized agency of the system.

(b) Note too that modern actors show extreme proclivity to avail themselves of the services of these advisory others. As the natural and spiritual environments are rationalized, anarchic uncertainties are tamed and transformed into rationalized uncertainties, with a myriad of others available to help proper agents deal with them. The exorbitant claims to effective and encompassing agency built into modern actors make them eager markets for this othering.

Three forms of otherhood have rapidly expanded. First, organized actors employ professionalized others, such as therapists or accountants or external consulting firms. Second, they show preference for employing those credentialed in the imagined principles of proper agency, via educational programs that are generally far removed from actual practical demands or competencies (Collins 1979; Berg 1970). Third, relatedly, actors themselves seek direct instruction in general principles of agency as much or more than training in actual practice.

Consultants without direct action responsibility are found everywhere the modern system reaches. Nation-states employ them and respond to their teachings in every modern policy domain, from family law, to education, medicine, and economics. Organizations structure themselves to depend upon a host of professionalized consultants in every sector, and further, internalize the relevant professionals. And modern individuals are well known for their rampant use of such informal and formal consultancy, helping to manage the mobilization of a proper self and its deployment over an (itself standardized) life course (Meyer 1987).

This ritualized and routinized otherhood might be thought to follow unproblematically from the interests of raw actorhood, on the assumption that the information carried by others is instrumentally useful in accomplishing actor goals. However, this representation is not very credible, for well-known empirical reasons (see, e.g., March 1988). That is, few studies can demonstrate the marginal utility of an economics consultant or a more professionally trained manager or a more highly educated employee, or of a training program in the abstract principles of self-management (Berg 1970). Modern actors nevertheless employ otherhood in the absence of demonstrated utility, or even in cases of highly suspect utility.

This practice becomes comprehensible if one sees the modern actor as mainly a legitimated agent for actorhood. Such an entity would obviously devote resources to the elaboration and demonstration of mobilized agency. Doing so may not help actual action – it may even interfere[8] – but openness to otherhood certainly helps with the construction of legitimated and accountable decisions, and for facilitating talk about rational action (Brunsson 1989).

9.5.2.2 The continuing scientization of nature and rationalization of the moral universe creates constant new discoveries of collective problems occasioning agentic pursuit and fueling the sweeping collective action of the modern system.

There is a continuing search for integrating scientific and legal/moral principles, to respond to inconsistencies, and to enable more effective agency. Differences in economic development for instance receive explication in terms of general economic laws, and are then subject to attempted agentic control.

This rationalization becomes an ongoing process, and fosters the extraordinary collective action that is a continuing characteristic, and sometimes even social problem, of the modern system. Thus, the nation-states of this system have been generators of waves and waves of religious and social movements. Human "actors" turn out to be able to mobilize on a large scale around a wide variety of issues, from the welfare of songbirds (Frank et al. 1999) to the worldwide movement for the protection of gay and lesbian rights (Frank and McEneaney 1999) to the abstract pursuit of world economic development (Chabbott 1999). The interstate system itself has been able to mobilize extraordinary levels of war and public commitment to war (notably, as with recent wars, mobilized more around abstract ideological visions than around clear raw-actor interests). Organizations have been able to pursue expansive collective visions: conventional actor theories can sometimes explain "private" behavior of this sort in terms of simple interests, but they have great difficulties explaining the worldwide rise of the various nonprofit structures of the contemporary world.[9]

In fact theories that see the modern system as made up of unremarkable raw actors have the greatest difficulty in explaining modern collective action in general. They tend instead to erect a supposed failure of collective action – in rather extraordinary denial of empirical evidence – as a descriptive nostrum and analytic problem. The actually massive collective action of the modern system becomes explicable if one situates the now standard "logic of collective action" (Olson 1965; Coleman 1990) within a broader logic of collective agency.[10] Specific agents share in the general social agency of the system. In negotiating the definitions and rules of this broader system, agents negotiate the bases of their own existence and authority. Nominally altruistic collective action can then readily be seen as the expression of a self-interest on the part of agents, but it is an interest often at odds with the self-interest of the selves they are to manage.

9.5.2.3 Much authority for collective action, and even social status, is tied to putatively disinterested agency for cultural standards, reflecting the peculiar structural idealism of the modern system.

The great enhancement of the centrality of "disinterested" professionalized others is a notable development of modern society, one difficult to account for in terms of interests or functional requirements. (Indeed demonstrations of functionality are conspicuous for their absence.) The definers and carriers of social agency – especially those more removed from direct responsibility for mundane self-interested actorhood – are granted substantial authority and prominence. The most canonical authority is that of the professional who serves no actor but rather the high truths of the rationalized natural and moral universe: pure otherhood, with no tainting by any particular (i.e., partly profane) actor. In fact, the admixture of pure agency with more mundane interests by professionals is a source of minor pollution-reactions. The therapist, accountant, or lawyer who must bring agency to the service of trivial individual problems is readily seen as tawdry; the scientist who must sacrifice larger concerns with high truth for the practical good of the corporation is readily seen as partly fallen; the social or physical scientist who entertains policy demands is readily seen as a lesser figure.

Naturally this system produces expansion of professionals beyond the requirements of function,[11] and it produces the centrality of professionals in the modern system of authority – surely a core feature of modern society. Power comes from many sources in the modern system, but authority seems to flow more from the relative purity of otherhood.

This relative proximity to high culture, and the putatively disinterested carrying of it, helps to account for peculiar idealist features of the modern stratification system, ones not adequately addressed in the literature (Meyer 1994b). The lowest status in this system is accorded to those categorized as simply self-interested actors; that is, those coded as merely working. A little higher are those certified agent-actors with more agency, in more rationalized and universalized structures; that is, those who manage work, or (receiving more status) provide services (if often invisible ones). High status is accorded to those who do not really work at all (in any conventional sense), or even manage work, but rather serve the great exogenous cultural principles: the professionals and scientists who are often agents of no real principal (Treiman 1977). These are people who get the Nobel prizes, or more prosaically, the highest prestige ratings in surveys. Reflective of this cultural structure, educational credentials everywhere become the master ingredient of status (with credentialism expanding in tandem with the increasing structuration of agentic actors). Further, the single biggest predictor of the relative prestige of an occupation is the educational credentialing that it represents.

Given this stratification system, the explosive expansion in numbers of professionals and scientists, along with professional and scientific authority (and discourse), becomes comprehensible. The inflated cultural system depicting humans and their groups as agent-actors creates a social world in which the most valued roles are those with little raw actorhood.

9.6 Summary and Conclusion

We have tried to contribute to a more substantive account of the modern actor by trying to recover a proper anthropological and historical distance from the modern system. The literatures that might actually situate such actors in history and culture – and thereby actually theorize them – have been strangely peripheralized (sometimes self-peripheralized) in current discourse. Cultural and symbolic anthropology are peripheralized precisely because they are seen as dealing with highly embedded social participants, wearing masks reflecting the authority of the gods – rather than being proper (and properly analyzable) actors. The religious history of the West is peripheralized as dealing with cultural matters irrelevant to the continuing operation of a world of now properly realized actors. Much political doctrine is similarly peripheralized as representing legal and institutional detail, or "ideas," irrelevant to social theory.

We think social theory should be concerned about these elisions. Modern social participants wear masks, too, now carrying the devolved authority of a high god. The modern mask is actorhood itself, and in wearing it modern participants acquire their agentic authority for themselves, each other, and the moral (and natural) universe (Berger, Berger, and Kellner 1973). They become agents for themselves, true, but under the condition that they are also agents for and under constructed rationalized and universalistic standards. These ideas help explain the distinctive features of the modern actor, we have suggested: its historical and anthropological peculiarity, standardization and professionalization, high structuration, isomorphism within and across types of actors, and extraordinary decoupling. Every one of these features is problematic in conventional realist theorizing – and in the more humanist cultural and interpretive work that has arisen in partial reaction.

The notion of culturally devolved agency also helps explain distinctive features of the modern system of actors. Generations of realist theories, starting from a narrow conception of the actor, have struggled to explain how collective action is possible. They have better conceptions of the blockages to collective action (and of the dynamics of raw actor interests) than of the contextual cultural forces that enable and facilitate it. The one-sided analytic preoccupation has been odd, given the demonstrated capacities and practices of the moderns in building imagined communities on expansive national and world scales – operating as others to each other and as agents for all sorts of nonactor interests, including the core high principles on which they all depend. Analysis of this matter is greatly furthered if one starts with the matrix of Western culture, and the idea that actorhood in the first place involves agentic authority devolved from a very distant and very high god. Legitimate actorhood has expanded continuously in this cultural system, and as part of its construction so has the capacity for expanded collective action. The dominant realist imagery has also erected a very peculiar "problem of social order" by seeing modern society as featuring a structure/agency tension between great raw social structural actors (principally the state) and raw subunit actors (especially individuals). This theorized tension is decentered (and downsized) if one sees actor agency as itself a central structure of the system: much of modern structuration exists in the formation, standardization, enactment, and celebration of agentic actorhood. It is further reconceptualized if one recognizes that central structures in the modern stratification system – its most distinctive feature a panoply of authoritative sciences and professions – build around relatively pure agency for high and universalistic collective principles.

Contemporary theorists constantly enjoin us to theorize modern society by "bringing actors back in." This injunction has coincided with little actual analysis of actorhood. To develop such analysis, we have argued, one must necessarily see modern individuals, organizations, and states as taking up standardized technologies of agentic authority, devolved from an elaborate Christian then post-Christian culture.

Notes

1. As indicated, by "realism" we invoke a contrast with more "phenomenological" or "constructivist" imagery. The underlying analytical dimension demarcates the degree to which units or relations under analysis are thought to be relatively generic (i.e., not very historically or contextually specific in "realist" imagery) versus highly constructed (i.e., quite historically or contextually generated); see Thomas, Meyer, Ramirez, and Boli (1987, chap. 1); Jepperson (1991). "Realism" also often entails actor-centric arguments that see activity as controlled by tightly connected incentives and resources. These may arise from the purposes of actors themselves (who may be conceived to be hard-wired [natural] systems [e.g., rational actors]), or from purposes built into wider networks or systems of control.

2. By "agency" we refer to legitimated representation of some legitimated principal, which may be an individual, an actual or potential organization, a nation-state, or abstract principles (like those of law or science, or more prosaically, high culture or even etiquette). Note that the concept "agency" directly draws attention to the devolution of external authority, and to the external legitimation and chartering of activity. We draw the concept from the standard principal/agent contrast, though we broaden the typical usage.

3. We should note that we see our discussion as solidaristic with some European efforts. Foucault's work (and related work) on technologies of the self is obviously directly relevant (Foucault 1979, 1990; Miller and Rose 1994; Miller and O'Leary 1987), with the idea that specific features of actorhood are generated by specific institutional structures. In this article we attend less to specific meso-institutional structures (such as prisons, asylums, clinics) and more to the basic institutional matrix of the modern Western polity. Most theorists have used agency

more as a means of isolating cultural rule systems, rather than studying the basic parameters of agentic actorhood as a topic in itself (e.g., Bourdieu [1977] has used agency as a theoretical entry in this way). We recognize that Luhmann (1982) developed an elaborate system theory of types of action in different institutional systems. We hesitate to position our work vis-a-vis his, except to say that Luhmann did not to our knowledge focus directly on the specifically agentic features of modern actorhood.

4. For a complementary explanatory sketch, see Meyer (1989).
5. By "rationalization" we refer (conventionally) to the cultural accounting of society and its environments in terms of articulated, unified, integrated, universalized, and causally and logically structured schemes (Weber 1927; Parsons 1966; Kalberg 1994).
6. We are focusing upon scientism – to science as a powerful post-Enlightenment ideology – rather than the actual scientific practices problematized by the "science studies" literature (e.g., Latour 1987; Barnes, Bloor, and Henry 1996). Concern for these meso- and microlevel features of science in principle complement our macroscopic ones. In fact, the ways in which the disorder and interestedness of actual scientific activity are cloaked in modern society – so stressed by the "science studies" literature – is a natural product of the extreme legitimacy and prestige of science in the modern polity. This status generates the loose coupling of image and doctrine to actual practice, in ways analyzed in the institutionalist literature about organizations (e.g., Meyer and Scott 1983).
7. By "raw actor" we intend to connote an entity pursuing rather unselfconsciously its built-in purposes – built in either through socialization or prior to socialization (e.g., by biology). These purposes can be nonlegitimated (e.g., some sexual ones), or legitimated self-interests (e.g., a person wanting a nice car).
8. See Brunsson (1989) for organizations, March (1988) for individuals (and organizations), Shenhav and Kamens (1991) for states.
9. The recent Rio conference on the environment, for instance, found many thousands of nonprofit organizations (including hundreds of international ones) eager to participate (Frank et al. 1999; see also Boli and Thomas 1999).
10. Olson (1965) indicated that his "logic of collective action," which specifies self-limiting features of collective action, might not obtain well in religious settings, among others. We are providing a rationale for this scope limitation, in part by specifying and generalizing the "religious" restriction. As we have argued, we see the cultural model of the Western system as religious in character – with substantial implications for expectations about collective action.

11. The literature on professions is well developed in its discussion of careerist interests and structures (e.g., Friedson 1986; Starr 1982), and in the exposure of the extraordinary arbitrariness and subjectivity involved in professional work (Latour 1987). It is almost helpless in discussing the extraordinary authority of these bodies (for partial exceptions see Abbott [1988] and Parsons [1954]). Usually there is an inclination to analyze the professions reductively and exclusively as successful conspiracies. This vision reflects fealty to the dominant analytic realism but it seems highly limited in substance.

References

Abbott, A. (1988). *The System of Professions*, Chicago, IL: University of Chicago Press.
Alexander, J. (1986). *Twenty Lectures on Sociological Theory*, New York, NY: Columbia University Press.
Anderson, B. (1991). *Imagined Communities*, London: Verso.
Barnes, B., D. Bloor, & J. Henry. (1996). *Scientific Knowledge*, London: Athlone.
Barrett, D. & D. Frank. (1999). Population Control for National Development: From World Discourse to National Policies. In J. Boli & G. M. Thomas, eds., *Constructing World Culture: International Nongovernmental Organizations Since 1875*. Stanford, CA: Stanford University Press, pp. 198–221.
Bellah, R. (1964). Religious Evolution. *American Sociological Review*, 29 (3), 358–74.
Berg, I. (1970). *Education and Jobs*, New York, NY: Praeger.
Berger, P. L., B. Berger, & H. Kellner. (1973). *The Homeless Mind*, New York, NY: Vintage.
Berkovitch, N. (1999). The International Women's Movement: Transformations of Citizenship. In J. Boli & G. M. Thomas, eds., *Constructing World Culture: International Nongovernmental Organizations Since 1875*. Stanford, CA: Stanford University Press, pp. 100–26.
Biersteker, T. (1992). The Triumph of Neoclassical Economics in the Developing World. In J. Rosenau & E. O. Czempiel, eds., *Governance without Government: Order and Change in World Politics*. Cambridge: Cambridge University Press, pp. 102–31.
Boli, J. (1987). World Polity Sources of Expanding State Authority and Organization, 1870–1970. In G. Thomas, J. W. Meyer, F. Ramirez, & J. Boli, *Institutional Structure: Constituting State, Society, and the Individual*. Newbury Park, CA: Sage, pp. 71–91.

Boli, J. & G. Thomas, eds. (1999). *Constructing World Culture: International Nongovernmental Organizations Since 1875*, Stanford, CA: Stanford University Press.

Bourdieu, P. (1977). *Outline of a Theory of Practice*, New York, NY: Cambridge University Press.

Boyle, E. H. & J. Meyer. (1998). Modern Law as a Secularized and Global Religious Model: Implications for the Sociology of Law. *Soziale Welt*, 49 (3), 213–32.

Brunsson, N. (1989). *The Organization of Hypocrisy: Talk, Decisions, and Action in Organizations*, New York, NY: Wiley.

Chabbott, C. (1999). Defining Development: The Making of the International Development Field, 1945–1990. In J. Boli & G. M. Thomas, eds., *Constructing World Culture: International Nongovernmental Organizations Since I 875*. Stanford, CA: Stanford University Press, pp. 222–48.

Coleman, J. S. (1973). *Power and the Structure of Society*, New York, NY: Norton.

Coleman, J. S. (1982). *Sociological Insight*, New York, NY: Oxford University Press.

Coleman, J. S. (1990). *Foundations of Social Theory*, Cambridge, MA: Harvard University Press.

Collins, R. (1979). *The Credential Society*, New York, NY: Academic Press.

Crozier, M. (1964). *The Bureaucratic Phenomenon*, Chicago, IL: University of Chicago Press.

Dahrendorf, R. (1967). *Society and Democracy in Germany*, New York, NY: W. W. Norton.

DiMaggio, P. & W. W. Powell. (1983). The Iron Cage Revisited: Institutional Isomorphism and Collective Rationality in Organizational Fields. *American Sociological Review*, 48(2), 147–60.

Dobbin, F., J. Sutton, J. Meyer, & W. R. Scott. (1993). Equal Opportunity Law and the Construction of Internal Labor Markets. *American Journal of Sociology*, 99(2), 396–427.

Dumont, L. (1986). *Essays on Individualism*. Chicago, IL: University of Chicago Press.

Edelman, L. (1990). Legal Environments and Organizational Governance. *American Journal of Sociology*, 95(6), 1401–40.

Eisenstadt, S. (1986). *The Origins and Diversity of Axial Age Civilizations*, Albany, NY: State University of New York Press.

Eisenstadt, S. (1987). *European Civilization in a Comparative Perspective*, Oslo: Norwegian University Press.

Feldman, M. & J. G. March. (1981). Information in Organizations as Signal and Symbol. *Administrative Science Quarterly*, 26(2), 171–86.

Finnemore, M. (1996a). *National Interests in International Society*, Ithaca, NY: Cornell University Press.

Finnemore, M. (1996b). Norms, Culture, and World Politics: Insights from Sociology's Institutionalism. *International Organization*, 50(2), 325–47.

Foucault, M. (1979). *Discipline and Punish*, New York, NY: Vintage.

Foucault, M. (1990). *The History of Sexuality*, New York, NY: Vintage.

Frank, D., A. Hironaka, J. Meyer, E. Schofer, & N. Tuma. (1999). The Rationalization and Organization of Nature in the World Culture. In J. Boli & G. M. Thomas, eds., *Constructing World Culture: International Nongovernmental Organizations Since 1875*. Stanford, CA: Stanford University Press, pp. 81–99.

Frank, D. & E. McEneaney. (1999). The Individualization of Society and the Liberalization of State Policies on Same-Sex Sexual Relations, 1985–1995. *Social Forces*, 77(3), 911–44.

Frank, D., J. Meyer, & D. Miyahara. (1995). The Individualist Polity and the Centrality of Professionalized Psychology. *American Sociological Review*, 60, 360–37.

Friedson, E. (1986). *Professional Powers*, Chicago, IL: University of Chicago Press.

Hall, J. (1986). *Powers and Liberties*, New York, NY: Penguin.

Hannan, M. & J. Freeman. (1989). *Organizational Ecology*, Cambridge, MA: Harvard University Press.

Hobsbawm, E. J., ed. (1983). *The Invention of Tradition*, Cambridge: Cambridge University Press.

Hofstede, G. (1980). *Culture's Consequences*, Beverly Hills, CA: Sage.

Inkeles, A. (1983). *Exploring Individual Modernity*, New York, NY: Columbia University Press.

Inkeles, A. & D. H. Smith. (1974). *Becoming Modern*, Cambridge, MA: Harvard University Press.

Jepperson, R. L. (1991). Institutions, Institutional Effects, and Institutionalism. In W. W. Powell & P. J. DiMaggio, eds., *The New Institutionalism in Organizational Analysis*. Chicago, IL: University of Chicago Press, pp. 143–63.

Jepperson, R. L. (1992). National Scripts: The Varying Construction of Individualism and Opinion Across Modern Nation-States. Ph.D. dissertation. Yale University, Department of Sociology.

Jepperson, R. L. & J. W. Meyer. (1991). The Public Order and the Construction of Formal Organizations. In W. W. Powell & P. J. DiMaggio, eds., *The New Institutionalism in Organizational Analysis*. Chicago, IL: University of Chicago Press.

Kalberg, S. (1994). *Max Weber's Comparative-Historical Sociology*, Cambridge: Cambridge University Press, pp. 204–31.

Latour, B. (1987). *Science in Action*, Cambridge, MA: Harvard University Press.
Laurent, A. (1983). The Cultural Diversity of Western Conceptions of Management. *International Studies of Management and Organization*, 13(1–2), 75–96.
Lerner, D. (1959). *The Passing of Traditional Society*, Glencoe, IL: Free Press.
Luhmann, N. (1982). *The Differentiation of Society*, New York, NY: Columbia University Press.
Mann, Michael. (1986). *The Sources of Social Power*, Cambridge: Cambridge University Press.
March, J. (1988). *Decisions and Organizations*, Oxford: Blackwell.
McNeely, C. (1995). *Constructing the Nation-State*, Westport, CT: Greenwood.
McNeill, W. (1963). *The Rise of the West*, Chicago, IL: University of Chicago Press.
Meyer, J. W. (1983). Conclusion: Institutionalization and the Rationality of Formal Organizational Structure. In J. W. Meyer & W. R. Scott, eds., *Organizational Environments*. Beverly Hills, CA: Sage, pp. 261–82.
Meyer, J. W. (1987). Self and Life Course: Institutionalization and its Effects. In G. Thomas, et al., eds., *Institutional Structure*. Newbury Park, CA: Sage, pp. 261–82.
Meyer, J. W. (1988). Society without Culture: A Nineteenth-Century Legacy. In F. Ramirez, ed., *Rethinking the Nineteenth Century*. New York, NY: Greenwood Press, pp. 193–201.
Meyer, J. W. (1989). Conceptions of Christendom: Notes on the Distinctiveness of the West. In M. Kohn, ed., *Cross National Research in Sociology*. Newbury Park, CA: Sage, pp. 395–413.
Meyer, J. W. (1994a). Rationalized Environments. In W. R. Scott, J. W. Meyer, et al., eds., *Institutional Environments and Organizations*. Newbury Park, CA: Sage, pp. 28–54.
Meyer, J. W. (1994b). The Evolution of Modern Stratification Systems. In D. B. Grusky, ed., *Social Stratification in Sociological Perspective*. Boulder, CO: Westview Press, pp. 730–7.
Meyer, J. W., J. Boli, G. M. Thomas, & F. O. Ramirez. (1997). World Society and the Nation-State. *American Journal of Sociology*, 103(1), 144–82.
Meyer, J. W., F. Ramirez, & Y. Soysal. (1992). World Expansion of Mass Education, 1870–1970. *Sociology of Education*, 65(2), 128–49.
Meyer, J. W. & B. Rowan. (1977). Institutionalized Organization: Formal Structure as Myth and Ceremony. *American Journal of Sociology* 83(2), 340–63.

Meyer, J. W. & W. R. Scott. (1983). *Organizational Environments*, Beverly Hills, CA: Sage.

Miller, P. & T. O'Leary. (1987). Accounting and the Construction of the Governable Person. *Accounting, Organizations and Society*, 12(3), 235–65.

Miller, P. & N. Rose. (1994). On Therapeutic Authority: Psychoanalytical Expertise under Advanced Liberalism. *History of the Human Sciences*, 7 (3), 29–65.

Needham, J. (1954). *Science and Civilization in China*, Cambridge: Cambridge University Press.

North, R. & R. Thomas. (1973). *The Rise of the Western World*, New York, NY: Cambridge University Press.

Olson, M. (1965). *The Logic of Collective Action*, New York, NY: Schocken Books.

Parsons, T. (1954). The Professions and the Social Structure. In T. Parsons, ed., *Essays in Sociological Theory*. Glencoe, IL: The Free Press, pp. 34–49.

Parsons, T. (1966). *Societies: Evolutionary and Comparative Perspectives*. Englewood Cliffs, NJ: Prentice-Hall.

Schofer, E. (1999). Science Associations in the International Sphere, 1875–1990: The Rationalization of Science and the Scientization of Society. In J. Boli & G. M. Thomas, eds., *Constructing World Culture: International Nongovernmental Organizations Since 1875*. Stanford, CA: Stanford University Press, pp. 249–66.

Scott, W. R., J. W. Meyer, & associates. (1994). *Institutional Environments and Organizations*, Thousand Oaks, CA: Sage.

Sewell, W. H. Jr. (1992). A Theory of Structure: Duality, Agency, and Transformation. *American Journal of Sociology*, 98(1), 1–29.

Shenhav, Y. & D. H. Kamens. (1991). The "Costs" of Institutional Isomorphism: Science in Non-Western Countries. *Studies of Science*, 21 (3), 527–45.

Starr, P. (1982). *The Social Transformation of American Medicine*, New York, NY: Basic Books.

Strang, D. & P. Chang. (1993). The International Labor Organization and the Welfare State: Institutional Effects on National Welfare Spending, 1960–80. *American Sociological Review*, 47(2), 235–62.

Sutton, J., F. Dobbin, J. Meyer, & W. R. Scott. (1994). Legalization of the Workplace. *American Journal of Sociology*, 99(4), 944–71.

Thomas, G. & J. W. Meyer. (1984). The Expansion of the State. *Annual Review of Sociology*, 10, 461–82.

Thomas, G., J. W. Meyer, F. Ramirez, & J. Boli. (1987). *Institutional Structure: Constituting State, Society, and the Individual*, Beverly Hills, CA: Sage.

Tilly, C. (1992). *Coercion, Capital, and European* States, Cambridge, MA: Basil Blackwell.

Treiman, D. (1977). *Occupational Prestige in Comparative Perspective*, New York, NY: Academic Press.

Varenne, H. (1977). *Americans Together*, New York, NY: Teachers College Press.

Wallerstein, I. (1974). *The Modern World System*, New York, NY: Academic Press.

Weber, M. (1927). *General Economic History*, New York, NY: Greenberg.

10 | Institutional Theory and World Society (2009)

J. MEYER[*]

Sociological institutional (or neoinstitutional) theory, as it has developed since the 1970s, has provided a useful perspective from which to understand the rise, nature, and impact of the modern world order or society. For many decades, social theories maintained postures that made it difficult to think of the world as a society, and theorists who did so (e.g., Peter Heintz 1972; Roland Robertson 1992; Niklas Luhmann 1975; Bull and Watson 1984) tended to be the exceptions. Rather than a society, the world was seen as anarchical (by realists in political science) or as an economy without a regulating polity (by world systems students following Wallerstein 1974).

The core problem was that the social sciences are themselves creatures of the post-Enlightenment nation-state system. Thus they tend, mostly implicitly (as in Parsons' work), to conceive of societies as coterminous with nations and states. Societies were interdependent systems managed by an over-riding sovereign organization. Since the world did not have a sovereign state, and global interdependence was recognized in only a limited way, the world was by definition not a society.

Institutional theory, particularly in its more sociological versions, dramatically changed that. Along with many other post-functionalist lines of thought, it emphasized a cultural conception of society as an "imagined community" (Anderson 1983), rather than a more realist model of actors involved in functional interdependencies. And it emphasized broad cultural themes and shifts in wider social environments as impacting actors

---

[*] This chapter reflects many themes from my earlier work, and from many collaborations. Its first sections parallel topics covered, vis-à-vis organization theory, in Meyer (2008). Work on the paper was supported by a grant (to Francisco Ramirez and John Meyer) from the Spencer Foundation (20060003). Ronald Jepperson provided many detailed comments and suggestions.
We have removed references to chapters in the book where this article was originally published.

of all sorts – organizations, but also individuals (Meyer and Rowan 1977). The application of this line of thought to conceptualizing a world society and its impact was straightforward. Institutional theory made it easy to conceive of the world as a society, and to analyze the impact of that society on all sorts of subunits, including national states. Further, in a point I emphasize below, institutional theory described and called attention to great movements in world society given neither description nor explanation in much more conventional social theory. So institutional theory, in addition to its explanatory role, has played a descriptive role. It calls attention to important features of the modern world order given little attention in earlier lines of thought.

World society, in this vision, is a good deal more than the set of actors (individuals, organizations, national states) envisioned in much more realist and functionalist social theory. And it is more than the transactions of power and exchange among such actors. The modern world is filled with shared understandings of nature, humans, and society. And it is filled with understandings of a directly collective reality in a physical, moral, and social world (Jepperson and Swidler 1993–4). Obviously, many understandings in the world are not shared, but vary across many dimensions. And many understandings are in no sense linked to conceptions of a common collective order, but rather envision only subunits. The surprising feature of the contemporary world is how much is shared, and how strong collectivity is perceived, not that global unification is in any sense universal.

Thus, world society is filled with associations, of little agency for action, speaking to great collective goods (as with the World Wildlife Fund and the environment, or Amnesty International, or a variety of treaty organizations). It is filled with supra-national professions, like the scientific and legal and social scientific and medical and educational elites, that speak great supra-national truths to all the actors of the world. It is filled with social movements along all these axes, half-organizations and half-professional or ideological. And it is filled with nation-states shifting from their role as actors within a world society to postures of agency for collective truth and virtue of this society: leading national states routinely parade themselves as instances of collective goods (the Americans illustrating enterprise and freedom; the Swedes sober community responsibility; the former communists equality).

All this prominent social material makes up an envisioned world society, of variable significance across social sectors and social regions. It is organized around collective goods – completely collective goods like the reified welfare of Mother Earth, and densely shared common interests like the health of the world exchange system. And orientation toward it clearly penetrates, in many social sectors, far down into ordinary social life, as local people and organizations respond to global environmental problems, or problems of violations of human rights. Much social theory is inattentive to the dramatic expansions of such orientations, and focused only on the internal dynamics of actors and their interdependencies. This has made it difficult for social scientists to explain whole great currents and movements of a more collective kind in the contemporary world (e.g., the environmental or human rights movement, or the worldwide movement for organizational reforms). Interestingly, the same limitations apply to the social scientific analyses of historic Christendom – often seen more as parts than as a culturally constituted whole – and have made it difficult to understand many aspects of the long-term "rise of the West" (see Mann 1986 for a related analysis). A continuing conceptual problem in the more realist social sciences is a very thin conception of culture: at the world level, the term is more likely to refer to some musical tastes than to the academic field of economics, or the highly developed doctrines of environmentalism.

I begin (I) by reviewing the distinctive features of sociological institutional theory, and in particular the more phenomenological versions that are useful in thinking about world society. Then I discuss (II) why this line of theorizing prospers in discussions of world society – that is, the features of world society that reflect processes theorized by the line of theory. In important ways, the kind of variables emphasized in institutional theory play very prominent roles in the post–World War II world. So the theory describes and calls attention to, as well as offers explanations of, major historical developments. (III) I then turn to a substantive review of the core theoretical themes or propositions involved. These involve the factors affecting the construction and expansion of modern "actorhood," creating powers and responsibilities for actors far beyond the plausible. The culture of the modern system greatly elaborates the imagined capacities and responsibilities of individuals, organizations, and national states, endowing them with extraordinarily agentic properties. (IV) This review leads to an emphasis on Durkheimian aspects of contemporary world society – the extent to which this society contains (and is in good part an imagined community constructed by) a collective cultural cosmology that penetrates very deeply into the identity and activity structures of the modern world. And it leads to an emphasis on the social forces that rapidly expand this cosmology, providing instruction and therapy and consulting advice for actors from individuals to national states.

10.1 Institutional Theories

As the social sciences developed after the Enlightenment period, they routinely conceptualized human activity as deeply institutionalized – highly embedded in collective cultural patterns. People were creatures of habit, groups of customs, and societies of culture. Analyses consisted of models, often evolutionary, of variations in these habits and cultures, and of their changes over time.

At the same time, however, the Enlightenment generated many ideas that "man," now possessing formerly divine powers, could use his developing knowledge of nature and society purposively, to accomplish his goals (Foucault 1994). Man in this connection meant, variously, individual human persons in liberal contexts, and nation-states in statist ones (Toulmin 1990). And over time it came to mean the bureaucracies derived from states, and the organizations constructed by individuals. In all these conceptions, persons, states, organizations, and bureaucracies were no longer seen as creatures of habit and culture: they were bounded and purposive and competent actors. In the twentieth century, indeed, the word habit disappeared from the social scientific vocabulary, and the word "actor" became central (Camic 1986). The choice of words is odd – in ordinary usage, it implies a person playing a role written by someone else. But in social science, it means something like a goal-oriented, bounded, integrated, technically effective entity.

With the rise of conceptions of modern society as built up around and by effective purposive actors, an intellectual division of labor developed. Primitive societies, the main focus of anthropology, were seen as embedded in culture. And to some extent, pre-modern societies in the west could be seen in the same way, as creatures of history. But in the social sciences focusing on modernity – economics, sociology, psychology, political science, and so on – preferred analyses increasingly traced causal processes to the bottom-line choices and preferences of human actors (Meyer 1988). Institutions remained, of course, but now these institutions were seen as choices of human actors, or as values deeply internalized by these actors. Modern humans and their groups, in short, created institutions and history, rather than being products of these elements.

With some simplification, one can call these emergent theoretical and normative emphases as realist, and I employ this term for them here. They have a micro-social emphasis, in that they stress the centrality of the subunit actors rather than the wider system (e.g., individuals in societies, nation-state actors in the world). And they are realist in that they tend to see the actors involved as quite hard-wired entities, and the relations and interactions among these actors as quite tangible expressions of the material forces of power and exchange.

World War II gave great impetus to this general line of thought. Notions of humans and their society as embedded in collective culture were disparaged with the stigmatization of corporatism and statism, and liberal conceptions of the actorhood of people and groups greatly strengthened. Individuals could be liberated, and social psychologies proliferated. Groups could be rational organizations, and organization theory blossomed. Societies, with rational decision-making and planning (Hwang 2006), could all develop and progress, and associated theories in economics and political science elaborated. The more culturally based institutions of the past and the primitive world could be overcome with education and rationality. In general, institutions, when recognized, got a bad reputation, as loci of inertia and irrationality: the unfortunate dependence of man on history, rather than history on man (Meyer 1988).

In this emergent social science of the postwar period, institutions were recognized, but as rather derivative structures. They were products of human action and decision, and could be produced and structured in rational ways by highly purposive (and often self-interested) actors. Society could be subjected to rational analysis, and the analyses used for policy purposes. So the dramatic twentieth-century expansion of the social sciences intensified, in the composition of university faculties (Frank and Gabler 2006) and student enrollments (Drori and Moon 2006).

By the early 1970s, the extreme liberal optimism involved in these patterns faded. Development theories of society, institutionalized as policy, did not produce spectacular progress. Rationalistic organizational theory ran up against constant empirical findings of great gaps between the plans and policies of formal organization and the realities of practice in informal structure (e.g., Dalton 1959; Meyer and Rowan 1977). And studies of individual persons demonstrated great inconsistencies between the theoretical autonomous actorhood of individuals and their practical embeddedness in taken-for-granted culture and relationships.

Thus in every social science (except anthropology and history, where the old institutionalisms never died out), new institutionalisms developed. Nation-states, formal organizations, and individuals – the "actors" of the new system – were conceived to be dependent on some sort of institutional structure. These new (or neo-) institutionalisms differed from the old one in one very crucial way. In the new or neo-version, institutional structures worked by affecting and controlling and constraining "actors" – that is, people and groups with real or imagined properties as fairly bounded, autonomous, purposive, rational, and sovereign entities, capable of considerable technical skill and enormous self-control, and possessed of discrete resources. So in this new scheme, national states, rather than being embedded in history and culture, became actors operating under an institutional frame. So also, organizations were seen as actors rather than groups, and were similarly seen to operate under institutional constraints and opportunities. And individual persons came similarly to be seen as highly agentic social actors.

10.1.1 The New Institutionalisms

An expanded recognition of the importance of institutional contexts in affecting social activity has characterized social scientific thinking over the last three decades. But there are sharp differences among lines of theorizing in the extent and character of the driving institutional contexts recognized, and in the degree to which social actors are thought to be affected, penetrated, or constituted by the institutional forces. Many modern social scientific issues are between institutionalisms, rather than between institutional thinking and entirely distinct lines of thought. The issues are reviewed in many discussions: Jepperson (2002) is especially relevant here, but also see the broad reviews by Scott (2001), and Hasse and Kruecken (2005).

For simplicity, I lay out the distinctions among institutionalisms on a single dimension, though multiple components are involved. At one pole, there is realist institutionalism, with (a) very strong conceptions of the priority, boundedness, autonomy, and rationality of actors, and limited conceptions of the effects of any institutions, (b) notions of institutions as clear and operative rules rather than diffuse meaning systems, and (c) very narrow or limited conceptions of the important institutional environments which constrain and empower actors. At the other pole, there is phenomenological institutionalism, with (a) notions of actors as constructed by institutional models and meanings, rather than as prior and fixed entities, (b) conceptions of institutions as cultural meanings rather than narrow organizational rules, and (c) very broad conceptions of institutions as general models constructing both actors and their activities. Thus:

At the realist extreme, we find ideas in economics that the whole modern system is made up of very strong actors and the single institutional rule of property rights (North and Thomas 1973). Parallel ideas in the political science field of international relations treat nation-states as actors in a completely anarchical context, except of the single institutional principle of state sovereignty (Krasner 1999). Both lines of thought have tended to soften over time (e.g., North 1981, Mokyr 1992), with the empirical recognition of more and more elements of institutional contexts. In both cases, the emphasis on a social world of strong actors and anarchic contexts is so strong that there is a tendency to see the putatively single institutional rules crucial to modernity (that is, property rights, or national sovereignty) as having arisen almost by accident (e.g., at Westphalia in the case of sovereignty), since actors themselves are unlikely to cooperate in any trustworthy fashion.

Less extreme positions in political science (and economics) add elements to the institutional environment, and conceive the social actors as somewhat more penetrated or penetrable (see Katzenstein, ed., 1996 for examples). Thus, political scientists imagine the environment contains "norms," and the actors involve may have created these norms (the more realist position) or become socialized to prior norms (slightly less realist). A norm might be "don't use chemical weapons," or "treat your enemies' emissaries civilly."

Standard middle-of-the-road institutionalism in political science conceives international society as a regime made up of a variety of organizations and rules (e.g., Krasner 1983), and as having a good deal of cultural content perhaps generated and controlled by professional epistemic communities (Haas 1992).

This line of thought is central in modern sociology. The locus classicus is DiMaggio and Powell (1983), and broader summaries can be found in Powell and DiMaggio (1991) and Scott (2001 and elsewhere). The "regime" is here called the "organizational field," and the cultural content is again understood to be controlled and generated by professions. By and large, thinking in this important sociological tradition has a realist cast. So the institutional environment controls and empowers actors through coercive organizational powers and professional norms (Scott 2001 has a related typology).

But DiMaggio and Powell (1983) added an additional element in discussing the impact of institutional rules on actors: they called it "mimetic isomorphism," by which actors incorporate institutional rules by taking them for granted without much decision or reflection. At this point, actors are no longer actors in the realist sense, and we are in the domain of more phenomenological institutionalism.

This line of sociological thought, as it arose in the 1970s, is commonly traced to Meyer and Rowan (1977, and elsewhere), which in turn has links back to earlier phenomenological thinking (esp. Berger and Luckmann 1967). Here, the conception of institution is very broad – whole edited and translated models of the world and effective activity in it, culturally (Czarniawska and Sevón, eds., 1996); and whole arrangements of organizations and roles and relations, structurally. And the actors in this institutional system are conceived as constructed and constituted by it, deriving much of their purpose, technical rationality, boundedness, and sovereignty from the institutional environment. So the line of thought is centrally sociological in character, in its analysis of the modern system, conceiving not only of social action as highly constructed, but social actors too: we will thus call the line of argument sociological institutionalism, or just institutionalism (see the review by Jepperson 2002).

As illustrative imagery, here, if a realist looks at the silver screen of social life and perceives a John Wayne, he imagines that this reflects a real true John Wayne. The sociological institutionalist supposes that what he sees is a very ordinary actor (perhaps even a wimp) playing the part of the John Wayne – a part written by a screenwriter who isn't an actor at all, and who may not know how many legs a horse has.

Of course, in the wider world society to which we attend, the "scriptwriter" is a historical-cultural drama. For example, a 900-year history builds the great institutional complex we call the university, with the deepest cultural legitimations (notions about nature, rationality, the truth, and so on) and the most diverse specific instantiations (e.g., detailed analyses of a specific flower, or the culture of teenagers). And the constructed actors are the individuals and groups taking identities as actors within this drama (e.g., the intellectual protagonists, as in Collins 1998). And the participants turn out, despite their exotic roles, to be ordinary people with clay feet. So we recognize, in the great gaps between the postures of the renowned intellectual "actors," and the realities of their daily life and practice, that a great deal of institutional construction has gone on.

As another example, a long much-discussed history produces the complex of legitimations and meanings we call capitalism, or the modern economy (Jepperson and Meyer 2007). Elaborate and intense interpretive scripts are written, so that all sorts of odd actor roles and identities are formed – a complex system of definitions turns friendly advice into expensive therapy, or a song into a worldwide commodity. And enormous energy is put into the playing of stressful roles (laborer, entrepreneur, and so on) far removed from ordinary human life.

Institutional theory has been central in sociological thinking about world society. It offers descriptive and explanatory imagery about the organization of this society, about how and why models of national and individual actors are generated, and about how they play out in practice.

The Red Line: But it must be emphasized that this theoretical perspective creates a certain discomfort in American sociology, and is often seen as in conflict with more realist perspectives. This is not really for theoretical or methodological reasons of a scientific character – the various institutional perspectives are not sharply inconsistent, and multivariate analyses can easily show the impact on particular outcomes of a wide variety of institutional forces. The problem is normative. The American economy, political system, and culture rest strikingly for their legitimation on principles of actorhood – particularly individual actorhood. The notion that actors are themselves constructions importantly violates a whole normative order that is deeply built into American social theory (e.g., Coleman 1986; see Jepperson and Meyer 2007 for an analysis). Thus the phenomenological tradition, starting exactly at the point where DiMaggio and Powell noted a shift from coercive and normative institutional influences on actors to mimetic isomorphism, has been the target of considerable tension of an ultimately normative sort (e.g., Hirsch 1997). In fact, DiMaggio (1988) later made a kind of apology for his transgression – an apology paralleled also by Scott (2006). There is a sort of red line, in American social theory, exactly between more realist mechanisms and the idea of mimetic isomorphism, which denies the ultimate primacy of humans seen as small gods (or "actors"). Interestingly, the issue is much less central in European thought, where there are many parallels to sociological institutionalism in the work of Foucault (e.g., 1991) and his followers (e.g., Rose and Miller 1992), of Luhmann (e.g., 1975) and the later system theorists, of all sorts of postmodern thinkers, and of Giddens (1984). The tensions about institutionalism in European thought reflect European tendencies toward functional models of collective purpose, often left-wing or critical ones. European intellectuals find it easy to understand that the individual is probably not a primordial purposive and rational or reasonable actor, but retain some belief that the king (or another sort of collective normative order) might be.

The tensions between institutional thinking and the modern normative emphasis on the priority and autonomy of actors have played out in many arenas of secondary relevance here. For instance, there is an odd reprise of the nineteenth-century discussions of free will versus determinism. The issue now is the tension between the idea of structural or institutional effects and the modern doctrines, highly legitimated, of human agency (see Sewell 1992, and an enormous subsequent literature, mostly American, on this oddly formulated problem).

If sociological institutionalism runs against some normative currents in American social science, the question arises of why it has prospered so well in recent decades, generating a good deal of social research and receiving much attention. The answer, centrally, relates to the extremely rapid globalization characteristic of the last half century.

10.2 Globalization, World Society, and Institutional Theory

The period since World War II has seen a dramatic increase in the long-term world tendency toward the actualities and perceptions of global integration. The world of conflicting but autonomous national states had run into disaster: it was seen as having created two crushing world wars, a massive global depression, gigantic deliberate destruction of human life including a Holocaust, and now a set of political conflicts between nuclear powers with the capacity to destroy life. It also confronted a most unruly set of social conditions, with much of the world escaping controlling empires and becoming independently acting national states. Further, rapid economic growth and change generated large-scale interdependencies no longer under secure (e.g., imperial) control. In view of the disasters of the century, the dramatically increased perceived interdependence, and the obvious fact that the primordial nationalist state was more problem than solution, new visions were obviously needed.

The natural resolution to the recognition of such expanding interdependencies, in the history of the Western system, has been the creation and expansion of larger-scale controlling state organization. For a variety of reasons, this solution was not viable in the period. A weak United Nations was built, and eventually a weak Western European organization. Some other regional associations and treaties were set up, too. But nothing remotely resembling a true world state was conceivable, and the intellectual fantasies about a world federation characteristic of the previous hundred years or so essentially disappeared.

Given the threats and opportunities of rapidly expanding interdependence, and the absence of any state-building possibilities, other coordinating social and cultural structures evolved. The parallels with the construction of the United States in the nineteenth century, as analyzed by Tocqueville (1836 [1969]), are striking.

A host of intergovernmental and especially non-governmental associations sprang up, devoted to the widest range of possible collective goods (Boli and Thomas 1999). On the governmental level, these were often far from classic self-interest associations, and espoused broad goals related to general matters of global concern: regulating the seabed or Antarctica, or supporting science or human rights. Nation-states in this sense functioned as script-writers for a new world rather than actors in it. This is even more true of the exponentially expanding non-governmental system, through which the broadest range of collective goods has been promulgated: global scientific and medical and educational associations (Doctors without Borders); organizations for the protection of human rights or endangered species (the World Wildlife Fund); advocates of global linguistic reform like Esperanto. These structures function primarily as script-writers, telling actors how to posture and behave in the good of the whole collectivity, rather than the interested actors of realist theory – I have sometimes called them "others," to contrast them with interested actor identities (Meyer 1999). The notion describes participants that function less as interested actors than as agents of collective goods and realities. They are thus less interested actors than significant or generalized others in the Meadian sense, addressing on general or universal principles what the imagined actors in the system should be like and what they should do.

The new global structures, and the societies within them, were at every point filled with rapidly expanding and globally integrating professions. These have been expanding exponentially around the world, carrying supra-national models of activity commonly defined as in the interests of the most universal and most collective goods. They generally lack political or economic control authority, but are renowned as script-writers and consultants, instructing and advising the national, organizational, and individual actors of the modern system. They are not really actors, in the standard senses, but rather agents of wider principles – they tell actors how to be and what to do (Meyer and Jepperson 2000). Thus the term "others." Social scientists are good examples. Economists provide universal prescriptions for progress and development, sociologists for human equality, and political scientists for proper governance. But similarly, medical professionals create worldwide standards, as do biologists and ecologists and engineers. And ultimately, actorhood management itself becomes a profession, and business schools with MBA programs spread all over the world (Sahlin-Andersson and Engwall, eds., 2002; Moon and Wotipka 2006).

The problems confronted by the collectively oriented associations, professions, and actors of the postwar world, and the absence of any real possibility for authoritative resolution, have driven the properties of the world society they came to imagine. First, inevitably many of the resolutions they could produce in order to be successful had to take a broadly cultural form: no authoritative organization was possible. Second, the cultural rules and ideas developed had to be selected to promote a dream of a shared and collective and unified world, not one filled with threatening conflicts. Third, the world culture generated clearly had to locate ideologically its action principles, not in the absent central organizations, but in properly tamed or constructed versions of the legitimated participants in world society: national states, first of all, but also individuals and organizations. Thus, a broadly coherent set of constraints produced the evolution of the modern world culture, eliminating or subordinating many themes (e.g., the class conflicts emphasized by the communists; or the excessively nationalist ideologies of the authoritarians; or the conflictful religious ideas arising out of previous world orders) that threatened possibilities for a new order.

Thus, we can consider how all these universalistic professionals, collective good organizations, and ordinary actors posturing as models and agents of the collective good worked to construct order in a rapidly integrating, but stateless world. Two core questions were involved. (1) First, on what bases could they construct rules and realities of the new world society that appeared so obviously necessary? An imagined and desired world order would obviously require rule systems, but the absence of a proper global state made positive law difficult to formulate and legitimate. (2) Second, what were the bottom-line components of the new system? The absence of a world state made it necessary to find or create loci of ultimate responsibility for the new order. An obvious possibility in the Western cultural system involved the formulation some very strong notions of rather sacralized actorhood, but who were the actors? Nationalism, and the sovereign national state, were very poor, partial, and delegitimated candidates, given the history.

The successful answers to these questions produced by the associations and professionals and posturing national agents giving birth to the new order have dominated the culture of world society throughout the postwar period. They reflect the same logics Tocqueville noted in interpreting an older American history. The answers take the form of formulations with something of a natural law character (in this case locating laws in science and rationality, rather than explicit religious ideas), given the absence of possible positive law bases.

(1) *Rationalization*: The bases of the rules that are to govern the new world society lie in the underlying laws of nature and rationality. Thus, the sciences and especially social sciences experience their extraordinary expansion throughout the period (Drori et al. 2003, 2006; Frank and Gabler 2006). They are thought to arise to deal with functional problems, and may play some role in this. But they are involved even with the ongoing reconstruction and development of the cosmology for the new order (Frank and Meyer 2007; Drori and Meyer 2006). Global social integration and legal order

are, thus, possible because humans act in a universe of common natural laws and social rationalities. This makes possible, for instance, a scientized global environment movement.

(2) *Ontology*: The underlying entities of the global social world, entitled to its protection and empowered to manage it, are human individuals (Thomas et al. 1987; Berger et al. 1974). They may operate through rational organizations, which derive from their choices. Or from national states, which similarly derive from their choices and are to respect their needs. Older notions not rooted directly in individual human rights and powers are delegitimated: nationalist models of corporate states, or bureaucratic or professional models of a Church (or university, or hospital, or business). The individual human, in principle, chooses a church, university, occupation, or even spouse.

The overall outcome of global cultural re-rooting of all of society away from collectives like the state onto the human individual has been an expansive transformation in the social identity of this individual. The widest range of kinds of people (indigenous people, children, handicapped people, and so on) are now accorded global rights as human individuals. The rights have been enormously expanded over time. And their character has changed: from being entitled to autonomy and protection, they are now empowered. They are seen as having the rights and capacities to manage the entire world, economically, socially, religiously, and politically.

These dominating cultural achievements of the postwar period clearly generate globally standardized models of the organization of society. We can note two dramatic dimensions of these. Both of them are core devices for integrating the two dominating elements noted above – the rationalization and scientization of the natural and social environments, and the fundamental ontological standing of the individual.

(3) *A Schooled World*: First, there is the universal, extraordinary and extreme expansion of education (especially higher education) in population coverage, content coverage, and penetrative pedagogy. The expanded rationalized laws of nature and society are melded onto the minds and bodies of the empowered and entitled young to an astonishing degree (Meyer et al. 1992; Schofer and Meyer 2005). And the whole enterprise has a strongly globalized and standardized flavor around the world.

(4) *An Organized World*: Second, there is the equally universal and extreme expansion of society as a collection of highly participatory formal organizations, with every sector of social life (including economy and state) coming to be organized in this fashion (Drori et al., eds., 2006). The organizations involved are hyper-rationalized, and also highly incorporative of the participatory individual. All sorts of alternative structures – traditional bureaucracies, traditional professions, property- and land-owning forms, and families in all their corporate forms – decline relative to the organized society.

Institutional theory is well adapted to both the description and the explanation of all these changes. In contrast, realist models (stressing the power of dominant states and economic organizations) have the greatest difficulty explaining why there are universities in New Guinea, thousands of formal organizations in Uganda, scientific establishments in the Congo, efforts at accounting transparency in Honduras, and symbolically recognized empowered individuals (with, e.g., gay and lesbian rights) everywhere.

Institutional theory can explain why the world generated so many models of proper actorhood during the period, why these models incorporated the elements they do (e.g., the modern individual), why the models have so much impact on putatively autonomous national states everywhere, and why explosions of science and the rationalities, organizations and education, and human rights and powers occur.

The continuing expansion of the world society on economic, political, social, and cultural dimensions through the whole postwar period has generated constant socio-cultural movements along the dimensions noted above. The professions and non-governmental associations, of course, continually expand. Then there is the rationalization of nature and society. The sciences expand, and new ones are created, and it becomes important to contemplate the question of ice on a moon of Jupiter. The social sciences expand even faster, and everything from childrearing to the diet of prehistoric man comes under their scrutiny. Similarly, there is a continuous expansion in the perceived rights and powers of individual persons: women, gay and lesbian rights, indigenous people's rights, the universal human entitlement to health and education and cultural choice, and powers of the young vis-à-vis their parents, their religious and military leaders, and even (tragically) their professors. And in consequence, education expands without a break, so that now about a fifth of a cohort of young people, worldwide, is enrolled in a university (Schofer and Meyer 2005). In parallel, rational organizations expand everywhere too, and global policing tracks their transparency and rationality on worldwide scales of degrees of corruption.

Stabilization and equilibrium would stop these dramatic changes, and would probably also partly undercut the institutional theories that best analyze them. By the logic of these theories, under stable conditions institutionalization works by locating cultural and social material in the proper motives and choices of constructed social actors. So after a period of time, the modern institutional system constructs a drama of realist actorhood. This tendency is analyzed in the work of researchers who study the rise of equal employment requirements for organizations (e.g., Dobbin et al. 1993, 1998; Edelman et al. 1992, 1999). These reflect great social and legal movements, but after institutionalization any ordinary organizational leader can, with the greatest assurance, explain why it is entirely rational for him to hire able women, minorities, and so on – and indeed, to have a program to do so more effectively. Order and realism are thus constructed and supported. Successful institutionalization has reconstructed actors so that they can give the properly motivated accounts of their proper activities. And when they do so, conventional realist social research can properly report these accounts as empirical findings and explanations.

A serious institutionalist would certainly find such accounts misleading, and would suppose the whole depicted realist world in fact rests on broadly institutionalized cultural models, but this idea would recede into the intellectual background of social thought, not the foreground of the business school. So it is well known that a factory in which everyone simply follows the rules will not work (rule-following is a classic oppositional union strategy) – participants have to believe in the enterprise to make it work. And it is well known that most social structures rely heavily on cultural credibility, not just organizational power: this understanding fuels the contemporary social psychological (and economic) emphasis on the importance of something called "trust" for the effective operation of modern social structures, and techniques are proposed to support such trust as a psychological property of individual persons. This is a deflection from the central idea that modern rationalized society depends very heavily on institutionalized models.

10.3 The Core Arguments of Institutional Theory

In giving an account of the rise, nature, and impact of the global society of the past half-century or more, institutional theory employs a very few very general ideas. These can be summarized simply, and they have proved to be quite convincing. Most of them, however, are strongly contested from realist perspectives, though as noted above there need not be any scientific conflict between lines of thought all of which can be true. These lines of thought often make different predictions, but that is a problem for substantive empirical research, not dogmatic resolutions. The real problem is rather a normative one, reflecting a need to stay on the right side of the red line: realist individualism is a reigning ideology of the modern system, and alternatives are seen as undercutting its legitimacy, or as improper and cynical depictions of actorhood in a cultural system resting on great respect for the competence and capacity of actors. So there is a good deal of tension about institutional propositions that in fact have obvious validity.

Argument 1: The Rise of World Models: Modern world society develops a great many models about what human actors – individuals, organizations, and national states – should be like. Far over and above the effects of political and economic powers and interests, these models are developed and elaborated by professions and associations organized around the collective good – and sometimes by established actors operating under collective good claims.

Clearly, there is no way to explain the great social changes of the postwar period that we have outlined above, starting with a realist picture emphasizing the great powerful states and corporations. These did not produce waves of human rights expansion (gay and lesbian rights; a worldwide right to education), nor did they generate global scientization, and social scientization. Nor did they generate huge worldwide waves of educational expansion, or organizational rationalization. All these social changes are better seen as products of scriptwriters – "others" – than as products of interested actors.

But these observations generate much intellectual tension. Realists, who tend to recognize a social world made up only of interested actors, have great difficulty analyzing all these "others." And because the issues are matters of normative tension, rhetoric becomes elaborate: there are defenses of a putative "old institutionalism" that properly recognized the role of power in rule-building (Hirsch and Lounsbury 1997; Stinchcombe 1997). One resolution is to imagine that the professionals, who generate much of the new and expanded cultural material, are doing so as self-interested projects, and manage to hoodwink all sorts of ordinary participants. But this is a weak account of the expanded professional authority of the modern system: it presents professionals as rational actors, but the rest of humanity as rubes.

A valiant attempt to see modern institutional rules as the product of hard-line social interests and functional requirements, with professionals serving mainly simply as mediators, is Stinchcombe's recent criticism of institutional theory (2001; see also 1997). He successfully finds examples that fit his realist arguments. For instance, rules in the construction business have to fit some very real constraints. But Stinchcombe does not attempt explanation of worldwide movements for gay and lesbian rights, or for education, scientization, and corruption control in the furthest peripheries of the world.

Note that a strong implication of Argument 1 is that the global models that arise in the modern system are models of the nation-state and other preferred actors as very nice and well-behaved, and thus as able in principle to get along well with each other. This follows from the Tocquevillian efforts of the professionals and the global associations to imagine and create a peaceful world order without a world state. The models do not stress the old evolutionary virtues of actors that successfully destroy each other.

Argument 2: The Impact of Global Models on Actors: Global models greatly impact the structures of the actors in world society – the national states, organizations, and individual identities involved. This assertion, the original and surprising core idea of institutional theory, is now very widely accepted. It is empirically obvious that the great changes we have discussed have taken place on a worldwide basis, and enter into the structures and policies of essentially every society in the world. No place now escapes education, rational organization, science, social science, and the at least symbolic recognition of the rights and powers of the expanded human individual.

The assertion is obviously true and powerful, but realists have much difficulty with any conception of social actors as highly constructed and penetrated, so there is much tension about the point. The realist demands explanation of why "actors" in the world incorporate the global models – and demands explanation assuming the boundedness and priority and rational self-interestedness of these actors. So instrumental motives must be invoked. Typically, the realist idea is that national societies incorporate world models because "the World Bank makes them do it," or "powerful states make them do it." These arguments completely fail empirically much of the time – it is difficult to say the Americans make a third world country sign treaties the Americans themselves do not sign. And empirically, countries dependent on the World Bank adopt fashionable policies at rates no different than autonomous countries. But the argument helps the realist maintain ideological realism.

One can see an expression of the tensions involved in the elaborate efforts of Mizruchi and Fein (1999) to understand the extraordinary popularity of the work of DiMaggio and Powell (1983). They adopt the posture of sociologists of science to investigate the question (a strategy often involved in special pleading in the social sciences). They discover that the key popularity of the work is in the red-line-crossing idea of "mimetic isomorphism," or taking-for-granted copying of established models. They see this idea as a marginal part of the original work, and thus its popularity as an odd distortion in the history of the science. Thus, the popularity of the work reflects from a kind of unfairness: the authors crossed the red line. Oddly enough, a related theme appears in the apology noted earlier by DiMaggio himself (1988; see also Scott 2006). Even more oddly, Mizruchi himself later came to employ the notion of mimetic isomorphism (Mizruchi et al. 2006).

For a sociological institutionalist, there is no problem in explaining the adoption of external models by actors. First, the expanded modern actor is built on external models in the first place, and readily adapts to their development. This is enhanced by the close supportive linkages between actors and the environments in which they are so deeply embedded. And it is enhanced by the routine incorporation by actors of the relevant professionals involved, who act as receptor sites for world models (Frank et al. 2000). Thus, Kogut and Macpherson show that countries with Chicago economists at their policy centers adopt preferred economic forms faster (2004) – presumably such economists were able to pick up the neoliberal themes coming down from Professor Sachs at Harvard more quickly.

Second, the "others" of world society constantly elaborate the models so that adoption is facilitated, providing constantly intensifying guidance on how to do the correct things. It becomes increasingly clear just how to do education, or health, or organizational reform.

The origins of the models around which modern actors form in the wider world environment help explain why the dominant adopted models in the postwar period have emphasized actorhood that is deeply virtuous in terms of the global collective good. Good nation-states are cooperative participants in global society. Good organizations are rational, transparent, and law-abiding. Good individuals are expanded, schooled, and empowered participants in the world.

Argument 3: Models are Decoupled from Each Other, from Internal Structure, and from Activity: External models flow into the structures of actors in highly decoupled ways. Policies and structures tend to be poorly linked to each other, and often poorly linked to internal subunits and to practices. This is true on an individual case-by-case basis even when at the systemic level there is a good deal of overall coherence.

The decoupling idea has the most massive empirical support in studies of individual actors as in the famous gaps between norms and behavior. It is a central finding in the study of organizations, as with the dramatic inconsistencies between formal and informal organization (Dalton 1959) and the studied inconsistencies and disjunctions between policy and practice (Brunsson 1985, 1989). It is a routine observation in studies of nation-states, with their strikingly low case-level associations between formal policies and actual practices (e.g., Hafner-Burton and Tsutsui 2005; Cole 2005). And it is well-theorized in institutionalist reasoning (Meyer and Rowan 1977). First, global models are elaborated as ideals to solve global problems of legitimation, not only to be useful in practice. Second, these models routinely reflect ideals beyond what is practicable in the most resourceful countries, let along impoverished peripheries. Thus, third, most actors do not have the capacity to conform to the best proprieties. Fourth, historic path dependencies and local interests may make conformity to standard models subject to some resistance. Finally, the adoption of exogenous models can create dialectic reactions. For instance, it is well understood that the long-term global emphasis on the importance and powers of individuals (e.g., democracy) creates some incentives to edit who the relevant individuals are, and thus has sometimes created impulses to genocide.

In fact, from an institutionalist point of view, decoupling is a necessary and stable feature of large-scale universalistic social organization (Brunsson 1989). And to maintain visions of universalistic rationality, modern actors devote enormous efforts at chronic reform activities (e.g., Brunsson and Olsen, eds., 1993). And when the reforms fail, they employ a very wide range of mechanisms to sustain hope for future reform (Brunsson 2006).

Realists have the greatest difficulty with the decoupling idea. They imagine that social structural rules arise because powerful political and economic actors want them in place, and want them implemented. If this doesn't happen, someone is cheating, or someone is asleep, and in any case great long-run stresses must be resolved. Permanent decoupling, as in the routine great inconsistencies between American criminal law and American criminal practice, is a problem for most realists. One can see the extreme tension, for instance, in an attack on a precursor of institutionalist thinking – the famously imagistic paper by Cohen, March, and Olsen called "A Garbage Can Model of Organizational Choice" (1972) – by Bendor et al. (2001) thirty years after the original paper was published. The original paper had some creative imagery about decoupling at its core, and was widely cited for this: it also had some illustrative simulation models that were given little subsequent attention. Unable to effectively attack the core imagery, Bendor et al. devote extraordinary effort to destroy the simulation models, clearly attempting to undercut the whole subsequent institutionalist development (2001: 189): "We believe it is possible to revitalize the [theory]... this operation would deprive the [theory] and the March-Olsen variant of the new institutionalism of a certain mystique. Without this bold move, however, there is little chance that these ideas will shed much enduring light on institutions." Crocodile tears lie thick on the page of the *American Political Science Review*.

Argument 4: Global Models Impact Internal Structure and Activity Independent of Their Adoption: Global institutional changes have pervasive effects, operating as waves running through the world (and through nominal actors in the world) rather than through point-by-point transmission through networks and organizational structures.

The point here is an obvious one about the world. An enormous amount of planned change doesn't get effectively organizationally implemented, given the extreme decouplings of the modern system. But an enormous amount of change happens anyway, impacting actors that have adopted corrected policies and actors that haven't done so. The inflated character of the modern actor means that internal components and behaviors are under systemic control more than under local actor control. The modern actor, constructed from the wider environment and maintained by linkages to that environment, has many internal components under environmental control. Being a properly modern rational actor, given inflated definitions, is possible only through a great deal of conformity, and by having many structural components (e.g., decisions) supported by the environment.

Thus Ramirez and his colleagues (e.g., Bradley and Ramirez 1996) study the impact of world norms on rapidly expanding female enrollments in higher education. They naturally observe pro-female policy changes in countries through the whole postwar period (perhaps greater in countries more closely tied to the world society). At the country level, such policy changes seem to have no direct effect at all: that is, countries with pro-female-education policies do not have more rapidly expanding female enrollment. Worldwide, female enrollments dramatically increase, but they increase in both adopters and non-adopters of virtuous policy. Exactly the same pattern appears in Abu Sharkh's (2002) cross-national study of child labor. Countries (especially well-linked-in ones) ratify International Labor Organization principles against child labor, but doing so has no effect on practices. But child labor declines sharply everywhere (especially in well-linked countries). Related findings characterize research on human rights (Cole 2005; Hathaway 2002; Hafner Burton and Tsutsui 2005). And similar results characterize studies of worldwide changes in demographic transitions (Bongaarts and Watkins 1996).

The key idea here is that modern social actors are highly expanded and highly constructed: their components reflect exogenous principles and forces rather than right functional relations. So change in the wider environment can flow in and around actors in wave-like patterns, only very partially affected by tight network and organizational relationships.

This Durkheimian point about the embeddedness of social actors in diffuse collective cultural environments has powerful implications for the study of large-scale and long-run social change in the current world society. We turn to a discussion of this point, and the presentation of one final argument in the discussion of world society from the point of view of institutional theory.

10.4 World Society, Institutional Theory, and Large-Scale Social Change

A striking feature of modern, highly developed, social science has been its inability to predict, or even analyze after the fact, a great deal of worldwide social change. It is precisely in the areas to which the institutional theory of world society most directly attends that the failure is most extreme.

Thus the world has experienced a dramatic and exponential expansion of all sorts of inter- and non-governmental organizational structure, without pause, through the whole postwar period (Boli and Thomas 1999; Drori et al. 2006). The expansion cuts across topic areas and regions of world society and involves organizations that penetrate far down into the world's societies, so that local persons and groups are dramatically more likely to be linked in than in the past. But one can study the social scientific literature on organizations theory and get no real hint of this dramatic change, and even long after the established fact get no real explanation.

Exactly the same sort of thing has gone on with the global expansion of the widest range of professions and professionals. Expansion goes on everywhere, and linking into world society. Lawyers and judges, supposedly prisoners of national boundaries, cite international precedents with abandon. Medical communication is worldwide, and so is managerialism. The social work people talk about global social policies, and routinely communication cross-nationally, in a way that was very implausible a few decades ago. The widest range of academic professionals is linked in to worldwide communication and citation patterns. Overall, the professionals are now a dominant category in the global occupational structure. But the social sciences – having no real explanation – continue to reason as if we were in the older world of workers and farmers and capitalists and owners. And nation-states. The problem, essentially, is the limited social scientific awareness that modern participants are acting in relation to a world society. When a supranational society is theorized, it is mainly seen as a production and exchange economy. But that conception cannot provide explanations of most of the crucial global expansions, which arise from a richly developed imagined world society (Anderson 1983).

The impact of all this machinery on the astonishing expansions and globalizations of science and social science is dramatic (Frank and

Gabler 2006). And so is the impact on the extraordinary career of human rights, which expands its domain in the most dramatic ways to cover new groups, new rights, and details down to the local ground of social life (Berkovitch 1999; Boyle 2002; Frank and McEneaney 1999; Ramirez et al. 1998; Soysal 1994; Tsutsui and Wotipka 2004). The social scientific analysis of these changes, and of the processes by which they occur, is impoverished. Social scientific thought can comprehend, for instance, a Saudi Arabia that sharply restricts the public roles of women. It cannot readily comprehend a Saudi Arabia with extraordinarily expanded female educational enrollments all the way through the university level (Bradley and Ramirez 1995).

Finally, the domestic consequences of all this – worldwide expansions in education and intra-societal formal organization, penetrating every society – have been extreme. But it is most difficult to find serious social scientific attempts, even unsuccessful ones, to try to explain rapid educational expansion in Malawi, and intensive organization-building in the Republic of Georgia (both countries without the supposedly necessary economic infrastructures).

The Durkheimian vision embodied in Argument 4 above can help explain both the problem and the solution here. Obviously, social scientific reasoning, especially in the American context, has stayed on the ideologically proper or realist side of the red line discussed above. Actors are taken very seriously as bounded, autonomous, prior, and purposive. So explanations of how and why they might change are restricted to realist mechanisms – organizational and network processes that bring new information and incentives into fixed structures. Thus, a leading social scientist might explain the unpredicted women's movement with demographic arguments (Stinchcombe 1968) about expanded education, lowered birth rates, and efficient domestic machinery. Or, shifting to a demand side, the scientist might imagine changed work force needs requiring women. None of this makes all that much sense in explaining such a broad social change running through the whole population, and none of it explains a women's movement in Thailand.

Argument 4 works much better. Changed postwar global ideologies about human rights apply everywhere, can easily be developed to cover many different populations (certainly including women), and are available to the widest array of intra-societal groups everywhere. Women can pick up the new story, or school teachers, or lawyers and legislators, or young female students. And all these people can adopt the new story in their thinking, their activities, or in very partial versions of each. If we assume that each actor in world society – individuals, organizations, or national states – is a composite of decoupled components, each exposed to and indeed dependent on the exogenous cultural environment, explanations for the diffusion of all sorts of broad ideological constructions are easy to generate and test. We can quickly understand the expansion of female educational enrollments in the most unlikely fields and countries (as per Bradley and Ramirez 1996, or Wotipka and Ramirez 2001).

The key idea is that as persons and groups and societies in the modern system become legitimated as "actors," they become very open systems (Meyer and Jepperson 2000), highly exposed to and embedded in their environments on many dimensions and through many pathways. Dependencies on wider cultural and organizational environments are built in at every point. So even if an organizational manager forgets to adapt to a changed principle – say, a favorable attitudes towards the employment of gay people – many internal participants will independently understand the new rule. And because the organization will probably have expanded its actorhood by employing many schooled professionals paid and trained to be attuned to the wider environment, the flow of the appropriate cultural material into the organization will probably be quite rapid.

The same points can be made about the modern nation-states, as expanded and empowered but by the same token deeply embedded actors (McNeely 1995). Their internal participants – increasing numbers of whom are highly professionalized and thus tied through schooling to the wider world order – rapidly bring in the culture of the wider system. And the same points can be made about the modern schooled individual, who quickly picks up the new social forms independent of internal preferences or of habituated activities.

Thus, the processes we have discussed above give an account of how the modern system turns people and groups and societies into organized and empowered and expanded actors. Plausible theories of an integrated but stateless system call for models of expanded actorhood. Classes of professional and associational model-producers quickly arise and expand, and the appropriate models of actorhood are produced. They diffuse throughout the world, as people and groups and societies find empowered actorhood an attractive prospect. Much decoupling and inconsistency results, but expanded actors are in the same way open systems, so the new cultural materials flow in anyway.

All these processes produce the strange world we now observe. It is a world with the most inflated claims about the rights and powers of human persons, the obligations and competencies of formal organizations in every sector of social life, and the extraordinary powers and responsibilities of national states. For all these structures, inflation produces expectations and standards far beyond any possible tightly coupled reality.

So no nation-state is really capable of being and doing what a nation-state now should be and do. All are failed states by the expanded modern criteria. Similarly, no organization can competently do all the things a modern organization should do according to expanded actorhood standards. And no individual is remotely competent to exercise all the powers and responsibilities a modern individual has: by now, all political, economic, social, and cultural outcomes are thought to be determined by, and in principle the responsibilities of, individual human persons seen as actors. Individual identities are enormously expanded and proliferated.

High aspirations and high self-esteem are everywhere, and have the highest legitimacy. Compared to them, reality looks mostly like failure. By expanded current standards, essentially all the actors in the world require the most extensive therapies. This produces the contemporary astounding demand for therapists – the professionals and organizations and helpful actors that created the expanded demand in the first place.

Argument 5: Expanded Modern Actorhood Creates Expanded Professionalism and Consultancy: Worldwide, we can observe the most dramatic increases in the sorts of professional occupations that provide advice and therapy to actors on the widest range of dimensions. Every sector of social life generates expanded professional consultants. This is obviously true for individuals, with huge and growing populations of consultants providing help: medical, psychological, educational, legal, economic, recreational, spiritual, and so on.

In the same way, organizations seem to need ever-expanding arrays of consulting help. Some of this can be internalized, with the incorporation of the relevant professionals. But much of it occurs in a globally-expanding market of consultants and consulting organizations. The consultants involved tend to cover most of the same domains dealt with by the therapists of the modern individual, suggesting the extent to which modern actorhood of every sort has many elements in common (Djelic and Sahlin-Andersson, eds., 2006; Sahlin-Andersson and Engwall, eds., 2002; Drori et al., eds., 2006).

And national states turn out to need advice and instruction on the widest variety of issues, so a great and growing set of international organizations and professionals arises to provide the appropriate services (McNeely 1995; Finnemore 1993).

Conflicts: The world social system we have described is built on visions of highly responsible participatory actors cooperating in an orderly global society. But in a number of ways, it can and does generate and intensify conflicts.

(1) By and large, the professionals and associations generating models for global society, and consultantship and therapies within this society, do so in ways that envision little conflict. These groups are rooted in the universalisms of science, social science, legal rights, education, rational organization, and so on. But of course many other participants in world society have their own visions of the global collective good, and produce more conflictful or less universalistic models of this good. So with expanding integration, and expanding actorhood, all sorts of religious, national, and ethnic leadership arises and mobilizes the expanding actors in directions that create conflicts. Economists do jihad for global progress, and sociologists for global equality, but other model-builders and advisors fill the same role with other forms of jihad.

(2) Models of expanding actorhood have built-in inconsistencies. First, there are the obvious inconsistencies between the expanded individual actor and the expanded organizational and nation-state actors. The individual is increasingly entitled to a self-chosen culture, and the organization to integrated cooperation.

Second, there are the legitimated inconsistencies between actors at each level. Individuals with expanded rights tread on each other's toes (in part generating the exceptional violence of American society, for example). Organizations are dramatically interpenetrated, with endless inconsistencies between, for example, professional and organizational obligations. Similarly, expanded national states have expanded possibilities for conflict with each other.

Third, there are the dramatic inconsistencies between actor powers and rights, on the one hand, and practical realities, on the other. The world society celebrates the equality of individuals and nations, but is extraordinarily unequal in fact – and with expanded integration, these inequalities increasingly come to be seen as inequities. The world's models of national societies emphasize possibilities for progress and internal equality that are unrealizable, and increasingly seen as unjust. Everywhere, there are the legitimate perceptions of world society, national societies, organizational life, and individual life as involving failure. A world of high self-regard is a world with many possibilities for failure and the perception of failure and injustice. Thus, the modern system is filled with well-constructed legitimation crises, though not of the sort Habermas (1975) may have had in mind. The crises involved provide much fuel for mobilization, and for the expansion of markets for consulting and the mobilization of helpful professional and associational "others."

All these kinds of inconsistency provide fuel for social mobilization, and often conflict. And the mobilizations and conflicts involved often have high world-recognized legitimacy, permitting much mobilization, great ideological formulations, and massive collective action.

In a well-known treatise, Mancur Olson (1965) noted the extreme difficulty with which systems of self-interested rational actors and actions could generate collective action. He noted that this problem might not exist with other forms of action – for example, religious actors and their activities. Since we obviously live in a world that has generated extraordinary levels of collective action, it may be fair to infer that our nominally secular social modern world is a highly religious one.

10.5 Modernity as a Quasi-Religious System

The social sciences have tended to take a micro-social and realist stance toward modern society. They have in recent decades brought "back in" actors. Individuals as actors, nation-states as actors, and all sorts of organizations as actors. The imagery about collective life is aggregative – social forces work by affecting and constraining these (often individual) actors, who then scheme, employing power to achieve their interests (Coleman 1986; see Jepperson and Meyer 2007 for an analysis). Society is an aggregated product of their struggles. Much of the thinking involved works from economic metaphors, as if modern people are competing for something to eat in a scarce environment. And indeed, the field of economics has gained a great deal of centrality: within political science and sociology, modified economic ways of thinking (e.g., "economic sociology") have also gained some prominence.

Central to all this thinking is a picture of the social world as made up of interested actors in some sort of organized or network relation to each other. The term "organizational field" is popular, as is the term "opportunity structure." The implication is indeed that the actors have strong interests and pursue them. The actors and their interests are prior, though in more sociological versions some network relationships and constraints on these may also be seen as exogenous – so the actors are very real actors, but are constrained (or sometimes empowered) by their embeddedness in organized social relations.

This scheme is applied very broadly. So, for example, the whole occupational structure is seen in light of economic metaphors – as a great labor market, in which people produce products which they then can exchange for other products (adding up to a Gross National Product). This is very strange, since in modern societies relatively few people engage in anything that might traditionally be defined as work or labor. And their jobs are often more organized around credentials than markets. And for most of them there is no very clear product, and certainly no clear exchange of products in any traditionally economic sense of "products." In modern societies, for instance, the most common jobs are positions like schoolteacher. Or manager. Indeed, most jobs lie entirely outside any sector with clear and tight links to a productive economy. They are in medicine, or education, or religion, or recreation, or the civil service, or the military, and both concepts and measures of "productivity" tend to be very opaque: very often operationalization consists simply of the tautological principle that if someone gets paid, they must have done something productive. From a traditional economic point of view, modern society is a ball game played without a ball: or with an elaborate set of sociocultural definitions substituting for a ball. The roles and identities of the participants, similarly, cannot be seen as dominated by exogenous and prior actorhood if the interests and purposes of these participants are centrally socioculturally constructed.

So at the least, it is useful to set up models which start at the other end of things – with the socioculturally constructing "others" rather than the "actors" that are their products, and with the rationalized and scientized environment (or ball game) within which they interact. This was the spirit of the renowned "garbage can model" discussed above (Cohen et al. 1972), and is very much the spirit of the sociological institutionalism which followed it. More broadly, it is the spirit of almost any phenomenological sociology or cultural anthropology, identifying the cultural worlds that inhabitants are acting within. A key idea of sociological institutionalism, is that modern cultural worlds identify these inhabitants as "actors."

If we do start with the cultural constructions, we immediately observe that they work not by defining seamless webs of cultural authority, as in the good old days of the oldest institutionalism. They work by defining "actors" at the front and center of the social stage. And they defined these actors as having interests and goals and relationships. These relationships occur in a very highly rationalized context, involving the scientized analyses of nature and very detailed models of organized social structure: extraordinary levels of differentiation isolate special sectors of social life, so actors can have goals difficult to think of in an earlier world (stamp collecting, skiing, possessing a house with ten thousand square feet, achieving recognition for eating hot dogs).

How is integration to be achieved in this constructed world? Clearly, money – rooted originally in economic imagery – plays a core role as a generalized medium of value (Jepperson and Meyer 2007; see Zelizer 1994 for instances of the fragmentation of this medium). Most of it is received for activities of little-known significance for traditionally conceived economic activity (teaching, for instance, or doing economic or sociological research). And most of it is spent for things of little significance in traditional productive economy terms. But it does permit a rough sociocultural translation of activity and meaning around the world: one can fairly definitively relate violin playing in Mongolia to grave robbing in Rome through the medium. Neither of these activities has economic meaning in any traditional sense. But being able to relate them so tightly to each other maintains a reality in which standardized human social actors, behaving in a standardized and rationalized world, enter into a common conceptualized or imagined polity. The logic here is deeper than economistic reasoning: fundamental human "actors" have many utilities in common, and these can be well indexed by a standard criterion of value. Thus more than a medium of economic exchange, money in the modern world society becomes an index of shared value and values.

All this has a highly constructed ceremonial quality. This, presumably, is an essential element of an integrated but stateless world polity.

10.6 Conclusions

Institutional theory provides something of a systemic picture describing and explaining some important features of the modern world society. It is a picture at dramatic odds with realist emphases on a world economy and power structure, and accounts for many things that realist notions cannot well explain (or simply ignore).

The institutionalist vision stresses the world as, in good part, a culturally imagined community, with elements that parallel religious visions. Cultural leaders from the schooled professions, and public good associations incorporating their ideas, rise to play prominent roles. The analogues with religious leaders from other integrated but decentralized systems are direct (e.g., nineteenth-century America; many periods in medieval Europe). And of course, participants who are interested actors in the world rise above their interests to enter the higher world of the collective good: Nations like the United States or Sweden support grand disinterested visions of the world order, much like the kings (who were religious as well as secular leaders) of the medieval world.

Beyond this, more traditionally religious elites also mobilize to make increasingly global claims. They try to reconstruct explicitly spiritual commonalities and unifying principles for a world society. And they try to put forward claims for the global recognition of spaces and themes. These efforts have been successful at mobilizing subgroups within world society, and conflicts among them (as in Islamic efforts to extend their claims to the larger world), but have been surprisingly unsuccessful in generating explicitly religious world themes on a global collective level. The contrast with the normative successes of elites rooted in more secular traditions – the supporters of scientific and rationalistic norms, and legal principles of human rights – is notable. Even the new "traditions" of a global order, such as World Heritage Sites, tend to be supported with more rationalistic discourses.

All the main elites support religious-like visions of a world of modern virtuous actors, saved by schooling and organizational reform to be valid participants in a transformed global community. Models of policy and identity arise – adoption will lead to universal progress and universal equality and justice. These models stress, not the need for participants in the world to abase themselves before a dominating organizational structure, but the empowerment and entitlement of the participants themselves as somewhat sacralized and legitimated "actors."

Naturally, the actors themselves find such models attractive, and adoption is very common. Individual self-regard rises around the world, and former peasantries come to hold and express opinions, and to mobilize. Groups turn into organizations, with purposes and policies and programs: they take on strategies for effective action. And national states greatly expand their powers and responsibilities – they now assume primary responsibility for national progress and justice.

But whether or not particular entities take on their full roles as actors, with the rights and powers involved, the same cultural standards are likely to penetrate them anyway. Expanded actors in the modern system are highly decoupled open systems, subject to pervasive cultural flows.

In any event, the expanded and rather religious actorhood that spreads around the world vastly transcends the realistic capabilities of the participating actors. It creates a greatly expanded set of persons and groups at the top of the world stratification system who are not exactly actors in the ordinary social scientific sense. They are "others," schooled in university knowledge of natural and rational law, and in their understanding of the rights and obligations of actors. They have much in common with religious functionaries everywhere. They make their living telling actors what to do, analyzing the failures of actors, and creating expanded new models of what actors should be like.

The outcome, obviously, is a world of rapid integration, much conflict, and very high levels of collective action. The integration, conflict, and collective action occur around models that are sometimes explicitly religious but more often secular dramas of science, rationality, and legal rights. Whether or not they are explicitly religious, they clearly have an ultimately religious or transcendental character.

References

Abu Sharkh, M. (2002). History and Results of Labor Standard Initiatives. PhD dissertation, Free University of Berlin.

Anderson, B. (1983). *Imagined Communities*, London: Verso.

Bendor, J., T. M. Moe, & K. W. Shotts. (2001). Recycling the Garbage Can: An Assessment of the Research Program. *American Political Science Review*, 95(1), 169–90.

Berger, P. L., B. Berger, & H. Kellner. (1974). *The Homeless Mind: Modernization and Consciousness*, New York, NY: Vintage Books.

Berger, P. L. & T. Luckmann. (1967). *The Social Construction of Reality*, New York, NY: Doubleday.

Berkovitch, N. (1999). *From Motherhood to Citizenship*, Baltimore, MD: Johns Hopkins University Press.

Berkovitch, N. & G. Thomas. (1999). *Constructing World Culture: International Non-Governmental Organizations Since 1875*, Stanford, CA: Stanford University Press.

Bongaarts, J. & S. C. Watkins. (1996). Social Interactions and Contemporary Fertility Transitions. *Population and Development Review*, 22(4), 639–82.

Boyle, E. H. (2002). *Female Genital Cutting: Cultural Conflict in the Global Community*, Baltimore, MD: Johns Hopkins University Press.

Bradley, K. & F. Ramirez. (1996). World Polity and Gender Parity: Women's Share of Higher Education, 1965–1985. In A. M. Pallas, ed., *Research in Sociology of Education and Socialization*, Vol. XI. Greenwich, CT: JAI Press, pp. 63–91.

Brunsson, N. (1985). *The Irrational Organization*, Chichester: Wiley.

Brunsson, N. (1989). *The Organization of Hypocrisy*, Chichester: Wiley.

Brunsson, N. (2006). *Mechanisms of Hope: Maintaining the Dream of the Rational Organization*, Copenhagen: Copenhagen Business School Press.

Brunsson, N. & J. P. Olsen. (1993). *The Reforming Organization*, London: Routledge.

Bull, H. & A. Watson, eds. (1984). *The Expansion of International Society*, Oxford: Oxford University Press.

Camic, C. (1986). The Matter of Habit. *American Journal of Sociology*, 91 (5), 1039–87.

Cole, W. (2005). Sovereignty Relinquished? Explaining Commitment to the International Human Rights Covenants, 1966–1999. *American Sociological Review*, 70(3), 472–95.

Collins, R. (1998). *The Sociology of Philosophies*, Cambridge, MA: Belknap Press.

Cohen, M., J. March, & J. Olsen. (1972). A Garbage Can Model of Organizational Choice. *Administrative Science Quarterly*, 17(1), 1–25.

Coleman, J. S. (1986). Social Theory, Social Research, and a Theory of Action. *American Journal of Sociology*, 91(6), 1309–35.
Czarniawska, B. & G. Sevón, eds. (1996). *Translating Organizational Change*, Berlin: de Gruyter.
Dalton, M. (1959). *Men Who Manage*, New York, NY: Wiley.
DiMaggio, P. (1988). Interest and Agency in Institutional Theory. In L. Zucker, ed., *Institutional Patterns and Organizations*. Cambridge, MA: Ballinger, pp. 3–21.
DiMaggio, P. & W. W. Powell. (1983). The Iron Cage Revisited: Institutional Isomorphism and Collective Rationality in Organizational Fields. *American Sociological Review*, 48(2), 147–60.
Djelic, M. & K. Sahlin-Andersson, eds. (2006). *Transnational Governance*, Cambridge: Cambridge University Press.
Dobbin, F. & J. R. Sutton. (1998). The Strength of a Weak State: The Employment Rights Revolution and the Rise of Human Resources Management Divisions. *American Journal of Sociology*, 104(2), 441–76.
Dobbin, F., J. R. Sutton, J. W. Meyer, & W. R. Scott. (1993). Equal Opportunity Law and the Construction of Internal Labor Markets. *American Journal of Sociology*, 99(2), 396–427.
Drori, G. S. & J. W. Meyer. (2006). Scientization: Making a World Safe for Organizing. In M. Djelic & K. Sahlin-Andersson, eds., *Transnational Governance: Institutional Dynamics of Regulation*. Cambridge: Cambridge University Press, pp. 31–52.
Drori, G. S., J. W. Meyer, & H. Hwang, eds. (2006). *Globalization and Organization: World Society and Organizational Change*, Oxford: Oxford University Press.
Drori, G. S., J. W. Meyer, F. O. Ramirez, & E. Schofer. (2003). *Science in the Modern World Polity*, Stanford, CA: Stanford University Press.
Drori, G. S. & H. Moon. (2006). The Changing Nature of Tertiary Education: Cross-National Trends in Disciplinary Enrollment, 1965–1995. In D. P. Baker & A. W. Wiseman, eds., *The Impact of Comparative Education Research on Institutional Theory*. Oxford: Elsevier Science Ltd.
Edelman, L. (1992). Legal Ambiguity and Symbolic Structures: Organizational Mediation of Civil Rights Law. *American Journal of Sociology*, 97(6), 1531–76.
Edelman, L., C. Uggen, & H. S. Erlanger. (1999). The Endogeneity of Legal Regulation: Grievance Procedures as Rational Myth. *American Journal of Sociology*, 105(2), 406–54.
Finnemore, M. (1993). International Organizations as Teachers of Norms. *International Organization*, 47(4), 565–97.

Foucault, M. (1991). Governmentality. In G. Burchell, C. Gordon, & P. Miller, eds, *The Foucault Effect: Studies in Governmentality*. Chicago, IL: University of Chicago Press, pp. 87-104.

Foucault, M. (1994). *The Order of Things: An Archeology of the Human Sciences*, New York, NY: Vintage Books.

Frank, D. J. & J. Gabler. (2006). *Reconstructing the University: Worldwide Changes in Academic Emphases over the 20th Century*, Stanford, CA: Stanford University Press.

Frank, D. J., A. Hironaka, & E. Schofer. (2000). The Nation-State and the Natural Environment Over the Twentieth Century. *American Sociological Review*, 65(1), 96–116.

Frank, D. J. & E. McEneaney. (1999). The Individualization of Society and the Liberalization of State Policies on Same-Sex Sexual Relations, 1984–1995. *Social Forces*, 77(3), 911–44.

Frank, D. J. & J. W. Meyer. (2007). University Expansion and the Knowledge Society. *Theory and Society*, 36(4), 287–311.

Giddens, A. (1984). *The Constitution of Society*, Berkeley, CA: University of California Press.

Haas, P. (1992). Epistemic Communities and International Policy Coordination. *International Organization*, 46(1), 1–35.

Habermas, J. (1975). *Legitimation Crisis*, Boston, MA: Beacon Press.

Hafner-Burton, E. & K. Tsutsui. (2005). Human Rights in a Globalizing World: The Paradox of Empty Promises. *American Journal of Sociology*, 110(5), 1373–411.

Hasse, R. & G. Kruecken. (2005). *Neo-Institutionalismus*. Rev. ed. Bielefeld: transcript Verlag.

Hathaway, O. A. (2002). Do Human Rights Treaties Make a Difference? *Yale Law Journal*, 111(8), 1935–2042.

Heintz, P. (1972). *A Macrosociological Theory of Societal Systems: With Special Reference to the International System*, Bern: Hans Huber Publishers.

Hirsch, P. M. (1997). Sociology Without Social Structure: Neoinstitutional Theory Meets Brave New World. *American Journal of Sociology*, 102(6), 1702–23.

Hirsch, P. M. & M. Lounsbury. (1997). Ending the Family Quarrel: Toward a Reconciliation of "Old" and "New" Institutionalism. *American Behavioral Scientist*, 40(4), 406–18.

Hwang, H. (2006). Planning Development: Globalization and the Shifting Locus of Planning. In G. Drori, J. Meyer, & H. Hwang, eds., *Globalization and Organization*. Oxford: Oxford University Press, pp. 69–90.

Jepperson, R. (1991). Institutions, Institutional Effects, and Institutionalism. In W. W. Powell & P. J. DiMaggio, eds., *The New Institutionalism in*

Organizational Analysis. Chicago, IL: University of Chicago Press, pp. 143-63.

Jepperson, R. (2002). The Development and Application of Sociological Neo-Institutionalism. In J. Berger & M. Zelditch, Jr., eds., *New Directions in Contemporary Sociological Theory.* Lanham, MD: Rowman and Littlefield, pp. 229-66.

Jepperson, R. & J. W. Meyer. (2007). Analytical Individualism and the Explanation of Macrosocial Change. In V. Nee & R. Swedberg, eds., *On Capitalism.* Stanford, CA: Stanford University Press, pp. 273-304.

Jepperson, R. & A. Swidler. (1993–4). What Properties of Culture Should We Measure? *Poetics,* 22(4), 359–71.

Katzenstein, P. J., ed. (1996). *The Culture of National Security: Norms and Identity in World Politics,* New York, NY: Columbia University Press.

Kogut, B. & J. M. Macpherson. (2004). The Decision to Privatize as an Economic Policy Idea: Epistemic Communities, Palace Wars, and Diffusion. Fontainebleau: INSEAD, unpublished paper.

Krasner, S. D., ed. (1983). *International Regimes,* Ithaca, NY: Cornell University Press.

Krasner, S. D. (1999). *Sovereignty: Organized Hypocrisy,* Princeton, NJ: Princeton University Press.

Luhmann, N. (1975). Die Weltgesellschaft. In N. Luhmann, *Soziologische Aufklärung 1: Aufsätze zur Theorie Sozialer Systeme.* Opladen: Westdeutscher Verlag, pp. 51–71.

Mann, M. (1986). *The Sources of Social Power,* Cambridge: Cambridge University Press.

McNeely, C. L. (1995). *Constructing the Nation-State: International Organization and Prescriptive Action,* Westport, CT: Greenwood Press.

Meyer, J. W. (1988). Society Without Culture: A Nineteenth Century Legacy. In F. Ramirez, ed., *Rethinking the Nineteenth Century.* New York, NY: Greenwood, pp. 193–201.

Meyer, J. W. (1999). The Changing Cultural Content of the Nation-State: A World Society Perspective. In G. Steinmetz, ed., *State/Culture: State Formation after the Cultural Turn.* Ithaca, NY: Cornell University Press, pp. 123–43.

Meyer, J. W. (2008). Reflections on Institutional Theories of Organizations. In R. Greenwood, C. Oliver, R. Suddaby, & K. Sahlin, eds., *The Sage Handbook of Organizational Institutionalism.* Thousand Oaks, CA: Sage, pp. 790–812.

Meyer, J. W., F. Ramirez, & Y. Soysal. (1992). World Expansion of Mass Education, 1870–1970. *Sociology of Education,* 65(2), 128–49.

Meyer, J. W. & B. Rowan. (1977). Institutionalized Organizations: Formal Structure as Myth and Ceremony. *American Journal of Sociology*, 83(2), 340–63.

Meyer, J. W. & R. Jepperson. (2000). The "Actors" of Modern Society: The Cultural Construction of Social Agency. *Sociological Theory*, 18(1), 100–20.

Mizruchi, M. S. & L. C. Fein. (1999). The Social Construction of Organizational Knowledge: A Study of the Uses of Coercive, Mimetic, and Normative Isomorphism. *Administrative Science Quarterly*, 44(4), 653–83.

Mizruchi, M. S., L. B. Stearns, & C. Marquis. (2006). The Conditional Nature of Embeddedness. *American Sociological Review*, 71(2), 310–33.

Mokyr, J. (1992). *The Lever of Riches*, Oxford: Oxford University Press.

Moon, H. & C. M. Wotipka. (2006). The World-Wide Diffusion of Business Education, 1881–1999. In G. Drori, J. Meyer, & H. Hwang, eds., *Globalization and Organization*. Oxford: Oxford University Press, pp. 121–36.

North, D. C. (1981). *Structure and Change in Economic History*, New York, NY: Norton.

North, D. C. & R. P. Thomas. (1973). *The Rise of the Western World*, Cambridge: Cambridge University Press.

Olson, M. (1965). *The Logic of Collective Action*, Cambridge, MA: Harvard University Press.

Powell, W. W. & P. M. DiMaggio, eds. (1991). *The New Institutionalism in Organizational Analysis*, Chicago, IL: University of Chicago Press.

Ramirez, F. O., Y. Soysal, & S. Shanahan. (1998). The Changing Logic of Political Citizenship: Cross-National Acquisition of Women's Suffrage. *American Sociological Review*, 62(5), 735–45.

Ramirez, F. O. & C. M. Wotipka. (2001). Slowly but Surely? The Global Expansion of Women's Participation in Science and Engineering Fields of Study, 1972–92. *Sociology of Education*, 74(3), 231–51.

Robertson, R. (1992). *Globalization: Social Theory and Global Culture*, London: Sage.

Rose, N. & P. Miller. (1992). Political Power Beyond the State: Problematics of Government. *British Journal of Sociology*, 43(2), 173–205.

Sahlin-Andersson, K. & L. Engwall, eds. (2002). *The Expansion of Management Knowledge*, Stanford, CA: Stanford University Press.

Schofer, E. & J. W. Meyer. (2005). The World-Wide Expansion of Higher Education in the Twentieth Century. *American Sociological Review*, 70(6), 898–920.

Scott, W. R. (2001). *Institutions and Organizations*, 2nd edn, Thousand Oaks, CA: Sage.

Scott, W. R. (2006). Approaching Adulthood: The Maturing of Institutional Theory. *Theory and Society*, Forthcoming. Stanford, CA: Dept. of Sociology, Stanford University.

Sewell, W. H., Jr. (1992). A Theory of Structure: Duality, Agency, and Transformation. *American Journal of Sociology*, 98(1), 1–29.

Soysal, Y. (1994). *Limits of Citizenship*, Chicago, IL: University of Chicago Press.

Stinchcombe, A. L. (1968). *Constructing Social Theories*, New York, NY: Harcourt, Brace & World.

Stinchcombe, A. L. (1997). On the Virtues of the Old Institutionalism. *Annual Review of Sociology*, 23(1), 1–18.

Stinchcombe, A. L. (2001). *When Formality Works*, Chicago, IL: University of Chicago Press.

Thomas, G., J. W. Meyer, F. Ramirez, & J. Boli. (1987). *Institutional Structure: Constituting State, Society, and the Individual*, Beverly Hills, CA: Sage.

Tocqueville, A. 1836 (1969). *Democracy in America*. J. P. Maier, ed., trans. G. Lawrence. Garden City, NY: Anchor Books.

Toulmin, S. (1990). *Cosmopolis: The Hidden Agenda of Modernity*, New York, NY: Free Press.

Tsutsui, K. & C. M. Wotipka. (2004). Global Civil Society and the International Human Rights Movement. *Social Forces*, 83(2), 587–620.

Wallerstein, I. (1974). Capitalist Agriculture and the Origins of the European World-Economy in the Sixteenth Century. Vol. I of *The Modern World-System*. New York, NY: Academic Press.

Zelizer, V. (1994). *The Social Meaning of Money*, New York, NY: Basic Books.

11 | Reflections on Part IV: The Construction of Actors

J. MEYER AND R. JEPPERSON

The neoinstitutional theory of this volume has analyzed the postwar Anglo-European institutional order as a system of constructed and "rationalized" social actors. It has offered arguments about the development and operation of this institutional structure, including into the neoliberal period that intensified following the end of communism. Chapter 9 provides arguments about how the modern and postmodern (European, now global) cultural system constructs modern actors as authorized agents for various interests. Chapter 10 discusses the system of actors and cultural "others" in the world society that emerged in the postwar period.

At the same time, in its metatheoretic discussion about trends in social theory, the neoinstitutionalism of this volume has explored the more abstract and doctrinal actor-centrism of much postwar social science. As Hwang and his collaborators document and analyze, the old human order of people, groups, and societies is commonly now promoted and labeled as made up of actors – individual, organizational, and national states (Hwang and Colyvas 2011, 2013; Hwang, Colyvas, and Drori 2019). They too make the point that much social science seems to take this expanded and empowered actorhood for granted, rather than analyzing it as an elaborate cultural project and postmodern social system. We reflect further on these points in this chapter, discussing (among other topics) the unrealism about actors that has accompanied an actor-centric social science.

11.1 Actors and Structures: A Reprise

By actors, analysts typically mean purposive, strategic, and fairly rational entities functioning within society: often the purposiveness is seen as self-interest rather than, for instance, the enactment of a role (or the conformity to [say] a divine will). An individual actor, compared with an ordinary person, has more bounded autonomy and capacity to choose and act. An organizational or nation-state actor has more sovereignty and capacity to make its own decisions. The core idea is built into the ambiguous term "agency," which refers to the right and capacity of the actors to choose: the denotation typically is agency for the interests of the self.

By structures, analysts mean all the organizational and cultural material in which such actors are embedded. At one ("realist") end of a theoretical continuum, actors are naturally filled with agency, and structures operate mainly to constrain it. At the other (institutionalist) end, the agency of actors – their capacity to choose and act – is constructed in a wider society, which may empower as much as constrain them.

Disputes about actors and structures tend to be normatively colored. Contemporary social norms require that actors be respected, and structural analyses – especially cultural ones – are often treated as normative violations: even very foolish and derivative participants are to be analyzed as real or potentially real actors. It's as if an emphasis on structure might weaken the moral fiber of people who urgently need to act. The whole discussion is a contemporary secular interpretation of the nineteenth-century controversies about free will and determinism.

Because of the ritual character of the disputes, the intellectual payoff has been very limited. In the same way that multiple levels of analysis are obviously relevant in affecting social life, variations among local participants as well as variations in settings obviously matter. There is very little to dispute in substance. Few structural theories conceive of a social world without variation in the activities of highly interested participants in society. However, many actor-centered theories (for instance, rational choice theories and many economic ones) try to claim monopoly status – as if all variation and change can be traced to one basic set of units, namely the rational individual person. This insistence seems to carry ideological energy.

11.2 The Reorganization of the Postwar Institutional Order Around Actorhood

The liberal world, expansive over the centuries, has been dominant since World War II, and dramatically hegemonic in the recent neoliberal period (Ruggie 1982, 1998). It attempts to construct and legitimate essentially every social institution – and every explanation in social theory – around agentic and rather self-interested actorhood. Consider the following domains.

Politics: Democracy is a globally preferred model, even more in principle than in practice, so almost all countries claim to be or to be becoming democracies (Hafner-Burton and Tsutsui 2005). The legitimating idea is that rational voters – the highlighted actors – choose, and their choices drive political society. To treat the system as "wired" by special interests is to delegitimate it (Lindblom 1977).

Economy: With the expansive and now global market economy, rational workers, owners, investors, inventors, and capitalists are to make choices (mostly self-interested ones), and these choices drive – and should drive – economic society.

Religion and Culture: In the same way, religious and cultural matters are to be decided by the choices of ordinary persons exercising their agency in specifying the properties of god(s) or the culture and language of the school curriculum. Most recently, national and ethnic identities come under the same regime. People are to be free to emigrate (though not yet always immigrate), to choose and change their citizenship (and maintain several), and to assert their own individual ethnocultural frames. Communal or legal structures that might constrain individuals from claiming to be Irish are weakened or eliminated as a matter of human rights (Lieberson and Waters 1988).

Family, Gender, and Sex: The old family systems come under sustained and global attack (Thornton 2005). Worldwide, modern persons tend to subscribe to doctrines of choice – in marriage, divorce, and childbearing (and abortion) – and within the family receive a good deal of individual freedom and protection from constraints now considered abusive. Sexual and gender identities and practices are to be free choices of individuals (Frank et al. 2010).

Organizations: Modern society is filled with formal organizational structures, in good part replacing older familial, professional, or bureaucratic forms. The essential definition of an organization, in the current legal and ideological framing, is that it is an actor, making choices (Coleman 1982; Perrow 1991; Bromley and Meyer 2015; Luhmann 2018). The organizations are understood, in dominant liberal models, to derive their actorhood from the individual actors who create and staff them, but they have the crucial properties as collectives themselves, operating under very widespread ideologies of accountability and liability.

Nation-states: Nation-states, too, are conceived as organizations making legitimate choices as actors, and both political processes and New Public Management ideologies celebrate their accountability and agency. In this case, the contemporary form replaces an older one, with very different sovereignty. Chapter 9 gives an analysis of the contemporary form.

The entities with the most exogenous standing – the individual and the national state – are those whose actorhood is most intensely emphasized. This is because individual persons and national states have been represented as the core ontological and moral agents in the cosmologies of the modern world (though the charisma of states has weakened in the neoliberal context) (Boli & Lechner 2001; Jepperson 2002). Social theories that are seen as over-emphasizing the role of structural forces in affecting human activity can be experienced as morally irresponsible as well as intellectually suspect – in effect absolving human actors from their natural responsibilities.

We can imagine how different social theory would be if it were addressed to something other than empowered human actors – highly schooled human actors in fact, educationally infused with a very strong orientation toward action in society. These are the people who are supposed to run the world and to do so in a very agentic way. And indeed, action theories of society may be especially prominent in the exploding professional schools – most recently, business and public policy schools – which are in the business of training students to be carriers of transcendental meaning (GDP growth, for instance). A social theory of human society taught to a class of peasants would look rather different. It would probably emphasize individual agency much less than do contemporary social theories taught to people who believe they are and should be actors.

This ideological role of social theory may be of use in supporting the secular religion of contemporary society, and in fitting well with prevailing normative logics, but it also has substantial costs. First, as explanatory theory, it understates cultural embeddedness and produces a greatly distorted picture of how society works and changes. Second, as ideology, it supports entirely unrealistic conceptions of how both actors and their structures are and should be organized: such conceptions are extraordinarily consequential and account for many aspects of contemporary society. We discuss these themes in turn.

11.3 Explanatory Distortions

Important modern social changes reflect broad cultural waves, cutting across locales, particular organizational settings, and particular arenas of social life. They are now often global in character. Actor-centered theories, stressing autonomous and bounded individuals (or the structures they create), fail utterly to predict or explain these massive developments. They have no good account for highly collective processes. It turns out that people and local settings are embedded in very general and widespread cultural meanings, and these meanings have changed in rather dramatic ways. Consider the following examples.

The Environment: A great environment movement arises, with pronounced roots in scientific analyses as much as in actually experienced environmental destruction (Meyer et al. 1997; Frank, Hironaka, & Schofer 2000; Hironaka 2014). It touches national societies everywhere (Ignatow 2007). Within these societies, many institutional structures are changed, often in rather diffuse ways. Schools and universities teach new material (Bromley et al. 2011; Frank et al. 2011). Political systems change priorities. Industries develop policies of corporate social responsibility, of varying seriousness (Tsutsui and Lim 2015). Opinion polls show long-term shifts in the views of all sorts of people in all sorts of places, in part independent of their interests and those dominant in their local settings. Leave aside the standard questions about how much of all this is "real," and how much it actually accomplishes needed changes: the point here is that a scientized global cultural drama is in play.

Human Rights: In exactly the same way, human rights principles have spread around the world. Change occurs in global institutions, with a profusion of treaties (Elliott 2007, and elsewhere). Change occurs in country after country, social sector after sector. Rights are discovered for children, women, indigenous people, gay and lesbian people, disabled people, immigrants, old people, and ethnic minorities of all stripes (Boli and Meyer 1978; Boyle 2002; Frank et al. 2010; Cole 2011). They are discovered in essentially every country. And more and more rights are discovered – not only basic rights to life and liberty, or political rights, or economic rights, but rights to all sorts of self-expression and cultural stances, and ultimately the strongly empowering rights that we see as constructing individual actorhood as a global social form. These developments reflect another cultural wave, one poorly predicted or explained by actor-centered theorizing. It has been difficult, without heroic assumptions, to see great worldwide forces of actor-centered interest and power behind worldwide movements supporting formerly very marginal gay and lesbian people, or indigenous people, or children.

Rationalized Social Organization: Dramatic cultural shifts also produce worldwide changes in social organization. Indeed, massive variations in local culture and resources can now be coded under the simple schemes emphasizing organizational expansion and accounting transparency (Bromley and Meyer 2015). For example, all the countries or organizations in the world can now be classified within unidimensional schemes, from better to worse, transparent to corrupt (e.g., by Business International and Transparency International).

Few of the great social changes that build the contemporary world are effectively predicted by actor-centered theorizing. It is essential to have theories of institutional change that see collective and cultural systems as real, and that can thus account for the worldwide penetration of societies by their themes.

11.4 Unrealism about Actors

We've stressed that actor-centered theories are basic ideology in contemporary societies. Expectations about the competence of these actors are built into social and cultural life of the liberal world to an extraordinary degree. The normative modern individual and organizational actor must possess cultural competence at an extreme level. The mythology involved here was central to the postwar rise of the liberal national society as canonical (Ruggie 1982). It became even more central in the neoliberal period (Ruggie 1998). Globalization and the weakening of the charisma of the national state challenged the folk theory of social order: In the absence of a world state, and highly legitimated national states, what forces would ensure order and progress (Rangan 2018)? Individuals, their creative efforts, and the effective organizations they might build were the panaceas.

But the expectations for putatively freed and empowered actors often extend far beyond realistic capabilities. Consider individual humans. Empirically, the individual is incompetent politically in the most obvious ways. Indeed, the discovery of this fact in the first major voting studies after World War II created a crisis in the field of political science, which had theorized a polity based on informed and competent citizens. So the discovery that the voters are uninformed, inattentive, and confused created a legitimacy problem (Lane and Sears 1964).[1] The problem is even greater in a global polity hopelessly organized.

Ordinary people are similarly uninformed and incompetent market participants. Normative expectations for personal budgeting, saving, and debt are demanding relative to the propensities of most people – as the housing bubble, student debt bubble, and savings level all show (and as the constant pleas for more rationality, attention, and prudence reveal).

Similarly, people are far from competent in religious, cultural, and social matters – and clearly unable to live up to the expanded contemporary conception of interpersonal and sexual competence. Sexual partners are unable to manage birth control or disease transmission. National and ethnic group members are revealed as very poorly informed about their history and culture (let alone those of other groups).

Shifting to the organizational actor, contemporary research shows again and again how far these structures are from the capacities assumed in realist theories. Leaders are often disastrously uninformed, obvious technical relationships fail, coordination is weak, and so on. Mild economic downturns reveal that many organizations survive only because of good times. A central concept in modern organization theory is the "decoupling" of actual practice from both norms and idealized pictures – an institutionalist idea and observation (Bromley and Powell 2012).

Similarly, the nation-states of the world are, in great numbers, routinely discovered to be "failed states" (Fukuyama 2014). The most obvious decisions – for example, military ones – are often made foolishly, and obvious collective obligations go unmet (Mann 2003; Hironaka 2017). The folk theory of the nation-state gives astonishing power and responsibility to states and state elites: empirical studies routinely find mediocre, ignorant, or corrupt incumbents in office. Political philosophers seeking Solomon or Solon meet Bush or Trump. And in its political role, the mass public, awash in vast political mythologies, hardly meets the standards presented in democratic theory, even as it is given occasional authority to "decide" on taxes or European integration.

Of course, all the commentators on individual, organizational, and national state failures are filled with advice and criticism. But it is interesting how little criticism goes to the myths of nation statehood, or to great power status – especially since the mythologies produce many devastatingly negative outcomes (Mann 2003, 2013; Hironaka 2017). Similarly, few modern commentators propose cutting back the fantasies of the modern organization – or the individual – as actor. It would be a normative violation to do so. There seems to be little interest in achieving a true realism, in the more standard sense of that term.

In response to the gaps between pretense and possibility, contemporary societies – especially more liberal ones like the United States – produce an explosion of consultants and therapists and teachers, as noted in Chapter 1 and analyzed in Chapter 10 (also see Hasse 2019). In other words, the liberal society generates an explosion, not only of rationalized actors but also of rationalized others – people who instruct actors in how to be actors, and who provide cover for their endless failures (Meyer 1996).

As it is recognized, worldwide, that regular people as produced by families and communities are not really up to proper actorhood, a gigantic education industry arises with explosions in enrollment unimaginable a few decades ago (Meyer et al. 1992; Schofer and Meyer 2005). Perhaps two-fifths of a birth cohort now makes it all the way to the university. And much of the education involved, beyond being one of the many expanded human rights, is now compulsory as a worldwide effort to make proper actors out of people.

The teachers, basically, are not constructed as actors: they are others to future actors. In the same way, a wide range of therapies and therapists develops to repair obvious failings in actorhood: again, the protagonists are professionalized others, not really analyzable as actors. They are agents of the others, not principally of their selves.

At organizational and national levels, a profusion of such consultants, teachers, and therapists arises, so that consulting becomes a major and rapidly growing profession. The consultant, only secondarily an actor in the system as it is conceptualized, functions as an other to organized actors. Similarly, at the national level, massive numbers of advisors and consultants appear, functioning as exoskeletal elements sustaining the pretenses of the putative great political actors (Hironaka 2017).

In a few decades, what is called the "service sector" – prominently composed of others rather than actors – has grown to be the most expanded arena of what is called the modern or developed "economy"

(Wyatt and Hecker 2006). In the organizational theories of the 1950s, these people were seen as marginal participants in the great industrial organization – "staff" people with educational degrees, at odds with the dominant "line" people who did the real work. In the organizational theories of the postmodern or "knowledge" society, they are the central participants, carrying the myths of actorhood so central to the contemporary models of the developed society (Bromley and Meyer 2015).

11.5 "Logics" of Action

In order to produce more realistic analyses of actors and action, some scholars have returned to the long-standing idea of distinguishing different so-called logics of action. The standard example, going back to Marx and classical economics, is provided by the capitalist firm. In the standard analysis, firms are driven by a "logic" of survival and profit-maximization. (So much so that firms have been called "monomaniacs" by critics.) This logic is different from, say, a logic of family solidarity and resource pooling, or a logic of community welfare provision, or a logic of professional expertise. Friedland and Alford (1991) called attention to such variations in a well-known paper, contrasting the logics that drive capitalism, democracy, family, and religion.

These ideas were clearly structuralist, as well as institutionalist, in character. A logic of action – organizing and operating principles – is intrinsic to the constructed identities associated with a given institutional sector (e.g., legally defined business firms operating in a competitive market). The identity dictates – and explains – main lines of action. The "actors" – firms, families, and democratic states – are enacting logics that derive from their basic identities. These ideas are basic parts of social science.

Multiple lines of work on "logics" have recently emerged. One version, dominant in American work, takes off from an expansion of the idea of "logics" as a way of either broadening actor-centric theorizing or merging it with an institutionalism. Here the wider environment is more or less taken for granted. One direction has pursued the way actors (generally seen as fairly competent) manage the varying institutional pressures they come under: a realist version is found in Oliver (1991), and an influential more culturalist version is found in Thornton et al. (2012). A closely parallel French version – seeing activity within a framework of multiple models – is "convention theory" (Boltansky and Thevenot 2006). The emphasis is often placed upon how coherent, purposive, and sometimes rational actors use cultural materials to build, exploit, resist, and change structures.

The more actor-and-micro-centric lines of work are producing interesting ideas and arguments on their own terms. However, they are sometimes put forward, not as micro-social studies of actors within institutional contexts, but as somehow foundational for institutions and institutional theory. This assumption is implausible, and reflects the essentializing of the micro-level discussed in Part 3 of this book. There is risk of losing the main point and explanatory power of the original structuralist idea of "logics." It is reasonable to see individual actors as managing structural frames; it is equally important to see the frames as constructing the identities and roles of the individuals. Activities, sometimes perceived as choices, affect history indeed – but history also constructs choices.

11.6 Conclusion

The term "actor" has come into common use in the social sciences. It reflects common cultural notions and is thus often undefined or poorly defined. It denotes a foundational ontological element of the contemporary liberal society – the uncaused cause that supposedly lies behind social reality and explains this reality. For that reason, the term is left opaque: an actor is attributed purpose and agency, and to define it too precisely would be to make a "structural" analysis, and would violate the core principles of actorhood.

Some of the special meanings and legitimations of actorhood formerly were attributed to the sovereign national state – a kind of sacred congregation (the Body of Christ) in the traditions of Christendom. But they were always also attributed to the individual soul-laden person (including, after discussion, female and indigenous persons). Both these especially validated entities – national state and individual – were seen as having direct ties to the sacred. The organizations created by states and individuals similarly, over time, acquired the properties of actorhood, if without a direct sacred standing.

Contemporary liberalism dramatically escalated the actorhood attributed to individual persons, and the organizations they create: to some extent it has reduced the formerly sacralized national state to the level of a less-sacred organization. (It is now obviously less heroic to die for one's country.)

The unrealistic properties of actorhood generate many of the institutions of the contemporary "knowledge society," whose strident claims about the possibilities of the human individual are accompanied by many social arrangements to tame and prop up these same individuals. In an emergent development, "populist" distancing from some globally institutionalized models have appeared. Some successes may portend substantial cultural changes, in so doing inviting institutional research (see e.g. Schofer, Lerch, and Meyer 2018; see also Chapter 12).

The liberal society has many attractions as well as hubris and hypocrisy. We have not been suggesting overall assessments or promoting projects for change. Our normative intention here is limited to a critique of contemporary social theory and advocacy for better theory.

Notes

1. Political science forgets and then periodically rediscovers ignorance in the mass public – a revealing cycle. The latest (and impressive) rediscovery of ignorance in the mass public is Achen and Bartels (2016).

References

Achen, C. H. & L. M. Bartels (2016). *Democracy for Realists*, Princeton, NJ: Princeton University Press.
Boli, J. & F. Lechner (2001). Globalization and World Culture. In N. Smelser & P. Baltes, eds., *International Encyclopedia of the Social and Behavioral Sciences*. Oxford: Elsevier, pp. 6261–6.
Boli-Bennett, J. & J. W. Meyer (1978). The Ideology of Childhood and the State: Rules Distinguishing Children in National Constitutions, 1870–1970. *American Sociological Review*, 43(6), 797–812.
Boltanski, L. & L. Thévenot (2006). *On Justification: Economies of Worth*, Princeton, NJ: Princeton University Press.
Boyle, E. (2002). *Female Genital Cutting: Cultural Conflict in the Global Community*, Baltimore, MD: Johns Hopkins University Press.
Bromley, P. & J. W. Meyer (2015). *Hyper-Organization: Global Organizational Expansion*, Oxford: Oxford University Press.
Bromley, P., J. W. Meyer, & F. Ramirez (2011). The Worldwide Spread of Environmental Discourse in Social Studies, History, and Civics

Textbooks, 1970–2008. *Comparative Education Review*, 55(4), 517–45.

Bromley, P. & W. W. Powell (2012). From Smoke and Mirrors to Walking the Talk: Decoupling in the Contemporary World. *The Academy of Management Annals*, 6(1), 483–530.

Brunsson, N. (1989). *The Organization of Hypocrisy*, Chichester: Wiley.

Cole, W. M. (2011). *Uncommon Schools: The Global Rise of Postsecondary Institutions for Indigenous Peoples*, Stanford, CA: Stanford University Press.

Coleman, J. S. (1982). *The Asymmetric Society*, Syracuse, NY: Syracuse University Press.

Elliott, M. A. (2007). Human Rights and the Triumph of the Individual in World Culture. *Cultural Sociology*, 1(3), 343–63.

Frank, D. J., B. J. Camp, & S. A. Boutcher (2010). Worldwide Trends in the Criminal Regulation of Sex, 1945 to 2005. *American Sociological Review*, 75(6), 867–93.

Frank, D. J. & J. Gabler (2006). *Reconstructing the University: Worldwide Changes in Academic Emphases over the Twentieth Century*, Stanford, CA: Stanford University Press.

Frank, D. J., A. Hironaka, & E. Schofer (2000). The Nation-State and the Natural Environment Over the Twentieth Century. *American Sociological Review*, 65(1), 96–116.

Frank, D. J., K. J. Robinson, & J. Olesen (2011). The Global Expansion of Environmental Education in Universities. *Comparative Education Review*, 55(4), 546–73.

Friedland, R. & R. Alford (1991). Bringing Society Back In: Symbols, Practices, and Institutional Contradictions. In W. Powell & P. DiMaggio, eds., *The New Institutionalism in Organizational Analysis*. Chicago, IL: University of Chicago Press, pp. 232–63.

Fukuyama, F. (2014.) *Political Order and Political Decay: From the Industrial Revolution to the Globalization of Democracy*, New York: Farrar, Straus, & Giroux.

Haack, P., J. Sieweke, & L. Wessel, eds. (2019). *Microfoundations of Institutions*, Bingley: Emerald Publishing.

Hafner-Burton, E. & K. Tsutsui (2005). Human Rights in a Globalizing World: The Paradox of Empty Promises. *American Journal of Sociology*, 110(5), 1373–411.

Hasse, R. (2019). What Difference Does it Make? An Institutional Perspective on Actors and Types Thereof. In H. Hwang, J. Colyvas, & G. Drori, eds., *Agents, Actors, Actorhood*. Bingley: Emerald Publishing, pp. 23–41.

Hironaka, A. (2014). *Greening the Globe: World Society and Environmental Change*, New York, NY: Cambridge University Press.

Hironaka, A. (2017). *Tokens of Power: Rethinking War*, New York, NY: Cambridge University Press.
Hwang, H. & J. Colyvas (2011). Problematizing Actors and Institutions in Institutional Work. *Journal of Management Inquiry*, 20(1), 62–66.
Hwang, H. & J. Colyvas (2013). "Actors, Actors! Actors? The Proliferation of the Actor and its Consequences." Annual meetings of the European Group for Organization Studies, Montreal.
Hwang, H., J. Colyvas, & G. S. Drori, eds. (2019). *Agents, Actors, Actorhood: Institutional Perspectives of the Nature of Agency, Action, and Authority*. Vol. 58 of *Research in the Sociology of Organizations*, Bingley: Emerald Publishing.
Ignatow, G. (2007). *Transnational Identity Politics and the Environment*, Lanham, MD: Lexington Books.
Jepperson, R. L. (2002). Political Modernities: Disentangling Two Underlying Dimensions of Institutional Differentiation. *Sociological Theory*, 20(1), 61–85.
Lane, R. & D. Sears (1964). *Public Opinion*, Englewood Cliffs, NJ: Prentice-Hall.
Lieberson, S. & M. Waters (1988). *From Many Strands*, New York, NY: Russell Sage Foundation.
Lindblom, C. (1977). *Politics and Markets*, New York, NY: Basic Books.
Luhmann, N. (2018). *Organization and Decision*, Cambridge: Cambridge University Press.
Mann, M. (2003). *Incoherent Empire*, London: Verso Books.
Mann, M. (2013). *Globalizations, 1945–2011*. Vol. IV of *The Sources of Social Power*, Cambridge: Cambridge University Press.
Meyer, J. W. (1996). Otherhood: The Promulgation and Transmission of Ideas in the Modern Organizational Environment. In B. Czarniawska & G. Sevón, eds., *Translating Organizational Change*. Berlin: De Gruyter, pp.241–52.
Meyer, J. W., D. Frank, A. Hironaka, E. Schofer, & N. Tuma (1997). The Structuring of a World Environmental Regime, 1870–1990. *International Organization*, 51(4), 623–51.
Meyer, J. W., F. Ramirez, & Y. Soysal (1992). World Expansion of Mass Education, 1870–1970. *Sociology of Education*, 65(2), 128–49.
Oliver, C. (1991). Strategic Responses to Institutional Processes. *Academy of Management Review*, 18(1), 145–79.
Perrow, C. (1991). A Society of Organizations. *Theory and Society*, 20(6), 725–62.
Rangan, S., ed. (2018). *Capitalism Beyond Mutuality*, Oxford: Oxford University Press.

Ruggie, J. G. (1982). International Regimes, Transactions, and Change: Embedded Liberalism in the Post-War Economic Order. *International Organization*, 36(2), 379–415.

Ruggie, J. G. (1998). Globalization and the Embedded Liberalism Compromise: The End of an Era? In W. Streeck, ed., *Internationale Wirtschaft, Nationale Demokratie*. Frankfurt: Campus, pp. 79–97.

Schofer, E., J. Lerch, & J. W. Meyer (2018). Illiberal Reactions to the University in the 21st Century. *Annual meetings of the American Sociological Association*, Philadelphia.

Schofer, E. & J. W. Meyer (2005). The World-Wide Expansion of Higher Education in the Twentieth Century. *American Sociological Review*, 70 (6), 898–920.

Thornton, A. (2005). *Reading History Sideways: The Fallacy and Enduring Impact of the Developmental Paradigm on Family Life*, Chicago, IL: University of Chicago Press.

Thornton, P. H., W. Ocasio, & M. Lounsbury (2012). *The Institutional Logics Perspective*, Oxford: Oxford University Press.

Tsutsui, K. & A. Lim, eds. (2015). *Corporate Social Responsibility in a Globalizing World*, Cambridge: Cambridge University Press.

Wyatt, I. D. & D. E. Hecker (2006). Occupational Changes During the 20th Century. *Monthly Labor Review*, 129(3), 35–57.

PART V

Conclusion

12 | Concluding Reflections:
Evolving Cultural Models in Global and National Society

R. JEPPERSON AND J. MEYER[*]

12.1 Introduction

As a conclusion to this volume, we analyze the cultural frameworks organizing social activity in three distinct periods within the postwar era. In part following Ruggie (1982, 1998), we distinguish a period of embedded liberalism, followed by a period of neoliberalism, and then a recent emergent post-liberal period.

Throughout the whole era, broadly liberal models of society are obviously central, emphasizing political and economic (and social and cultural) freedom of individuals and their associations. The period of embedded liberalism (1945~1980) idealized a world of bounded and sovereign nation-states operating under liberal norms of individual citizenship and free economic action. A more aggressive neoliberal period (~1980–2010) consolidated in the 1980s and then intensified following the end of the Cold War. A globalized world of free human economic and social action was imagined and partly enacted, weakening and transcending national boundaries and domestic solidarities. The practical excesses and legitimacy failures of neoliberalism appear to have generated a third, post-liberal, period (~2010). This period has maintained the economic and cultural libertarianism of the previous period in many respects. At the same time reactive post-liberalisms have arisen, asserting national, ethnic, familial, and religious identities.

Our objective in this chapter is to narrate what one might see if one pays attention to the institutionalization of evolving cultural assumptions – the primary focus of this volume's line of thought. Changing cultural models, operating in a world society, produce changes in national and subnational structures. As institutional theories were useful

---

[*] We thank John Boli for comments on an earlier draft of this chapter.

in analyzing the effects of liberal models, they are likely to be useful in understanding waves of post-liberalism.

12.2 The Immediate Postwar Period and Social Theory

In reaction to the disasters of the first half of the twentieth century, dramatic postwar efforts arose in public discourse and policies to build a new world order. There were very high levels of interdependence and perceived interdependence, on a global scale. Economic, political, social, cultural, and military dimensions and conflicts knit together people within countries, and countries in the world. British, European, Soviet, and US elites circulated multiple ideas for establishing international coordination, under considerable pressure and tension. A state-like overarching organization that might bring order was not remotely plausible. Further, the old European world of statist, corporatist, and imperial structures was in disrepute: it had created calamitous wars, economic breakdown, and extraordinary violations of basic human rights and needs.

The entities still standing were the United States (US) and the Union of Soviet Socialist Republics (USSR).[1] The emergent Cold War competition intensified the roles of both. Europe liberalized and integrated with US influence. The old European imperial system broke down, given European postwar weakness, a world nationalist upsurge, and US opposition. The USSR established a kind of imperial control in Eastern Europe. An explosion of global collective activity followed in the Anglo-European core, then emanating outward globally. The activity in that core took a broadly liberal form, stressing the capacities of individuals and organizations seen as empowered actors to create an order of justice and progress. (The Wilsonian emphases in the US emerging again with the UN vision are apparent.) Sweeping cultural myths stressed the potential rational action of individuals, organizations, and national states, in scientized social and natural environments. The proper society was to be a "knowledge society" (Etzioni 1968; Bell 1973). Individual persons everywhere were to be schooled to an extent previously unimaginable; science, universities, and "planning" were all to expand. Organizations – governmental, for-profit, and nonprofit – were to be built up and properly rationalized, and in fact soared in number all the way up through the global level (Boli and Thomas 1999; Bromley and Meyer 2015).

The enormous changes initiated in the postwar period were thus embedded in taken-for-granted culture. Much social science also took for granted the changes as necessary and functional, and thus became unable really to explain them and their global sweep. Some conventional theories saw postwar developments as arising naturally out of the needs (and sometimes conflicts) of the postwar era. Other theories saw the eventual system as product of the prior interests of powerful economic and political forces – the so-called old institutionalism (Stinchcombe 1997).[2] Such lines of theory miss the striking visions – and the urgency, the *bricolage,* the shifts of course – building the contemporary order. And such theories cannot account well for new characteristics of the emergent cultural frame and institutional order: for example, the mobilization around "human rights," and the related rapid development of liberation movements. Or for the global character of these changes. Or for the disconnections between sweeping changes in doctrine and radically disjointed practice: we live in a world that celebrates human equality to a previously unknown extent, but in which extreme inequalities are routine.

In reaction, the neoinstitutionalism of this volume called attention to an extraordinary pretense of the new culture: namely, that it is not a culture but rather the natural purposes of individuals, the unexceptional missions of organizations, and the obvious priorities of national and world societies. To produce a more realistic analysis, neo-institutionalism reached back to a *very* "old institutionalism" of traditional social science, seeing persons and organizations and national societies as embedded in matters of habit, custom, and culture (Chapters 2, 6–8). It saw the cultural materials of postwar society as highly rationalized – theorized, systematized, formalized – and as institutionalized in the "actor" structures of a new society, one that established an heroic status for individuals and organizations (Chapters 9–11).

In the postwar period of seventy-odd years, the world and national cultures have evolved – there has been real dynamism. The changes have altered the construction of social arenas, modifying the individual and organizational and national entities involved. There is a directionality to the evolution: an organization around liberal ideas, a radical intensification of them, and now a period containing reactions against them. We turn to this evolution, organizing our account around the three periods we distinguish.[3]

12.3 Embedded Liberalism

After the horrors of nationalistic fascism, Anglo-European elites were desperate to institutionalize peaceful relations among sovereign national states, and motivated to protect the rights and needs of the individual human person. These twin foundational principles were intensified by a quickly emerging Cold War competition, with an opponent committed neither to peaceful interstate relations nor to some core dimensions of cultural individualism.

With great urgency, then, a massive burst of global institution-building followed, broadly employing liberal ideologies and social theories. The period that consolidated, running from roughly 1945 into the 1980s, was labeled as "embedded liberalism" by Ruggie (1982). He referred to the liberal priority of free trade, but set in a state system that would allow individual countries to regulate their economies (including capital controls) and to establish domestic welfare programs as they saw fit. Stepping back further, the imagery was one of national states undertaking social "development" under the management of their states, with free and participating citizenries. The development would have economic, political, and social dimensions, all shaped and interrelated at national levels. The nonmetropolitan world was included in this universalistic imagery: these areas were "underdeveloped" and could "modernize."

International Organization: Embedded liberalism was institutionalized in central organizations, but of course nothing resembling a national state. First, to embody the new intended global political order, there was a whole system of structures around the emergent United Nations. Second, to embody the new global economic order, there was a network of structures around the emergent World Bank and treaty system. Extending from both these centers, a massive array of international organizations arose: inter-governmental, nongovernmental, and for-profit multinationals. All these enterprises grew exponentially (Bull and Watson 1985; Boli and Thomas 1999; Bromley and Meyer 2015). The NGOs especially took up the universalist liberal ideology and sought to disseminate and reinforce it. But the whole system created an institutional context in which many worldwide pressures surged around the globe. Neoinstitutional theories provided useful descriptions and possible explanations.

A Transnational Rationalized Culture: Beyond and parallel to the explosion of global formal organization there was a similar exponential expansion of a rationalizing cultural system, extending globally, transforming the definition of social reality within which both interstate and intrastate structures were to function (Lechner and Boli 2005; Boli and Lechner 2015). First, the natural and social worlds were scientized: the expansion of scientific authority and activity was rapid and global (Drori et al. 2003). There was more science (and imagined science), covering more and more aspects of nature and society, and carrying more and more social authority. Absent the laws of a world state, the natural laws of science (real and imagined) provided cultural underpinning for a globalized world. And because the new system confronted dramatic social challenges, the social sciences expanded even more rapidly than the natural ones (Drori and Moon 2006; Frank and Gabler 2006). In the postwar vision, social scientists could foster the "knowledge society," as well as contribute to the "modernization" of the so-called developing countries.[4] Now a good graduate student anywhere could suggest proper rules for anywhere else in the world, based for instance (and remarkably) on the imagined universal applicability of neoclassical economics.

Second, the period also emphasized the primordial standing of the individual human person (in reaction to fascism and communism, and reflecting US predominance). Human rights became a main theme of the period (Lauren 2003; Stacy 2009), and global treaty language invoked more rights for more kinds of people (Elliott 2007, 2011, 2014). At the beginning, the main emphasis, in reaction to a horrific history, was the idea of equal rights of racial and ethnic groups. But expansions brought in women, children, gay and lesbian people, disabled people, old people, indigenous people, immigrants, and so on: all entitled, all ultimately equal. The contrast between such global visions and very unequal practical realities was and is extreme: the decoupling and inconsistency involved have been dynamic, generating a wide range of now familiar social movements.

12.3.1 Domestic Effects

The evolving doctrines and organizations of the international system generated waves of corresponding change at domestic levels – this topic being a main focus of neoinstitutional theory. Thus the explosion of formal organization in the international system generated or paralleled radical expansions of formalization in organizational structures throughout the world (Drori et al. 2006; Bromley and Meyer 2015).[5]

The effect is especially striking in the world's peripheries, where formalization, decoupled from practice, vastly exceeds what might previously have been thought functional or even plausible.

Similar effects have occurred within more cultural dimensions. Local knowledge systems were penetrated and standardized with their linkages to a transnational cultural order. Conceptions of nature were transformed everywhere with widespread scientization; environmental movements spread (Hironaka 2014). The world human rights movement found extraordinary reproduction in national legal and policy and cultural systems – extending eventually into formerly suppressed matters such as gay and lesbian rights (Frank et al. 2010). These changes cannot realistically be seen as reflecting local pressures: indeed they are often at such odds with local norms that implementation is a remote prospect. But the global norms during this period of high legitimacy nevertheless had long-term effects on local realities (Cole and Ramirez 2013).

The human rights revolution conjoined with global scientization produced the most extraordinary global social change of the whole period: the massive worldwide expansion of education. Mass education expanded everywhere, so that nearly universal enrollment (if not necessarily student and teacher attendance) could be found in distant peripheries (Meyer et al. 1992). University expansion was even more extreme (Schofer and Meyer 2005): Botswana eventually reached an enrollment rate higher than the UK's 1950 level.

The powerful individualist thrust of the liberal period produced remarkable destruction of less rationalized community at every level. (a) The traditional family was weakened with liberalized divorce, easier abortion, stigmatization of within-family domination, celebration of rights of women and children, and rejection of family controls over marriage. (b) Communal work relations were weakened via clear property rights and labor contracts. Communal employment practices were seen as discriminatory. The professions and their structures (schools, hospitals) were reconstructed, losing autonomy. (c) Political and economic structures based on communal ethnic solidarities lost legitimacy.

12.3.2 Isomorphism and Variations

The period of embedded liberalism produced a clear model of what all societies in the world should look like in principle, and domestic societies tended to incorporate this model – in law, policy, and theory, if not necessarily in practice. Proper "development" meant the institutions of progressive liberal society, above and beyond economic growth. (a) There should be a democratic, efficient, and active state. In practice almost all countries, often implausibly, adopted this model as a constitutional form or at least a goal. (b) There should be markets in labor, capital, and commodities (perhaps subject to regulation). (c) There should be freedom for individuals to make choices, independent of familial, communal, ethnic, racial, or religious constraints. (d) Cultural matters, such as religion and language, should rest on the choices of free individuals.

Education, improved organization, and planning would bring about the appropriate condition or trajectory. And in fact national plans sprang up almost everywhere (Hwang 2006). Naturally, there was great variation in the actual influence of the model: the Iron Curtain symbolized a sharp boundary, for instance. But the communist countries did claim to embody popular will, and some claimed to be democracies. And they generally claimed to support free social lives in noneconomic areas, and often free cultural choices.

Other variations reflected standard patterns of institutional diffusion. The richer national societies shaped evolving world models in many areas, but then were often able to resist elements of them too. For instance, path dependence was especially strong in the US hegemon, which exported liberal models but maintained many deviations in matters of race, culture, social life, and political organization. At the other end of the development scales, peripheral societies came under many incentives to conform to proper ideals in policies – for example, in transforming traditional legal systems into modern forms, even if having almost no capacity to implement the models in practice (Boyle and Meyer 1998).

Of course the models themselves contained internal variations and inconsistencies. The liberal boundary between equal citizenship and unequal economic life could be drawn in a welfare state format in Scandinavia, and as a market society in Anglo democracies. In parallel, there were substantial variations in the valuation of collective as opposed to individual goods.

Seeing the dramatic changes in national and world societies, neo-institutional theory – emphasizing the diffusion of liberal models of actors and action – developed rapidly. Realist models of social change did not much attend to the sweeping spread of extraordinary ideals so disconnected from immediate realities, and their intellectual preferences provided weak resources for explanation of the spread.

12.4 Neo-Liberalism

Economic interdependence, and crises associated with it, continued to expand through the whole earlier liberal period. The Cold War conflict, sharply codified and articulated, continued. Both reinforced the awareness of "globalization." An oil crisis called attention to economic interdependence, and "stagflation" to seeming failures of national responses, including Keynesian economic policy. Political crises were everywhere, and long-lasting civil wars supported by the contending powers were routine (Hironaka 2005). In a world that celebrated visions of human rights and human equality, the persistent extreme inequalities – social, political, and economic – rapidly became conceptualized as injustices to be corrected by international action.

One reaction was to seek a new international order managing world inequalities in a modest welfare-state-like manner – the Brandt Commission of 1977 is representative. Poor countries advocated this response. Rich ones demurred, but generated and supported international aid of various sorts: a whole international governmental and nongovernmental organizational system expanded.

A more dominant reaction – especially strong in the United States and the United Kingdom – was to call for the liberation of business and finance. The economic crises of the 1970s provided an opening for long-consolidated liberal ideas to surge out from think tanks, institutes, and consultancies, attacking the collectivist practices that had developed during the 1930s, World War II, and the immediate postwar period (Steger and Roy 2010; Carter 2020: Ch. 12). A triumphalist and insistent "neoliberal" model consolidated in the 1970s and 1980s, rapidly becoming a dominant ideology and a core component of a second distinctive postwar period (Ruggie 1998). Now the economy was to be, in effect, disembedded from society.

We will call attention to two additional characteristics of the neoliberal period beyond its intensification of political, social, and economic liberalism. First, it was characterized by an acceleration of anti-elitism. Second, the earlier "rights revolution" of liberalism intensified

Concluding Reflections 305

into anti-traditional liberation movements. Together, economism, a consolidating anti-elitism, and liberation from traditional constraint provided a new cultural frame shaping social activity.

Before we discuss these neoliberal characteristics, we wish to mention dynamics of the prior liberal period that remained operative.

12.4.1 Continuities from Embedded Liberalism

First, scientific activity continued to expand: domains of social life little penetrated by scientific knowledge came under scientific scrutiny. Would-be experts addressed a widened range of issues formerly treated as matters of local culture: for example, family practices, child-rearing, marriage practices, sexuality, recreation, exercise, and diet.

Second, projects of social rationalization continued. Economies were subject to world standards and norms of transparency (as with the notorious Structural Adjustment Programs). Political systems were evaluated according to norms of democracy, human rights, and corruption. Social systems were to support free individual status and rights for women, children, migrants, and so on. And cultural arrangements were to celebrate free individual choices – and ideally tolerance. Naturally decoupling remained extreme (Bromley and Powell 2012), and practices (and local norms) remained far from the global theoretical ideals.

Third, elites at the world level attained more connection and integration. The elites, networked via expanded educational and organizational systems, had a great deal in common. They often identified more easily with each other than with national compatriots – a detachment of great consequence for the eventual development of "populist" reactions (Goodhart 2017). The old principle that it was difficult to sustain multi-national firms because of putative cultural differences disappeared, and such firms multiplied. Perhaps managers came from different backgrounds, but they all could have MBAs from Wharton (Meyer et al. 2015).

12.4.2 Main Characteristics of the Neoliberal Period (1): Economic Libertarianism

Extreme notions of the virtues of markets quickly took hold as central ideologies in academic economics and in public discourse, eventually producing a "market fundamentalism" (Harvey 2005; Appelbaum 2019). The managed and mixed economies of embedded liberalism were now to be unfettered. (The rich countries sought the dream world of neoclassical economics, says Milanovic [2019:192].) Analysts describe a rapid transition from more to less controlled capitalisms in the rich core (e.g., Luttwak 1998; Reich 2007). In Britain and the United States, an earlier demonization of government reemerged: famously, government was the problem not the solution (Ronald Reagan), and there was no such thing as "society" to protect, in any case (Margaret Thatcher). Manic privatizations, deregulations, and pushes for yet freer trade formed an antipode to the more collectivist urgency of the immediate postwar period. At the global level, the United Nations became less central, and the World Bank (and IMF) much more central.

Scholars have delineated a number of political and socioeconomic consequences of the ensuing neoliberal policy regime. Many analysts have argued that business elites were able to attain even more dominance within challenged and fractured states (e.g., Crouch 2004).[6] Corporatism was weakened across the rich world (as well as unions in many countries), reducing (or removing) the presence of labor as an organized interest and hence countervailing power (e.g., Lindvall and Sebring 2005; Streeck 2010). Scholars have found a substantial expansion of capital incomes relative to employment incomes (e.g., Piketty 2014), and an associated explosion of income and wealth inequality in the rich capitalist countries (e.g., Milanovic 2016). Social scientists have discussed how globalization and technological development imperiled the economic security of some population segments while facilitating others: in the less integrated national economies, any rising tide no longer lifted all boats (e.g., Reich 1992, 2007). Many have described a rollback of welfare state provisions in some polities (e.g., Mann 2013: Ch. 6); some scholars have depicted a broader "undermining of citizenship," understood broadly as societal membership as well as political efficacy (e.g., Crouch 1999; Hobsbawm 1999; Reich 2007).

With a vast imagined economy (Chapter 7), economism became both a dominant social theory and a standard idiom. A broader pseudo-economic rationalization of organizations eventually developed: an expansion of pricing and shadow pricing, of formal accounting of time and resource flows – for universities, governments, and nonprofits as well as business firms (Bromley and Meyer 2015). A wide range of social institutions did not have clear economic accounting and hence lost legitimacy as possible collective goods:[7] local communities, "Main Street," unions, newspapers, and industries. Whole cities could be abandoned – for example, Detroit in the United States – or entirely transformed into enclaves for the rich, for example, due to job and housing market forces (e.g., San Francisco). Such developments were most conspicuous in the US, which went farthest in the direction of a market society.

12.4.3 Characteristics (2): The Departure from Statism and a Broader Anti-Elitism

In subordinating and delegitimating the formerly charismatic national state to the more universalistic rules of real or imagined markets, the period departed from embedded liberalism in a radical way. The immediate postwar period had maintained a "myth of the state" (Cassirer 1966) in the Anglo-European core, along with a more limited actual practice of "planning" (Judt 2005). A strong role for the state had "seemed the only sensible route out of the abyss," says Judt (2005:77). This mid-century collectivist moment, even characterizing the United States, was now supplanted by a mythology of self-sufficient markets.

Skepticism about governmental elites was part of a developing broader anti-elitism. Trust in the elites of multiple social sectors was dropping everywhere (Lipset and Schneider 1983; Inglehart 1997). A period of seeming "deference" (or at least begrudging acceptance) – at one time remarked upon for both England and the United States (Almond and Verba 1963; Shils 1982: Ch. 7 [1968]; Halsey 1978) – was confined to the immediate postwar era. It did not survive the cultural revolution of the 1960s and the era of popular "empowerment" that followed. The great elevation of the imagined capacities of the "masses" – a long-developing change in folk epistemology – went hand-in-hand with the diminution of elites. The mid-century imagery of elite guidance, management, and protection weakened greatly.

Related, the period was also characterized by an institutional and social dis-integration of the elites of the different societal sectors – that is, political, economic, media, religious, military, and entertainment sectors. The Depression, World War II, and the immediate postwar reconstruction had integrated elites that were already attached by class and ethnic ties (Marwick 1986). "Power elites" were apparent, described (perhaps with exaggeration) by various analysts (e.g., Mills 1956; Domhoff 1970). The cultural tumult of the 1960s and the economic tumult of the 1970s weakened these mid-century linkages. Integrated "establishments" had slowly dissolved, with the degree and pacing of dis-integration depending of course upon national institutional heritage.

Neoliberal ideology established no clear role of "statesmanship" for business elites, and these elites quickly left behind any felt responsibilities for it. Outside of a few business celebrities, business elites remained strangely invisible, given their power and authority. By the 1990s analysts were remarking upon the "secession" of such elites (and the rich generally) from the broader society (e.g., Reich 1992). Attempts to reintegrate elites through movements arose (e.g., Davos, or Corporate Social Responsibility). These efforts produced more world integration (discussed earlier) but little discernible domestic societal re-engagement (Reich 2020).

And of course there are the elitism-dissolving technologies – viz., the Web and social media, and the displacement of older media elites. Technology along with ideology has finally brought forth the mass society, preparing the way for a full-fledged emergence of so-called populist movements.

12.4.4 Characteristics (3): Sociocultural Libertarianism

The economic libertarianism of the period was accompanied by an intensified sociocultural one. Social life was to be more free, too, with expanded mobility possibilities, and with greatly broadened norms of family and sexual and gender relations. Individual persons were to be "free to choose" religion, language, national identity, and all forms of self-expression. The result was an identity explosion (Frank and Meyer 2002). Ideas of human rights shifted to emphasize the empowerment of individuals to make choices and take action, rather than simple assertions of entitlements: even students were to be trained in empowerment rather than subordinated to cultural authority and canons (Bromley et al. 2011). The emphasis on individual choice led to the further weakening of the authority of traditional communal structures: the family, local communities, religious bodies, and national citizenship. Individuals came to expect liberation from traditional practices. Importantly, the changed norms involved were all codified in explicitly global ways, in an expanding array of treaties and international organizations. Thus, transnational human rights gained standing against citizenship rights: according to the emergent norms, people could expect to be able to move and function anywhere (Soysal 1994; Jacobson 1995).

In one sense the term "libertarianism" is deceptive in characterizing these cultural developments. The movements called for liberation from traditional norms and customs. But for success the movements required institutionalization – and often achieved it, in law and in organizational rules. People's behavior in many work settings is now tightly regulated by entirely new norms and rules; family life proceeds within more formal rules and informal norms; sexual interaction is under more legal control.

Hence it seems an exaggeration to say (as some do) that the neoliberal period moved in an amoral direction. For instance, in his discussion of the evolution of capitalism, Milanovic says that morality was "gutted" and moral controls were "outsourced" merely to law (2019:180ff). While this argument may apply to the evolution of political economy, it doesn't address the neoliberal period as a whole. After all, the period sustained and globalized the rights and equality revolution, and moral norms were extended further into a number of domains: gender and sexuality, family, organizational roles, and the protection of individual and collective identities.

12.5 Post-Liberalism

Great cracks in the neoliberal model appeared, and in the period since around 2010 various anti- and post-liberal reactions emerged on both global and national scales. The neoliberal system supported high levels of economic inequality and insecurity, and some economic disasters: such outcomes were seen as more unjust as world integration increased. Similarly, international political domination became more apparent, and more problematic in terms of both justice and efficacy (e.g., US interventionism). Socially, increased migration and its legitimation produced strong reactions, as did cultural conflict among multiple legitimated groups and ideas (e.g., between liberal and "neotraditional" groups).

In retrospect the neoliberal period may look like an instance of manic and triumphalist over-reach, in various ways self-destructive.

There is much awareness that neoliberalism weakened greatly toward the end of the first decade of the twenty-first century, and that the Anglo-European societies, and the world generally, are entering a new era (Steger and Roy 2010: Ch. 6, Mann 2013: Chs. 10–12, Kuttner 2018: Ch. 11). The cultural models emerging in the new era are not yet settled, and there is much conflict between continuingly expanding liberalism and its critics. This conflict is perhaps the distinctive characteristic of the emergent period. Accordingly, along with others we employ the label "post-liberalism."[8]

Depictions of a new period are disparate. We'll begin with a list of forces often mentioned as causes of transition. Then we turn to our core interest, the cultural frames that may be developing and then structuring ideologies and movements.

12.5.1 Forces Structuring a Post-Liberal Period

Various potential transformative forces have been suggested:

1. Analysts often emphasize the 2008 economic crisis created by the less-regulated global and domestic economies. The crisis clearly reduced the legitimacy of some extreme economistic doctrines.
2. Associated lines of argument emphasize the intra- and inter-national inequalities produced by market and financial globalization. (While inter-national inequalities modestly declined in the neoliberal period, intra-national inequalities generally increased, with some very visible effects [e.g., homelessness].)
3. Related and broader, some analysts call attention to a conflict of interest between so-called cosmopolitan elites, committed to economic globalization and relatively open immigration, and working- and middle-class populations attached to more protected national economies and welfare states (Goodhart 2017; Guilluy 2019). Cosmopolitan elites have promoted a globalization that has threatened wide ranges of jobs, pressuring many communities outside of metropolitan centers. And they have allowed immigration waves that have challenged national integration and politicized national citizenship benefits anew.[9]
4. In some countries representative democracy has had great difficulties as a policy system, both in coping with new or intensified issues

Concluding Reflections 311

and in avoiding policy stalemates in a context of political party dealignment. A broadly shared conception of democratic chaos has reemerged, along with a broadened range of conceived "failed states."[10]

5. The liberating society of liberalism and neoliberalism deconstructed a wide range of traditional social controls and cultural canons, occasioning "neo-traditionalist" reactions and "culture wars."
6. The shock of the September 2001 attack in New York precipitated a rapid assembly of "security states" in the United States and Europe, changing the nature of states and their relationship to citizenries, and inducing new forms of citizen distrust. Talk of a possible "clash of civilizations," and especially an Islamic threat, rapidly replaced a decade of "end of the Cold War" enthusiasm.
7. Some observers emphasize that the quasi-imperial blunders and arrogance of the United States have themselves tarnished the liberal model. In any case, the relative dominance and the prestige of this country have clearly declined, opening wider the door for alternative societal models.
8. Challengers distinguishing themselves from the liberal order, serving as possible alternative models and competing for influence, have in fact arisen: India, Russia, Islamic societies, and China.

All the above developments seem powerful, and we will make no attempt to weigh their relative import. We would merely add: By the second decade of the twenty-first century, the Anglo-European societies, and to some extent the entire world, had experienced a half-century or so of the dual libertarian revolution, economic and cultural. That dual revolution had produced societies with difficulties of mass economic inclusion, with no "myth of the state," with a generalized anti-elitism, and with a whole array of empowered "actors" (perhaps with nowhere to go). A new historical period should not be surprising.

12.5.2 Emergent Post-Liberal Ideologies

In any event, the neoliberal global cultural regime showed more and more weaknesses, and formerly muted oppositions were articulated with increasing force. There are multiple projects contending within a loosened space, freer from global geopolitical and social controls. In addition, the previous cultural core of the world system – the Anglo-

European societies – is now composed of notably "post-heroic" societies (H. Muenkler quoted by Anderson 2009:274). Their charisma has drained away substantially, both internally and externally, and they exert less world authority. The global institutions they sponsored have also lost credibility and centrality.

So, the world capitalist system – always suspect from the left – came under much broader attack as a creature of dominance, inequality, and ecological destruction. Radical demands for social control from the left were paralleled by increasing attacks from the old conservative right (e.g., the Vatican) – but also from centrist demands for justice, basic human rights, and ecological balance.

In the same way, it became possible to attack "liberal" democracy, and alternatives were put forward as putative general models in Russia, China, Brazil, Turkey, Hungary, and elsewhere. The world had always been full of autocrats with democratic pretenses: now they emerge with grandiose depictions of alternatives (Kuttner 2018; Snyder 2018; Przeworski 2019). Related, a wave of restrictions on the activities of international nongovernmental organizations occurred (Bromley et al. 2019).

Further, the social and cultural institutions of liberalism came under stronger attack. Attacks on the rights of homosexuals, women, children, immigrants, and religious and ethnic minorities arose in many national contexts.

Finally, attacks intensified on the core underlying institutions of a global liberal order. Criticisms of science and its "undemocratic" authority were widespread around the world – including the centers of the US government. Similar criticisms of expanded and putatively impractical education have grown around the world (Schofer et al. 2019). At both global and national levels, efforts to weaken or control the large multinational firms have become more common, as have attacks on governmental and nongovernmental organizations (Meyer et al. 2015; Bromley et al. 2019). In addition, the rationalized structures of national states – putatively turned into proper organizations rather than bureaucracies in the neoliberal period – came under criticism everywhere.

The anti-elitism and "confidence gap" long-developed during liberalism and neoliberalism broadened into a skepticism about or dismissal of expertise – a shift in folk epistemology, especially pronounced in the historically subjectivist and anti-intellectual United States (Hofstadter

Concluding Reflections

1962). An "intellectual egalitarianism" has developed, says one analyst (Nichols 2018). We assume that this epistemic shift is occurring worldwide, associated with individual and group empowerment.[11] By now, schooled individuals are equipped with greatly expanded notions of intuition and competence, encouraging them to declare "opinions" on every topic with great confidence. Humans have often been prolific opiners; now such opining is more legitimated. So we assume that research would find deference to expert knowledge declining everywhere, as well as the number of subjects treated as expert domains; related, we assume that distinctions between expert and layperson are blurring in a great many domains, including those traditionally associated with science. Related, notions of high, middle, and low culture (or equivalent distinctions) are now far less legitimated (even in post-aristocratic Europe). Of course a proliferation of confident claims on every topic is now powered by technology offering mass communication entirely free of elite mediation or professional norms (e.g., Kakutani 2018).

12.5.3 Resulting Post-Liberal Movements

The bases of post-liberalism have not consolidated into a single oppositional culture at the world level, and for the most part not at the national level either. Political nationalisms try to resurrect the old charismatic state. Ethnic and cultural nationalisms propose new political geographies. Religious alternatives to liberalism are mobilized (as in India, and with Islamic mobilizations). All these movements produce variously grounded attacks on immigrants and putative outsiders. Rather than left/right, the above movements appear to coalesce within two historically familiar cultural frames: "populist" and "communal."

Populist.[12] A great many movements imagine a governing sociopolitical "system" that is thought to be unresponsive or incompetent or corrupt. The movements seek a more direct influence of "the people" – a vague but standard conception. Many of the current anti-system movements do echo the movements labeled populist in the past.[13] The re-emergence of this old ideological frame now should not be surprising, given decades of attacks on government, of diminution of elites, of elevation of the imagined capacities of the mass public, and of policy difficulties (real and perceived).

The "populist" category is a very broad one, containing diverse subsets. Some movements remain democratic but show less commitment to representative democracy (Przeworski 2019), with more desire for direct input (e.g., more use of plebiscites). In contrast, other movements are anti-democratic in seeing constitutional and legal procedures as blockages of a popular rule. In such cases there is the familiar recourse to authoritarianism – the idea that an autonomous leader, freed from impediments (such as rules), is necessary for addressing the people's interests.

Then there is the set of "right-wing" anti-liberal populisms now dotted across the map, showing limited commitment to parliamentary democracy, tolerance, deliberation, cosmopolitanism, and rationalism (Kuttner's list [2018:260–263]). Some scholars would place the current United States in this "right-wing populist" set (or at least its current Republican Party). Most analysts would distinguish this set from the quasi- or pseudo-democratic polities such as Russia, Turkey, Poland, and Hungary.

Some insurgent movements may be labeled populist simply because they oppose the agendas of governing elites. Those voting for Brexit or engaged in the French "Yellow Vest" protests may be so labeled. But Goodhart (2017) has argued persuasively that some such mobilizations are protests against "cosmopolitan" elite inattention to economic security and to the consequences of immigration (see also Judis 2016).

Finally, regional autonomy movements are sometimes labeled as populist. These movements may be better placed within the next broad grouping.

Communal. A second main category of post-liberal movements reflects the "ideology of cultural authenticity" (Boli and Lechner 2015) that intensified throughout the postwar period. This cultural frame is the long-standing one originating in nationalism:[14] the guiding idea is that distinct cultures should have the opportunity to self-govern and thereby live in accordance with distinctive practices and valued traditions.

The emergent period reveals a mobilization around cultural boundaries of every sort – ethnicity, race, sex, sexuality, religion, locality, and ethnicized political alignments. This so-called new tribalism (Barber 1996), producing a "separatist impulse" both globally and within polities (Gitlin 1995), can be post-liberal in various ways. It may be mono-cultural, or antidemocratic, or anti-neoliberal-economy, or neotraditional. Some communal mobilization conflicts with individualism, as with religiously grounded movements emphasizing the authority of Christian (or Orthodox), Islamic, or Hindu traditions. And of course communal mobilizations may be anti-tolerance, whether within polities or on a world scale.

Both cultural frames, populist and communal, have resonance and applicability around the world (see Goodhart 2017: ch.3 for European populisms, Kurtz 2007 for religious movements, Chirot 2011 for ethnic ones). Their diffusion is aided by a now-global public space, facilitating rapid copying of rhetorics and models. The models are sharply distinct from those that neoinstitutional theory called attention to in the past. They tend to depict a dismantling of some of the more rationalized structures of the liberal era. And their highly varied nature leads one to expect a continuation of a cultural deglobalization already underway.

12.6 Conclusion

The postwar world was one of massive liberal and neoliberal expansion, with visions of a world society, emanating from an Anglo-European core, institutionalized in extended organization and reflected in discourse. That world took its ideologies and social theories very seriously: they were real, or to be made real, and they were perhaps even natural. Freed from superstition and culture and constraint, humans would finally be more rational actors and society might move toward a proper "knowledge society."

Neoinstitutional theory calls attention to this vision *as an institutionalized cultural matter*. Social life took new form under this cultural canopy, generating explosive expansion of science, education, and organization. But the mundane realities produced were often quite distinct from the imagined society, generating the now-familiar waves of mobilizations for justice or equality or more freedom. Movements then invariably generated counter-movements attached to different standards: for example, perceived sex or gender discrimination has produced reforms celebrated in some places but abhorrent in others.

Such cultural dramas now proceed in a world filled with empowered human "actors." Individuals and groups worldwide are entitled to authenticity and self-governance. In addition, they are empowered not only by ideology but also with transformative technology – for example, the Web and social media for individuals, genetic and AI projects for scientists and corporations, powerful weaponry, now including cyberweaponry, for a widened range of collectivities. Yet in this hyperworld of entitled and empowered actors a whole range of social control processes are not even discussable.

While empowerment seems to outrun control in the emergent post-liberal period, the shift away from dominant liberal and neoliberal models to a more fragmented set of alternatives doesn't represent a return to the raw "Realist" international order depicted by some political scientists. Rather, the shift represents diverse sets of political, religious, social, and economic cultural models. These models can produce waves of post-liberal global diffusion. Some are certainly capable of institutionalization – after all, populist authoritarianism, theocracy, and a mono-ethnic polity are all familiar institutionalized forms (to suggest just some examples). If institutionalized, any form will constitute identities (including "actors") distinct from those of high liberalism and neoliberalism. (Any form will remain only partially reflected in mundane social realities, as always.)

Despite this new world, the default intellectual imageries in Anglo-European social theory remain those of economics, social psychology, and psychology (or one or another normative philosophy). Those imageries do not provide much help for describing the changing world, let alone explaining it. So those theoretic defaults sustain great space for a more realistic social imagery, one that sees humans as always dependent upon and operating within taken-for-granted but varying cultural frames.

Notes

1. The United States was producing forty-odd percent of the world's goods and services and had some sixty percent of the world's capital stock. The USSR by 1945 had re-established a huge army and controlled a vast expanse in central and eastern Europe.
2. In some of these theories it is imagined that the order is a successful construction by the actors that the new order actually produced – thereby getting the causation turned around.
3. We sketch the periods, and suggest some transitional forces. We don't attempt a proper historical account of transitions between periods.

4. In retrospect, a remarkably reified and uniform vision. Weiner (1966) is representative.
5. By "formalization" we refer to increases in the number of entities calling themselves organizations, in the number of social domains filled by organizations, and in the number of rules and roles within them (Drori et al. 2006:2–3).
6. Iversen and Soskice (2019) argue that this common idea is an exaggeration, on the grounds that business power is constrained by the relative immobility of many businesses – especially those dependent upon regional knowledge and talent centers – as well as by global business competition. This rebuttal represents a minority position, at least so far.
7. Anticipated by Daniel Bell in his discussion of the "limits of the economizing mode" (1973:279–287), and earlier by Galbraith (1958).
8. We use the term in an historical sense, to denote a period, not a political philosophy.
9. Hence reactivating "cosmopolitan/local" and "center/periphery" cleavages emphasized in mid-twentieth-century sociology but less prominent in recent times (e.g., Shils 1982 [1961, 1962]; Lipset and Rokkan 1967).
10. For example, Fukuyama has now written about "political decay," and detects a substantial amount in the United States as well as other locations (Fukuyama 2014).
11. We have not seen materials sufficient to allow much confidence about country variation. Our impression is that an expansion of subjectivism and the decline of epistemic elites is less often remarked upon for Western Europe, where elitism seems to have persisted more. As an aside, we note one cross-national survey that shows American respondents having the highest confidence in their own individual scientific knowledge (when compared within 140 nationalities), while showing a middling level of trust in scientists (www.sciencemag.org/news/2019/06/global-survey-finds-strong-support-scientists).
12. We thank Michael Mosher for ideas and materials on contemporary populism.
13. We draw upon the analyses provided in Ionescu and Gellner (1969).
14. For example, Wilsonian ideology featured the idea of self-governance of distinct culture groups (even if the idea of culture was racialized).

References

Almond, G. & S. Verba (1963). *The Civic Culture*, Boston, MA: Little, Brown, & Co.

Anderson, P. (2009). *The New Old World*, London: Verso.

Appelbaum, B. (2019). *The Economists' Hour*, New York, NY: Little, Brown, & Co.
Barber, B. (1996). *Jihad vs. McWorld*, New York, NY: Ballantine.
Bell, D. (1973). *The Coming of Post-Industrial Society*, New York, NY: Basic Books.
Boli, J. & F. J. Lechner (2015). Globalization and World Culture. In J. D. Wright, ed., *International Encyclopedia of the Social and Behavioral Sciences*, 2nd ed. Amsterdam: Elsevier, pp. 225–32.
Boli, J. & G. Thomas (1999). *Constructing World Culture: International Non-Governmental Organizations Since 1875*, Stanford, CA: Stanford University Press.
Boyle, E. & J. W. Meyer (1998). Modern Law as a Secularized and Global Model: Implications for the Sociology of Law. *Soziale Welt*, 49(3), 213–32.
Bromley P. & J. W. Meyer (2015). *Hyper-Organization: Global Organizational Expansion*, Oxford: Oxford University Press.
Bromley, P., J. W. Meyer, & F. O. Ramirez (2011). Student-Centeredness in Social Science Textbooks: Cross-National Analyses, 1970–2005. *Social Forces*, 90(2), 547–70.
Bromley, P. & W. W. Powell (2012). From Smoke and Mirrors to Walking the Talk: Decoupling in the Contemporary World. *Academy of Management Annals*, 6(1), 483–530.
Bromley, P., E. Schofer, & W. Longhofer (2019). Contentions over World Culture: The Rise of Legal Restrictions on Foreign Funding to NGOs, 1994–2015. *Social Forces*, soz138: https://doi.org/10.1093/sf/soz138.
Bull, H. & A. Watson, eds. (1985). *The Expansion of International Society*, Oxford: Oxford University Press.
Carter, Z. D. (2020). *The Price of Peace*, New York, NY: Random House.
Cassirer, E. (1966). *The Myth of the State*, New Haven, CT: Yale University Press.
Chirot, D. (2011). *Contentious Identities*, New York, NY: Routledge.
Cole, W. M. & F. O. Ramirez (2013). Conditional Decoupling: Assessing the Impact of National Human Rights Institutions, 1981 to 2004. *American Sociological Review*, 78(4), 702–25.
Crouch, C. (1999). *Social Change in Western Europe*, Oxford: Oxford University Press.
Crouch, C. (2004). *Post-Democracy*, London: Polity.
Domhoff, G. W. (1970). *The Higher Circles*, New York, NY: Random House.
Drori, G., J. W. Meyer, & H. Hwang, eds. (2006). *Globalization and Organization*, Oxford: Oxford University Press.
Drori, G., J. W. Meyer, F. O. Ramirez, & E. Schofer (2003). *Science in the Modern World Polity: Institutionalization and Globalization*, Stanford, CA: Stanford University Press.

Drori G. & H. Moon (2006). The Changing Nature of Tertiary Education: Cross-national Trends in Disciplinary Enrollment, 1965–1995. In D. Baker & A. Wiseman, eds., *The Impact of Comparative Education Research on Institutional Theory*. Amsterdam: Elsevier Science, pp. 157–86.

Etzioni, A. (1968). *The Active Society*, New York, NY: The Free Press.

Frank, D., B. Camp, & S. Boutcher (2010). Worldwide Trends in the Criminal Regulation of Sex, 1945 to 2005. *American Sociological Review*, 75(6), 867–93.

Frank, D. J. & J. Gabler (2006). *Reconstructing the University: Worldwide Changes in Academic Emphases over the Twentieth Century*, Stanford, CA: Stanford University Press.

Frank, D. J. & J. W. Meyer (2002). The Profusion of Individual Roles and Identities in the Postwar Period. *Sociological Theory*, 20(1), 86–105.

Fukuyama, F. (2014). *Political Order and Political Decay*, New York, NY: Farrar, Straus, & Giroux.

Galbraith, J. K. (1958). *The Affluent Society*, Boston, MA: Houghton Mifflin.

Gitlin, T. (1995). *The Twilight of Common Dreams*, New York, NY: Metropolitan Books.

Goodhart, D. (2017). *The Road to Somewhere: The Populist Revolt and the Future of Politics*, London: Hurst & Co.

Guilluy, C. (2019). *Twilight of the Elites*. New Haven, CT: Yale University Press.

Halsey, A. H. (1978). *Change in British Society*, Oxford: Oxford University Press.

Harvey, D. (2005). *A Brief History of Neoliberalism*, Oxford: Oxford University Press.

Hironaka, A. (2005). *Neverending Wars*, Cambridge: Cambridge University Press.

Hironaka, A. (2014). *Greening the Globe*, Cambridge: Cambridge University Press.

Hobsbawm, E. (1999). *On the Edge of the New Century*, New York, NY: The New Press.

Hofstadter, R. (1962). *Anti-Intellectualism in American Life*, New York, NY: Vintage.

Hwang, H. (2006). Planning Development: Globalization and the Shifting Locus of Planning. In G. Drori, J. W. Meyer, & H. Hwang, eds., *Globalization and Organization*, Oxford: Oxford University Press, pp.69–90.

Inglehart, R. (1997). Postmaterialist Values and the Erosion of Institutional Authority. In J. S. Nye, P. D. Zelikow, & D. C. King,

eds., *Why People Don't Trust Government*. Cambridge, MA: Harvard University Press.
Ionescu, G. & E. Gellner (1969). *Populism*, New York, NY: Macmillan Publishers.
Iversen, T. & D. Soskice (2019). *Democracy and Prosperity*, Princeton: Princeton University Press.
Jacobson, D. (1995). *Immigration and the Decline of Citizenship*, Baltimore, MD: Johns Hopkins University Press.
Judis, J. (2016). *The Populist Explosion*, New York, NY: Columbia Global Reports.
Judt, T. (2005). *Postwar*, London: Penguin Books.
Kakutani, M. (2018). *The Death of Truth*, New York, NY: Tim Duggan Books.
Kurtz, L. (2007). *Gods in the Global Village*, 2nd ed. Newbury Park, CA: Pine Forge Press.
Kuttner, R. (2018). *Can Democracy Survive Global Capitalism?* New York, NY: W. W. Norton.
Lauren, P. G. (2003). *The Evolution of International Human Rights: Visions Seen*, Philadelphia, PA: University of Pennsylvania Press.
Lechner, F. & J. Boli (2005). *World Culture*, Hoboken, NJ: Wiley-Blackwell.
Lindvall, J. & J. Sebring (2005). Policy Reform and the Decline of Corporatism in Sweden. *West European Politics*, 28(5), 1057–74.
Lipset, S. M. & S. Rokkan (1967). *Party Systems and Voter Alignments*, New York, NY: The Free Press.
Lipset, S. M. & W. Schneider (1983). *The Confidence Gap*, New York, NY: The Free Press.
Luttwak, E. (1998). *Turbo-Capitalism*, London: Weidenfeld & Nicholson.
Mann, M. (2013). *The Sources of Social Power, vol. 4: Globalizations, 1945–2011*, Cambridge: Cambridge University Press.
Marwick, A. (1986). The Upper Class in Britain, France, and the U.S. Since the First World War. In A. Marwick, ed., *Class in the Twentieth Century*. Brighton: Harvester Press.
Meyer, J. W., S. Pope, & A. Isaacson (2015). Legitimating the Transnational Corporation in a Stateless World Society. In K. Tsutsui & A. Lim, eds., *Corporate Social Responsibility in a Globalizing World*. Cambridge: Cambridge University Press, pp. 27–72.
Meyer, J. W., F. O. Ramirez, & Y. Soysal (1992). World Expansion of Mass Education, 1870–1970. *Sociology of Education*, 65(2), 128–49.
Milanovic, B. (2016). *Global Inequality*, Cambridge, MA: Harvard University Press.
Milanovic, B. (2019). *Capitalism Alone*, Cambridge, MA: Harvard University Press.

Mills, C. W. (1956). *The Power Elite*, Oxford: Oxford University Press.
Nichols, T. (2018). *The Death of Expertise*, Oxford: Oxford University Press.
Piketty, T. (2014). *Capital in the Twenty-First Century*, Cambridge, MA: Harvard University Press.
Przeworski, A. (2019). *Crises of Democracy*, Cambridge: Cambridge University Press.
Reich, R. (1992). *The Work of Nations*, New York, NY: Vintage Books.
Reich, R. (2007). *Supercapitalism*, New York, NY: Knopf.
Reich, R. (2020). *The System*, New York, NY: Knopf.
Ruggie, J. (1982). International Regimes, Transactions, and Change: Embedded Liberalism in the Postwar Economic Order. *International Organization*, 36(2), 379–415.
Ruggie, J. (1998). Globalization and the Embedded Liberalism Compromise: The End of an Era? In W. Streeck, ed., *Internationale Wirtschaft, Nationale Demokratie: Herausforderungen für die Demokratietheorie*. Frankfurt: Campus, pp. 79–97.
Schofer, E., J. Lerch, & J. W. Meyer (2019). *Illiberal Reactions to the University in the 21st Century*, New York, NY: Annual Meetings of the American Sociological Association.
Schofer, E. & J. W. Meyer (2005). The World-Wide Expansion of Higher Education in the Twentieth Century. *American Sociological Review*, 70(6), 898–920.
Shils, E. (1982). *The Constitution of Society*, Chicago, IL: University of Chicago Press.
Snyder, T. (2018). *The Road to Unfreedom*, New York, NY: Tim Duggan Books.
Soysal, Y. N. (1994). *Limits of Citizenship*, Chicago, IL: University of Chicago Press.
Stacy, H. M. (2009). *Human Rights for the 21st Century: Sovereignty, Civil Society, Culture*, Stanford, CA: Stanford University Press.
Steger, M. B. & R. K. Roy (2010). *Neoliberalism*, Oxford: Oxford University Press.
Stinchcombe, A. (1997). On the Virtues of the Old Institutionalism. *Annual Review of Sociology*, 23(1), 1–18.
Streeck, W. (2010). *Re-Forming Capitalism: Institutional Change in the German Political Economy*, Oxford: Oxford University Press.
Weiner, M., ed. (1966). *Modernization*, New York, NY: Basic Books.

Index

Abell, Peter, 111, 143
Actors
 agentic actorhood (*See* Agentic actorhood)
 collective culture and, 130–31
 conflicts involving, 269–70
 cultural construction of (*See* Cultural construction of actors)
 cultural elaborateness and dependence, 10–11
 cultural rules of actorhood, 212–13
 defined, 281–82, 290
 economics, increased focus on in, 246–47, 270–71
 emergence of concept, 246
 empowerment of, 315–16
 environmental movement, inability of actor-centered theories to predict or explain, 285
 focus on actorhood in institutional theory, 126, 127–29, 270–73
 human rights, actorhood and, 128
 human rights, inability of actor-centered theories to predict or explain, 285–86
 individuals as, 6–8, 128 (*See also* Individuals)
 institutionalism and, 54–56
 institutionalization of behavior, 9–10
 isomorphic actors, 226–27
 levels of actors, inconsistences between, 269
 liberalism, actorhood and, 7, 290–91
 "logics" of action, 289–90
 monopolistic nature of actor-centered theories, 282
 nation-states as, 128 (*See also* Nation-states)
 nature, rationalization by science and, 214–15, 218, 231–32
 neoliberalism, actorhood and, 7
 nonactors, as agents for, 220
 not embedded in culture, viewed as, 209–10
 organizations as, 14, 128 (*See also* Organizations)
 political science, increased focus on in, 246–47, 270–71
 practical realities, inconsistences between actors and, 270
 psychology, increased focus on in, 246–47
 rationalized social organization, inability of actor-centered theories to predict or explain, 286
 raw actors, 236
 realism and, 210
 religion, and rationalization of, 218, 231–32
 sacred nature of attributes, 290
 scripts and, 9–10
 social change, inability of actor-centered theories to predict or explain, 285–86
 social sciences, increased focus on in, 246–47, 270–71, 281
 sociological neoinstitutionalism and, 100–2
 sociology, increased focus on in, 246–47, 270–71
 structures versus, 282
 as system of social agency, 211
 tension with institutional theory, 252
 unrealistic expectations of, 286–89, 291
 world society, actorhood and, 258 (*See also* World society)
Agency. *See* Agentic actorhood
Agentic actorhood
 agency defined, 235

Index

authorized agents, 211
  collective action and, 234–35
  consultants and, 230
  corporate social entities and, 223
  cultural authority, agents for, 220–21
  disinterested agency and, 232–33
  heightened structuration of actors, 228–29
  as historical construction, 221–22
  implications for understanding social structure, 224
  individuals and, 223–24
  isomorphic actors, 226–27
  liberalism and, 222, 223–24
  nature, rationalization by science and, 213–15, 231–32
  nonactors, agents for, 220
  other actors, agents for, 219–20
  overview, 234, 235, 281–82
  principal-agent tension, 224–26
  principle, agents for, 220–21
  professionals and, 230
  religion, and rationalization of, 216–17, 231–32
  scripts and, 226–27
  self, agents for, 218–19
  services from "others," 230–31
  structural elements of actors, decoupling of, 227–28
  system of social agency, actors as, 211
  transformation into "otherhood," 229–30
  variations in, 222–23
Alford, R., 289
Almond, Gabriel, 93
Anderson, Perry, 179
Anthropology
  culture and, 28
  individual, role of, 7, 201
  institutions, continued centrality of, 246
  reductionism in, 7
Atomism, 160

Barrett, Deborah, 87, 104
Barton, A., 200
Bell, Daniel, 127, 182
Bendor, J., 263

Berger, Joseph, 102, 103
Berger, Peter, 5, 7, 47, 52–53, 71, 132
Berkovitch, Nitza, 104
Blau, P., 200
Boli, John, 67–68, 85, 89–90, 110
Botswana, education in, 302
Boudon, R., 145
Boudon-Coleman diagram, 140–41, 145–47, 150, 156, 160
Brandt Commission, 304
Braudel, F., 179, 190
Brazil, attacks on democracy in, 312
Brenner, Robert, 173–74
Brexit, 314
Brunsson, N., 14
Buckley, Walter, 58–59
Bureaucracy, organization versus, 14
Burt, R., 151

Calvin, John, 154
Calvinism, 145, 149–50
Campbell, Donald, 196
Canada, differences from United States, 4
Capital, 185
Capitalism
  enterprise, centrality of, 174–75
  globalization, conflation with, 185–86
  modernity, conflation with, 178–79, 180–81
  post-liberal attacks on, 312
  Protestantism and, 141, 156–60
  rationalization and, 174–75
Catholic Mass, 58
Chase-Dunn, Christopher, 112
China
  democracy, attacks on, 312
  post-liberalism, role in, 311
  Western culture contrasted, 212–13
Christianity
  changes in cultural models arising from, 171–73
  economics and, 176
  human rights and, 212
  individual and, 172
  nature and, 172
  "Protestant Ethic Thesis" deflecting from broader context of, 171
  Protestantism (*See* Protestantism)
  Puritanism, 150

Christianity (cont.)
  rationalization and, 172–73, 180
  science and, 172
  systemic model, shift from liturgical model to, 172
  as Western cultural framework, 212
  world society compared, 245
Citizenship, institutional development and, 48
Class conflict
  game theory and, 162
  institutional formation and, 48
  institutionalization of, 43–44
Class structure, 27, 30
Cohen, M., 263
Cold War, 298
Coleman, James, 91, 110, 140, 141, 143, 145–47, 158
Collins, R., 145, 158, 176, 177–78
Colyvas, J., 126
Communal movements, 314–15
Communism, 303
Companies. See Organizations
Congo, science in, 257
Consultants
  agentic actorhood and, 230
  individuals and, 268–69
  nation-states and, 268–69
  organizations and, 268–69
  in response to unrealistic expectations of actors, 288–89
Contextual analysis, 200
Convention theory, 289–90
Corporations. See Organizations
Cultural construction of actors
  abstract, 209
  overview, 9, 18, 210–12
  sociological neoinstitutionalism and, 212
Cultural institutionalism
  functionalism and, 11
  incorporation of new cultural schemes, 11
  institutionalized doctrine and, 10
  mainstream acceptance of, 126–27
  marginalization of culture and, 5–6, 17, 129–30
  overview, 3, 132–33
  phenomenology and, 5

political science and, 4
reemergence of institutions, 7–8
social change and, 8
sociological neoinstitutionalism (See Sociological neoinstitutionalism)
sociology and, 4
Culture
  actorhood, collective culture and, 130–31
  actors viewed as not embedded in, 209–10
  anthropology and, 28
  collective-level conception, absence of, 130
  expressive aspects of, 29
  individual as primary actor in, 6–8
  institutionalization, conflation with, 45–46
  liberalism and, 283
  marginalization in social theory, 5–6, 17, 129–30, 233
  moral meaning and, 28–29
  nature and, 28
  neoliberalism, socio-cultural libertarianism in, 308–9
  in nineteenth-century analysis, 28–30
  rules of, 30
  society as cultural system, 29
  transcendental meaning and, 28–29
"Culture wars," 311

Dahrendorf, R., 43–44
Davis, J.A., 200
Davis, J.J., 200
Deal, Terrence, 79
Decoupling
  of models in world society, 262–63
  organizations and, 13, 74–75
  realism and, 263
  of structural elements of actors, 227–28
Deep socialization, 43
Deinstitutionalization, 48
Derivative structures, institutions as, 247
Determinism, 252
DiMaggio, Paul, 79, 97, 250, 251–52, 261
Division of labor, 27, 30, 33
Dobbin, Frank, 76, 88–89, 97, 198

Index

Dornbusch, Sanford, 73
Douglas, Mary, 58
Downward causation, 196–97
Durkheim, Emile, 37, 55, 161, 199–200

Economics
  actors, increased focus on, 246–47, 270–71
  broadening of causal forces, 175–76
  capital and, 185
  capitalism (*See* Capitalism)
  Christianity and, 176
  default intellectual imagery of, 316
  Europe, economic history of, 173–78
  free trade, 300
  imagined economy, expansion of, 184–85
  individual, role of, 7, 173–74, 177–78, 188, 201
  "knowledge economy," 127
  knowledge systems and, 176–77
  liberalism and, 283
  longer period of time, causal forces operating over, 175–77
  management of firms and, 183
  monetarization and, 181–84
  neoliberalism, economic libertarianism in, 305–7
  new institutionalisms in, 248
  non-economic institutions and, 182
  "Protestant Ethic Thesis" and, 154
  rationalization and, 179–80, 188
  realist institutionalism and, 249
  reductionism in, 7
  service sector, 288–89
  sociopolitical control over, 182
Economism
  capital and, 185
  in European economic history, 173–74, 177–78
  individualism and, 188
  modernity and, 178–79, 180–81
  neoliberalism and, 306–7
Education
  embedded liberalism and, 302
  expansion of, 266
  functionalism and, 81–82
  in Germany, 107
  individual and, 12–13, 89–90
  institutionalization, nature and effects of, 72–73
  modernization and, 80–82
  myth and, 70, 71–72, 100
  political participation and, 199–200
  principal-agent tension in, 224–25
  rationalization and, 180
  in response to unrealistic expectations of actors, 288
  socialization, role of, 70–72
  theoretical research program (TRP) and, 96
  women in, 264
  world society and, 256
Eisenstadt, S.N., 4, 141–42, 154
Elster, J., 143
Embedded liberalism
  Communism versus, 303
  crises in, 304
  domestic effects of, 301–2
  education and, 302
  environmental movement and, 302
  family and, 302
  human rights and, 301, 302
  individual and, 299–300, 301, 302
  institution-building and, 300
  intergovernmental organizations and, 300
  international organization and, 300
  isomorphisms of, 303–4
  model of, 302–3
  neoliberalism, continuities in, 305
  non-governmental organizations and, 300
  overview, 297
  sexuality and, 302
  transnational rationalized culture and, 300–1
  variations of, 303–4
  weakening of traditional structures, 302
Empirical research, 12
Environmental movement
  actor-centered theories, inability of to predict or explain, 285
  embedded liberalism and, 302
  transformation of nation-states and, 87
  world society and, 15–16
Esser, Hartmut, 140, 145

Europe. *See also specific country*
  economic history of, 173–78
  modernity in, 178–81
  religious culture in, 170–73
Evolving cultural models
  embedded liberalism (*See* Embedded liberalism)
  neoliberalism (*See* Neoliberalism)
  overview, 18, 297, 299
  post-liberalism (*See* Post-liberalism)
Exchange system, 181–82

"Failed states," 128, 268, 287, 310–11
Family
  embedded liberalism and, 302
  liberalism and, 283
Fein, L.C., 261
Finnemore, Martha, 98
Firms. *See* Organizations
Fligstein, Neil, 76, 98
Foucault, M., 235–36, 252
France
  institutionalization in, 40
  organizational definition of state and, 31
  railroads in, 88–89
  "Yellow Vest" protests in, 314
Frank, David, 87, 94, 95, 104
Freeman, J., 146
Free will, 252
Friedland, R., 289
Functionalism
  education and, 81–82
  overview, 11, 109

Galileo, 180
Game theory, 162
"Garbage can" model, 263, 272
Gellner, Ernest, 181
Gender
  deinstitutionalization and, 48
  liberalism and, 283
Germany
  corporate social entities in, 223
  education in, 107
  individualism in, 93
Ghana, institutions in, 41
Globalization
  capitalism, conflation with, 185–86
  individualism and, 187, 188–89
  levels of analysis in, 198–99
  rationalization and, 186
  of science, 265–66
  of social sciences, 265–66
  sociological neoinstitutionalism and, 67–68
Goffman, E., 45, 47, 52–53
Goodhart, D., 314
Gorski, P.S., 153
Granovetter, M., 151

Hacking, Ian, 132
Haiti, voting in, 40
Hamilton, Gary, 77
Hannan, Michael, 80, 84, 97, 143–44, 146
Hechter, M., 143
Hedström, P., 140–41, 143, 145–46, 147
Hernes, G., 145
Hicks, J.R., 182
History
  individual, role of, 7, 201
  institutions, continued centrality of, 246
  reductionism in, 7
Holism, 160
Homans, G., 149
Honduras, accounting in, 257
Human rights
  actor-centered theories, inability of to predict or explain, 285–86
  actorhood and, 128
  Christianity and, 212
  embedded liberalism and, 301, 302
  expansion of, 265–66
  individual and, 13, 128
  post-liberal attacks on, 312
  world society and, 16
Hungary, attacks on democracy in, 312, 314
Hwang, H., 126, 281

Ideological role of social theory, 284
Imagined economy, expansion of, 184–85
India, post-liberalism and, 311

Index

Individualism. *See also* Individuals
  agentic actorhood and, 223–24
  as collective-level construction, 90–91
  economism and, 188
  evolution of, changes in individual identity over, 94–95
  globalization and, 187, 188–89
  institutional theory and, 201–2, 204
  levels of analysis and, 200–1
  liberalism and, 189, 201
  methodological individualism (*See* Methodological individualism)
  multilevel analysis versus, 202
  mythology of, 188–89
  neoliberalism and, 201
  organizations, expanded individualism in, 78–79
  sexuality and, 95
  suicide and, 199
  variations in, 93–94
  women and, 94, 111
Individual-level causal processes, 148–49
Individuals. *See also* Individualism
  as actors, 6–8, 128
  agentic actorhood and (*See* Agentic actorhood)
  anthropology, role in, 7, 201
  changes in individual identity over evolution of individualism, 94–95
  Christianity and, 172
  consultants and, 230, 268–69
  "contemporary identity explosion," 95
  cultural authority, as agents for, 220–21
  culture, as primary actor in, 6–8
  deemphasis of cultural aspect, problems with, 34
  economics, role in, 7, 173–74, 177–78, 188, 201
  education and, 12–13, 89–90
  embedded liberalism and, 299–300, 301, 302
  empirical research findings, 12–13
  heightened structuration of, 228–29
  history, role in, 7, 201
  human rights and, 13, 128
  individual-level enactment, 90–91
  inflation of claims on, 268
  institutional formation and, 48
  as isomorphic actors, 226–27
  levels of analysis and, 198
  liberalism and, 284
  "life courses" and, 92–93
  modernity and, 90–91, 110
  myth and, 34
  nation-states and, 87
  nature, rationalization of and, 215
  as new cultural rule, 30
  in nineteenth-century analysis, 27–28, 34
  nonactors, as agents for, 220
  other actors, as agents for, 219–20
  political reconstruction of society around, 89–90
  principal-agent tension in, 225–26
  principle, as agents for, 220–21
  professionals and, 230, 268–69
  "Protestant Ethic Thesis" and, 171
  psychology, role in, 7, 201
  realism and, 34
  religion, and rationalization of, 216–17
  research problems, 34–35
  scripts and, 92–93
  self, as agents for, 218–19
  as social construction, 201
  sociology, role in, 7, 68–69, 201
  structural elements, decoupling of, 227–28
  theoretical research program (TRP) and, 98–99
  unrealistic expectations of, 286–88
Inkeles, Alex, 90
Institutional causal processes, 148–49, 153–55
Institutional effects, 49, 56
Institutional explanations, 49
Institutionalism
  actors and, 54–56
  conceptualization of, 38
  cultural institutionalism (*See* Cultural institutionalism)
  individualist/phenomenological line of theory, 52
  individualist/realist line of theory, 51

Institutionalism (cont.)
  levels of analysis and, 49–50, 51
  microtranslation and, 55, 61–62
  "new institutionalisms," 38
  organizational analysis and, 53
  other arguments distinguished, 54
  psychology and, 52–53
  rational choice theory versus, 55
  rules in, 53–54
  socially constructed units and, 49–51, 61
  sociological neoinstitutionalism (See Sociological neoinstitutionalism)
  sociology and, 52
  straightforward representation of, 38
  structuralist/phenomenological line of theory, 52
  structuralist/realist line of theory, 51
Institutionalization
  absence of reproductive processes versus, 43
  action versus, 43–44, 55–56
  of class conflict, 43–44
  conceptualization of, 38
  contextuality and, 45
  culture, conflation with, 45–46
  cultures, 46
  deep socialization versus, 43
  degrees of, 47–48
  as distinct social property, 38
  education and, 72–73
  formal organization versus, 44–45
  forms of, 46–47
  holistic comparison of, 60
  legitimacy versus, 44
  macro level of analysis and, 45, 59
  other forms of reproduction versus, 43
  political institutionalization, 60
  as process, 39–40
  regimes, 46
  social entropy versus, 43
  as social reproductive process, 38
  "taken-for-grantedness" and, 48
  total institutionalization, 47
  vulnerability to social intervention, 47–48
Institutional racism, 37
Institutional theory. *See also specific topic*
  actorhood, focus on, 126, 127–29, 270–73
  concept of world society arising from, 243–44
  core arguments regarding world society, 259
  cultural institutionalism (*See* Cultural institutionalism)
  defined, 49
  individualism and, 201–2, 204
  liberalism as institutionalized cultural matter in, 315
  models in world society and, 258–59
  sociological neoinstitutionalism (*See* Sociological neoinstitutionalism)
  success in explaining world society, 257
  tension with actors, 252
Institutions. *See also specific institution*
  absence of thought and, 58
  anthropology, continued centrality in, 246
  centrality, relative to, 41
  conceptualization of, 38
  conceptual vagueness regarding, 37–38
  context, relative to, 40
  definition of, 44
  deinstitutionalization, 48
  denotation of, 37
  derivative structures, treated as, 247
  development, 48
  dimension of relationship, relative to, 41
  examples of, 39
  formation, 48
  history, continued centrality in, 246
  institutional change, 48–49
  operation of, 41–42
  overview, 17, 56
  reinstitutionalization, 49
  as relative property, 40–41
  secondary levels, relative to, 40–41
  as social pattern, 39–40
  "taken-for-grantedness," 42
  voting as, 40
Interdependence in postwar period, 298
Intergovernmental organizations, 253–54, 265, 300
International Labor Organization, 264

Index 329

International Monetary Fund (IMF), 41, 306
International Relations, 98, 112
Isomorphic actors, 226–27
Iversen, T., 317

Japan
  corporate social entities in, 223
  cultural institutionalism in, 5
Jones, E.L., 173, 174

Kamens, David, 70
Katzenstein, Peter, 98
Kincaid, H., 143
"Knowledge economy," 127
"Knowledge society," 127, 298, 315
Knowledge systems, 176–77
Kogut, B., 261
Kruecken, G., 14

Lakatos, Imre, 105
Landes, David, 151, 158, 177–78
Lazarsfeld, P., 200
Levels of analysis
  blurring of, 199
  complexity of, 196
  contextual analysis and, 200
  downward causation and, 196–97
  in globalization, 198–99
  hierarchy of, 196–97
  individual and, 198
  individualism and, 200–1
  individual-level causal processes, 148–49
  institutional causal processes, 148–49, 153–55
  mixed levels, 198
  multilevel analysis (*See* Multilevel analysis)
  nation-state and, 198
  nesting of, 198
  organization and, 198
  social-organizational causal processes, 148–49, 151–52
  in social sciences, 197–99
  sociology, evolution in, 199–201
  upward causation and, 196–97
Lévi-Strauss, Claude, 58
Liberalism
  actorhood and, 7, 290–91
  agentic actorhood and, 222, 223–24
  culture and, 283
  economics and, 283
  embedded liberalism (*See* Embedded liberalism)
  family and, 283
  gender and, 283
  hegemony of, 282–83
  individualism and, 189, 201
  individuals and, 284
  as institutionalized cultural matter, 315
  nation-states and, 284
  neoliberalism (*See* Neoliberalism)
  organizations and, 283
  political science and, 283
  post-liberalism (*See* Post-liberalism)
  religion and, 283
  sexuality and, 283
Libertarianism
  economic libertarianism, 305–7
  socio-cultural libertarianism, 308–9
Life course, 92–93
Lindenberg, S., 145, 147
Lipset, S.M., 4
"Logics" of action, 289–90
Luckmann, Thomas, 5, 7, 47, 52–53, 71, 132
Luhmann, N., 235–36
Lüthy, Herbert, 158

Macpherson, J.M., 261
Malawi, education in, 266
Management of firms, 183
Mann, Michael, 174, 175–76, 177–78, 179, 181
March, J., 132, 263
Marginalization of culture in social theory, 5–6, 17, 129–30, 233
Marx, Karl, 154, 180–81, 184, 227, 289
McClelland, David, 145
McEneaney, Elizabeth, 95
McLean, P.D., 153
Mead, G.H., 102
Meier, F., 14
Menzel, H., 200
Merton, Robert, 71, 72, 200

Methodological individualism
  dominance of in recent theory, 143–44, 160–61, 162, 201
  limitations of, 17, 170, 187–89, 203–4
  multilevel analysis versus, 144
  "Protestant Ethic Thesis" and, 141, 144–45, 187–88
  Protestantism and, 91, 110–11
  rebuttal of, 141, 142
  social change, inability to predict or explain, 203–4
Microfoundations, 156–60, 202–3
Microtranslation, 55, 61–62
Milanovic, B., 309
Mimetic isomorphism, 250, 251–52, 261
Miyahara, David, 94
Mizruchi, M.S., 261
Models in world society
  decoupling of, 262–63
  impact independent from adoption of, 263–64, 266–68
  impact on actors, 260–62
  institutional theory and, 258–59
  overview, 16
  political form and responsibility, 84–86
  rise of, 259–60
Modernity
  capitalism, conflation with, 178–79, 180–81
  economism and, 178–79, 180–81
  education, modernization and, 80–82
  in Europe, 178–81
  individuals and, 90–91, 110
  nation-states, modernization and, 80–82
  as quasi-religious system, 270–73
Mokyr, Joel, 176–77, 190
Monetarization, 181–84, 272–73
Moral meaning, culture and, 28–29
Multilevel analysis
  abstract, 139
  causal processes, 147–49
  individualism versus, 202
  individual-level causal processes, 148–49

  institutional causal processes, 148–49, 153–55
  macro-macro causation, 140–41
  macro- versus micro-level causation, 141
  methodological individualism versus, 144
  microfoundations and, 156–60, 202–3
  overview, 17–18, 160–62
  "Protestant Ethic Thesis" and, 156
  social-organizational causal processes, 148–49, 151–52
  theoretical explanations regarding, 142–43
Myth
  education and, 70, 71–72, 100
  individualism, mythology of, 188–89
  individuals and, 34
  nation-states and, 287–88
  in neoliberalism, 307
  organizations and, 74, 97
  states and, 32

Nation-states
  as actors, 128
  agentic actorhood and (See Agentic actorhood)
  consultants and, 230, 268–69
  cultural authority, as agents for, 220–21
  embedding within "world polity," 83–84
  empirical research findings, 14–15
  environment, transformation of nation-states and, 87
  heightened structuration of, 228–29
  individuals and, 87
  inflation of claims on, 268
  as isomorphic actors, 226–27
  "isomorphic expansion" of, 84
  levels of analysis and, 198
  liberalism and, 284
  modernization and, 80–82
  multiple types of modern polities, 87–89
  myth and, 287–88
  nature, rationalization of and, 215
  nonactors, as agents for, 220

Index 331

other actors, as agents for, 219–20
"post national membership" and, 87
principle, as agents for, 220–21
professionals and, 230, 268–69
"Protestant Ethic Thesis" and, 154
religion, and rationalization of, 216–17
self, as agents for, 218–19
similarities among, 84
social change and, 267
society, conflation with, 243
structural elements, decoupling of, 227–28
theoretical research program (TRP) and, 97–98
transformation of, 86–87
unrealistic expectations of, 287–88
"world polity" and, 82–83
Nature. *See also* Science
actorhood, rationalization of nature and, 214–15, 218, 231–32
"axial tension" of society with, 212–13
Christianity and, 172
culture and, 28
environmental movement (*See* Environmental movement)
individual and rationalization of, 215
nation-state and rationalization of, 215
new entities and interests arising from rationalization of, 214–15
organization and rationalization of, 215
rationalization by science, 213–15, 231–32
Neoliberalism
actorhood and, 7
anti-elitism in, 304–5, 307–8
anti-statism in, 307–8
anti-tradition nature of, 304–5
crises in, 309–10
economic libertarianism in, 305–7
economism and, 306–7
elites and, 305, 307–8
embedded liberalism, continuities from, 305
individualism and, 201
myth in, 307

overview, 297
political consequences of, 306
rise of, 304
science and, 305
social rationalization and, 305
socio-cultural libertarianism in, 308–9
socio-economic consequences of, 306
Netherlands, Protestantism in, 154
New Guinea, education in, 257
"New institutionalisms," 38
"New tribalism," 314–15
9/11 attacks, 311
Non-economic institutions, 182
Non-governmental organizations, 253–54, 265, 300
North, Douglass, 175, 181

"Old institutionalism," 299
Oliver, C., 289
Olsen, J., 132, 263
Olson, Mancur, 236, 270
"Ontological truism," 142, 159, 197
Opportunity structure, 271
Organizational field, 250, 271
Organizations
as actors, 14, 128
agentic actorhood and (*See* Agentic actorhood)
appropriateness and, 108
boundedness of, 73
bureaucracy versus, 14
consultants and, 230, 268–69
cross-national variation, 77
cultural authority, as agents for, 220–21
de-bureaucratization of, 79
decoupling and, 13, 74–75
deemphasis of cultural aspect, problems with, 32–33
different types of, 75
empirical research findings, 13–14
expanded individualism in, 78–79
"ground rules of economic life," institutional construction of, 75–76
heightened structuration of, 228–29
increasing standardization in, 78
inflation of claims on, 268

Organizations (cont.)
  instrumentality and, 108
  integration of, 73
  as isomorphic actors, 226–27
  Japanese organizational practices, 79–80
  levels of analysis and, 198
  liberalism and, 283
  linkage of organizational elements and institutional structures, 74–75, 79–80
  models of, 13–14
  myth and, 74, 97
  nature, rationalization of and, 215
  as new cultural rule, 30
  in nineteenth-century analysis, 32–33
  nonactors, as agents for, 220
  operation of, 41–42
  as organized actor, 14
  orthodoxy and, 108
  other actors, as agents for, 219–20
  personnel administration, 80, 108
  principal-agent tension in, 225–26
  principle, as agents for, 220–21
  professionals and, 230, 268–69
  rationalization and, 74, 107–8
  realism and, 32–33
  reform waves, 108
  religion, and rationalization of, 216–17
  research problems, 34–35
  social change and, 267
  societal sectoralization in, 78
  structural elements, decoupling of, 227–28
  theoretical research program (TRP) and, 96–97
  time, variation over, 77–79
  unrealistic expectations of, 287–88
Orloff, A.S., 146

Padgett, J.F., 153
Parsons, Talcott, 4, 55, 71, 72, 184, 189
Path dependence, 303
Perrow, Charles, 97
Personnel administration, 80, 108
Phenomenology
  cultural institutionalism and, 5

  institutionalism and, 61
  phenomenological institutionalism, 249, 250
Poland, attacks on democracy in, 314
Polanyi, K., 182
Political institutionalization, 60
Political science
  actors, increased focus on, 246–47, 270–71
  cultural institutionalism and, 4
  liberalism and, 283
  new institutionalisms in, 248
  realist institutionalism and, 249
  theoretical research program (TRP) and, 98
Populism, 313–14
Post-liberalism
  anti-elitism and, 312–13
  capitalism, attacks on, 312
  challengers to liberal order, role of, 311
  communal movements and, 314–15
  cosmopolitan elites, role of, 310
  "culture wars," impact of, 311
  democracy, attacks on, 312
  democracy, role of, 310–11
  forces creating, 310–11
  human rights, attacks on, 312
  inequality, impact of, 310
  new models in, 316
  9/11 attacks, impact of, 311
  overview, 297
  populism and, 313–14
  realism versus, 316
  rise of, 309–10
  science, attacks on, 312
  2008 economic crisis, impact of, 310
  United States, role of, 311
Powell, Walter, 79, 97, 250, 251–52, 261
Professionals
  agentic actorhood and, 230
  individuals and, 268–69
  nation-states and, 268–69
  organizations and, 268–69
  in response to unrealistic expectations of actors, 288
  world society and, 254, 265
"Protestant Ethic Thesis" (Weber)
  Boudon-Coleman diagram and, 145–47, 150, 156

Index 333

broader context of Christianity, deflection from, 171
collective action and, 155
economic activity and, 154
individual and, 171
individual-level causal processes and, 149–51
institutional causal processes and, 153–55
methodological individualism and, 141, 144–45, 187–88
multilevel analysis and, 156
nation-state and, 154
polity and community and, 153–54
science and, 155
social-organizational causal processes and, 151–52
Protestantism
  Calvinism, 145, 149–50
  capitalism and, 141, 156–60
  in historical context, 170–71
  methodological individualism and, 91, 110–11
  Puritanism, 150
  Reformation, 141–42, 145, 153–55
Prussia, organizational definition of state and, 31
Psychology
  actors, increased focus on, 246–47
  default intellectual imagery of, 316
  individual, role of, 7, 201
  institutionalism and, 52–53
  reductionism in, 7
Puritanism, 150

Racism, institutional, 37
Ramirez, Francisco, 58, 85, 89–90, 94, 109–10, 111, 264
Rational choice theory, 55, 282
Rationalization
  capitalism and, 174–75
  Christianity and, 172–73, 180
  defined, 189, 236
  economics and, 179–80, 188
  education and, 180
  embedded liberalism, transnational rationalized culture and, 300–1
  globalization and, 186
  nature, rationalization by science, 213–15, 231–32

neoliberalism, social rationalization and, 305
organizations and, 74, 107–8
of religion, 216–17, 231–32
science and, 180
world society and, 255–56
Raw actors, 236
Reagan, Ronald, 306
Realism
  actors and, 210
  collective action and, 234–35
  decoupling of models and, 263
  defined, 235
  individual and, 34
  institutionalism and, 61
  organization and, 32–33
  post-liberalism versus, 316
  realist institutionalism, 248–49
  social change, inability to predict or explain, 259–60, 266
  in social sciences, 247
  state and, 31
  world models and, 260–61
  world society, difficulty in explaining, 257
Reductionism, 7, 201
Reformation, 141–42, 145, 153–55
Reinstitutionalization, 49
Religion
  actorhood, rationalization of religion and, 218, 231–32
  "axial tension" of society with, 212–13
  Christianity (*See* Christianity)
  Europe, religious culture in, 170–73
  individual and rationalization of, 216–17
  liberalism and, 283
  modernity as quasi-religious system, 270–73
  nation-state and rationalization of, 216–17
  organization and rationalization of, 216–17
  Protestantism (*See* Protestantism)
  rationalization of, 216–17, 231–32
  reinstitutionalization and, 49
Robinson, W.S., 199–200
Rowan, Brian, 13, 73, 74–75, 79, 250
Roy, William, 132, 133–34

Verba, Sidney, 93
Voting as institution, 40

Wallerstein, Immanuel, 82–83, 97–98, 148, 173–74, 179
Weber, Max, 17, 37, 76, 91, 107–8, 141, 144–45, 149–51, 154, 155, 171, 174–75, 179, 189, 190. *See also* "Protestant Ethic Thesis" (Weber)
Weick, Karl, 13
Welfare state, 304
White, H., 151
Wippler, R., 145, 147
Women
  in education, 264
  individualism and, 94, 111
  social change and, 8, 266–67
World Bank, 186, 261, 300, 306
World society
  actorhood and, 258
  Christianity compared, 245
  complexity of, 245
  components of, 244, 255
  concept arising from institutional theory, 243–44
  conflicts in, 269–70
  constraints on, 254–55
  core arguments of institutional theory, 259
  cultural system, society as, 29
  education and, 256
  emergence of, 252–53
  empirical research findings, 15–16
  environment and, 15–16
  expansion of, 257–58, 265–66
  human rights and, 16
  intergovernmental organizations and, 253–54, 265
  lack of controlling organization, 253
  models in (*See* Models in world society)
  as more than sum of actors, 244
  in nineteenth-century analysis, 27
  non-governmental organizations and, 253–54, 265
  ontology of, 256
  organization of, 256–57
  "others" and, 15, 253–54, 259–60
  overview, 18, 245–46
  professionals and, 254, 265
  rationalization and, 255–56
  realism, difficulty in explanation by, 257
  rules of, 255
  sociological neoinstitutionalism and, 243
  stabilization of, 258
  state versus society dichotomy, 27
  success of institutional theory in explaining, 257
  United States, parallels with, 253

Zelditch, Morris, 72, 102, 103
Zetterberg, H.L., 145
Zucker, Lynne, 75, 106